# *TEXT BOOK*

## An Introduction to
## Literary Language

# TEXT BOOK

## An Introduction to Literary Language

**Robert Scholes**
Brown University

**Nancy R. Comley**
Queens College, CUNY

**Gregory L. Ulmer**
University of Florida

**St. Martin's Press**
New York

Senior Editor: Nancy Perry
Project Editor: Vivian McLaughlin
Production Supervisor: Julie Toth
Text design: Bill Smith Studio
Cover design: Darby Downey

Library of Congress Catalog Card Number: 87–060579
Copyright © 1988 by St. Martin's Press, Inc.
All rights reserved.
Manufactured in the United States of America.
21098
fedcba

For information, write to:
St. Martin's Press, Inc.
175 Fifth Avenue
New York, NY 10010

ISBN: 0–312–00251–3
Instructor's Edition ISBN: 0–312–01311–6

## ACKNOWLEDGMENTS

Maya Angelou, "Graduation," from I KNOW WHY THE CAGED BIRD SINGS by
Maya Angelou. Copyright © 1969 by Maya Angelou. Reprinted by permission
of Random House, Inc.

W. H. Auden, "Let Us Honor," Copyright 1934 and renewed 1962 by W. H.
Auden. Reprinted from W. H. AUDEN: COLLECTED POEMS edited by Edward
Mendelson, by permission of Random House, Inc., and Faber and Faber Ltd.

Roland Barthes, selections from A LOVER'S DISCOURSE by Roland Barthes.
English translation copyright © 1978 by Farrar, Straus and Giroux, Inc. Re-
printed by permission of Hill & Wang, a division of Farrar, Straus and Giroux,
Inc.

Bruno Bettelheim, "Hansel and Gretel," from THE USES OF ENCHANTMENT:
THE MEANING AND IMPORTANCE OF FAIRY TALES by Bruno Bettelheim.
Copyright © 1975, 1976 by Bruno Bettelheim. Reprinted by permission of
Alfred A. Knopf, Inc.

André Breton, "Broken Line," from THE POEMS OF ANDRÉ BRETON, translated
by J. P. Cauvin.

Roger Brown, reprinted with permission of The Free Press, a Division of Macmillan, Inc., from WORDS AND THINGS by Roger Brown. Copyright © 1958,
1968 by The Free Press.

Ernst Cassirer, "Names and Magic," from LANGUAGE AND MYTH by Ernst

Copyrights and acknowledgments continue at the back of the book on pages
286–288, which constitutes an extension of the copyright page.

# $\mathcal{A}$ Letter to the Instructor

The title of this textbook is not a joke. It is meant to signify our intention to offer an alternative approach to the traditional course called "Writing About Literature" or "Introduction to Literature." By substituting the concept of *text* for the traditional concept of *literature*, we accomplish a number of things. We allow for the presentation of a wider range of material and a broader spectrum of approaches to literary study. And we close or reduce the gaps that have separated reading from writing, creative from critical work, and literature from ordinary language.

In this book the traditional literary genres have their places. We attend to narrative, dramatic, and poetic texts—but not in isolation from explanatory, meditative, and persuasive texts. We discuss reading and interpretation, but we do not restrict ourselves to those modes of study. Our aim is to help students to feel at home in the universe of textuality: to understand the workings of power and pleasure in all kinds of texts.

We begin with the simplest and most accessible materials and concepts, working from story and scene through metaphor, intertextuality, and experiment. We introduce concepts from linguistics and literary theory at appropriate points. But this is not a book *about* literature; it is a text for working *with* literature. Textual interaction is the guiding principle throughout. At any point, including, of course, the end, you may profitably bring in supplementary material. This is an inclusive, not an exclusive, approach. It is, however, presented in a highly developmental manner. Later sections assume the mastery of concepts and techniques stressed in the earlier sections. We guarantee that students using this book will have interesting discussions and will produce interesting texts themselves. And that is what it is all about.

Sincerely,


Robert Scholes
Nancy R. Comley
Gregory L. Ulmer

# Acknowledgments

First of all, we would like to thank Nancy Perry, whose patience, in the face of an unprecedented degree of loopiness, never flagged. Then Tom Broadbent, who, in Paleolithic times, it seems, made us an offer we couldn't refuse. And Lori Lefkovitz, who kept the faith and told us firmly what worked and what didn't. Others who assisted in various ways were David Bleich, Indiana University; Kitty Chen Dean, Nassau Community College; Sandra K. Fisher, SUNY Albany; Richard Gebhardt, Findlay College; Michael Holzman, University of Southern California; Joseph Kruppa, University of Texas at Austin, Deborah Linderman, Smith College; Frank O'Hare, Ohio State University; Marie Secor, Pennsylvania State University; Elisa Kay Sparks, Clemson University; and William Sheidley, University of Connecticut.

# Contents

# *A Letter to the Student*

You may, of course, have read our letter to your instructor—just as your instructor has undoubtedly read this letter to you. Other people's mail has a special fascination. Nevertheless, in these few paragraphs we will assume that you have just opened this book for the first time and want to know why: why you are using this book of all books, and what you may get out of using it. We consider these fair questions and will try to answer them fairly, but first we must warn you that verbal education is a lot like physical education. You build your mind in the same way you build your body: through your own efforts. We can provide the most interesting and useful material for you to work on, based on the most recent information about language and literature, but the benefits to you will depend on your own efforts. "No pain, no gain," as the iron-pumpers say.

Our goal is to help you to a better mastery of your verbal environment. We all live in a world that constantly bombards us with texts. To survive—and above all to do more than just survive: to flourish—we need to deal with all kinds of texts surely and confidently. This book is called *Text Book* because it offers an entrance into the world of textuality: to the higher and more developed forms of reading and writing.

As you enter this book you will find all kinds of texts: some are usually called "literary" and some are not. This mixture is essential to our method. We do *not* want to offer you a collection of "master" works that ask for your passive submission, but a set of texts that you can work and play with, increasing your own understanding of fundamental textual processes and your own ability to use the written word. We hope to help you feel more at home in the house of language, and we are confident that a better command of written language will contribute to a better life. That is saying a lot, we realize, but we want you to know that, though this book is often playful, we are serious about its purpose. It is different from other books, and that has made it harder to write—and more fun. We have worked on it for years, trying to make it as effective and attractive as we could.

Come on in and see for yourself.

Sincerely,

Robert Scholes
Nancy R. Comley
Gregory L. Ulmer

# TEXT BOOK

## An Introduction to Literary Language

# Chapter 1
# Texts and People

In this chapter we will explore the ways in which people and their actions get into texts. Human events can be recounted (narrative) or enacted (drama), but either way they become *textualized*, taking on a certain formal structure that is found in much the same form in every culture: the structure of stories, which extends from personal anecdotes to literary novels and plays. That this should be the case is interesting in itself, but even more interesting is the way this formal structure returns into our lives, shaping our thoughts and actions. If you have ever found yourself wondering how something that was happening to you would sound in the telling, you know what we mean. If you have ever wondered how some experience in your life would "come out," you were applying a concept from storytelling to the interpretation of your own experience, even as it was happening: because experience does not "come out"—it just goes on and on.

The point of all this is that texts and life exist in a very complex relationship. Our thinking and even our feeling are shaped by texts in ways that we are dimly aware of in our normal day-to-day existence. We all use narrative structures and dramatic devices every day in our thoughts and in our actions—living out stories, playing roles, recounting events, enacting gestures and deeds. To learn more about how narrative and dramatic texts work, then, is to be a little more conscious of our own situations, a little more in control of our own lives.

The reading, discussion, and writing opportunities presented in this chapter are designed to help you strengthen your command of narrative and dramatic processes, building on the awareness you already have—having come this far in life—of narrative and dramatic forms. We will present you with some texts designed to reveal connections between these "literary" forms and ordinary life, and with some opportunities to move back and forth between the forms, developing your awareness and mastery of textual processes.

# *Story and Storyteller*

## Natural Narrative

### *Mary Louise Pratt*

*We think of literature as something special, as something above or beyond the way we use language in our daily lives—and so, in certain respects, it is. Literature is language used with special care and precision, or special energy and imagination. But the forms taken by literary works, and even the language used by poets and playwrights, are based on forms and ways of speaking that we all use, all the time. Literature is different from other uses of language, but it is also the same; it overlaps ordinary speech. Most approaches to the study of literature emphasize the differences, concentrating on the unique powers of literature. Without denying that these powers exist, we are taking the opposite tack in this book. We are going to emphasize the continuities, showing how literary forms and uses of language are connected to the ways that we use language on ordinary occasions. The point of doing it this way is to show that the passage from ordinary language to literature can be negotiated by any of us. It is not some impassable abyss that only a genius can leap. It is a craft, a skill, that will yield to study, effort, and practice. Our presentation begins with the anecdote, a basic form of storytelling that links the personal narratives we tell one another with the literary narratives produced by professional writers.*

*A few years ago Mary Louise Pratt, a literary critic, discovered that the great novels of world literature were similar in their structure to the personal narratives exchanged among people with very little formal education. She based her discovery on studies of inner-city speech by the sociolinguist William Labov. In the following selection we have reprinted a section of the second chapter of her book,* A Speech-Act Theory of Literary Discourse, *in which she presents Labov's work and discusses its significance.*

*For our purposes, the most important thing to learn from Pratt is the six-part structure of the ordinary personal narrative. You will find versions of this structure—or interesting deviations from it—in every kind of text that presents a story.*

Much of Labov's research over the past ten years has been devoted to documenting dialect variations in American English and above all to exploring the ways in which those divisions reflect and reinforce a    1 speaker's place in the class hierarchy of the larger speech community. He has concentrated especially on those dialects of American English considered by most Americans to be not only nonstandard but also substandard. In his first book, *The Social Stratification of English in New York City* (1966), Labov showed that phonological variation in the speech of New Yorkers could not be systematically specified independently of the social pressures acting on the speakers in the given speech situation. This was an important realization for linguistics since it provided support for building information about social context into the grammar.

Labov's interest in oral narrative stems mainly from a study of Black English Vernacular (BEV), "that relatively uniform dialect spoken by the majority of black youth in most parts of the United States today, especially in the inner city areas" (Labov, 1972:xiii). The project, which resulted in the volume of essays titled *Language in the Inner City* (1972), was originally undertaken to find out whether dialect differences had anything to do with the consistent reading problems of inner city black children. It was conducted in Harlem. As he analyzed the phonological and grammatical differences between BEV and Standard English, Labov made an important observation:

> The major reading problems did not stem from structural interference in any simple sense. . . . The major causes of reading failure are political and cultural conflicts in the classroom, and dialect differences are important because they are symbols of this conflict. We must then understand the way in which the vernacular culture uses language and how verbal skills develop in this culture. (Labov, 1972:xiv)

BEV speakers had trouble reading not because they lacked verbal skills (the contrary proved to be the case) but because the verbal skills they had were of no use in school. All this seems a far cry from aesthetics, and it is true that Labov's interest in "verbal art" rose from his research quite indirectly. I quote here Labov's own description of this development. The passage is long but worthwhile as an introduction to my own discussion to follow:

> In the course of our studies of vernacular language, we have developed a number of devices to overcome the constraints of the face-to-face interview and obtain large bodies of tape-recorded casual speech. The most effective of these techniques produce *narratives of personal experience*, in which the speaker becomes deeply involved in rehearsing or even reliving events of his past. The "Danger of Death" question is the prototype and still the most generally used: at a certain point in the conversation, the inter-

viewer asks, "Were you ever in a situation where you were in serious danger of being killed, where you said to yourself—*'This is it'?*" In the section of our interview schedule that deals with fights, we ask "Were you ever in a fight with a guy bigger than you?" When the subject says "Yes" we pause and then ask simply, "What happened?" The narratives that we have obtained by such methods form a large body of data on comparative verbal skills, ranging across age levels, classes and ethnic groups. Because they occur in response to a specific stimulus in the interview situation, they are not free of the interactive effect of the outside observer. The form they take is in fact typical of discourse directed to someone outside of the immediate peer group of the speaker. But because the experience and emotions involved here form an important part of the speaker's biography, he seems to undergo a partial reliving of that experience, and he is no longer free to monitor his own speech as he normally does in face-to-face interviews. (1972:354–55)

Labov was fascinated by the high degree of verbal virtuosity displayed by many of his informants in these narratives and by the high value placed on that virtuosity by the vernacular speech communities. This interest and the fact that, despite cultural differences, the narratives had great structural similarities led him to attempt a structural description of the oral narrative of personal experience as a speech act. The results of his study are found in two papers, "Narrative Analysis: Oral Versions of Personal Experience" (1967), written in collaboration with Joshua Waletzky, and "The Transformation of Experience in Narrative Syntax," in *Language in the Inner City*. (Unless otherwise specified, all subsequent references are to the latter article.) Before presenting Labov's analysis of these narratives, let me offer two contrasting examples, both taken from Labov's data. The first is a story told by a middle-aged white male speaker from Martha's Vineyard:

(1)

I never believed a whole lot in licking. I was never—
with my children, and I never—when it was with my animals,
dogs; I never licked a dog, I never had to. A dog knew
what I meant; when I hollered at a dog, he knew the—what
I meant. I could—I had dogs that could do everything
but talk. And by gorry, sir, I never licked 'em.
    I never come nearer bootin' a dog in my life. I
had a dog—he was a wonderful retriever, but as I say he
could do everything but talk. I could waif him that way,

I could waif him on, I could waif him anywhere. If I                10
shot a crippled duck he went after it; he didn't see it
in the water, he'd always turn around look at me, and I'd
waif him over there, if the duck was there, or if it was
on the other side of where we're on, I could waif him
straight ahead, and he'd turn and he'd go. If he didn't           15
see me, he'd turn around, he'd look at me, and I'd keep
a-waifin' him on. And he'd finally catch sight of him,
and the minute he did, you know, he would beeline and
get that duck.

 I was gunnin' one night with that dog—we had to           20
use live decoys in those days—a fellow named Jack Bumpus
was with me; I was over at a place called Deep Bottom,
darker than pitch. And—uh—heard a quackin' off shore.
And I said to Jack, "keep quiet. There's one comin' in."
And uh—finally Jack said to me, "I think I see 'im." I           25
said, "Give 'im a gun. Give 'im a gun. Try it."

 So he shot, and this duck went for the shore with
his wings a-goin' like that for the shore. Went up on the
shore. Well this dog never lost a crippled duck on shore,
he'd take a track just the same as a hound would take a           30
rabbit track. And I sent him over. I said, "Go ahead."

 So he went over there. And—gone a while and come
back and he didn't have the duck. And that was unusual—
I said, "You git back there and get that duck!" And he
went back there; and he stayed a little while longer,            35
longer than he did the first time, and he come back and
he didn't have the duck.

 And I never come nearer shootin' a dog. By gorry,
I come pretty near. *"You git back there and get that
duck!"* And that dog went back there, and he didn't come         40
back. And he didn't come back. By gorry, we went over
there—I walked over there, and here he was; one of my
tame ducks that I had tethered out there had got the
strap off her leg, and had gone out there, and when
this fellah shot he hadn't hit the duck. The duck                45
came to the shore, he hadn't hit the duck; but the
duck was scared and come for the shore. My dog was
over there, and he had his paw right on top of that
duck, holdin' him down just as tight as could be, and—
by gorry, boy, I patted that dog, I'll tell you if I             50
had ever walloped that dog I'd have felt some bad. He
knew more'n I did; the dog knew more than I did. He

knew that was that tame duck; he wasn't gonna pick him
up in his mouth and bring him, you know. He was just
holdin' him right down on the ground.                           55
                                    (Labov, 1967:14–15)

The second is a fight story told by a black adolescent male from Harlem
referred to as Larry:

(2)

An' then, three weeks ago I had a fight with this other dude
outside. He got mad 'cause I wouldn't give him a cigarette
Ain't that a bitch? (Oh yeah?)
Yeah, you know, I was sittin' on the corner an' shit, smokin'
my cigarette, you know. I was high, an' shit. He walked over          5
to me:
        "Can I have a cigarette?"
He was a little taller than me, but not that much. I said:
        "I ain't got no more, man."
'Cause, you know, all I had was one left. An' I ain't gon'            10
give up my last cigarette unless I got some more. So I said:
        "I don't have no more, man."
So he, you know, dug on the pack, 'cause the pack was in my
pocket. So he said:
        "Eh, man, I can't get a cigarette, man? I mean—I mean        15
we supposed to be brothers, an' shit."
So I say:
        "Yeah, well, you know, man, all I got is one, you dig it?"
An' I won't give up my las' one to nobody. So you know, the
dude, he looks at me, an' he—I 'on' know—he jus' thought            20
he gon' rough that motherfucker up. He said:
        "I can't get a cigarette."
I said:
        "Tha's what I said, my man."
You know, so he said:
        "What you supposed to be *bad* an' shit?"                    25
So I said:
        "Look here, my man, I don't think I'm bad, you understand?
But I mean, you know, if I had it, you could git it. I like
to see you with it, you dig it? But the sad part about it,           30
you got to do without it. That's all, my man."
So the dude, he 'on' to pushin' me, man.
(Oh, he pushed you?)

An' why he do that? *Everytime somebody fuck with me*, why
they do it? I put that cigarette down, an' boy let me tell you. I          35
beat the shit outa that motherfucker. I tried to *kill* 'im—over
one cigarette! I tried to *kill* 'im. Square business! After I got
through stompin' him in the face, man, you know, all of a
sudden I went crazy! I jus' went crazy. An' I jus' wouldn't stop
hittin' the motherfucker. Dig, it, I couldn't stop hittin'                40
'im, man, till the teacher pulled me off o' him. An' guess
what? After all that I gave the dude the cigarette, after
all that. Ain't that a bitch?
(How come you gave 'im the cigarette?)
I 'on' know. I jus' gave it to him. An' he smoked it, too!                 45
                                        (Labov, 1972:356–58)

Labov's (1972) analysis of these "natural narratives," as they are   4
commonly called, will seem self-evident to literary critics, and it is for
precisely this reason that I want to outline it here. Labov defines narrative as:

> one method of recapitulating past experience by matching a verbal
> sequence of clauses to the sequence of events which (it is inferred)
> actually occurred. . . . Within this conception of narrative, we can
> define a *minimal narrative*, as a sequence of two clauses which are
> *temporally ordered*: that is, a change in their order will result in a
> change in the temporal sequence of the original semantic interpreta-
> tion. (p. 360)

Narrative clauses are clauses with a simple preterite verb or, in some   5
styles, a verb in the simple present. Here is an adult "danger of death"
narrative which consists of four such ordered clauses: (This and all
further examples in this chapter are taken from Labov's data.)

(3) Well, this person had a little too much to drink and he attacked
me and the friend came in and she stopped it.

Narratives like (3), which consist only of narrative clauses, are not very
interesting, nor are they very common. A fully developed natural narrative, according to Labov, is made up of the following sections:

1. abstract
2. orientation
3. complicating action
4. evaluation

5. result or resolution
6. coda

"A complete narrative," he concludes, "begins with an orientation, proceeds to the complicating action, is suspended at the focus of evaluation before the resolution, concludes with the resolution, and returns the listener to the present time with the coda." I shall summarize briefly Labov's description of the six sections:

*Complicating action* and *resolution* are, of course, the core of the 6 narrative. The former begins with the first narrative clause in the speech act; the latter usually ends with the last such clause.

The *abstract* is a short (usually one or two sentence) summary of the 7 story that narrators generally provide before recounting the story proper. The abstract "encapsulates the point of the story." In narrative (1) above, the single sentence "I never come nearer bootin' a dog in my life" has this function; in narrative (2), lines 1–2 are the abstract.

The *orientation* serves to "identify in some way the time, place, 8 persons, and their activity or situation" and occurs immediately before the first narrative clause, as a rule. The orientation often includes "an elaborate portrait of the main character" as in (1), whose narrator describes at length the prowess of his retriever before going on to the situation orientation (11. 20–22). In (2), some information is already available in the abstract, and the orientation section (11. 4–5) gives a more detailed picture of the situation. Syntactically, orientations often contain many past progressive verbs "sketching the kind of thing that was going on before the first event of the narrative occurred or during the entire episode."

The *coda*'s general function is to "close off the sequence of com- 9 plicating actions and indicate that none of the events that followed were important to the narrative." In addition to this mechanical function, "a good coda . . . leaves the listener with a feeling of satisfaction and completeness that matters have been rounded off and accounted for." Labov notes a number of forms codas can take. Sometimes they consist of a single sentence like "And that was that"; sometimes they "bring the narrator and the listener back to the point at which they entered the narrative," as does this coda, which closes out a story in which the teller was saved from drowning:

(4) And you know, that man who picked me out of the water? He's a detective in Union City, and I see him every now and again.

and this coda to a fight story:

(5) Ever since then I haven't seen the guy 'cause I quit. I quit, you know. No more problems.

In narrative (1) above, the narrative proper ends at "just as tight as could be" (1.49) and the coda, starting with a pause and the phrase "by gorry," echoes the abstract ("If I had ever walloped. . . .") and provides an additional explication and recapitulation of the story's climax. In narrative (2), the fight story ends with the teacher's intervention, and the coda, beginning with "Guess what?" (1.41), contains additional information about the ultimate effects of the events, as in (5) above. The narrator of (2), like that of (1), echoes the abstract in the coda, here by repeating the line "Ain't that a bitch?"

*Evaluation* is considered by Labov to be "perhaps the most impor- 10 tant element in addition to the basic narrative clause." By evaluation, Labov means "the means used by the narrator to indicate the point of the narrative, its raison d'être: why it was told and what the narrator was getting at." He elaborates:

> There are many ways to tell the same story, to make very different points, or to make no point at all. Pointless stories are met (in English) with the withering rejoinder, "So what?" Every good narrator is continually warding off this question; when his narrative is over, it should be unthinkable for a bystander to say, "So what?" Instead, the appropriate remark would be "He did?" or similar means of registering the reportable character of the events of the narrative. (p. 366)

> To identify the evaluative portion of a narrative, it is necessary to know why this narrative—or any narrative—is felt to be tellable; in other words, why the events of the narrative are reportable. Most of the narratives cited here concern matters that are always reportable: danger of death or of physical injury. These matters occupy a high place on an unspoken permanent agenda. . . . The narrators of most of these stories were under social pressure to show that the events involved were truly dangerous and unusual, or that someone else really broke the normal rules in an outrageous and reportable way. Evaluative devices say to us: this was terrifying, dangerous, weird, wild, crazy; or amusing, hilarious and wonderful; more generally, that it was strange, uncommon, or unusual—that is, worth reporting. (p. 371)

The evaluation of a natural narrative is usually concentrated in one 11 section immediately preceding the resolution. However, as Labov notes, evaluative devices are generally strung throughout the entire narrative, forming what he calls "a secondary structure." Labov's discussion of evaluation is long, and I shall only partially summarize here his preliminary typology of the evaluative devices used by his informants. Again, the examples are Labov's.

A.   *Evaluative commentary*

The narrator interrupts the progress of the narrative with a statement reaffirming the tellability of the story or assessing the situation. Such commentary may be

1.   *External*: The narrator himself asserts the point of the story as in statements like "it was quite an experience" or "it was the strangest feeling" and so on.

2.   *Internal*: The evaluative statements are embedded in the story. The narrator may

a.   present the statement as having occurred to him at the time in the story, e.g., "I just closed my eyes, I said, 'O my God, Here it is!'"

b.   present the evaluation as statements addressed by himself to another character. Larry's evaluation, addressed (in rhymed couplets, no less) to his adversary (11.28–31) is an example of this type.

c.   attribute evaluative remarks to a witness or neutral observer in the story as in this example, referring to a knife wound: "And the doctor says, 'Just about this much more' he says, 'and you'd a been dead!'"

(a) to (c), you will notice, involve progressively deeper embedding of the evaluation in the story. As Labov notes, the more deeply embedded the evaluation, the more effective it is.

B.   *Sentence-internal evaluation devices*

1.   *Intensifiers*: These are devices superimposed or added onto the basic narrative syntax without affecting the unmarked (simple past) form of the narrative verb phrase. Examples:

a.   gestures.

b.   expressive phonology such as lengthened vowels ("a loooong time").

c.   repetition; there are many examples in (1) and (2).

d.   ritual interjections like "Well, sir," "By gorry," and so on.

2.   *Comparators*: These are devices which involve the use of some verb phrase construction other than the simple past of the narrative clause. They include negatives, futures, modals, questions, commands, comparatives, and others.

The category called Comparators merits some explanation. Labov 12 observed that complex auxiliary constructions tended to be concentrated in the evaluation sections of natural narratives, and he concluded upon analysis that most, if not all, verb constructions that depart from the simple past tense in natural narrative can be shown to be performing an evaluative role. The Comparators do so by referring to hypothetical events that are then compared to the observed events. Comparators, in other words, "draw upon a cognitive background considerably richer than the set of events which were observed." Negatives, for example, talk about what didn't happen but could have; futures allude to what could happen but hasn't yet; modals refer to hypothetical events; questions and commands are attempts to produce future events and function often as disguised threats in narratives, implying future consequences (see, for example, narrative (2) above). Generally speaking "a comparator moves away from the line of narrative events to consider unrealized possibilities and compare them with events that did occur." Labov uses the following evaluation taken from a schoolboy's narrative of a fight with "the baddest girl in the neighborhood" to exemplify the evaluative role played by complex auxiliary structures:

(6) So I says to myself, "There's *gonna* be times my mother won't give me money, because we're a poor family and I *can't* take this every time she *don't* give me any money." So I say, "Well, I just *gotta* fight this girl. She *gonna hafta* whup me. I hope she *don't* whup me (emphasis mine).

The passage contains four negatives, four futures, and three modals, all involving speculation about hypothetical events or situations which are compared to the present state of affairs. In the resolution of the story which follows, the simple narrative syntax is restored:

(7) I hit the girl, powww! I put something on it. I win the fight.

Larry's fight narrative above (11.7–12 and elsewhere) is similarly organized. The grammatical comparative of course always performs an evaluative function, as do similes and metaphors. Interestingly, such overt comparisons are found mainly in the syntax of older, more highly skilled narrators like that of (1) (see for example, 11. 7, 30, 52).

One of the most striking aspects of Labov's model, as I suggested 13 earlier, is its self-evidence. I think it is self-evident for two reasons. First, the oral narrative of personal experience is a speech act exceedingly familiar to us all, regardless of what dialect we speak. We all spend enormous amounts of conversational time exchanging anecdotes, though these may only occasionally involve fights or danger of death. Most speakers of English have a distinctive speech style for this type of narration with special intonation and in many cases special grammatical constructions not used in other contexts.* We are all perfectly aware of the "unspoken agenda" by which we assess an experience's tellability. We know that anecdotes, like novels, are expected to have endings. We know that for an anecdote to be successful, we must introduce it into the conversation in an appropriate way, provide our audience with the necessary background information, keep the point of the story in view at all times, and so on. And as with any speech situation, literary or otherwise, we form firm judgments all the time about how "good" an anecdote was and how well it was brought off by its teller; in fact, we are expected to express this judgment as soon as an anecdote ends. We recognize narrative expertise when we hear it, and when narrative speech acts fail, we can almost always say why: the experience was trivial, the teller longwinded, or we "missed the point." Should anyone be in doubt about any of these points, I would urge him to spend an hour some day listening to real "everyday language," watching for narratives and for people's responses to them.

The second reason Labov's analysis seems so obvious is that his 14 subdivision of the narrative into six main components corresponds very closely indeed to the kind of organization we are traditionally taught to observe in narrative literature. Every high school student knows that novels and plays have an introduction, a gradual rising action, a climax followed by a swift dénouement and resolution with the option of an epilogue at the end. That novels and natural narratives both have a structurally similar "narrative core" is not so surprising, since both are attempts to render experience. . . .

---

* For example, adverbial constructions like "down we fell" or "over it went" are apparently exclusively narrative. In many languages, including North American English, speakers often switch to the present tense for narration or alternate between present and simple past as in "so yesterday he comes into my office and I told him he was fired." Many North American English dialects use irregular first person forms like "I says," "I comes," "I runs" exclusively for narration. Needless to say, these phenomena are much in need of study, but their very existence strongly supports the hypothesis that, independent of any literary considerations, narration must be identified as a speech act in its own right.

# For Discussion and Writing

1. *Complicating action* and *resolution* are two elements of narrative
   that Pratt does not discuss at length, because she assumes that "every
   high school student knows that novels and plays have an introduction, a gradual rising action, a climax followed by a swift dénouement and resolution with the option of an epilogue at the end." Is
   she right? Do you know these things? In any case, it might be a good
   idea to review your understanding by discussing the complicating
   action and resolution of the two complete examples Pratt quotes
   from Labov. Try to summarize the *action* of each narrative, ignoring
   the other elements of the speech act. Can you locate a "rising"
   action, climax, and dénouement or resolution in both cases?

2. What makes a good anecdote good? Discuss the two examples given
   by Pratt. How much depends upon the events narrated and how
   much upon the way the narrator handles such matters as abstract,
   orientation, evaluation, and coda?

3. Take Pratt's example (3), which presents a whole story in a single
   sentence, and make something of it. That is, retell it as a full-fledged
   anecdote, using all six elements and adding descriptive details that
   will make it interesting. (This can be done as a group project.)

4. In preparation for writing your own anecdote (5), your instructor
   may ask you to tell your anecdote to the class, or to a group of
   students. As you listen to one another's anecdotes, take note of the
   evaluative commentary used by each speaker. You might want to
   discuss the writing strategies necessary to substitute for gestures
   used by the speaker to emphasize a point. Remember, it is not easy to
   convey a tone of voice in writing.

5. Write an anecdote based on personal experience. Your narrative may
   concern something that happened to you, or it may concern something that you witnessed but that happened to someone else. You
   may, like most of Labov's speakers, tell about a situation when you
   felt yourself to be in danger, but, as Labov points out, memorable
   events can be "weird, wild, crazy; or amusing, hilarious and wonderful" as well. After you have written out your anecdote, refer to
   Pratt's list of six parts of the anecdote to make sure that yours is
   formally complete.

# Agassiz and the Fish

## Ezra Pound

*This selection comes from a book about poetry called* The A B C of Reading *by Ezra Pound. Pound is arguing that the study of poetry should become more like scientific study. He uses an anecdote to make his point.*

The proper METHOD for studying poetry and good letters is the method of contemporary biologists, that is careful first-hand examination of the matter, and continual COMPARISON of one "slide" or specimen with another. 1

No man is equipped for modern thinking until he has understood the anecdote of Agassiz[1] and the fish: 2

A post-graduate student equipped with honors and diplomas went to Agassiz to receive the final and finishing touches. The great man offered him a small fish and told him to describe it. 3

Post-Graduate Student: 'That's only a sunfish.' 4

Agassiz: 'I know that. Write a description of it.' 5

After a few minutes the student returned with the description of the Ichthus Heliodiplodokus, or whatever term is used to conceal the common sunfish from vulgar knowledge, family of Heliichtherinkus, etc., as found in textbooks of the subject. 6

Agassiz again told the student to describe the fish. 7

The student produced a four-page essay. Agassiz then told him to look at the fish. At the end of three weeks the fish was in an advanced state of decomposition, but the student knew something about it. 8

By this method modern science has arisen, not on the narrow edge of medieval logic suspended in a vacuum. 9

## For Discussion and Writing

1.  Compare Pound's anecdote to the "natural" narratives presented by Pratt. First of all, consider the structure of Pound's presentation. Can you discover the six elements of narrative in Pound's anecdote? What, if anything, makes this anecdote especially literary?

2.  What is the connection between the anecdote and the point Pound is trying to make about how to study poetry?

[1] Louis Agassiz (1807–73), the most influential American naturalist of his day, taught at Harvard University.

3. Why do you suppose Pound brings in the notion of "mediaeval logic" in his last sentence, and why does he say it is "suspended in a vacuum"? What has all this got to do with the point he is trying to make?

4. Considering Pound's anecdote and the "natural" narratives presented by Pratt, do you find the differences or the similarities between them more important? Develop your views in a brief written paper, illustrating with appropriate quotations and analysis of specific points.

# The Use of Force

### *William Carlos Williams*

*The following selection is a personal experience recounted by the American poet William Carlos Williams. Williams was a physician, a general practitioner, and this is a story drawn from his practice.*

They were new patients to me, all I had was the name, Olson. Please    1
come down as soon as you can, my daughter is very sick.

When I arrived I was met by the mother, a big startled looking    2
woman, very clean and apologetic who merely said, Is this the doctor?
and let me in. In the back, she added. You must excuse us, doctor, we
have her in the kitchen where it is warm. It is very damp here sometimes.

The child was fully dressed and sitting on her father's lap near the    3
kitchen table. He tried to get up, but I motioned for him not to bother,
took off my overcoat and started to look things over. I could see that they
were all very nervous, eyeing me up and down distrustfully. As often, in
such cases, they weren't telling me more than they had to, it was up to
me to tell them; that's why they were spending three dollars on me.

The child was fairly eating me up with her cold, steady eyes, and no    4
expression to her face whatever. She did not move and seemed, inwardly,
quiet; an unusually attractive little thing, and as strong as a heifer in
appearance. But her face was flushed, she was breathing rapidly, and I
realized that she had a high fever. She had magnificent blonde hair, in
profusion. One of those picture children often reproduced in advertising
leaflets and the photogravure sections of the Sunday papers.

She's had a fever for three days, began the father and we don't know    5
what it comes from. My wife has given her things, you know, like people

do, but it don't do no good. And there's been a lot of sickness around. So we tho't you'd better look her over and tell us what is the matter.

As doctors often do I took a trial shot at it as a point of departure.   6
Has she had a sore throat?

Both parents answered me together, No . . . No, she says her throat   7
don't hurt her.

Does your throat hurt you? added the mother to the child. But the   8
little girl's expression didn't change nor did she move her eyes from my face.

Have you looked?                                                           9

I tried to, said the mother, but I couldn't see.                          10

As it happens we had been having a number of cases of diphtheria in   11
the school to which this child went during that month and we were all, quite apparently, thinking of that, though no one had as yet spoken of the thing.

Well, I said, suppose we take a look at the throat first. I smiled in my  12
best professional manner and asking for the child's first name I said, come on, Mathilda, open your mouth and let's take a look at your throat.

Nothing doing.                                                            13

Aw, come on, I coaxed, just open your mouth wide and let me take a  14
look. Look, I said opening both hands wide, I haven't anything in my hands. Just open up and let me see.

Such a nice man, put in the mother. Look how kind he is to you.  15
Come on, do what he tells you to. He won't hurt you.

At that I ground my teeth in disgust. If only they wouldn't use the  16
word "hurt" I might be able to get somewhere. But I did not allow myself to be hurried or disturbed but speaking quietly and slowly I approached the child again.

As I moved my chair a little nearer suddenly with one catlike move-  17
ment both her hands clawed instinctively for my eyes and she almost reached them too. In fact she knocked my glasses flying and they fell, though unbroken, several feet away from me on the kitchen floor.

Both the mother and father almost turned themselves inside out in  18
embarrassment and apology. You bad girl, said the mother, taking her and shaking her by one arm. Look what you've done. The nice man . . .

For heaven's sake, I broke in. Don't call me a nice man to her. I'm  19
here to look at her throat on the chance that she might have diphtheria and possibly die of it. But that's nothing to her. Look here, I said to the child, we're going to look at your throat. You're old enough to under-stand what I'm saying. Will you open it now by yourself or shall we have to open it for you?

Not a move. Even her expression hadn't changed. Her breaths how-  20
ever were coming faster and faster. Then the battle began. I had to do it. I had to have a throat culture for her own protection. But first I told the

parents that it was entirely up to them. I explained the danger but said that I would not insist on a throat examination so long as they would take the responsibility.

If you don't do what the doctor says you'll have to go to the hospital, 21 the mother admonished her severely.

Oh yeah? I had to smile to myself. After all, I had already fallen in 22 love with the savage brat, the parents were contemptible to me. In the ensuing struggle they grew more and more abject, crushed, exhausted while she surely rose to magnificent heights of insane fury of effort bred of her terror of me.

The father tried his best, and he was big man but the fact that she was 23 his daughter, his shame at her behavior and his dread of hurting her made him release her just at the critical times when I had almost achieved success, till I wanted to kill him. But his dread also that she might have diphtheria made him tell me to go on, go on though he himself was almost fainting, while the mother moved back and forth behind us raising and lowering her hands in an agony of apprehension.

Put her in front of you on your lap, I ordered, and hold both her 24 wrists.

But as soon as he did the child let out a scream. Don't, you're hurting 25 me. Let go of my hands. Let them go I tell you. Then she shrieked terrifyingly, hysterically. Stop it! Stop it! You're killing me!

Do you think she can stand it, doctor! said the mother.                        26

You get out, said the husband to his wife. Do you want her to die of 27 diphtheria?

Come on now, hold her, I said.                                                28

Then I grasped the child's head with my left hand and tried to get the 29 wooden tongue depressor between her teeth. She fought, with clenched teeth, desperately! But now I also had grown furious—at a child. I tried to hold myself down but I couldn't. I know how to expose a throat for inspection. And I did my best. When finally I got the wooden spatula behind the last teeth and just the point of it into the mouth cavity, she opened up for an instant but before I could see anything she came down again and gripping the wooden blade between her molars she reduced it to splinters before I could get it out again.

Aren't you ashamed, the mother yelled at her. Aren't you ashamed to 30 act like that in front of the doctor?

Get me a smooth-handled spoon of some sort, I told the mother. 31 We're going through with this. The child's mouth was already bleeding. Her tongue was cut and she was screaming in wild hysterical shrieks. Perhaps I should have desisted and come back in an hour or more. No doubt it would have been better. But I have seen at least two children lying dead in bed of neglect in such cases, and feeling that I must get a diagnosis now or never I went at it again. But the worst of it was that I too had got beyond reason. I could have torn the child apart in my own fury and enjoyed it. It was a pleasure to attack her. My face was burning with it.

The damned little brat must be protected against her own idiocy, one 32 says to one's self at such times. Others must be protected against her. It is a social necessity. And all these things are true. But a blind fury, a feeling of adult shame, bred of a longing for muscular release are the operatives. One goes on to the end.

In a final unreasoning assault I overpowered the child's neck and 33 jaws. I forced the heavy silver spoon back of her teeth and down her throat till she gagged. And there it was—both tonsils covered with membrane. She had fought valiantly to keep me from knowing her secret. She had been hiding that sore throat for three days at least and lying to her parents in order to escape just such an outcome as this.

Now truly she was furious. She had been on the defensive before but 34 now she attacked. Tried to get off her father's lap and fly at me while tears of defeat blinded her eyes.

## For Discussion and Writing

1. Later in this book, we will discuss more formally the question of how to produce "interpretations" of literary texts. For the moment we can think of interpretation simply as an extension of what Labov calls evaluation. It is a matter of explaining the significance or meaning of the events narrated. In Williams's story there is actually very little evaluation. You might confirm this by checking the text of the story against the six Labovian features of narrative. The absence of overt evaluation in many literary texts is a way of drawing the reader into the creative process. The reader must supply an appropriate evaluation for the events in order to complete the narrative structure.

   With this in mind, how do you evaluate or interpret the events in this story. What is the story about? What does it mean? You might begin by locating anything in the text that does seem to you to belong to orientation or evaluation. What about the title, for instance? Would you consider that a step toward an interpretation of the story? Try to develop, either in writing or in discussion, a full evaluation or interpretation of the story.

2. At this point, you might begin discussing the similarities and differences between the natural narratives of Labov and Pratt and the literary anecdote or story as exemplified by "The Use of Force."

What seem to you to be the important features common to both types of narrative, and what differences do you find notable? Which seem to you the most important—the similarities or the differences?

# The Kiss

*Kate Chopin*

*This selection is a short story by the American writer Kate Chopin, who lived in Louisiana a century ago. She was unique for her time, in that she wrote frequently about a powerful female sexuality trapped within an elaborate code of manners.*

It was still quite light out of doors, but inside with the curtains drawn and the smouldering fire sending out a dim, uncertain glow, the room was full of deep shadows. 1

Brantain sat in one of these shadows; it had overtaken him and he did not mind. The obscurity lent him courage to keep his eyes fastened as ardently as he liked upon the girl who sat in the firelight. 2

She was very handsome, with a certain fine, rich coloring that belongs to the healthy brune type. She was quite composed, as she idly stroked the satiny coat of the cat that lay curled in her lap, and she occasionally sent a slow glance into the shadow where her companion sat. They were talking low, of indifferent things which plainly were not the things that occupied their thoughts. She knew that he loved her—a frank, blustering fellow without guile enough to conceal his feelings, and no desire to do so. For two weeks past he had sought her society eagerly and persistently. She was confidently waiting for him to declare himself and she meant to accept him. The rather insignificant and unattractive Brantain was enormously rich; and she liked and required the entourage which wealth could give her. 3

During one of the pauses between their talk of the last tea and the next reception the door opened and a young man entered whom Brantain knew quite well. The girl turned her face toward him. A stride or two brought him to her side, and bending over her chair—before she could suspect his intention, for she did not realize that he had not seen her visitor—he pressed an ardent, lingering kiss upon her lips. 4

Brantain slowly arose; so did the girl arise, but quickly, and the newcomer stood between them, a little amusement and some defiance struggling with the confusion in his face. 5

"I believe," stammered Brantain, "I see that I have stayed too long.    6
I—I had no idea—that is, I must wish you good-by." He was clutching his
hat with both hands, and probably did not perceive that she was extending her hand to him, her presence of mind had not completely deserted
her; but she could not have trusted herself to speak.

"Hang me if I saw him sitting there, Nattie! I know it's deuced    7
awkward for you. But I hope you'll forgive me this once—this very first
break. Why, what's the matter?"

"Don't touch me; don't come near me," she returned angrily. "What    8
do you mean by entering the house without ringing?"

"I came in with your brother, as I often do," he answered coldly, in    9
self-justification. "We came in the side way. He went upstairs and I came
in here hoping to find you. The explanation is simple enough and ought
to satisfy you that the misadventure was unavoidable. But do say that you
forgive me, Nathalie," he entreated, softening.

"Forgive you! You don't know what you are talking about. Let me    10
pass. It depends upon—a good deal whether I ever forgive you."

At that next reception which she and Brantain had been talking    11
about she approached the young man with a delicious frankness of
manner when she saw him there.

"Will you let me speak to you a moment or two, Mr. Brantain?" she    12
asked with an engaging but perturbed smile. He seemed extremely unhappy; but when she took his arm and walked away with him, seeking a
retired corner, a ray of hope mingled with the almost comical misery of
his expression. She was apparently very outspoken.

"Perhaps I should not have sought this interview, Mr. Brantain; but—    13
but, oh, I have been very uncomfortable, almost miserable since that
little encounter the other afternoon. When I thought how you might have
misinterpreted it, and believed things"—hope was plainly gaining the
ascendancy over misery in Brantain's round, guileless face—"of course, I
know it is nothing to you, but for my own sake I do want you to
understand that Mr. Harvy is an intimate friend of long standing. Why, we
have always been like cousins—like brother and sister, I may say. He is
my brother's most intimate associate and often fancies that he is entitled
to the same privileges as the family. Oh, I know it is absurd, uncalled for,
to tell you this; undignified even," she was almost weeping, "but it
makes so much difference to me what you think of—of me." Her voice
had grown very low and agitated. The misery had all disappeared from
Brantain's face.

"Then you do really care what I think, Miss Nathalie? May I call you    14
Miss Nathalie?" They turned into a long, dim corridor that was lined on
either side with tall, graceful plants. They walked slowly to the very end
of it. When they turned to retrace their steps Brantain's face was radiant
and hers was triumphant.

Harvy was among the guests at the wedding; and he sought her out in 15
a rare moment when she stood alone.

"Your husband," he said, smiling, "has sent me over to kiss you."    16

A quick blush suffused her face and round polished throat. "I sup- 17
pose it's natural for a man to feel and act generously on an occasion of
this kind. He tells me he doesn't want his marriage to interrupt wholly
that pleasant intimacy which has existed between you and me. I don't
know what you've been telling him," with an insolent smile, "but he has
sent me here to kiss you."

She felt like a chess player who, by the clever handling of his pieces, 18
sees the game taking the course intended. Her eyes were bright and
tender with a smile as they glanced up into his; and her lips looked
hungry for the kiss which they invited.

"But, you know," he went on quietly, "I didn't tell him so, it would 19
have seemed ungrateful, but I can tell you. I've stopped kissing women;
it's dangerous."

Well, she had Brantain and his million left. A person can't have 20
everything in this world; and it was a little unreasonable of her to expect it.

# For Discussion and Writing

1. This is a sophisticated story of a sophisticated world. Begin your
   study of it by comparing its structure to that of "natural" narratives.
   Does it have all six of Labov's analytic elements? Discuss what is
   omitted, compressed, or rearranged in this story.

2. Retell the story as a personal narrative recounted by Mr. Harvy.
   Imagine him in his club, telling this tale to a small circle of intimate
   friends. You will have to develop his character and motivation a bit
   to do this, but try to keep your additions in harmony with the
   material in Chopin's version of this story. Aim for a "complete"
   narrative, with all six Labovian elements.

3. In a written essay take up the question of the relationship between
   "natural" narratives and "literary" narratives, exploring both their
   similarities and differences. Use Pratt and Chopin as your primary
   sources, but feel free to add material from Pound and Williams if you
   have studied their anecdotes as well. Try to reach some conclusion
   about which is more important: the differences or the similarities
   between popular and literary storytelling.

# Character and Confrontation

## Spring Awakening
## (a scene from the play)

*Frank Wedekind*

*In the previous section the object of study was the basic structure of narrative texts. Beginning with personal or "natural" narrative, we considered the ways in which Labov's six elements of narrative can be applied to texts of every size and shape. In the present section we will approach the study of dramatic texts through the ways in which they resemble and differ from narrative, using Labov's six elements as the basis of our comparison.*

*To begin with, let us consider a sample of dramatic literature that is drawn closely from ordinary life. The following selection is a scene from a play by Frank Wedekind, written in Germany over half a century ago. In this scene Wedekind presents the drama that occurs when a girl insists that her mother tell her the "facts of life." Later, you may wish to consider how such domestic scenes have changed in the past seventy years, but to begin you should simply read the scene over a couple of times and be prepared to act it out or stage a reading of it in class. You should know that until quite recently it was common for children in Germany and in the United States to be told that babies were delivered by The Stork, who was often pictured in cartoons flying along holding a baby's diapers or swaddling clothes in his beak, with the infant dangling down beneath him.*

SCENE II.
*Wendla's room, empty. Mrs. Bergmann, her hat on, her shawl round her shoulders, a basket on her arm, enters with beaming face.*

*Mrs. Bergmann* —Wendla! Wendla!
*Wendla* —[*Appearing, half dressed, at the other door.*]  What is it, Mother?
*Mrs. Bergmann* —Up already, dear? Well! That's nice of you.
*Wendla* —Have you been out already?
*Mrs. Bergmann* —Hurry up now and get dressed! You must go straight down to Ina's and take this basket to her.
*Wendla* —[*Finishing dressing during the following.*] Have you been at Ina's? How is Ina feeling? Isn't she ever going to get better?

*Mrs. Bergmann*  —Just think, Wendla: the stork came to her last night and brought her a new little boy!

*Wendla*  —A boy?—A boy?—Oh, that's grand!—So it was for that she's been sick so long with influenza!

*Mrs. Bergmann*  —A splendid boy!

*Wendla*  —I've got to see him, Mother!—So now I'm an aunt for the third time—one niece and two nephews!

*Mrs. Bergmann*  —And what fine nephews they are!—That's just the way of it when one lives so close to the church roof.—It'll be just two [and a half?] years to-morrow since she went up those steps in her wedding-dress!

*Wendla*  —Were you with her when he brought him, mother?

*Mrs. Bergmann*  —He had just that minute flown away again!—Don't you want to pin a rose on here? [*At the front of her dress*.]

*Wendla*  —Why didn't you get there a little bit sooner, Mother?

*Mrs. Bergmann*  —Why, I do believe, almost, that he brought you something too—a brooch or something like that.

*Wendla*  —[*Losing patience*.] Oh, it's really too bad!

*Mrs. Bergmann*  —But I tell you that he did bring you a brooch too!

*Wendla*  —I've got brooches enough. . . .

*Mrs. Bergmann*  —Why, then be happy, darling. What are you troubled about?

*Wendla*  —I'd like to have known, so much, whether he flew in by the window or down the chimney.

*Mrs. Bergmann*  —You must ask Ina about that. [*Laughing*.] You must ask Ina about that, dear heart! Ina will tell you all about it exactly. Didn't Ina spend a whole half-hour talking to him?

*Wendla*  —I'll ask Ina as soon as I get down there.

*Mrs. Bergmann*  —Be sure you don't forget, you angel child! Really, I'm interested myself in knowing if he came in by the window or the chimney!

*Wendla*  —Or how about asking the chimney-sweep, rather?—The chimney-sweep must know better than anybody whether he flies down the chimney or not.

*Mrs. Bergmann*  —No, not the chimney-sweep, dear; not the chimney-sweep! What does the chimney-sweep know about the stork? He'll fill you chuck-full of nonsense he doesn't believe himself. . . . Wha-what are you staring down the street so at?

*Wendla*  —A man, mother, three times as big as an ox!—with feet like steamboats—!

*Mrs. Bergmann*  —[*Plunging to the window*.] Impossible! Impossible!

*Wendla*  —[*Right after her*.] He's holding a bedstead under his chin and fiddling "The Watch on the Rhine" on it—now he's just turned the corner. . . .

*Mrs. Bergmann* —Well! You are and always were a little rogue! To put your simple old mother into such a fright!—Go get your hat. I wonder when you'll ever get any sense! I've given up hope!

*Wendla* —So have I, Mother; so've I. It's pretty sad about my sense! Here I have a sister who's been married two and a half years; here I am an aunt three times over; and I haven't the least idea how it all happens! . . . Don't be cross, motherkin! don't be cross! Who in the world should I ask about it but you? Please, Mother dear, tell it to me! Tell me, darling motherkin! I feel ashamed at myself! Please, please, mother, speak! Don't scold me for asking such a thing. Tell me about it—how does it happen—how does it all come about?—Oh, you can't seriously expect me still to believe in the stork when I'm fourteen!

*Mrs. Bergmann* —But, good Lord, child, how queer you are! What things do occur to you! Really, I just can't do that!

*Wendla* —But why not, mother? Why not? It can't be anything ugly, surely, when everyone feels so glad about it!

*Mrs. Bergmann* —Oh, oh, God defend me!—Have I deserved to——Go and put your things on, girl,—put your things on.

*Wendla* —I'm going . . . and supposing your child goes out now and asks the chimney-sweep?

*Mrs. Bergmann* —Oh, but that's enough to drive me crazy!—Come, child, come here: I'll tell you. . . . Oh, Almighty Goodness!—only not to-day, Wendla! To-morrow, day after, next week, whenever you want, dear heart!

*Wendla* —Tell it to me to-day, mother. Tell it to me now; now, at once. Now that I've seen you so upset, it's all the more impossible for me to quiet down again until you do!

*Mrs. Bergmann* —I just can't, Wendla.

*Wendla* —Oh, but why can't you, motherkin?—Here I'll kneel at your feet and put my head in your lap. Cover my head with your apron and talk and talk as if you were sitting all soul alone in the room. I won't move a muscle, I won't make a sound; I'll keep perfectly still and listen, no matter what may come!

*Mrs. Bergmann* —Heaven knows, Wendla, it isn't my fault! The good God knows me.—Come, in His name!—I will tell you, little girl, how you came into this world—so listen, Wendla. . . .

*Wendla* —[*Under her apron.*] I'm listening.

*Mrs. Bergmann* —[*Incoherent.*] But it's no use, child! That's all! I can't justify it.—I know I deserve to be put in prison,—to have you taken from me . . .

*Wendla* —[*Under her apron.*] Pluck up heart, Mother!

*Mrs. Bergmann* —Well, then, listen. . . .

*Wendla* —[*Trembling.*] O God, O God!

*Mrs. Bergmann* —To have a child—you understand me, Wendla?——

*Wendla*   —Quick, mother! I can't bear it much longer!

*Mrs. Bergmann*   —To have a child—one must love the man—to whom one is married—love him, I say,—as one can only love a man! You must love him so utterly—with all your heart—that—that—it can't be told! You must love him, Wendla, as you at your age can't possibly love anyone yet. . . . Now you know.

*Wendla*   —[*Getting up.*] Great—God—in Heaven!

*Mrs. Bergmann*   —Now you know what tests lie before you!

*Wendla*   —And that is all?

*Mrs. Bergmann*   —God help me, yes, all!—Now pick up the basket there and go down to Ina. You'll get some chocolate there, and cakes with it.—Come here—let me just look you over—laced boots, silk gloves, sailor-blouse, a rose in your hair. . . . But your little dress is really getting too short now, Wendla!

*Wendla*   —Have you got meat for dinner already, motherkin?

*Mrs. Bergmann*   —God bless you and keep you!—I must find time to sew another breadth of ruffles round your skirt.

*CURTAIN*

# For Discussion and Writing

1. Stage a reading of the scene.

2. Plays are meant to be acted. We often forget this little fact when we encounter the texts of plays in books. A printed play is more like a printed story than an acted play is. For one thing, a printed play usually has stage directions. At this point we would like you to consider the full range of differences between narration and enactment as ways of representing events. What seem to you the special strengths and limitations of each form? What do plays have that stories don't—and vice versa? Base your answers on the texts you have already considered in this course. You might also consider the difference between your private reading of Wedekind's text and the public staging or reading of it that you have just witnessed. The point of this inquiry is to refine your understanding of the ways that these different forms go about putting events into texts. If you have a preference for one form over the other, try to explain your reasons for holding this position.

3. Write your own version of a contemporary scene in which a child (of either sex) asks a parent (of either sex) about the facts of life. Remember to specify the age of the child. (How old is Wendla?)

4. Using Wedekind's scene as a source, write a personal narrative in which Wendla (or her mother) tells a friend about this moment in her life. You will have to decide how long after the scene this telling takes place, since narration is always some distance after the events narrated, and the length of this distance can affect the telling.

# The Kiss (dialogue from the story)

## *Kate Chopin*

*This selection should look familiar to you. It consists of all of the spoken dialogue from Kate Chopin's little story, "The Kiss." Look this material over before considering the assignment.*

*Brantain:* I believe, I see that I have stayed too long. I—I had no idea—that is, I must wish you good-by.

*Harvy:* Hang me if I saw him sitting there, Nattie! I know it's deuced awkward for you. But I hope you'll forgive me this once—this very first break. Why, what's the matter?

*Nathalie:* Don't touch me; don't come near me. What do you mean by entering the house without ringing?

*Harvy:* I came in with your brother, as I often do. We came in the side way. He went upstairs and I came in here hoping to find you. The explanation is simple enough and ought to satisfy you that the misadventure was unavoidable. But do say you forgive me, Nathalie.

*Nathalie:* Forgive you! You don't know what you're talking about. Let me pass. It depends upon—a good deal whether I ever forgive you.

*Nathalie:* Will you let me speak to you a moment or two, Mr. Brantain?

*Nathalie:* Perhaps I should not have sought this interview, Mr. Brantain; but—but, oh, I have been very uncomfortable, almost miserable since that little encounter the other afternoon. When I thought how you might have misinterpreted it, and believed things—of course, I know it is nothing to you, but for my sake I do want you to understand that Mr. Harvy is an intimate friend of long standing. Why, we have always been like cousins—like brother and sister, I may say. He is my brother's most intimate associate and often fancies that he is entitled to the same privileges as the family. Oh, I know it is absurd, uncalled for, to tell you this; undignified even, but it makes so much difference to me what you think of—of me.

*Brantain:* Then you really do care what I think, Miss Nathalie? May I call you Miss Nathalie?

*Harvy:* Your husband has sent me over to kiss you.

*Harvy:* I suppose it's natural for a man to feel and act generously on an occasion of this kind. He tells me he doesn't want his marriage to interrupt wholly that pleasant intimacy which has existed between you and me. I don't know what you've been telling him, but he has sent me over here to kiss you.

*Harvy:* But you know, I didn't tell him so, it would have seemed ungrateful, but I can tell you. I've stopped kissing women; it's dangerous.

## For Discussion and Writing

Your task is to add everything that is needed to make this into a play that is as complete as the story from which it has been taken. You might begin by considering what is missing from this version that is in the story, using Labov's formula to aid your investigation. Then consider how to compensate for what is lacking. Some of the things you should consider adding are these:

    a. scene divisions and settings

    b. stage directions

    c. additional dialogue (monologue? soliloquy?)

    d. additional characters (a confidante? a commentator?)

You should undertake your revision of the dialogue with a staged production in mind: something that could be performed in class.

# Character Contests

*Erving Goffman*

---

*A personal narrative or a dramatic scene can be thought of as a form imposed upon the chaos of life—and we are often encouraged to think of literature in this way. But in fact, as sociologists have been demonstrating for some time, such forms are already present in life itself. Because life is social, it often has many of the features of a scene played before an audience. No one has developed this view more eloquently than Erving Goffman, a sociologist who has studied the dramatic or literary aspects of ordinary human interaction.*

*Ordinary interaction is not always ordinary, of course, and Goffman has argued persuasively that the smooth running of society requires a rhythm of crisis and relaxation, a rhythm caused by attempts of individuals to live out the roles or characters that they have adopted in order to function within a social structure. Our characters, says Goffman, are illusions encouraged by society. Our behavior in moments of crisis or confrontation depends upon our feeling that what we do will reveal what we are. Goffman puts it this way:*

> And now we can begin to see character for what it is. On the one hand, it refers to what is essential and unchanging about the individual—what is *characteristic* of him. On the other, it refers to attributes that can be generated and destroyed in a few fateful moments.
>
> (*Interaction Ritual*, p. 238)

*Because we want to have a good character—to be known as brave, or honest, or faithful—we try to behave in moments of stress so as to enact bravery, honesty, or fidelity. For Goffman one of the most interesting social moments arrives when the characters of two individuals are at stake in a contest. In the following selection from* Interaction Ritual *he develops and illustrates the concept of "character contest," which is one of the forms of life that is also a form of art.*

Starting with the notion of fateful occupational duties, we can view action as a kind of self-oriented evocation in ritualized form of the moral scene arising when such duties are exercised. Action consists of chancy tasks undertaken for "their own sake." Excitement and character display, the by-products of practical gambles, of serious fateful scenes, become in the case of action the tacit purpose of the whole show. However, neither fateful duties nor action tell us very much about the mutual implications that can occur when one person's display of character directly bears upon another's, nor do we learn about the framework of understanding we possess for dealing with such occurrences. For this we must turn to interpersonal action. 1

During occasions of this kind of action, not only will character be at stake, mutual fatefulness will prevail in this regard. Each person will be at least incidentally concerned with establishing evidence of strong character, and conditions will be such as to allow this only at the expense of the character of the other participants. The very field that the one uses to express character may be the other's character expression. And at times the primary properties at play may themselves be openly made a convenience, pointedly serving merely as an occasion for doing battle by and for character. A *character contest* results; a special kind of moral game. 2

These engagements occur, of course, in games and sports where opponents are balanced and marginal effort is required to win. But character contests are also found under conditions less obviously designed for contesting, subjecting us all to a stream of little losses and 3 gains. Every day in many ways we can try to score points, and every day in many ways we can be shot down. (Perhaps a slight residue remains from each of these trials, so that the moment one individual approaches another, his manner and face may betray the consequences that have been usual for him, and subtly set the interaction off on a course that develops and terminates as it always seems to do for him.) Bargaining, threatening, promising—whether in commerce, diplomacy, warfare, card games, or personal relations—allow a contestant to pit his capacity for dissembling intentions and resources against the other's capacity to rile or cajole the secretive into readability. Whenever individuals ask for or give excuses, proffer or receive compliments, slight another or are slighted, a contest of self-control can result. Similarly, the tacit little flirtations occurring between friends and between strangers produce a contest of unavailability—if usually nothing more than this. And when banter occurs or "remarks" are exchanged, someone will have out-poised another. The territories of the self have boundaries that cannot be literally patrolled. Instead, border disputes are sought out and indulged in (often with glee) as a means of establishing where one's boundaries are. And these disputes are character contests.

If the significance of character contests is to be appreciated, how- 4 ever, we must turn from games and skirmishes to constitutive features of social life. We must examine the investment an individual is obliged to make in legitimate expectations that happen to be his own, especially informal ones, and the means available in society for establishing authority, invidious position, dominance, and rank. In the interplay of righteousness and ranking, a code is to be found that cuts to the center of the self and is worth attempting to formulate ideally.

When two persons are mutually present, the conduct of each can be 5 read for the conception it expresses concerning himself and the other. Co-present behavior thus becomes mutual treatment. But mutual treatment itself tends to become socially legitimated, so that every act, whether substantive or ceremonial, becomes the obligation of the actor and the expectation of the other. Each of the two participants is transformed into a field in which the other necessarily practices good or bad conduct. Moreover, each will not only desire to receive his due, but find that he is obliged to exact it, obliged to police the interaction to make sure that justice is done him.

When a contest occurs over whose treatment of self and other is to 6 prevail, each individual is engaged in providing evidence to establish a definition of himself at the expense of what can remain for the other. And this dispute will embarrass not only the desire for a satisfactory place in the definitions that prevail, but also the right to be given such a place and the duty to insist thereon. A "matter of principle" is involved, that is, a rule whose sanctity derives not only from the actual conduct that is guided by it, but also from its symbolic implication as one of a whole set of rules, the system itself being in jeopardy. Insisting on a desirable place is thus covered and strengthened by insisting on one's rightful place, and this is further hardened by the obligation to do so, lest the whole pattern of rules deteriorate. *Honor* can thus be engaged, namely, that aspect of personal make-up that causes the individual dutifully to enjoin a character contest when his rights have been violated—a course he must follow in the very degree that its likely costs appear to be high.[1]

The game typically starts with one player offending against a moral    7
rule, the particular application of which the other player is pledged to maintain personally, usually because he or those he identifies with are the targets of the offense. This is the "provocation." In the case of minor infractions, the offender is likely to offer an immediate apology, which restores both the rule and the honor of the offended; the offended need only convey acceptance to abort the whole game—in fact, he may apologize himself at the same time, or accept apology before it is offered, demonstrating again the great concern of persons to stay out of this kind of action. (An important structural issue here is that it is easier to proffer an excuse and apology in one's capacity as guardian of the other's rights, when this is self-initiated, than it is to accept an affront in one's capacity as protector of one's own sanctity.) A similar termination of the game occurs when the offended conveys a mild challenge (enough to show he is not without honor), drawing the offender's attention to what has happened, which is followed by a sequence of apology and acceptance. "Satisfaction" is asked for and given, and little character is generated, although each party can once again affirm that he is a properly socialized person with proper piety regarding the rules of the game. Even, however, where the offense is uncommon and deep, serious consequences can be avoided. The offended person can openly express his feeling that the offender is not the sort of person whose acts need be taken seriously; [2] the offender, on being challenged, can back down with wit, so that while one part of him becomes defamed, it is another part of him that is doing

---

[1] The leading case here is the sixteenth-century duel of honor. A gentleman stood by his honor, but only a small number of others were socially qualified to oblige him to satisfy his honor by means of a duel, and then, of course, the problems of arranging mutually satisfactory time, place, and equipment were so great that in countries like England few duels actually did get fought. See F. Bryson, *The Point of Honor in Sixteenth-Century Italy: An Aspect of the Life of the Gentleman* (Publications of the Institute of French Studies, Inc., Columbia University, New York, 1935); R. Baldick *The Duel* (London, Chapman and Hall, 1965).

[2] Tellers have foiled bank robberies by simply refusing to take seriously the threat-note to them by would-be armed robbers. Similarly policemen have countered pistol threats against themselves by simply turning their backs on the gunman, thereby removing the basis for contest. (See *San Francisco Chronicle*, July 26, 1965, p. 3, "Cop Turns His Back—And Disarms a Gunman.")

the defaming—and doing it so well as to undercut the challenger's claim of having self-restorative work to do.

Since a challenge can be communicated and declined with the 8 slightest of cues, one finds here a general mechanism of interpersonal social control. An individual who has moved slightly out of line is reminded of the direction he is taking and its consequences before any serious damage has been done. The same mechanism seems to be employed in the establishment of a pecking order regarding various kinds of rights.

If the contest is to begin in earnest, the challenge conveyed by the 9 offended must be serious, and the other player must pointedly decline to give satisfaction. When both of these responses are present they together transform retrospectively the meaning of the initial offense, reconstituting it into the beginning of what is sometimes called a "run-in." This is always a two-party affair, unlike an "incident," which may centrally involve only one person. Moral combat results, with properties of character brought into play as something to be lost and gained.[3] Run-ins involve the victim himself in all the phases of the sanctioning process. In this court, the plaintiff must act as judge and executioner. As is characteristic of action in general, the unaided individual is here the efficacious unit of organization.

It should be apparent that the meaning of these various moves 10 derives in part from the orientation the player brings to them and the readings he retrospectively makes of them. Therefore there will be leeway in defining the situation, and a certain degree of mutual consent will be required before a full-fledged run-in can occur.

In today's world, when a run-in does happen, a character contest is 11 likely to follow immediately, if indeed it is to occur. In myth and ritual, however, the parties often withdraw to meet again at a designated place, voluntarily keeping an appointment with fate, of both the corporeal and the characterological kind. In either case, bystanders are necessary and always must carefully refrain from interfering. (This ensures that the contest will be reputed as "fair," a valid scene for the play of character.)

When the run-in has occurred and the contest begun, the charac- 12 terological implications of the play can unfold in different ways, and not necessarily with "zero-sum" restrictions.

---

[3] Traditional duels were more complex because of the choice-of-weapons rule. Were the offended party to challenge the offender to a duel the latter would ordinarily have the choice of weapons, an unfair advantage for someone who had already done wrong. And so the offended party would openly insult the offender, "giving him the lie," and with this provocation the original offender would then be forced to challenge the offended. Through this extensive cooperation, choice of weapon could be lodged on the right side.

One party can suffer a clear-cut defeat on the basis of properties of 13
character: he proves to have been bluffing all along and is not really
prepared to carry out his threatened deed; or he loses his nerve, turns tail
and runs, leaving his opponent in the comfortable position of not having
to demonstrate how seriously he was prepared to carry through with the
contest; or he collapses as an opponent, abases himself and pleads for
mercy, destroying his own status as a person of character on the tacit
assumption that he will then be unworthy as an opponent and no longer
qualify as a target of attack.

Both parties can emerge with honor and good character affirmed— 14
an outcome carefully achieved, apparently, in most formal duels of
honor, a considerable achievement since injury was also usually avoided.

And presumably both parties can lose, just as one party may lose 15
while the other gains little. Thus, that ideal character contest, the
"chicken run," may end with both vehicles swerving, neither vehicle
swerving, or one swerving so early as to bring great dishonor to its driver
but no particular credit to the opponent.

Obviously, the characterological outcome of the contest is quite 16
independent of what might be seen as the "manifest" result of the fray.
An overmatched player can gamely give everything he has to his hopeless
situation and then go down bravely, or proudly, or insolently, or gracefully, or with an ironic smile on his lips.[4] A criminal suspect can keep his
cool in the face of elaborate techniques employed by teams of police
interrogators, and later receive a guilty sentence from the judge without
flinching. Further, a well-matched player can grimly suffer while his
opponent stoops to dishonorable but decisive techniques, in which case
a duel is lost but character is won. Similarly, an individual who pits
himself against a weak opponent may acquire the character of a bully
through the very act of winning the match. And a bully who ties is lost
indeed, as this news story from Fresno, California illustrates:

> A barmaid and a bandit played a game of "chicken" with
> loaded pistols early yesterday and although no shots were fired, the
> barmaid won.
>
> The action took place at The Bit, a proletarian beer and wine
> oasis on the southern fringe of town, where lovely Joan O'Higgins
> was on duty behind the bar.
>
> Suddenly a towering bandit walked into the establishment,

---

[4] One of the reasons unexpected rescues are employed in action stories is that
only in this way can the hero be given a chance to demonstrate that even in the
face of quite hopeless odds he will not cry uncle. Second leads are allowed to
prove this the hard way, being expendable in the plot.

ordered a beer, flashed a small pistol and commanded Miss O'Higgins to clean out the cash register.

The barmaid placed $11 on the bar, an amount that failed to satisfy the bandit, whose height was estimated at six feet five.

"Give me the rest," he demanded.

Barmaid O'Higgins reached into a drawer for the main money bag and the .22 caliber pistol beneath it.

She pointed the gun at the man and asked:

"Now, what do you want to do?"

The bandit, realizing that he had met his match in The Bit, blinked at the sight of the gun and left, leaving his beer and the $11 behind.[5]

## For Discussion and Writing

1. Goffman suggests that we make up and enact fictions about ourselves—that our real lives are penetrated by fictional concepts. Do you agree or disagree? If there are any aspects of Goffman's essay that you find difficult to understand or to accept, present them for discussion.

2. According to Goffman, when two people have a "run in" in real life, this takes a form quite similar to a scene from a play. Does your own experience support this view? Can you recall a run-in that you have either seen or participated in yourself? Could it be re-enacted as a dramatic scene? Can you describe how this might be done?

3. Character contests involve what Goffman calls the "boundaries" or "borders" of the self. They also involve matters of "honor" or "principle." Discuss the scene from Frank Wedekind's *Spring Awakening* (above, pp. 22–25) in Goffman's terms. In what sense does that scene record a "character contest?" Are matters of honor, principle, or boundaries of the self at stake in that scene? Is there a winner or a loser?

4. Consider Kate Chopin's story, "The Kiss," as a character contest. What is at stake? Who wins or loses?

5. Consider W. C. Williams's story, "The Use of Force," as a character contest. What is at stake? Who wins or loses?

[5] *San Francisco Chronicle*, July 14, 1966.

6. The "run-in" is an especially dramatic form of character contest. Which of the anecdotes you studied earlier can be described as a run-in? Rewrite a personal anecdote of your own in the form of a dramatic run-in, so that a reader will have no trouble assigning gains and losses to the characters involved. Use the dramatic rather than the narrative form of presentation.

7. In the run-in between the "bandit" and the "barmaid" the bandit is described as "towering" and the barmaid as "lovely." How important to the success of the story as a story are these details?

8. Suppose the barmaid had shot and killed the bandit. Would the result make as good a story? What would be lost with respect to this event's quality as a "character contest"?

9. How important are the barmaid's exact words to the function of this episode as a little drama or character contest?

10. Here is a brief but complete newspaper item about an event similar to the run-in between bandit and barmaid. Your task is to make a complete little drama out of this, with three scenes:
    1. The bandits before the raid.
    2. The shop before, during, and after the raid.
    3. The bandits after they have fled.
Try to make any gains or losses of character apparent, but try also to make your presentation as affective and amusing as possible. In particular, you should consider how this event may have changed the characters of the two bandits and the relationship between them.

# French Robbers Flee Barrage of Pastries

*United Press International*

St. Etienne, France—Two would-be robbers were driven away from 1 a pastry shop by a hail of creme pies, cakes and pastries thrown by the 65-year-old owner, her daughter and two grandchildren, police said.

The two men armed with a tear-gas bomb and a pistol entered 2 Armand Davier's pastry shop Sunday in the industrial city on the Loire River in southeastern France and demanded the contents of the cash box, officers said.

They ran from a fusillade of pies and cakes hurled at them by the ₃ owner, her daughter and two grandchildren, police said.

# The Stronger
## *August Strindberg*

*The following one-act play was written almost a hundred years ago by the Swedish playwright, August Strindberg, who is known for his dramatizations of psychological and sexual problems within and around family life. This particular play is unusual in several respects. Only one character speaks, while the others (and one other in particular) listen and react. The speaking character tells and interprets a narrative of events involving her, her husband, and the woman she is addressing. The title of the play suggests that the events that are narrated—and their narration on this occasion—constitute a character contest over which woman is "the stronger." As you read you will need to put some effort into reconstructing a narrative of the events that have preceded the play.*

Characters

*Mrs. X.*, actress, married
*Miss Y.*, actress, unmarried
*A Waitress*

*Scene: A corner of a ladies' café (in Stockholm in the eighteen eighties). Two small wrought-iron tables, a red plush settee and a few chairs. Miss Y. is sitting with a half-empty bottle of beer on the table before her, reading an illustrated weekly which from time to time she exchanges for another. Mrs. X. enters, wearing a winter hat and coat and carrying a decorative Japanese basket.*

*Mrs. X*  Why, Millie, my dear, how are you? Sitting here all alone on Christmas Eve like some poor bachelor.
*Miss Y looks up from her magazine, nods, and continues to read.*
*Mrs. X*  You know it makes me feel really sad to see you. Alone. Alone in a café and on Christmas Eve of all times. It makes me feel as sad as when once in Paris I saw a wedding party at a restaurant. The bride was reading a comic paper and the bridegroom playing billiards with the witnesses. Ah me, I said to myself, with such a beginning how

will it go, and how will it end? He was playing billiards on his wedding day! And she, you were going to say, was reading a comic paper on hers. But that's not quite the same.

*A waitress brings a cup of chocolate to Mrs. X and goes out.*

*Mrs. X* Do you know, Amelia, I really believe now you would have done better to stick to him. Don't forget I was the first who told you to forgive him. Do you remember? Then you would be married now and have a home. Think how happy you were that Christmas when you stayed with your fiancé's people in the country. How warmly you spoke of domestic happiness! You really quite longed to be out of the theatre. Yes, Amelia dear, home is best—next best to the stage, and as for children—but you couldn't know anything about that.

*Miss Y's expression is disdainful. Mrs. X sips a few spoonfuls of chocolate, then opens her basket and displays some Christmas presents.*

*Mrs. X* Now you must see what I have bought for my little chicks. [*Takes out a doll.*] Look at this. That's for Lisa. Do you see how she can roll her eyes and turn her head. Isn't she lovely? And here's a toy pistol for Maja. [*She loads the pistol and shoots it at Miss Y, who appears frightened.*]

*Mrs. X* Were you scared? Did you think I was going to shoot you? Really, I didn't think you'd believe that of me. Now if *you* were to shoot *me* it wouldn't be so surprising, for after all I did get in your way, and I know you never forget it—although I was entirely innocent. You still think I intrigued to get you out of the Grand Theatre, but I didn't. I didn't, however much you think I did. Well, it's no good talking, you will believe it was me . . . [*Takes out a pair of embroidered slippers.*] And these are for my old man, with tulips on them that I embroidered myself. As a matter of fact I hate tulips, but he has to have tulips on everything.

*Miss Y looks up, irony and curiosity in her face.*

*Mrs. X* [*putting one hand in each slipper*] Look what small feet Bob has, hasn't he? And you ought to see the charming way he walks—you've never seen him in slippers, have you?

*Miss Y laughs.*

*Mrs. X* Look, I'll show you. [*She makes the slippers walk across the table, and Miss Y laughs again.*]

*Mrs. X* But when he gets angry, look, he stamps his foot like this. "Those damn girls who can never learn how to make coffee! Blast! That silly idiot hasn't trimmed the lamp properly!" Then there's a draught under the door and his feet get cold. "Hell, it's freezing, and the damn fools can't even keep the stove going!" [*She rubs the sole of one slipper against the instep of the other. Miss Y. roars with laughter.*]

*Mrs. X* And then he comes home and has to hunt for his slippers, which Mary has pushed under the bureau . . . Well, perhaps it's not right to make fun of one's husband like this. He's sweet anyhow, and a good, dear husband. You ought to have had a husband like him, Amelia. What are you laughing at? What is it? Eh? And, you see, I know he is faithful to me. Yes, I know it. He told me himself—what *are* you giggling at?—that while I was on tour in Norway that horrible Frederica came and tried to seduce him. Can you imagine anything more abominable? [*Pause.*] I'd have scratched her eyes out if she had come around while I was at home. [*Pause.*] I'm glad Bob told me about it himself, so I didn't just hear it from gossip. [*Pause.*] And, as a matter of fact, Frederica wasn't the only one. I can't think why, but all the women in the Company seem to be crazy about my husband. They must think his position gives him some say in who is engaged at the Theatre. Perhaps you have run after him yourself? I don't trust you very far, but I know he has never been attracted by you, and you always seemed to have some sort of grudge against him, or so I felt.

*Pause. They look at one another guardedly.*

*Mrs. X* Do come and spend Christmas Eve with us tonight, Amelia—just to show that you're not offended with us, or anyhow not with me. I don't know why, but it seems specially unpleasant not to be friends with you. Perhaps it's because I did get in your way that time . . . [*slowly*] or—I don't know—really, I don't know at all why it is.

*Pause. Miss Y. gazes curiously at Mrs. X.*

*Mrs. X [thoughtfully]* It was so strange when we were getting to know one another. Do you know, when we first met, I was frightened of you, so frightened I didn't dare let you out of my sight. I arranged all my goings and comings to be near you. I dared not be your enemy, so I became your friend. But when you came to our home, I always had an uneasy feeling, because I saw my husband didn't like you, and that irritated me—like when a dress doesn't fit. I did all I could to make him be nice to you, but it was no good—until you went and got engaged. Then you became such tremendous friends that at first it looked as if you only dared show your real feelings then—when you were safe. And then, let me see, how was it after that? I wasn't jealous—that's queer. And I remember at the christening, when you were the godmother, I told him to kiss you. He did, and you were so upset . . . As a matter of fact I didn't notice that then . . . I didn't think about it afterwards either . . . I've never thought about it—I didn't think about it afterwards either . . . I've never thought about it—until *now*! [*Rises abruptly.*] Why don't you say something? You haven't said a word all this time. You've just let me go on talking. You have sat there with your eyes drawing all these thoughts out of me—they

were there in me like silk in a cocoon—thoughts . . . Mistaken
thoughts? Let me think. Why did you break off your engagement?
Why did you never come to our house after that? Why don't you
want to come to us tonight?

*Miss Y makes a motion, as if about to speak.*

**Mrs. X**  No. You don't need to say anything, for now I see it all. That was
why—and why—and why. Yes. Yes, that's why it was. Yes, yes, all
the pieces fit together now. That's it. I won't sit at the same table as
you. [*Moves her things to the other table.*] That's why I have to em-
broider tulips, which I loathe, on his slippers—because you liked
tulips. [*Throws the slippers on the floor.*] That's why we have to
spend the summer on the lake—because you couldn't bear the sea-
side. That's why my son had to be called Eskil—because it was your
father's name. That's why I had to wear your colours, read your
books, eat the dishes you liked, drink your drinks—your chocolate,
for instance. That's why—oh my God, it's terrible to think of, terrible! Everything, everything came to me from you—even your passions. Your soul bored into mine like a worm into an apple, and ate
and ate and burrowed and burrowed, till nothing was left but the skin
and a little black mould. I wanted to fly from you, but I couldn't. You
were there like a snake, your black eyes fascinating me. When I
spread my wings, they only dragged me down. I lay in the water with
my feet tied together, and the harder I worked my arms, the deeper I
sank—down, down, till I reached the bottom, where you lay in waiting like a giant crab to catch me in your claws—and now here I am.
Oh how I hate you! I hate you, I hate you! And you just go on sitting
there, silent, calm, indifferent, not caring whether the moon is new
or full, if it's Christmas or New Year, if other people are happy or unhappy. You don't know how to hate or to love. You just sit there without moving—like a cat at a mouse-hole. You can't drag your prey out,
you can't chase it, but you can out-stay it. Here you sit in your corner—you know they call it the rat-trap after you—reading the papers
to see if anyone's ruined or wretched or been thrown out of the Company. Here you sit sizing up your victims and weighing your chances—like a pilot his shipwrecks for the salvage. [*Pause.*] Poor Amelia!
Do you know, I couldn't be more sorry for you. I know you are miserable, miserable like some wounded creature, and vicious because
you are wounded. I can't be angry with you. I should like to be, but
after all you are the small one—and as for your affair with Bob, that
doesn't worry me in the least. Why should it matter to me? And if
you, or somebody else, taught me to drink chocolate, what's the difference? [*Drinks a spoonful. Smugly.*] Chocolate is very wholesome
anyhow. And if I learnt from you how to dress, *tant mieux!*—that
only gave me a stronger hold over my husband, and you have lost

what I gained. Yes, to judge from various signs, I think you have now lost him. Of course, you meant me to walk out, as you once did, and which you're now regretting. But I won't do that, you may be sure. One shouldn't be narrow-minded, you know. And why should nobody else want what I have? [*Pause.*] Perhaps, my dear, taking everything into consideration, at this moment it is I who am the stronger. You never got anything from me, you just gave away—from yourself. And now, like the thief in the night, when you woke up I had what you had lost. Why was it then that everything you touched became worthless and sterile? You couldn't keep a man's love—for all your tulips and your passions—but I could. You couldn't learn the art of living from your books—but I learnt it. You bore no little Eskil, although that was your father's name. [*Pause.*] And why is it you are silent—everywhere, always silent? Yes, I used to think this was strength, but perhaps it was because you hadn't anything to say, because you couldn't think of anything. [*Rises and picks up the slippers.*] Now I am going home, taking the tulips with me—*your* tulips. You couldn't learn from others, you couldn't bend, and so you broke like a dry stick. I did not. Thank you, Amelia, for all your good lessons. Thank you for teaching my husband how to love. Now I am going home—to love him.

*Exit.*

## For Discussion and Writing

1.  Discuss the history of the relationships that have led to this little scene. That is, from the evidence given in the play, construct the story of the relevant portions of the characters' lives.

2.  Discuss Goffman's theory of character contests as a way of interpreting the play. To do this, you must examine what is enacted and said in the play in the light of Goffman's concepts of why and how people behave the way they do. How much of what happens in the play can be explained by Goffman's theory? Are there aspects of the play that seem to elude Goffman's theory—perhaps things that belong to art rather than life?

3.  Write a revised version of the play in which Miss Y does all the talking and Mrs. X is silent. To do this you should make the following assumptions: first, that Mrs. X's monologue is simply a version of events interpreted in a way that is satisfying for Mrs. X; second that Miss Y would not only interpret the "same" events differently, she might also remember the events differently and might even remem-

ber somewhat different events; that is, you should assume that something happened between Mr. X and Miss Y that roughly corresponds to the description provided by Mrs. X, but may not correspond to that description in every respect. Your job is to keep the same large structure—an affair between Mr. X and Miss Y that ended with Mr. X still married to Mrs. X—but allow Miss Y to tell a version of the events that shows her to be "the stronger." We say there arc two sides to every story. This is your chance to show what that expression means.

4. Assume that the waitress overhears this whole scene and that she knows more about the history of the Xs and Miss Y than emerges from Mrs. X's speeches. Has the waitress known Mr. X intimately? You decide. At any rate, your assignment here is to narrate the waitress's version of this scene. Assume she is telling a friend about it—or writing a letter to a friend about it—and go on from there.

# Aristotle and the Advertisers: The Television Commercial as Drama (passages from the essay)

### Martin Esslin

*Dramatic form not only shapes our social behavior but confronts us regularly as a form of persuasive manipulation. A major literary critic, Martin Esslin, has even argued that much of television advertising is dramatic in structure. Centuries ago Aristotle pointed out that dramatic plots can be reduced to two simple forms and two complex developments of those forms. In one basic form the fortunes of the central character or protagonist (hero, heroine) are improved during the course of the action. This is the basic comic plot. In the other simple form—the tragic—the protagonist experiences a fall in fortune.*

*The more complex plots involve a reversal in the course of the hero or heroine's fortunes: first a rise, followed by a fall; or first a fall, then a rise. Aristotle's word for such a reversal of fortune was* peripeteia. *In classic drama, reversals were often brought about by the intervention of a god, whose descent from the heavens was simulated by lowering the god or goddess onto the stage with a machine like a derrick or backhoe. The Latin term for such a "god from a machine" is* deus ex

machina, *a term we still use for divine intervention or other mechan-*
*ical methods of reversing a character's fortunes in a play.*

*Aristotle also believed that plots are more interesting if they lead to*
*a change from ignorance to knowledge. He called such a change recog-*
*nition or* anagnorisis, *and the new way of thinking brought about by*
*recognition he called* dianoia. *He was surely right about the impor-*
*tance of these features, for they are the basis of every detective story as*
*well as of Aristotle's favorite play, the* Oedipus *of Sophocles. In a*
*murder mystery the* anagnorisis *and* dianoia *lead to the* peripeteia *of the*
*murderer. The structures Aristotle identified are still very much with*
*us, so it should come as no surprise that Martin Esslin finds them*
*active in TV commercials. Here are selections from his essay "Aristotle*
*and the Advertisers":*

We have all seen it a hundred times, and in dozens of variations: that short    1
sequence of images in which a husband expresses disappointment and
distress at his wife's inability to provide him with a decent cup of coffee
and seems inclined to seek a better tasting potion outside the home,
perhaps even at the bosom of another lady; the anxious consultation,
which ensues between the wife and her mother or an experienced and
trusted friend, who counsels the use of another brand of coffee; and
finally, the idyllic tableau of the husband astonished and surprised by the
excellence of his wife's new coffee, demanding a second—or even a
third!—cup of the miraculously effective product.

A television commercial. And, doubtless, it includes elements of    2
drama, yet is it not too short, too trivial, too contemptible altogether to
deserve serious consideration? That seems the generally accepted opinion. But in an age when, through the newly discovered technologies of
mechanical reproduction and dissemination, drama has become one of
the chief instruments of human expression, communication, and indeed,
thought, all uses of the dramatic form surely deserve study. If the television commercial could be shown to be drama, it would be among the
most ubiquitous and the most influential of its forms and hence deserve
the attention of the serious critics and theoreticians of that art, most of
whom paradoxically still seem to be spellbound by types of drama (such
as tragedy) that are hallowed by age and tradition, though practically
extinct today. And surely, in a civilization in which drama, through the
mass media, has become an omnipresent, all-pervasive, continuously
available, and unending stream of entertainment for the vast majority of
individuals in the so-called developed world, a comprehensive theory,
morphology, and typology of drama is urgently needed. Such a theory
would have to take cognizance of the fact that the bulk of drama today is
to be found not on the stage but in the mechanized mass media, the
cinema, television, and in most civilized countries, radio; that, both on

the stage and in the mass media, drama exists in a multitude of new forms, which might even deserve to be considered genres unknown to Aristotle—from mime to musicals, from police serials to science fiction, from westerns to soap opera, from improvisational theatre to happenings—and that, among all these, the television commercial might well be both unprecedented and highly significant.

The coffee commercial cited above, albeit a mere thirty to fifty    3 seconds in length, certainly exhibits attributes of drama. Yet to what extent is it typical of the television commercial in general? Not all TV commercials use plot, character, and spoken dialogue to the same extent. Nevertheless, I think it can be shown that most, if not all, TV commercials are essentially dramatic, because basically they use mimetic action to produce a semblance of real life, and the basic ingredients of drama— character and a story line—are present in the great majority of them, either manifestly or by implication.

Take another frequently occurring type: a beautiful girl who tells us    4 that her hair used to be lifeless and stringy, while now, as she proudly displays, it is radiantly vital and fluffy. Is this not just a bare announcement, flat and undramatic? I should argue that, in fact, there is drama in it, implied in the clearly fictitious character who is telling us her story. What captures our interest and imagination is the radiant girl, and what she tells us is an event which marked a turning point in her life. Before she discovered the miraculous new shampoo she was destined to live in obscurity and neglect, but now she has become beautiful and radiant with bliss. Are we not, therefore, here in the presence of that traditional form of drama in which a seemingly static display of character and atmosphere evokes highly charged, decisive events of the past that are now implicit in the present—the type of drama, in fact, of which Ibsen's *Ghosts* is a frequently cited specimen?

What, though, if the lady in question is a well-known show business    5 or sporting personality and hence a *real* rather than a fictitious character? Do we not then enter the realm of reality rather than fictional drama? I feel that there are very strong grounds for arguing the opposite: for film stars, pop singers, and even famous sporting personalities project not their real selves but a carefully tailored fictional image. There has always, throughout the history of drama, been the great actor who essentially displayed no more than a single, continuous personality rather than a series of differing characters (witness the harlequins and other permanent character types of the *commedia dell'arte*; great melodrama performers like Frédéric Lemaître; great comics like Chaplin, Buster Keaton, Laurel and Hardy, or the Marx Brothers; or indeed, great film stars like Marilyn Monroe or John Wayne—to name but a very few). Such actors do not enact parts so much as lend their highly wrought and artistically crafted fictitious personality to a succession of roles that exist merely to display that splendid artifact. Hence if Bob Hope or John Wayne appear as spokesmen for banking institutions, or Karl Malden as the advocate of a credit card, no one is seriously asked to believe that they are informing us of their real experience with these institutions; we all know that they are speaking a preestablished, carefully polished text, which, however brief it may be, has been composed by a team of highly skilled professional writers, and that they are merely lending them the charisma of their long-established—and fictional—urbanity, sturdiness, or sincerity.

There remains, admittedly, a residue of nondramatic TV commer-  6
cials: those which are no more than newspaper advertisements displaying a text and a symbol, with a voice merely reading it out to the less literate members of the audience, and those in which the local car or carpet salesman more or less successfully tries to reel off a folksy appeal to his customers. But these commercials tend to be the local stations' fill-up material. The bulk of the major, nationally shown commercials are profoundly dramatic and exhibit, in their own peculiar way, in minimal length and maximum compression, the basic characteristics of the dramatic mode of expression in a state of particular purity—precisely because here it approaches the point of zero extension, as though the TV commercial were a kind of differential calculus of the aesthetics of drama.

Let us return to our initial example: the coffee playlet. Its three-beat  7
basic structure can be found again and again. In the first beat the exposition is made and the problem posed. Always disaster threatens: persistent headaches endanger the love relationship or success at work of the heroine or hero (or for headaches read constipation, body odor, uncomfortable sanitary pads, ill-fitting dentures, hemorrhoids, lost credit cards, inefficient detergents that bring disgrace on the housewife). In the second beat a wise friend or confidant suggests a solution. And this invariably culminates in a moment of insight, of conversion, in fact the classical anagnorisis that leads to dianoia and thus to the peripeteia, the turning point of the action. The third beat shows the happy conclusion to what was a potentially tragic situation. For it is always and invariably the hero's or heroine's ultimate happiness that is at stake: his health or job or domestic peace. In most cases there is even the equivalent of the chorus of ancient tragedy in the form of an unseen voice, or indeed, a choral song, summing up the moral lesson of the action and generalizing it into a universally applicable principle. And this is, almost invariably, accompanied by a visual epiphany of the product's symbol, container, trademark, or logo—in other words the allegorical or symbolic representation of the beneficent power that has brought about the fortunate outcome and averted the ultimate disaster; the close analogy to the *deus ex machina* of classical tragedy is inescapable.

All this is compressed into a span of from thirty to fifty seconds.  8
Moreover such a mini-drama contains distinctly drawn characters, who,

while representing easily recognizable human types (as so many characters of traditional drama), are yet individualized in subtle ways, through the personalities of the actors portraying them, the way they are dressed, the way they speak. The setting of the action, however briefly it may be glimpsed, also greatly contributes to the solidity of characterization: the tasteful furnishings of the home, not too opulent, but neat, tidy, and pretty enough to evoke admiring sympathy and empathy; the suburban scene visible through the living room or kitchen window, the breakfast table that bears witness to the housewifely skills of the heroine—and all subtly underlined by mood music rising to a dramatic climax at the moment of anagnorisis and swelling to a triumphant coda at the fortunate conclusion of the action. Of all the art forms only drama can communicate such an immense amount of information on so many levels simultaneously within the span of a few seconds. That all this has to be taken in instantaneously, moreover, ensures that most of the impact will be subliminal—tremendously suggestive while hardly ever rising to the level of full consciousness. It is this which explains the great effectiveness of the TV commercial and the inevitability of its increasing employment of dramatic techniques. Drama does not simply translate the abstract idea into concrete terms. It literally incarnates the abstract message by bringing it to life in a human personality and a human situation. Thus it activates powerful subconscious drives and the deep animal magnetisms that dominate the lives of men and women who are always interested in and attracted by other human beings, their looks, their charm, their mystery.

## For Discussion and Writing

1. Look back at the various narratives and dramas you have already considered, from the personal narratives of Pratt to the character contests of Goffman. Which of them have clear reversals, recognitions, or both? Is Aristotle right? Are the texts with reversals and recognitions the most interesting? Discuss any exceptions you find. It would be especially useful to consider your own dramatizations and personal narratives in the light of Aristotle's views.

2. Watch commercials on TV until you find one that follows the Aristotelian principles described by Esslin. If you have access to a VCR, record the commercial you are going to use so that you can study it carefully. If not, do the best you can. You may have to see a commercial several times before you can complete your project.
   This project has two parts. First, develop a written version of your chosen commercial, in the form of a play, with stage directions

and everything else you would need for someone to act out the commercial. (An alternative to this would be to have someone with access to a VCR provide a written version that the whole class could use.) Second, write an alternative version of the same commercial, in which some event happens or something is said that subverts or destroys the commercial function of the play. Try to make the smallest changes possible that will achieve the result that is being aimed at here. With some help from your classmates, act out your altered version.

# Chapter 2

# Texts, Thoughts, and Things

In this chapter we ask you to shift your attention from the large or "macro" structures of narrative and drama to the small or "micro" structure of language itself. In particular we will focus on a single crucial element of language: the creative principle of metaphor.

A friend of ours who became a writer and teacher himself told us that his whole attitude toward language was changed when a teacher said to him—somewhat brutally—"Words are razor blades. You use them as if they were bricks." The point, of course, was that careless, clumsy use of language could be dangerous: that a certain awareness, a certain delicacy, is demanded by language. A razor blade can be a tool, a weapon, or a hazard, but you ignore its sharp edges at your peril. The point was forcefully made by the teacher's own use of the blade of metaphor, drawing the student's attention to a potential danger in language that he had overlooked.

We do not intend to draw any blood here, nor do we recommend wounding people to get their attention, but we hope this fragment of an anecdote will help explain why we have singled out metaphor as a dimension of language that should receive special attention. The reading and writing work in this chapter is designed to help you develop your awareness of the presence and function of metaphor in all sorts of texts. This awareness should help you attain greater precision and power as a writer. It should also enhance your pleasure and ability as a reader. Metaphor is at the heart of the creative process embodied in human language.

# The Linguistic Basis of Metaphor

It is widely understood that metaphor is a basic element of poetry. It is also true, however, that metaphor is a fundamental building block of ordinary language and of such forms of written prose as the essay. We begin our investigation of metaphor with two passages from a book called *Words and Things* by the psycholinguist Roger Brown.

In the first passage Brown uses the case of the Wild Boy of Aveyron as a way of directing our attention to the linguistic problem of names for things—or nouns, as we call them. By clarifying for us the way in which nouns refer not to individual things but to "universals," or categories of things, Brown lays the basis for an understanding of metaphor.

In a metaphor the name of one thing is applied to another, so that, as in certain chemical reactions, there is an exchange of particles between the two. That is, when we say, "Words are razor blades," certain defining attributes of the category *razor blades* are transferred to the category *words*: namely, delicacy and dangerousness. This is the way metaphor works. In the second passage included here, Brown helps us to understand why. He also suggests that all nouns are to some extent metaphorical. Language grows by a kind of metaphorical extension. Metaphor is thus not an ornament added on top of language, but a principle built in at the most fundamental level of linguistic behavior.

## "What Words Are: Reference and Categories"

### Roger Brown

"A child of eleven or twelve, who some years before had been seen  1
completely naked in the Caune Woods seeking acorns and roots to eat, was met in the same place toward the end of September 1797 by three sportsmen who seized him as he was climbing into a tree to escape from their pursuit." In these words Dr. Jean-Marc-Gaspard Itard began his first report on the education of the wild boy found in the Department of Aveyron. The discovery of a human creature who had lived most of his life outside of all human society excited the greatest interest in Paris.

Frivolous spirits looked forward with delight to the boy's astonishment at the sights of the capital. Readers of Rousseau expected to see an example of man as he was "when wild in woods the noble savage ran." There were even some who counted on hearing from the boy mankind's original unlearned language—they conjectured that it was most likely to be Hebrew. The savage of Aveyron disappointed all of these expectations. He was a dirty, scarred, inarticulate creature who trotted and grunted like a beast, ate the most filthy refuse, and bit and scratched those who opposed him. In Paris he was exhibited to the populace in a cage, where he ceaselessly rocked to and fro like an animal in the zoo, indifferent alike to those who cared for him and those who stared. The great psychiatrist Pinel, who taught France to treat the insane as patients rather than as prisoners, was brought to examine the boy. After a series of tests Pinel pronounced him a congenital idiot unlikely to be helped by any sort of training.

2  Many came to believe that the so-called savage was merely a poor subnormal child whose parents had recently abandoned him at the entrance to some woods. However, a young physician from the provinces, Dr. Itard, believed that the boy's wildness was genuine, that he had lived alone in the woods from about the age of seven until his present age of approximately twelve, and there was much to support this view. The boy had a strong aversion to society, to clothing, furniture, houses, and cooked food. He trotted like an animal, sniffed at everything that was given him to eat, and masticated with his incisors in the same way as certain wild beasts. His body showed numerous scars, some of them apparently caused by the bites of animals and some which he had had for a considerable time. Above all, a boy of his general description had been seen running wild in the same forest some five years earlier.

3  Dr. Itard had read enough of Locke and Condillac to be convinced that most of the ideas a man possesses are not innate but, rather, are acquired by experience. He believed that the apparent feeble-mindedness of the boy of Aveyron was caused by his prolonged isolation from human society and his ignorance of any language and that the boy could be cured by a teacher with patience and a knowledge of epistemology. Itard asked for the job. He had been appointed physician to the new institute for deaf mutes in Paris and so asked to take Victor there to be civilized and, most interesting for us, to learn the French language. Permission was granted and Itard worked with the boy, whom he called Victor, for five years. Itard had little success in teaching Victor to speak. However, he had considerable success in teaching Victor to understand language and, especially, to read simple words and phrases. . . .

4  In teaching Victor to understand speech, Itard found that he must, in the beginning, set aside the question of meaning and simply train the boy to identify speech sounds. In the first period after his capture Victor paid

no attention to the human voice but only to sounds of approach or movement in his vicinity—noises that would be important to a creature living in the forest. Itard devised an instructive game for teaching Victor to distinguish one vowel from another. Each of the boy's five fingers was to stand for one of five French vowels. When Itard pronounced a vowel, Victor was to raise the appropriate finger. Victor was blindfolded and the vowels were pronounced in an unpredictable order so that if the boy made correct responses it must be because he could distinguish the vowels. In time Victor learned to play the game, but he was never very good at it. Thus Itard decided that the boy's vision was more acute than his hearing and thought he might be taught to read more easily than he could be taught to understand speech.

Again Itard came up with an ingenious game designed to teach Victor   5 to identify the forms of the written and printed language, even though he could not yet understand their meanings. The same collection of words was written on two blackboards, making the order of words on one board unrelated to the order on the other. Itard would point to a word on his board and it was Victor's task to point to its counterpart on the other board. When the boy made a mistake, teacher and pupil "spelled" the word together; Itard pointed to the first letter of his word and Victor did the same with his supposed match, and they proceeded in this fashion until they came to two letters where Victor saw a difference. After a time Victor could read quite a large number of words, some of them very much alike. As yet, however, this was not reading with understanding but simply the identification of empty forms.

The time had come to teach Victor something about the meanings of   6 words. Itard arranged several objects on a shelf in the library, including a pen, a key, a box, and a book. Each thing rested on a card on which its name was written, and Victor had already learned to identify the names. Itard next disarranged the objects and cards and indicated to Victor that he was to match them up again. After a little practice the boy did this very well. Itard then removed all the objects to a corner of the room. He showed Victor one name and gave him to understand that he was to fetch the object named. Victor also learned this very quickly, and Itard grew increasingly optimistic.

The next test went badly at first. Itard locked away in a cupboard all   7 of the particular objects with which Victor had practiced, but made sure that there were in his study other objects of the same kinds—other pens, keys, boxes, and books. He then showed Victor a word, e.g., *livre*, and indicated that the boy was to bring the referent. Victor went to the cupboard for the familiar book and finding the cupboard locked had to give up the task. He showed no interest in any other book. The same failure occurred with the other words. Victor had understood each word to name some particular thing rather than a category of things.

Itard then spread out a variety of books, turning their pages to show    8
what they had in common. He indicated that the word *livre* could go
with any of them. After this lesson, when shown the word *livre*, Victor
was able to fetch a book other than the specific book of his training.
However, he did not correctly constitute the book category at once, for
he brought a handful of paper at one time and a pamphlet and magazine
at another. As his errors were corrected, however, he learned to distinguish books from other sorts of publications and also to recognize
such categories as are named *key, pen*, and *box*. The crucial test for
understanding of the referent category was always Victor's ability to
identify new instances.

Itard next approached the difficult problem of conveying an under-    9
standing of words that name qualities and relations rather than objects
that have size, shape, and weight. He took out two books, one large and
one small, and Victor promptly labelled each with the word *livre*. Itard
then took Victor's hand and spread it flat on the front of the large volume
showing how it failed to cover the full surface. The same hand spread out
on the smaller book did cover that surface. Victor then seemed puzzled
as if wondering that one word should name these two different objects.
Itard gave him new cards labelled *grand livre* and *petit livre* and matched
them with the appropriate books. Now came the test to see whether
Victor had learned specific habits or had abstracted a general relationship. Itard produced two nails, one large and one small, and asked that
the cards *grand* and *petit* be correctly assigned. Victor learned this
relationship and others besides.

Itard had another good idea for verbs that name actions. He took a    10
familiar thing, e.g., a book, and made it the object of some action—
pounding it or dropping it or opening it or kissing it. In each case he gave
the boy the appropriate verb in the infinitive form. The test was for the
boy to label such actions when their object was changed, e.g., to a key or
a pen. This too Victor learned.

The end of all this imaginative teaching was that Victor learned to    11
read with understanding quite a large number of words and phrases. He
would obey simple written commands and also use the word cards to
signal his own desires. In addition to all this he assumed the manners and
appearance of a civilized young man. However, Itard's final word was
discouraging. Although Victor had been greatly improved by education,
diminishing returns on his efforts convinced Itard that the boy was
performing to the limits permitted by his intellectual endowment and
these limits, unfortunately, were subnormal.

### Reference and Categories

When Dr. Itard wanted to give Victor some idea of the meanings of    12
words, he hit upon a way of showing that each word stood for some-

thing, that each word had a referent. This is the sort of thing each of us would do to convey to a small child the meanings of his first words; it is also the usual recourse in trying to communicate with a foreigner who understands no English. The use of language to make reference is the central language function which is prerequisite to all else. It is the beginning of the psychology of language and is, accordingly, the focus of this book.

What Victor learned about reference was at first too specific. Words 13 do not name particular things as Victor thought; they name classes or categories. Someone who properly understands the word *book* is prepared to apply it to any and all particular books. I see in the room where I sit a novel in a highly colored dust jacket and quite near it one numbered volume of a sober encyclopedia; on the floor is a Penguin paperback, and asleep in the hall the telephone directory. Although they differ in many respects, all of these are, nevertheless, books. They have the printed pages and stiff covers that define the category.

Actually we do not badly stretch the notion of the category if we 14 treat even a single particular book as a category. The single book, the single anything, is a category of sense impressions. Victor must have seen the book that was used in his early training on many occasions, in various positions, and from different angles. At one time a book is a rectangular shape lying on a table; at another time the same book is only the back of a binding on the library shelf. While it is possible to say that these various experiences constitute a category, that category must be distinguished from the sort named by *book* in general. The various appearances of one book have a continuity in space-time that makes us think of them as one thing preserving its identity through change. The various individual books around my room do not have this kind of continuity. So let us agree to call all referents categories but to distinguish the particular referent from the general by calling it an "identity" category.

Itard's later training procedures show that not all referents are ob- 15 jects with size, shape, and weight. Actions like dropping and kissing are referents and so are such qualities as large and small or red and green. Clearly too, these referents are categories. The act of dropping changes many of its characteristics from one occasion to the next but preserves something invariant that defines the action. Any sort of recurrence in the non-linguistic world can become the referent of a name and all such recurrences will be categories because recurrences are never identical in every detail. Recurrence always means the duplication of certain essential features in a shifting context of non-essentials.

It is quite easy to see that the referents of words are categories but 16 somewhat less easy to see that language forms, the names of referents, are also categories. Variations in the production of a language form are probably more obvious in the written or printed version than in the spoken. Differences of handwriting and of type are so great that it is actually difficult to specify what all the renderings of one word have in common. Even the individual letter is a category of forms changing considerably in their numerous productions. Variations in pronunciation are also certainly ubiquitous but our early extensive training in disregarding the dimensions of speech that are not significant for distinguishing English words causes us to overlook them. So long as phonetic essentials are preserved we identify utterances as the same, although they change greatly in loudness, pitch, quaver, breathiness, and the like. From acoustic studies we know that even one speaker "repeating" the same vowel does not produce identical sounds. Itard's productions of the French vowels cannot have been identical from one time to another and neither, we may be sure, were the "matched" words he wrote on the two blackboards. In these first games Victor was learning to categorize the empty forms of language, to pick out the essential recurrent features and to overlook the non-essential variations.

## For Discussion and Writing

1. It is easy to understand Brown when he says that the word *book* refers to a "category" that includes all the books that one could possibly encounter. But things get more complicated when he says that any particular book is also a category—what he calls an "identity category." Reconsider Brown's fourteenth paragraph and discuss the notion of "identity category." Define this term in your own words, and illustrate your definition with examples.

2. Every word, even every letter, says Brown, is also a "category of forms." Looking over paragraph 16, define "category of forms" in your own words, and illustrate the way in which a word may be described as a "category of forms."

# "What Words Are: Metaphor"

### *Roger Brown*

When someone invents a new machine, or forms a concept, or buys     1
a dog, or manufactures a soap powder his first thought is to name it. These names are almost never arbitrary creations produced by juggling the sounds of the language into a novel sequence. We think hard and ask

our friends to help us find a "good" name, a name that is appropriate in that its present meaning suggests the new meaning it is to have.

Sometimes new words are introduced by borrowing words or mor- 2 phemes[1] from classical languages. The biological sciences have been especially partial to this practice as *photosynthesis, streptoneura*, and *margaritifera* testify. In order to savor the appropriateness of these names a classical education is required and so, for most of us, they are functionally arbitrary.

The usual method of creating a new name is to use words or mor- 3 phemes already in the language; either by expanding the semantic range of some word or by recombining morphemes. Every word has a history of former meanings and, traced back far enough, an ancestor that belongs to another language. The modern French *lune* derives from the Latin *lux*. The extension of the Latin word for *light* to the moon is appropriate and may once have been experienced as appropriate. Today, however, because of phonetic change and loss of the earlier meaning, the metaphor in *lune* must be overlooked by most French speakers even as we overlook the metaphor in our *moon* which is a remote cognate of Latin *mensis* for month. Both languages arrived at their word for the moon by metaphorical means, though the metaphors are constructed on different attributes of the referent—its luminosity for the French, its periodic cycle for the English. In both cases the whole process dates so far back that the appropriateness of these names like that of *margaritifera* or *photosynthesis* is evident only to scholars.

Many new names are still very familiar in an older reference and so 4 their appropriateness to the new referent is easy to see. There are dogs called *Spot* or *Rover*; detergents and soaps are called *Surf, Rinso*, and *Duz*; one kind of personality is said, by clinical psychologists, to be *rigid*. Compounds like *overcoat, railroad train*, and *fireplace* have familiar constituents. While the origins of these names are obvious enough they probably are not ordinarily noticed. It seems to be necessary to take a special attitude toward language, quite different from our everyday attitude, to discern the metaphors around us.

The metaphor in a word lives when the word brings to mind more 5 than a single reference and the several references are seen to have something in common. Sometime in the past someone or other noticed that the foot of a man bears the same relation to his body as does the base of a mountain to the whole mountain. He thought of extending the word *foot* to the mountain's base. This word *foot* then referred to two categories. These categories share a relational attribute which makes them one category. Within this superordinate category, which we might name *the*

---

[1] morpheme: the smallest unit of meaning in any given language. In English the word *dog* is a morpheme. The word *dogged* adds a second morpheme—Editor.

*foundations* or *lower parts of things*, are two subordinate categories—
the man's foot and the mountain's base. These two remain distinct within
the larger category because the members of each subordinate category
share attributes that are not shared with the members of the other
subordinate category. The *man's foot* is made of flesh and has toes,
which is not true of the base of any mountain. Thus far the relationship is
like that of any set of superordinate and subordinate categories, e.g.,
*polygons* as superordinate to triangles and squares. The subordinates
have something in common which makes them species of one genus but
they are distinct because members of one subordinate have still more in
common. Metaphor differs from other superordinate-subordinate relations in that the superordinate is not given a name of its own. Instead, the
name of one subordinate is extended to the other and this, as we shall
see, has the effect of calling both references to mind with their differences as well as their similarities. The usual superordinate name, e.g.,
polygons, calls to mind only the shared attributes of the various varieties
of polygon.

The use of *foot* to name a part of the mountain results in the    6
appearance of *foot* in certain improbable phrase contexts. One hears, for
the first time, the *foot of the mountain* or *mountain's foot*. Until someone saw the similarity that generated the metaphor these sayings were
not heard. They cause the metaphor to live for others who have not
noticed the similarity in question. The anatomical reference is called to
mind by the word *foot* which has been its unequivocal name. The
context *of the mountain* is one in which this word has never appeared.
The phrase suggests such forms as *peak* or *top* or *slope* or *height* or *base*;
it is a functional attribute of all these. Only one of these forms has a
referent that is like the anatomical foot and that one is *base*. There is a
click of comprehension as the similarity is recognized and some pleasure
at the amusing conceit of a mountain with toes, a mountain anthropo-
morphized. If the metaphor was created for a poem about the mountain
climber's struggle with his almost human antagonist—the mountain itself—then the metaphor might figure importantly in communicating the
sense of the poem.

This metaphor blazed briefly for the person who created it and it    7
lights up again when anyone hears it for the first time, but for most of us
it is dead. This is because with repetition of the phrase *foot of the
mountain* the word *foot* loses its exclusive connection with anatomy.
The word may be used of mountain as often as of man. When that is true
there is nothing in the phrase *foot of the mountain* to suggest a man's foot
and so the phrase is experienced as a conventional name for the lower
part of a mountain. Part of the phrase is accidentally homophonic with
part of the phrase *foot of a man* but there is no more reason for one to
call the other to mind than there is for *board of wood* to remind us of

*board of directors, bored with psycholinguistics,* or *bored from within.*
In the interest of univocal reference we attend to the context in which
each form occurs and do not consider the meanings it might have in
other contexts.

The word *foot,* in isolation, is ambiguous. It has many referents    8
including the mountainous and the anatomical. That special attitude
toward language which brings out the potential metaphors now seems to
me to involve attending to forms in isolation, deliberately ignoring context. In this last sentence, for instance, consider the word *attending* and
disregard its surroundings. *Attending* names at least two kinds of behavior; there is "attending a lecture" and "attending to a lecture." The
latter behavior is notoriously not the same as the former. In the sentence
above only the intellectual attention sense of *attending* comes to mind;
the other is ruled out by context.

A metaphor lives in language so long as it causes a word to appear in    9
improbable contexts, the word suggesting one reference, the context
another. When the word becomes as familiar in its new contexts as it was
in the old the metaphor dies. This has happened with *foot of the mountain.* Sometimes there is a further stage in which the older set of contexts
dies altogether and also the older reference. In these circumstances one
speaks of a historical semantic change in the word. The term *strait-laced*
is applied nowadays to people who follow an exceptionally severe,
restrictive moral code. An older sense can be revived by placing the term
in one of its older contexts; "Mrs. Mather was miserable in her strait-
laced bodice." In the days when people laced their clothing *strait* meant
*tight* and to be *strait-laced* was literally to be rather tightly trussed up. It
is not difficult to see the attributes of this condition that resulted first in a
metaphor and then in a semantic change. Whether one is tightly laced
into his clothing or into his conscience he will feel confined, he may
strain against his bonds and burst them, or, when no one else is about, he
may secretly relax them a little. The metaphor is so rich that we should
not be surprised to find it in poetry as well as in the history of linguistic
change.

In fact there exists a poem founded on the very similarities that    10
caused strait-laced to change in meaning.

# Delight in Disorder

## *Robert Herrick*

A sweet disorder in the dress
Kindles in clothes a wantonness.
A lawn about the shoulders thrown
Into a fine distraction;
An erring lace, which here and there                 5
Enthrals the crimson stomacher;
A cuff neglectful, and thereby
Ribbands to flow confusedly;
A winning wave, deserving note,
In the tempestuous petticoat;                        10
A careless shoestring, in whose tie
I see a wild civility;—
Do more bewitch me, than when art
Is too precise in every part.

Herrick lived in seventeenth century England, through the period of 11
Puritan rule into the restoration of Charles II. F. W. Bateson . . . points
out that the poem reproduced above is concerned with more than disorder of costume. It is not only the clothes but also the wearers that Herrick
would have *sweet, wanton, distracted, erring, neglectful, winning, tempestuous, wild,* and *bewitching.* The poem is a plea for disorder of
manners and morals as well as of dress. It is a statement of anti-Puri-
tanism.

How does Herrick communicate these depth meanings? The poem 12
by its title professes to be concerned with dress. The word *disorder* can
be applied to dress, to manners, to politics, to morals, or even to a man's
wits. The fact that we are reading a poem makes us receptive to multiple
meanings but the title alone does not indicate what secondary meanings,
if any, are relevant. In the first line *sweet* sounds a trifle odd since it is not
often said of disorder in dress. *Sweet* starts several auxiliary lines of
thought having to do, perhaps, with girl friends, small children, and
sugar cane. Only one of these is reinforced by what follows. *Kindles* and
*wantonness* in the second line rule out children and sugar cane.
Thoughts about girls and loose behavior are supported by words like
*distraction, enthrals,* and *tempestuous.* All of these words can be used in
talking about clothes. However, their choice is improbable enough to call
for some explanation. Since the improbable words are all drawn from a
set of terms having to do with girls and their behavior a second group of
consistent references is created.

A scientist might call Herrick's message ambiguous since he uses 13
words that have several different referents and does not clearly sort these
out with criterial contexts. Behind that judgment is the assumption that
the poet intends, as a scientist might, to call attention to just one kind of
reference. In fact, however, Herrick wanted to talk simultaneously about
clothing, ladies, and morality and to do so in a very compact way. Rather
than string out three unequivocal vocabularies he uses one vocabulary
which is able to make three kinds of reference.

When a poet uses simile he explicitly invites us to note the sim- 14
ilarities and differences in two referents as in "My love is like a red, red
rose." When he uses metaphor a word is used in a context that calls for a
different word as in "The *lion* of England" or "My *rose* smiled at me."
The context evokes one reference, the word another and the meaning is
enriched by their similarities and differences. *Lion* and *king, rose* and
*love* concentrate on similarities. There is an extraordinary sentence of
e. e. cummings' . . . in which the difference in the two references is the
main thing: "And although her health eventually failed her she kept her
sense of humor to the *beginning*." The most probable word for final
position in that sentence is *end*. This is not only different from *beginning*, it is the antonym. The probability of *end* is so great that the reader
is bound to anticipate it. Finding instead its antonym almost makes us feel
reprimanded. Our worldly outlook has made us too prone to think of
death as the end.

## For Discussion and Writing

1. At the end of paragraph 4, Brown says that "it seems to be necessary
   to take a special attitude toward language, quite different from our
   everyday attitude, to discern the metaphors around us." Try to
   define or describe the attitude Brown is discussing.

2. Adopting the attitude of a student of metaphor, examine the metaphors that Brown himself employs—as in the first sentence of paragraph 7, for instance. Does his use of metaphor differ from that of a
   poet like Robert Herrick?

3. Examine more closely the poem by Herrick. Brown has discussed the
   major system of metaphor in the poem, but the poetic text is en-
   livened by other instances of metaphoric language. Discuss the range
   of meaning evoked by some of the following words in the poem:
   kindles (line 2)
   enthrals (line 4)
   flow, wave, tempestuous (lines 8, 9, 10)
   How do you understand a phrase like "wild civility"?

4. Produce, in your own words, a working definition of metaphor, with some appropriate illustrative examples. You will need some clear notion of metaphor to begin your study of the workings of this feature of language in poems, dreams, essays, and advertisements.

# *Metaphor in Three Poems*

Metaphor is a vital principle of all language, but it is especially important in poetry. If metaphors grow like weeds—in ordinary language—poets cultivate them, extend them, and combine them to make new hybrids that might never occur in nature but are exotic and exciting in those formal gardens we call poems.

Our study of the workings of metaphor will take us ultimately to essays, arguments, and advertising—back toward ordinary life. But we begin with three short poems, as laboratory specimens designed to illustrate some of the principles of metaphoric language. Please read them carefully and consider the questions for discussion and writing after each poem.

## Separation

### *W. S. Merwin*

Your absence has gone through me
Like thread through a needle.
Everything I do is stitched with its color.

## For Discussion and Writing

1. It has been said that a good simile or metaphor is both unexpected and appropriate. Consider Merwin's poem in the light of this view. How would you expect someone to complete the phrase "Your absence has gone through me like . . ."?

2. If someone said "Your absence has gone through me like a dagger," that would signify that separation is painful. What does Merwin's metaphor signify?

# "Let us honor . . ."

## W. H. Auden

Let us honor if we can
The vertical man
Though we value none
But the horizontal one.

## For Discussion and Writing

This very small poem was sent by Wystan Hugh Auden to his friend Christopher Isherwood, and later appeared at the beginning of a volume of Auden's poetry. The poem depends upon the use of two words that are nearly synonyms (*honor* and *value*) and two words that form an abstract, geometrical opposition (*vertical* and *horizontal* ). The reader is invited to make his or her own interpretive distinction between the meanings of *honor* and *value* and also to supply some concrete interpretations for *vertical* and *horizontal*. One way to do this is simply to rewrite the poem by filling in the blanks:

Let us _____ if we can
The _____ man
Though we _____ none
But the _____ one.

The assumption you must make in filling in these blanks is that *horizontal* and *vertical* are metaphors for something: for instance, death and life, slackness and probity. By supplying your interpretation, you collaborate in the completion of the poem.

Compare your version with others. Are some more satisfying than others? Is any one so satisfying that you feel like adopting it as "correct" and labeling the others wrong? Are any so unsatisfying that you want to rule them out entirely? Does the idea of interpretation as a collaborative or creative activity please or displease you? Discuss these matters.

# Metaphors

*Sylvia Plath*

I'm a riddle in nine syllables,
An elephant, a ponderous house,
A melon strolling on two tendrils.
O red fruit, ivory, fine timbers!
This loaf's big with its yeasty rising.                5
Money's new-minted in this fat purse.
I'm a means, a stage, a cow in calf.
I've eaten a bag of green apples,
Boarded the train there's no getting off.

## For Discussion and Writing

1. This poem is a riddle, with each line providing a metaphoric clue to
   its solution. Solve the riddle, and consider how the relationships
   between the metaphors contribute to its solution.

2. Compose your own riddle poem to present to the class for solution.
   Your subject should be something with which the class is familiar,
   such as a physical or emotional state (sleepiness, hunger, happiness,
   envy), or a place (classroom, fast-food restaurant), or a thing (car, TV,
   pizza). To get started, make a list of the qualities of your subject that
   first come to mind. Consider which quality or qualities best describe
   your subject, and concentrate on developing metaphors that will
   make your audience experience your subject from your point of
   view.

# Metaphor and Dream

For centuries people have believed that dreams are messages from somewhere, perhaps in a code that disguises their meaning. In our century a new theory of dreams has dominated discussion, the theory developed by Sigmund Freud. According to Freud, dreams are messages from the human unconscious, in a code designed to pass the censorship of our conscious mind. These messages, which have to do with our most primal needs and desires—especially those relating to sexuality—must be censored because we do not wish to admit that we could even "think" such things, since they conflict with our status as civilized, reasonable beings.

Freud has a name for the psychic process or mechanism that transforms our desires into acceptable shape. He calls it the *dream-work*. For our purposes Freud's dream-work is interesting on two counts. First, it operates much as do those linguistic devices called figures of speech, of which metaphor is especially important. Second, Freud calls the process of making sense of dreams *interpretation*, and what he means by interpretation is very close to what literary critics mean by the interpretation of poems.

Dreams and poems are texts that work in similar ways—to a certain extent. We are concerned here with both the similarities and the differences. But before discussing them, we should examine Freud's own definitions of his key terms. We have numbered and arranged these definitions here, but the language is Freud's (from the English translation of his *Introductory Lectures on Psychoanalysis*) except where indicated by square brackets:

# From Introductory Lectures on Psychoanalysis

### Sigmund Freud

1. *Latent* and *manifest*

We will describe what the dream actually tells us as the *manifest dream-content* and the concealed material, which we hope to reach by pursuing the ideas that occur to the dreamer, as the *latent dream-thoughts*.

## 2.    *Dream-work* and *work of interpretation*

The work which transforms the latent dream into the manifest one is called the *dream-work*. The work which proceeds in the contrary direction, which endeavors to arrive at the latent dream from the manifest one, is our work of *interpretation*. This work of interpretation seeks to undo the dream-work.

## 3.    *Condensation*

The first achievement of the dream-work is *condensation*. . . . Condensation is brought about (1) by the total omission of certain latent dream elements, (2) by only a fragment of some complexes in the latent dream passing over into the manifest one and (3) by latent elements which have something in common being combined and fused into a single unity in the manifest dream. . . . The dream-work tries to condense two different thoughts by seeking out (like a joke) an ambiguous word in which the two thoughts may come together.

## 4.    *Displacement*

The second achievement of the dream-work is displacement. . . . It manifests itself in two ways: in the first, a latent element is replaced not by a component part of itself but by something more remote—that is, by an allusion; and in the second, the psychical accent is shifted from an important element on to another which is unimportant, so that the dream appears differently centered and strange.

## 5.    *Imagery*

The third achievement of the dream-work is psychologically the most interesting. It consists in transforming thoughts into visual images. [Freud suggests that we can imagine how this works by trying to translate a political editorial into pictures.] In so far as the article mentioned people and concrete objects you will replace them easily and perhaps even advantageously by pictures; but your difficulties will begin when you come to the representation of abstract words and of all those parts of speech which indicate relations between thoughts—such as particles, conjunctions and so on. In the case of abstract words . . . you will recall that most abstract words are "watered-down" concrete ones, and you will for that reason hark back as often as possible to the original concrete meaning of such words. Thus you will be pleased to find that you can represent the "possession" of an object by a real, physical sitting down on it.

*As we can see from Freud's definitions, the dream-work functions in order to conceal meaning. But it conceals meaning in order to express it. Its motto might be, "Better disguised expression than no expression at all." The language of poetry uses metaphor and other ways of displacing and condensing meaning for similar ends. In most poetry, however, meanings are displaced and condensed consciously, so as to give the reader an active role in constructing meanings for a poetic text, through the process that we call interpretation.*

*Poetic meaning, however, is not simply a matter of a poet's having a clear meaning and then disguising it. A poem is often a search for meaning on the part of the poet, who seeks—like the dream-work—to find signs and symbols for feelings that lie too deep within his or her psyche to have a definite mental shape. Poetic metaphor, then, is a way of pointing to meanings that can only be made clear by an act of interpretation.*

*You will have a chance to do some interpreting of poetic texts later on, but now we would like you to consider briefly some instances of poets using metaphor in a way especially close to the manner in which Freud says the dream-work functions. These poets, who called themselves "surrealists," tried to push metaphor to the point of nonsense, as a way of allowing the unconscious to speak in images. In the next section you will have a chance to examine for yourself the relationship between poems and dreams.*

# *Surrealist Metaphor*

How far can metaphor be extended? If all naming is metaphorical, moving toward the unknown by analogies with what is already known and safely named, perhaps a poet can suggest new realities by metaphorically linking unusual or incompatible things. The surrealist movement in art and literature is based on disrupting our habitual sense of reality so as to allow us glimpses of a deeper reality. Consider, for instance what the surrealist poet André Breton (1896–1966) said about the images that combine to make metaphors:

> For me, the strongest is one that presents
> the highest degree of arbitrariness . . . ; one
> that requires the longest time to translate
> into practical language, either because it
> contains an enormous dose of apparent                      5
> contradiction, or because one of the terms
> is strangely hidden, or because it appears
> to unravel feebly after heralding itself as
> sensational . . . , or because it very naturally
> lays the masque of the concrete upon abstract             10
> things, or vice versa, or because it implies
> the negation of some elementary physical
> property, or because it unleashes laughter.

(Cauvin and Caws, xix)

If a balanced view of poetic metaphor insists on images that are combined in a way that is both surprising *and* appropriate, the surrealists take an extreme position in favor of the surprising combination, as in the following lines from one of Breton's poems:

> . . . there go the fuses blown again
> Here's the squid with his elbows on the window sill
> And here wondering where to unfold his sparkling sewer grill
> Is the clown of the eclipse in his white outfit
> Eyes in his pocket. . . .

The impossibility of a squid leaning elbows (of all things) on a window sill is perhaps the most striking thing about this language. Its parts just won't go together to form a "normal" image. But the possibility that this bizarre image is a metaphor for something else is both tantalizing and a little threatening. Is there some particular meaning that we are intended to decode? And are we stupid if we can't discover it?

Above all, the surrealists want to disabuse their readers of the notion that they have hidden a correct meaning behind every metaphor. They have allowed their unconscious minds to interrupt the logic of consciousness. If meanings have been generated, the surrealist poet and his or her readers will have to look for them together. Breton hopes that his images will have a high degree of arbitrariness, that they will require time and effort to be translated into "practical language." Notice that he does not say that they should be impossible to translate, only that they should offer resistance. Breton would like the reader's unconscious to enter into the process of translation. He wants us to play with his images until we begin to see how to connect and interpret them. Try, for instance, playing with the "clown of the eclipse" until you generate some reason for him to have "eyes in his pocket."

## For Discussion

At this point it will be helpful for you to compare what Breton said in the quotation above (p. 66) to Freud's description of the dream-work quoted in the previous section (pp. 63–64). If we reduce Breton's statement to its purely descriptive notions, we get something like this:
1. apparent contradiction
2. hidden term
3. concrete for abstract
4. abstract for concrete
5. negation of physical property

This is not the same as Freud's list, by any means, but there is some overlap. Discuss these five processes until you understand what is meant by each one, and then compare this list to Freud's description of the dream-work. Note both the common features and the differences. This development of your analytical terminology will help you in doing the assignments to come.

# Two Poems

*Some of our finest poets have been influenced by the surrealists. Both W. S. Merwin and Wallace Stevens like to develop metaphoric images that set our ordinary perceptions back on their heels. In one of his poems Stevens tells us, in words very similar to Breton's, that "The poem must resist the intelligence/Almost successfully." The "almost" is important, but most of the major modern poets have believed that the intelligence must be "resisted" in order to free the imagination to discover things that mere intelligence would not notice. This is one reason why some poems are difficult—not to embarrass their readers but to challenge us and stimulate our own creativity.*

*Read the following two poems by Breton and Stevens with this in mind, and consider the points raised for discussion.*

# Broken Line
for Raymond Roussel

*André Breton*

We plain bread and water in the prisons of the sky
We the paving stones of love all the interrupted signals
Who personify the charms of this poem
Nothing expresses us beyond death
At this hour when night puts on its polished ankle-boots to go out      5
We take our time as it comes
Like a party wall adjoining that of our prisons
Spiders bring the ship into the harbor
One has only to touch there is nothing to see
Later you shall learn who we are                                        10
Our labors are still well protected
But it's dawn on the last shore the weather is worsening
Soon we'll carry our cumbersome luxury elsewhere
We'll carry the luxury of the plague elsewhere
We a little hoarfrost on human firewood                                15
And that's all
Brandy dresses wounds in a cellar through the vent from which one
    glimpses a road lined with great empty patience-docks

Don't ask where you are
We plain bread and water in the prisons of the sky
Card game under the stars                                          20
We scarcely lift the veil by its edge
The mender of crockery is working on a ladder
He looks young despite the concession
We wear yellow mourning for him
The pact is not yet signed                                         25
The sisters of charity provoke
Escapes on the horizon
Perhaps we palliate at the same time evil and good
Thus it is that the will of dreams is done
People you who could                                               30
Our rigors become lost in the regret of all that crumbles
We are the popular idols of the more terrible seduction
Ragman Morning's hook on flowery tatters
Casts us to the fury of long-toothed treasures
Don't add anything to the shame of your own pardon                 35
'Tis enough to arm toward a bottomless end
Your eyes with these ridiculous tears that relieve us
The belly of words is golden this evening and nothing is in vain any
    more

# For Discussion and Writing

1. Breton's poem is called "Broken Line," and it celebrates, among
   other things, "the interrupted signals/Who personify the charms of
   this poem." Speculate, for a moment, on the connections among
   broken lines, interrupted signals, and poetic charms.

2. Certain individual lines of Breton's poem can provoke interesting
   thoughts if we simply meditate on what they mean to *us*, without
   worrying about whether these meanings are "intended" or "correct." Using one of the following lines from the poem (or any other
   single line of your choice) write a few sentences on what the line
   means to you or what it leads you to think about:
       line 13  Soon we'll carry our cumbersome luxury elsewhere
       line 28  Perhaps we palliate at the same time evil and good
       line 29  Thus it is that the will of dreams is done
       line 32  We are the popular idols of the more terrible seduction
       line 35  Don't add anything to the shame of your own pardon

3. Many of Breton's lines would not be shocking or difficult at all if one or two words were changed to give the line a consistent topic. Consider the following revisions, for instance:

    line  8  Spiders bring the ship into the harbor
                Tugboats bring the ship into the harbor
    line 22  The mender of crockery is working on a ladder
                The mender of crockery is working on a pot
    line 32  We are the popular idols of the more terrible seduction
                We are the popular idols of the more fashionable seduction
    line 35  Don't add anything to the shame of your own pardon
                Don't add anything to the shame of your own crime.

By giving these—and other—lines a simple prose sense we can begin to see how the surrealistic effect is managed—and we can also see why some of these lines are simply startling while others are both startling and interesting. Discuss the lines presented here, and then write a paper in which you extend your research in this direction: Take a line from Breton's poem and translate it—with minimal change—into simple prose. Then discuss the differences between the meanings of the two versions of the line. Perform the same operation with one or two additional lines. Use your analyses as the basis for some speculation about the method and uses of surrealist poetry.

4. Go back to the poem by Robert Herrick quoted by Roger Brown on p. 57. Starting with the title, make a few changes in every line so as to turn "Delight in Disorder" into a surrealist poem. Try to produce something in the spirit of Breton. Don't worry if the lines lose their rhythm or rhyme. In class, exchange poems and discuss the most interesting poems or lines with their authors. The point of this exercise is to confront the problems of interpretation and the problems of composition together.

5. Reconsider Breton's "Broken Line" in the light of his discussion of the metaphoric image. Try to locate the specific devices he mentions in his own poetic lines. For instance, is line 8 a case of "negation of some elementary physical property" or a line that "appears to unravel feebly after heralding itself as sensational"—or both?

# Domination of Black

## *Wallace Stevens*

At night, by the fire,
The colors of the bushes
And of the fallen leaves,
Repeating themselves,
Turned in the room,                                          5
Like the leaves themselves
Turning in the wind.
Yes: but the color of the heavy hemlocks
Came striding.
And I remembered the cry of the peacocks.                    10

The colors of their tails
Were like the leaves themselves
Turning in the wind,
In the twilight wind.
They swept over the room,                                    15
Just as they flew from the boughs of the hemlocks
Down to the ground.
I heard them cry—the peacocks.
Was it a cry against the twilight
Or against the leaves themselves                             20
Turning in the wind,
Turning as the flames
Turned in the fire,
Turning as the tails of the peacocks
Turned in the loud fire,                                     25
Loud as the hemlocks
Full of the cry of the peacocks?
Or was it a cry against the hemlocks?

Out of the window,
I saw how the planets gathered                               30
Like the leaves themselves
Turning in the wind.
I saw how the night came,
Came striding like the color of the heavy hemlocks.
I felt afraid.                                               35
And I remembered the cry of the peacocks.

# For Discussion and Writing

In some respects this resembles a surrealist poem. Its images are striking, unexpected. The poem resists interpretation, but it is not meant to resist successfully. For one thing, we can locate a single situation in the poem: a person in a room, with a fire going in a fireplace, in autumn, at night, thinking about darkness. We can also find certain images repeated in the poem, giving it a higher degree of coherence than a surrealist poem.

To interpret the poem, we need to understand how the images are connected. How, for instance, are autumn leaves and peacocks' tails connected? There are only a few clusters of images in the poem: the autumn leaves, the hemlock bushes, the peacocks, the firelight, and the darkness. Write a short paper in which you express in your own words the meaning of the poem. Among other things, you should explore the connections among images, the meaning of the title, and the significance of the cry of the peacocks.

# *Poetic Uses of Metaphor*

What follows is a minianthology of poems selected because each of them is short and makes some interesting use of metaphor. Some of them are about the poetic process and about metaphor in particular. Others are about other things but employ similes or other kinds of metaphoric process as a way of presenting their ideas.

If you have attended to the previous work on metaphor in this book, you should be in a position now to write an essay on the way metaphors work in poetry. We ask you, then, to write such an essay, using the following minianthology as your source for examples. You are not being asked to write an interpretation of each poem, but to draw from the poems certain metaphors to illustrate your discussion.

In writing your essay you should consider some of the following matters:

1. Why do poets use metaphors so frequently?
2. What does the use of metaphor have to do with the "difficulty" of poetry?
3. What does the use of metaphor have to do with the pleasures of poetry?
4. What makes an interesting metaphor interesting?
5. How do metaphors contribute to the power of poetry to move us emotionally or to amuse us?

In the course of your discussion, you should consider some specific metaphors drawn from these poems, exploring and explaining the meanings generated by each metaphor. In the case of an extended comparison, you should examine the way that the details of description apply to both the things being compared. For instance, Robert Francis's poem "Pitcher" describes what a baseball pitcher does in such a way that it becomes a metaphor for what a poet does. The result changes our way of thinking about both activities: pitching and writing poetry. But the effectiveness of the poem depends upon the way that the details of the description support both ends of the comparison, and that is the sort of analysis that you should make in your essay. To make it, of course, you have to understand that the comparison is being made—that the description is not just description but metaphoric. You need to be an alert reader and to read each poem over until you have a real grip on its meanings. If the poet is the pitcher, you are the batter—but in this case you can make him keep on throwing the same pitch until you really get a hold of it.

Remember, you are not being asked to go through each poem and write about what it means. You are being asked to draw from the poems the material that will enable you to produce your own essay on why and how poets use metaphors.

## "Doesn't he realize . . ."

*Ono no Komachi*
*Translated from Japanese by*
K. Rexroth and I. Atsumi

Doesn't he realize
that I am not
like the swaying kelp
in the surf,
where the seaweed gatherer
can come as often as he wants.

## Word

*Stephen Spender*

The word bites like a fish.
Shall I throw it back free
Arrowing to that sea
Where thoughts lash tail and fin?
Or shall I pull it in
To rhyme upon a dish?

## Pitcher

*Robert Francis*

His art is eccentricity, his aim
How not to hit the mark he seems to aim at,

His passion how to avoid the obvious,
His technique how to vary the avoidance.

The others throw to be comprehended. He                5
Throws to be a moment misunderstood.

Yet not too much. Not errant, arrant, wild,
But every seeming aberration willed.

Not to, yet still, still to communicate
Making the batter understand too late.                  10

# Ars Poetica

### X. J. Kennedy

The goose that laid the golden egg
Died looking up its crotch
To find out how its sphincter worked.

Would you lay well? Don't watch.

# Cottonmouth Country

### Louise Glück

Fish bones walked the waves off Hatteras.
And there were other signs
That Death wooed us, by water, wooed us
By land: among the pines
An uncurled cottonmouth that rolled on moss
Reared in the polluted air.
Birth, not death, is the hard loss.
I know. I also left a skin there.

# A Sort of a Song
### *William Carlos Williams*

Let the snake wait under
his weed
and the writing
be of words, slow and quick, sharp
to strike, quiet to wait,                     5
sleepless.

—through metaphor to reconcile
the people and the stones.
Compose. (No ideas
but in things) Invent!                        10
Saxifrage is my flower that splits
the rocks.

# Praise in Summer
### *Richard Wilbur*

Obscurely yet most surely called to praise,
As sometimes summer calls us all, I said
The hills are heavens full of branching ways
Where star-nosed moles fly overhead the dead;
I said the trees are mines in air, I said          5
See how the sparrow burrows in the sky!
And then I wondered why this mad *instead*
Perverts our praise to uncreation, why
Such savor's in this wrenching things awry.
Does sense so stale that it must needs derange     10
The world to know it? To a praiseful eye
Should it not be enough of fresh and strange
That trees grow green, and moles can course in clay,
And sparrows sweep the ceiling of our day?

# How Soft This Prison Is

## *Emily Dickinson*

How soft this Prison is
How sweet these sullen bars
No Despot but the King of Down
Invented this repose

Of Fate if this is All
Has he no added Realm
A Dungeon but a Kinsman is
Incarceration—Home.

# Moving in Winter

## *Adrienne Rich*

Their life, collapsed like unplayed cards,
is carried piecemeal through the snow:
Headboard and footboard now, the bed
where she has lain desiring him
where overhead his sleep will build                               5
its canopy to smother her once more;
their table, by four elbows worn
evening after evening while the wax runs down;
mirrors grey with reflecting them,
bureaus coffining from the cold                                   10
things that can shuffle in a drawer,
carpets rolled up around those echoes
which, shaken out, take wing and breed
new altercations, the old silences.

# Eating Poetry

*Mark Strand*

Ink runs from the corners of my mouth.
There is no happiness like mine.
I have been eating poetry.

The librarian does not believe what she sees.
Her eyes are sad                                                    5
and she walks with her hands in her dress.

The poems are gone.
The light is dim.
The dogs are on the basement stairs and coming up.

Their eyeballs roll,                                               10
their blond legs burn like brush.
The poor librarian begins to stamp her feet and weep.

She does not understand.
When I get on my knees and lick her hand,
she screams.                                                       15
I am a new man.
I snarl at her and bark.
I romp with joy in the bookish dark.

# Inscription Facing Western Sea

*W. S. Merwin*

Lord of each wave comes in
campaign finished ten thousand miles
years clashes winds dead moons
riderless horses no messages
he lays down flag bowing quickly and retires            5
his flag
sun waits to take him home
flag fades
sand
stars gather again to watch the war                     10

# Of Mere Being

## *Wallace Stevens*

The palm at the end of the mind,
Beyond the last thought, rises
In the bronze decor,

A gold-feathered bird
Sings in the palm, without human meaning,                5
Without human feeling, a foreign song.

You know then that it is not the reason
That makes us happy or unhappy.
The bird sings. Its feathers shine.

The palm stands on the edge of space.                   10
The wind moves slowly in the branches.
The bird's fire-fangled feathers dangle down.

# *Metaphor as a Basis for Thought*

In the last section we considered metaphor as a way of structuring poetry. Here we will be looking not only at metaphor as a way of structuring prose but also at the ways in which metaphor structures our thinking. How this structuring is revealed in our everyday language has been of primary interest to linguists George Lakoff and Mark Johnson. The material presented here is from their book *Metaphors We Live By*.

## Concepts We Live By

### *George Lakoff and Mark Johnson*

Metaphor is for most people a device of the poetic imagination and the rhetorical flourish—a matter of extraordinary rather than ordinary language. Moreover, metaphor is typically viewed as characteristic of language alone, a matter of words rather than thought or action. For this reason, most people think they can get along perfectly well without metaphor. We have found, on the contrary, that metaphor is pervasive in everyday life, not just in language but in thought and action. Our ordinary conceptual system, in terms of which we both think and act, is fundamentally metaphorical in nature. 1

The concepts that govern our thought are not just matters of the intellect. They also govern our everyday functioning, down to the most mundane details. Our concepts structure what we perceive, how we get around in the world, and how we relate to other people. Our conceptual system thus plays a central role in defining our everyday realities. If we are right in suggesting that our conceptual system is largely metaphorical, then the way we think, what we experience, and what we do every day is very much a matter of metaphor. 2

But our conceptual system is not something we are normally aware of. In most of the little things we do every day, we simply think and act more or less automatically along certain lines. Just what these lines are is by no means obvious. One way to find out is by looking at language. Since communication is based on the same conceptual system that we use in thinking and acting, language is an important source of evidence for what that system is like. 3

Primarily on the basis of linguistic evidence, we have found that most of our ordinary conceptual system is metaphorical in nature. And 4 we have found a way to begin to identify in detail just what the metaphors are that structure how we perceive, how we think, and what we do.

To give some idea of what it could mean for a concept to be   5 metaphorical and for such a concept to structure an everyday activity, let us start with the concept ARGUMENT and the conceptual metaphor ARGUMENT IS WAR. This metaphor is reflected in our everyday language by a wide variety of expressions:

# Argument Is War

> Your claims are *indefensible*.
> He *attacked every weak point* in my argument.
> His criticisms were *right on target*.
> I *demolished* his argument.
> I've never *won* an argument with him.
> You disagree? Okay, *shoot*!
> If you use that *strategy*, he'll *wipe you out*.
> He *shot down* all of my arguments.

It is important to see that we don't just *talk* about arguments in   6 terms of war. We can actually win or lose arguments. We see the person we are arguing with as an opponent. We attack his positions and we defend our own. We gain and lose ground. We plan and use strategies. If we find a position indefensible, we can abandon it and take a new line of attack. Many of the things we *do* in arguing are partially structured by the concept of war. Though there is no physical battle, there is a verbal battle, and the structure of an argument—attack, defense, counterattack, etc.—reflects this. It is in this sense that the ARGUMENT IS WAR metaphor is one that we live by in this culture; it structures the actions we perform in arguing.

Try to imagine a culture where arguments are not viewed in terms of   7 war, where no one wins or loses, where there is no sense of attacking or defending, gaining or losing ground. Imagine a culture where an argument is viewed as a dance, the participants are seen as performers, and the goal is to perform in a balanced and aesthetically pleasing way. In such a culture, people would view arguments differently, experience them differently, carry them out differently, and talk about them differently. But *we* would probably not view them as arguing at all: they would simply be doing something different. It would seem strange even to call what they were doing "arguing." Perhaps the most neutral way of describing this difference between their culture and ours would be to say that we have a discourse form structured in terms of battle and they have one structured in terms of dance.

This is an example of what it means for a metaphorical concept, 8 namely, ARGUMENT IS WAR, to structure (at least in part) what we do and how we understand what we are doing when we argue. *The essence of metaphor is understanding and experiencing one kind of thing in terms of another*. It is not that arguments are a subspecies of war. Arguments and wars are different kinds of things—verbal discourse and armed conflict—and the actions performed are different kinds of actions. But ARGUMENT is partially structured, understood, performed, and talked about in terms of WAR. The concept is metaphorically structured, the activity is metaphorically structured, and, consequently, the language is metaphorically structured.

Moreover, this is the *ordinary* way of having an argument and 9 talking about one. The normal way for us to talk about attacking a position is to use the words "attack a position." Our conventional ways of talking about arguments presuppose a metaphor we are hardly ever conscious of. The metaphor is not merely in the words we use—it is in our very concept of an argument. The language of argument is not poetic, fanciful, or rhetorical; it is literal. We talk about arguments that way because we conceive of them that way—and we act according to the way we conceive of things.

# Some Further Examples

We have been claiming that metaphors partially structure our everyday 10 concepts and that this structure is reflected in our literal language. Before we can get an overall picture of the philosophical implications of these claims, we need a few more examples. In each of the ones that follow we give a metaphor and a list of ordinary expressions that are special cases of the metaphor. The English expressions are of two sorts: simple literal expressions and idioms that fit the metaphor and are part of the normal everyday way of talking about the subject.

### *Theories (and Arguments) Are Buildings*
Is that the *foundation* for your theory? The theory needs more *support*. The argument is *shaky*. We need some more facts or the argument will *fall apart*. We need to *construct* a *strong* argument

for that. I haven't figured out yet what the *form* of the argument will be. Here are some more facts to *shore up* the theory. We need to *buttress* the theory with *solid* arguments. The theory will *stand* or *fall* on the *strength* of that argument. The argument *collapsed*. They *exploded* his latest theory. We will show that theory to be without *foundation*. So far we have put together only the *framework* of the theory.

### Ideas Are Food

What he said *left a bad taste in my mouth*. All this paper has in it are *raw facts, half-baked ideas, and warmed-over theories*. There are too many facts here for me to *digest* them all. I just can't *swallow* that claim. That argument *smells fishy*. Let me *stew* over that for a while. Now there's a theory you can really *sink your teeth into*. We need to let that idea *percolate* for a while. That's *food for thought*. He's a *voracious* reader. We don't need to *spoon-feed* our students. He *devoured* the book. Let's let that idea *simmer on the back burner* for a while. This is the *meaty* part of the paper. Let that idea *jell* for a while. That idea has been *fermenting* for years.

With respect to life and death IDEAS ARE ORGANISMS, either PEO- 11
PLE or PLANTS.

### Ideas Are People

The theory of relativity *gave birth to* an enormous number of ideas in physics. He is the *father* of modern biology. Whose *brainchild* was that? Look at what his ideas have *spawned*. Those ideas *died off* in the Middle Ages. His ideas will *live on* forever. Cognitive psychology is still in its *infancy*. That's an idea that ought to be *resurrected*. Where'd you *dig up* that idea? He *breathed new life into* that idea.

### Ideas Are Plants

His ideas have finally come to *fruition*. That idea *died on the vine*. That's a *budding* theory. It will take years for that idea to *come to full flower*. He views chemistry as a mere *offshoot* of physics. Mathematics has many *branches*. The *seeds* of his great ideas were *planted* in his youth. She has a *fertile* imagination. Here's an idea that I'd like to *plant* in your mind. He has a *barren* mind.

### Ideas Are Products

We're really *turning (churning, cranking, grinding) out* new ideas. We've *generated* a lot of ideas this week. He *produces* new ideas at an astounding rate. His *intellectual productivity* has decreased in recent years. We need to *take the rough edges off* that idea, *hone it down*, *smooth it out*. It's a rough idea; it needs to be *refined*.

### Ideas Are Commodities

It's important how you *package* your ideas. He won't *buy* that. That idea just won't *sell*. There is always a *market* for good ideas. That's a *worthless* idea. He's been a source of *valuable* ideas. I wouldn't *give a plugged nickel for* that idea. Your ideas don't have a chance in the *intellectual marketplace*.

### Ideas Are Resources

He *ran out of* ideas. Don't *waste* your thoughts on small projects. Let's *pool* our ideas. He's a *resourceful* man. We've *used up* all our ideas. That's a *useless* idea. That idea will *go a long way*.

### Ideas Are Money

Let me put in my *two cents' worth*. He's *rich* in ideas. That book is a *treasure trove* of ideas. He has a *wealth* of ideas.

### Ideas Are Cutting Instruments

That's an *incisive* idea. That *cuts right to the heart of* the matter. That was a *cutting* remark. He's *sharp*. He has a *razor* wit. He has a *keen* mind. She *cut* his argument *to ribbons*.

### Ideas Are Fashions

That idea went *out of style* years ago. I hear sociobiology *is in* these days. Marxism is currently *fashionable* in western Europe. That idea is *old hat*! That's an *outdated* idea. What are the new *trends* in English criticism? *Old-fashioned* notions have no place in today's society. He keeps *up-to-date* by reading the New York Review of Books. Berkeley is a center of *avant-garde* thought. Semiotics has become quite *chic*. The idea of revolution is no longer *in vogue* in the United States. The transformational grammar *craze* hit the United States in the mid-sixties and has just made it to Europe.

### Understanding Is Seeing;
### Ideas Are Light-Sources;
### Discourse Is a Light-Medium

I *see* what you're saying. It *looks* different from my *point of view*. What is your *outlook* on that? I *view* it differently. Now I've got the *whole picture*. Let me *point something out* to you. That's an *insightful* idea. That was a *brilliant* remark. The argument is *clear*. It was a *murky* discussion. Could you *elucidate* your remarks? It's a *transparent* argument. The discussion was *opaque*.

### Love Is a Physical Force
### (Electromagnetic, Gravitational, etc.)

I could feel the *electricity* between us. There were *sparks*. I was *magnetically drawn* to her. They are uncontrollably *attracted* to each other. They *gravitated* to each other immediately. His whole life *revolves* around her. The *atmosphere* around them is always *charged*. There is incredible *energy* in their relationship. They lost their *momentum*.

### Love Is a Patient

This is a *sick* relationship. They have a *strong, healthy* marriage. The marriage is *dead*—it can't be *revived*. Their marriage is *on the mend*. We're getting *back on our feet*. Their relationship is *in really good shape*. They've got a *listless* marriage. Their marriage is *on its last legs*. It's a *tired* affair.

### Love Is Madness

I'm *crazy* about her. She *drives me out of my mind*. He constantly *raves* about her. He's gone *mad* over her. I'm just *wild* about Harry. I'm *insane* about her.

### Love Is Magic

She *cast her spell* over me. The *magic* is gone. I was *spellbound*. She had me *hypnotized*. He has me *in a trance*. I was *entranced* by him. I'm *charmed* by her. She is *bewitching*.

### Love Is War

He is known for his many rapid *conquests*. She *fought for* him, but his mistress *won out*. He *fled from* her *advances*. She *pursued* him *relentlessly*. He is slowly *gaining ground* with her. He *won* her hand in marriage. He *overpowered* her. She is *besieged* by suitors. He has to *fend* them *off*. He *enlisted the aid* of her friends. He *made an ally* of her mother. Theirs is a *misalliance* if I've ever seen one.

### Wealth Is a Hidden Object

He's *seeking* his fortune. He's flaunting his *new-found* wealth. He's a *fortune-hunter*. She's a *gold-digger*. He *lost* his fortune. He's *searching for* wealth.

### Significant Is Big

He's a *big* man in the garment industry. He's a *giant* among writers. That's the *biggest* idea to hit advertising in years. He's *head and shoulders above* everyone in the industry. It was only a *small* crime. That was only a *little* white lie. I was astounded at the *enormity* of the crime. That was one of the *greatest* moments in World Series history. His accomplishments *tower over* those of *lesser* men.

### Seeing Is Touching; Eyes Are Limbs

I can't *take* my eyes *off* her. He sits with his eyes *glued to* the TV. Her eyes *picked out* every detail of the pattern. Their eyes *met*. She never *moves* her eyes *from* his face. She *ran* her eyes *over* everything in the room. He wants everything *within reach of* his eyes.

### The Eyes Are Containers for the Emotions

I could see the fear *in* his eyes. His eyes were *filled* with anger. There was passion *in* her eyes. His eyes *displayed* his compassion. She couldn't *get* the fear *out* of her eyes. Love *showed in* his eyes. Her eyes *welled* with emotion.

### Emotional Effect Is Physical Contact

His mother's death *hit* him *hard*. That idea *bowled me over*. She's a *knockout*. I was *struck* by his sincerity. That really *made an impression* on me. He *made his mark on* the world. I was *touched* by his remark. That *blew me away*.

### Physical and Emotional States Are Entities Within a Person

He has a pain *in* his shoulder. Don't *give* me the flu. My cold has *gone from my head to my chest*. His pains *went away*. His depression *returned*. Hot tea and honey will *get rid of* your cough. He could barely *contain* his joy. The smile *left* his face. *Wipe* that sneer *off* your face, private! His fears *keep coming back*. I've got to *shake off* this depression—it keeps *hanging on*. If you've got a cold, drinking lots of tea will *flush it out* of your system. There isn't a *trace* of cowardice *in* him. He hasn't got *an honest bone in his body*.

### Vitality Is a Substance

She's *brimming* with vim and vigor. She's *overflowing* with vitality. He's *devoid* of energy. I don't *have* any energy *left* at the end of the day. I'm *drained*. That *took a lot out of* me.

### Life Is a Container

I've had a *full* life. Life is *empty* for him. There's *not much left* for him *in* life. Her life is *crammed* with activities. *Get the most out of life*. His life *contained* a great deal of sorrow. Live your life *to the fullest*.

### Life Is a Gambling Game

I'll *take my chances*. The *odds are against me*. I've got an *ace up my sleeve*. He's *holding all the aces*. It's a *toss-up*. If you *play your cards right*, you can do it. He *won big*. He's a real *loser*. Where is he when the *chips are down*? That's my *ace in the hole*. He's *bluffing*. The president is *playing it close to his vest*. Let's *up the ante*. Maybe we need to *sweeten the pot*. I think we should *stand pat*. That's *the luck of the draw*. Those are *high stakes*.

In this last group of examples we have a collection of what are called 12 "speech formulas," or "fixed-form expressions," or "phrasal lexical items." These function in many ways like single words, and the language has thousands of them. In the examples given, a set of such phrasal lexical items is coherently structured by a single metaphorical concept. Although each of them is an instance of the LIFE IS A GAMBLING GAME metaphor, they are typically used to speak of life, not of gambling situations. They are normal ways of talking about life situations, just as using the word "construct" is a normal way of talking about theories. It is in this sense that we include them in what we have called literal expressions structured by metaphorical concepts. If you say "The odds are against us" or "We'll have to take our chances," you would not be viewed as speaking metaphorically but as using the normal everyday language appropriate to the situation. Nevertheless, your way of talking about, conceiving, and even experiencing your situation would be metaphorically structured.

# The Partial Nature of Metaphorical Structuring

Up to this point we have described the systematic character of meta- 13 phorically defined concepts. Such concepts are understood in terms of a number of different metaphors (e.g., TIME IS MONEY, TIME IS A MOVING OBJECT, etc.). The metaphorical structuring of concepts is necessarily partial and is reflected in the lexicon of the language, including the phrasal lexicon, which contains fixed-form expressions such as "to be without foundation." Because concepts are metaphorically structured in a systematic way, e.g., THEORIES ARE BUILDINGS, it is possible for us to use expressions (*construct, foundation*) from one domain (BUILDINGS) to talk about corresponding concepts in the metaphorically defined domain (THEORIES). What *foundation*, for example, means in the metaphorically defined domain (THEORY) will depend on the details of how the metaphorical concept THEORIES ARE BUILDINGS is used to structure the concept THEORY.

The parts of the concept BUILDING that are used to structure the 14 concept THEORY are the foundation and the outer shell. The roof, internal rooms, staircases, and hallways are parts of a building not used as part of the concept THEORY. Thus the metaphor THEORIES ARE BUILDINGS has a "used" part (foundation and outer shell) and an "unused" part (rooms, staircases, etc.). Expressions such as *construct* and *foundation* are instances of the used part of such a metaphorical concept and are part of our ordinary literal language about theories.

But what of the linguistic expressions that reflect the "unused" part 15 of a metaphor like THEORIES ARE BUILDINGS? Here are four examples:

> His theory has thousands of little rooms and long, winding corridors.
> His theories are Bauhaus in their pseudofunctional simplicity.
> He prefers massive Gothic theories covered with gargoyles.
> Complex theories usually have problems with the plumbing.

These sentences fall outside the domain of normal literal language and are part of what is usually called "figurative" or "imaginative" language. Thus, literal expressions ("he has constructed a theory") and imaginative expressions ("His theory is covered with gargoyles") can be instances of the same general metaphor (THEORIES ARE BUILDINGS).

Here we can distinguish three different subspecies of imaginative (or 16 nonliteral) metaphor:

> Extensions of the used part of a metaphor, e.g., "These facts are the bricks and mortar of my theory." Here the outer shell of the building is referred to, whereas the THEORIES ARE BUILDINGS metaphor stops short of mentioning the materials used.

> Instances of the unused part of the literal metaphor, e.g., "His theory has thousands of little rooms and long, winding corridors."

Instances of novel metaphor, that is, a metaphor not used to structure part of our normal conceptual system but as a new way of
thinking about something, e.g., "Classical theories are patriarchs
who father many children, most of whom fight incessantly." Each
of these subspecies lies outside the *used* part of a metaphorical
concept that structures our normal conceptual system.

We note in passing that all of the linguistic expressions we have given 17
to characterize general metaphorical concepts are figurative. Examples
are TIME IS MONEY, TIME IS A MOVING OBJECT, CONTROL IS UP,
IDEAS ARE FOOD, THEORIES ARE BUILDINGS, etc. None of these is
literal. This is a consequence of the fact that only *part* of them is used to
structure our normal concepts. Since they necessarily contain parts that
are not used in our normal concepts, they go beyond the realm of the
literal.

Each of the metaphorical expressions we have talked about so far 18
(e.g., the time *will come*; we *construct* a theory, *attack* an idea) is used
within a whole system of metaphorical concepts—concepts that we
constantly use in living and thinking. These expressions, like all other
words and phrasal lexical items in the language, are fixed by convention.
In addition to these cases, which are parts of whole metaphorical systems, there are idiosyncratic metaphorical expressions that stand alone
and are not used systematically in our language or thought. These are
well-known expressions like the *foot* of the mountain, a *head* of cabbage,
the *leg* of a table, etc. These expressions are isolated instances of metaphorical concepts, where there is only one instance of a used part (or
maybe two or three). Thus the *foot* of the mountain is the only used part
of the metaphor A MOUNTAIN IS A PERSON. In normal discourse we do
not speak of the *head, shoulders*, or *trunk* of a mountain, though in
special contexts it is possible to construct novel metaphorical expressions based on these unused parts. In fact, there is an aspect of the
metaphor A MOUNTAIN IS A PERSON in which mountain climbers will
speak of the *shoulder* of a mountain (namely, a ridge near the top) and of
*conquering, fighting*, and even *being killed by* a mountain. And there are
cartoon conventions where mountains become animate and their peaks
become heads. The point here is that there are metaphors, like A MOUN-
TAIN IS A PERSON, that are marginal in our culture and our language;
their used part may consist of only one conventionally fixed expression
of the language, and they do not systematically interact with other
metaphorical concepts because so little of them is used. This makes them
relatively uninteresting for our purposes but not completely so, since
they can be extended to their unused part in coining novel metaphorical
expressions, making jokes, etc. And our ability to extend them to unused
parts indicates that, however marginal they are, they do exist.

Examples like the *foot* of the mountain are idiosyncratic, unsystema- 19
tic, and isolated. They do not interact with other metaphors, play no
particularly interesting role in our conceptual system, and hence are not
metaphors that we live by. The only signs of life they have is that they can
be extended in subcultures and that their unused portions serve as the
basis for (relatively uninteresting) novel metaphors. If any metaphorical
expressions deserve to be called "dead," it is these, though they do have
a bare spark of life, in that they are understood partly in terms of
marginal metaphorical concepts like A MOUNTAIN IS A PERSON.

It is important to distinguish these isolated and unsystematic cases 20
from the systematic metaphorical expressions we have been discussing.
Expressions like *wasting time, attacking positions, going our separate
ways*, etc., are reflections of systematic metaphorical concepts that structure our actions and thoughts. They are "alive" in the most fundamental
sense: they are metaphors we live by. The fact that they are conventionally fixed within the lexicon of English makes them no less alive.

## For Discussion and Writing

1.  Lakoff and Johnson begin by defining what they call *metaphorical
    concepts*. Exactly what do they mean by this expression? What is the
    difference between a metaphor and a metaphorical concept? Base
    your explanation on a discussion of the "further examples" pre-
    sented in the text.

2.  In paragraph 18 Lakoff and Johnson discuss the metaphor *foot of the
    mountain*. Compare their discussion with Roger Brown's treatment
    of this same metaphor. Sum up in your own words the points each
    essay makes using this same example. Do these two views comple-
    ment each other, or are they in conflict at any point?

3.  In Sylvia Plath's poem "Metaphors" we can find references to com-
    mon expressions such as "big as a house" and "big as an elephant."
    Find other references to common metaphors in any of the other
    poems in this text. What happens when a poet works with a common
    metaphorical concept? What role do the normally unused parts of
    such concepts play in the construction of poetic metaphors?

4.  In your local newspaper or in a national news or sports magazine,
    find an editorial in which metaphor plays an important part, either
    because many metaphorical expressions are used in it or because the
    whole piece is based on one or more metaphorical concepts, or both.
    Write an essay in which you discuss the way metaphor functions in

your chosen editorial. That is, show how metaphors are presented to influence the reader's response or how metaphorical concepts have operated to structure the writer's thinking.

5. Take one of Lakoff and Johnson's examples of a metaphorical concept, such as "ideas are fashions" or "love is madness," and use it to structure a short essay in which you explore, through the examples given, the cultural attitude that is reflected there. Feel free to provide additional examples of your own.

# *Metaphorical Concepts*

Metaphorical concepts function in every aspect of life, from business to health. The following two selections will serve to illustrate some of the ways in which metaphorical thinking shapes our thought and our actions in areas that seem a long way from poetry, such as business and medicine. The first selection is an article that appeared recently in the financial section of the *New York Times*. It was written by a management consultant from a major business school and addressed to an audience of corporate executives and would-be executives. It illustrates the way a particular set of metaphorical concepts—drawn from sports—operates in the thinking of corporate America.

The second selection is by the cultural critic and writer Susan Sontag. It consists of two short pieces from her book *Illness as Metaphor*, in which she explores the ways in which certain metaphors of disease have operated to shape thinking about quite different matters—political affairs, for instance.

# A New Game for Managers to Play
## *Robert W. Keidel*

As the football season gradually gives way to basketball, corporate 1 managers would do well to consider the differences between these games. For just as football mirrors industrial structures of the past, basketball points the way to the corporate structure of the future.

It's the difference between the former chief executive officer of 2 I.T.T., Harold Geneen, the master football coach who dictates his players' roles and actions, and Donald Burr, the People Express Airlines chief executive officer, who puts his players on the floor and lets them manage themselves.

Football is, metaphorically, a way of life in work today—the corpo- 3 rate sport. This is reflected in the language many managers use:

"It's taken my staff and me a sizable chunk of time, but we now have 4 a solid game plan for the XYZ job. Jack, I want you to quarterback this thing all the way into the end zone. Of course, a lot of it will be making the proper assignments—getting the right people to run interference and the right ones to run with the ball. But my main concern is that we avoid mistakes. No fumbles, no interceptions, no sacks, no penalties. I don't want us to have to play catch-up; no two-minute drills at the end. I want the game plan executed exactly the way it's drawn. When we're done we want to look back with pride at a win—and not have to Monday-morning-quarterback a loss."

Does this football language represent more than just a convenient    5 shorthand? Almost certainly it does, because the metaphors we use routinely are the means by which we structure experience. Thus, football metaphors may well reflect—and reinforce—underlying organizational dynamics. But football, despite its pervasiveness, is the wrong model for most corporations.

Consider the scenario above. Planning has been neatly separated    6 from implementation; those expected to carry out the game plan have had no part in creating it. Also, the communication flow is one-way: from the head coach (speaker) to the quarterback (Jack)—and, presumably, from the quarterback to the other players. And the thrust of the message is risk-averse; the real name of the game is control—minimizing mistakes. But perhaps most significant is the assumption of stability—that nothing will change to invalidate the corporate game plan. "No surprises!" as Mr. Geneen likes to say.

Stability is a realistic assumption in football, even given the sport's    7 enormous complexity, because of the time available to coaches—between games and between plays. A pro football game can very nearly be programmed. Carl Peterson, formerly with the Philadelphia Eagles and now president of the United States Football League's champions, the Baltimore Stars, has estimated that managing a game is 75 percent preparation and only 25 percent adjustment.

Thus, football truly is the realm of the coach—the head coach, he    8 who calls the shots. (Most pro quarterbacks do not call their own plays.) As Bum Phillips has said in tribute to the head coach of the Miami Dolphins, Don Shula, "He can take his'n and beat your'n, or he can take your'n and beat his'n."

But football is not an appropriate model for most businesses pre-    9 cisely because instability is an overwhelming fact of life. Market competition grows ever more spastic, product life-cycles shrink unimaginably and technology courses on paths of its own.

In this milieu, corporate "players" simply cannot perform effec-    10 tively if they must wait for each play to be called for them, and remain in fixed positions—or in narrowly defined roles—like football players; increasingly, they need to deploy themselves flexibly, in novel combinations.

Thirty years ago it may have been possible to regard core business    11 functions—R&D, manufacturing and marketing—as separate worlds, with little need for interaction. R&D would design the product and then lob it over the wall to manufacturing; manufacturing would make the product and lob it over another wall to the customer.

No need to worry about problems that do not fit neatly into the 12 standard departments; these are inconsequential and infrequent. And when they do arise, they are simply bumped up the hierarchy to senior management—the head coach and his staff.

In effect, performance is roughly the sum of the functions—just as a 13 football team's performance is the sum of the performances of its platoons—offense, defense and special teams. Clearly, this view of the corporation is anachronistic. Yet it remains all too common.

Business's "season" is changing, and a new metaphor is needed. 14 While football will continue to be a useful model for pursuing machinelike efficiency and consistency—that is, for minimizing redundancies, bottlenecks and errors—this design favors stability at the expense of change. Since now more than ever businesses must continuously innovate and adapt, a more promising model is basketball.

To begin with, basketball is too dynamic a sport to permit the rigid 15 separation of planning and execution that characterizes football. Unlike football teams, basketball teams do not pause and regroup after each play. As the former star player and coach Bill Russell has noted, "Your game plan may be wiped out by what happens in the first minute of play." Success in basketball depends on the ability of the coach and players to plan and adjust while in motion. Such behavior requires all-around communication—just as basketball demands all-around passing, as opposed to football's linear sequence of "forward," one-way passing.

Basketball also puts a premium on generalist skills. Although dif- 16 ferent players will assume somewhat different roles on the court, all must be able to dribble, pass, shoot, rebound and play defense. Everyone handles the ball—a far cry from what happens on the gridiron. Indeed, basketball is much more player-oriented than football—a sport in which players tend to be viewed as interchangeable parts.

If football is a risk-averse game, basketball is risk-accepting. In bas- 17 ketball, change is seen as normal, not exceptional; hence, change is regarded more as the source of opportunities than of threats. Mr. Geneen has claimed that "Ninety-nine percent of all surprises in business are negative."

Mr. Geneen's perspective is classic football and is tenable in stable, 18 "controllable" environments. But such environments are becoming rare. The future increasingly belongs to managers like Mr. Burr or James Treybig, the founder of Tandem Computers, who thrive on change rather than flee from it.

We need fewer head coaches and more player-coaches, less scripted 19 teamwork and more spontaneous teamwork. We need to integrate planning and doing—managing and working—far more than we have to date. Are you playing yesterday's game—or tomorrow's?

## For Discussion and Writing

1. In paragraph 5 Keidel makes an important point about metaphor. Try to restate it in your own terms. What does he mean by *structure* in the expression "the means by which we structure experience"?

2. Keidel is arguing that corporate managers should replace one set of metaphors with another. Why do you suppose he doesn't suggest getting rid of metaphor altogether and thinking of business *as* business?

3. If you have ever played an organized sport, you know that coaches use metaphors. That is, they talk about sports in terms of something else. Discuss some of the metaphors you have encountered within the world of sports. If you have ever had a coach whose speech was memorable, try to describe what you remember about the way he or she spoke. A coach (who shall remain nameless here) of a college soccer team used to crack up his team by telling them to "pair up in three"—not a metaphor exactly, but a piece of almost surrealist speech. You must have encountered similar poetic phrases. Share them with your classmates—especially any notable uses of metaphor. Where do most sports metaphors come from?

4. Write an essay in which you describe any common aspect of life in terms of one or two sports. That is, begin with an idea of this order: "Marriage is more like tennis than like boxing." Then explore all the parallels and contrasts between your subject matter and the sport (or sports) you have chosen as the basis for your metaphors. Some functions of life that you might wish to consider are school, family, friendship, love, and work, but choose something that interests you and discuss it in terms of appropriate sporting metaphors.

# Illness as Metaphor

*Susan Sontag*

Two diseases have been spectacularly, and similarly, encumbered by    1
the trappings of metaphor: tuberculosis and cancer.

The fantasies inspired by TB in the last century, by cancer now, are    2
responses to a disease thought to be intractable and capricious—that is, a
disease not understood—in an era in which medicine's central premise is
that all diseases can be cured. Such a disease is, by definition, mysterious.
For as long as its cause was not understood and the ministrations of
doctors remained so ineffective, TB was thought to be an insidious,
implacable theft of a life. Now it is cancer's turn to be the disease that
doesn't knock before it enters, cancer that fills the role of an illness
experienced as a ruthless, secret invasion—a role it will keep until, one
day, its etiology becomes as clear and its treatment as effective as those of
TB have become.

Although the way in which disease mystifies is set against a backdrop    3
of new expectations, the disease itself (once TB, cancer today) arouses
thoroughly old-fashioned kinds of dread. Any disease that is treated as a
mystery and acutely enough feared will be felt to be morally, if not
literally, contagious. Thus, a surprisingly large number of people with
cancer find themselves being shunned by relatives and friends and are
the object of practices of decontamination by members of their house-
hold, as if cancer, like TB, were an infectious disease. Contact with
someone afflicted with a disease regarded as a mysterious malevolency
inevitably feels like a trespass; worse, like the violation of a taboo. The
very names of such diseases are felt to have a magic power. In Stendhal's
*Armance* (1827), the hero's mother refuses to say "tuberculosis," for fear
that pronouncing the word will hasten the course of her son's malady.
And Karl Menninger has observed (in *The Vital Balance*) that "the very
word 'cancer' is said to kill some patients who would not have suc-
cumbed (so quickly) to the malignancy from which they suffer." This
observation is offered in support of anti-intellectual pieties and a facile
compassion all too triumphant in contemporary medicine and psychia-
try. "Patients who consult us because of their suffering and their distress
and their disability," he continues, "have every right to resent being
plastered with a damning index tab." Dr. Menninger recommends that
physicians generally abandon "names" and "labels" ("our function is to
help these people, not to further afflict them"—which would mean, in
effect, increasing secretiveness and medical paternalism. It is not naming

as such that is pejorative or damning, but the name "cancer." As long as a particular disease is treated as an evil, invincible predator, not just a disease, most people with cancer will indeed be demoralized by learning what disease they have. The solution is hardly to stop telling cancer patients the truth, but to rectify the conception of the disease, to demythicize it.

When, not so many decades ago, learning that one had TB was 4 tantamount to hearing a sentence of death—as today, in the popular imagination, cancer equals death—it was common to conceal the identity of their disease from tuberculars and, after they died, from their children. Even with patients informed about their disease, doctors and family were reluctant to talk freely. "Verbally I don't learn anything definite," Kafka wrote to a friend in April 1924 from the sanatorium where he died two months later, "since in discussing tuberculosis . . . everybody drops into a shy, evasive, glassy-eyed manner of speech." Conventions of concealment with cancer are even more strenuous. In France and Italy it is still the rule for doctors to communicate a cancer diagnosis to the patient's family but not to the patient; doctors consider that the truth will be intolerable to all but exceptionally mature and intelligent patients. (A leading French oncologist has told me that fewer than a tenth of his patients know they have cancer.) In America—in part because of the doctors' fear of malpractice suits—there is now much more candor with patients, but the country's largest cancer hospital mails routine communications and bills to outpatients in envelopes that do not reveal the sender, on the assumption that the illness may be a secret from their families. Since getting cancer can be a scandal that jeopardizes one's love life, one's chance of promotion, even one's job, patients who know what they have tend to be extremely prudish, if not outright secretive, about their disease. And a federal law, the 1966 Freedom of Information Act, cites "treatment for cancer" in a clause exempting from disclosure matters whose disclosure "would be an unwarranted invasion of personal privacy." It is the only disease mentioned.

All this lying to and by cancer patients is a measure of how much 5 harder it has become in advanced industrial societies to come to terms with death. As death is now an offensively meaningless event, so that disease widely considered a synonym for death is experienced as something to hide. The policy of equivocating about the nature of their disease with cancer patients reflects the conviction that dying people are best spared the news that they are dying, and that the good death is the sudden one, best of all if it happens while we're unconscious or asleep. Yet the modern denial of death does not explain the extent of the lying and the wish to be lied to; it does not touch the deepest dread. Someone who has had a coronary is at least as likely to die of another one within a few years as someone with cancer is likely to die soon from cancer. But no one thinks of concealing the truth from a cardiac patient: there is nothing shameful about a heart attack. Cancer patients are lied to, not just because the disease is (or is thought to be) a death sentence, but because it is felt to be obscene—in the original meaning of that word: ill-omened, abominable, repugnant to the senses. Cardiac disease implies a weakness, trouble, failure that is mechanical; there is no disgrace, nothing of the taboo that once surrounded people afflicted with TB and still surrounds those who have cancer. The metaphors attached to TB and to cancer imply living processes of a particularly resonant and horrid kind. . . .

TB was understood, like insanity, to be a kind of one-sidedness: 6 a failure of will or an overintensity. However much the disease was dreaded, TB always had pathos. Like the mental patient today, the tubercular was considered to be someone quintessentially vulnerable, and full of self-destructive whims. Nineteenth- and early-twentieth-century physicians addressed themselves to coaxing their tubercular patients back to health. Their prescription was the same as the enlightened one for mental patients today: cheerful surroundings, isolation from stress and family, healthy diet, exercise, rest.

The understanding of cancer supports quite different, avowedly 7 brutal notions of treatment. (A common cancer hospital witticism, heard as often from doctors as from patients: "The treatment is worse than the disease.") There can be no question of pampering the patient. With the patient's body considered to be under attack ("invasion"), the only treatment is counterattack.

The controlling metaphors in descriptions of cancer are, in fact, 8 drawn not from economics but from the language of warfare: every physician and every attentive patient is familiar with, if perhaps inured to, this military terminology. Thus, cancer cells do not simply multiply; they are "invasive." ("Malignant tumors invade even when they grow very slowly," as one textbook puts it.) Cancer cells "colonize" from the original tumor to far sites in the body, first setting up tiny outposts ("micrometastases") whose presence is assumed, though they cannot be detected. Rarely are the body's "defenses" vigorous enough to obliterate a tumor that has established its own blood supply and consists of billions of destructive cells. However "radical" the surgical intervention, however many "scans" are taken of the body landscape, most remissions are temporary; the prospects are that "tumor invasion" will continue, or that rogue cells will eventually regroup and mount a new assault on the organism.

Treatment also has a military flavor. Radiotherapy uses the meta- 9 phors of aerial warfare; patients are "bombarded" with toxic rays. And chemotherapy is chemical warfare, using poisons.* Treatment aims to "kill" cancer cells (without, it is hoped, killing the patient). Unpleasant side effects to treatment are advertised, indeed overadvertised. ("The agony of chemotherapy" is a standard phrase.) It is impossible to avoid damaging or destroying healthy cells (indeed, some methods used to treat cancer can cause cancer), but it is thought that nearly any damage to the body is justified if it saves the patient's life. Often, of course, it doesn't work. (As in: "We had to destroy Ben Suc in order to save it.") There is everything but the body count.

The military metaphor in medicine first came into wide use in the 10 1880s, with the identification of bacteria as agents of disease. Bacteria were said to "invade" or "infiltrate." But talk of siege and war to describe disease now has, with cancer, a striking literalness and authority. Not only is the clinical course of the disease and its medical treatment thus described, but the disease itself is conceived as the enemy on which society wages war. More recently, the fight against cancer has sounded like a colonial war—with similarly vast appropriations of government money—and in a decade when colonial wars haven't gone too well, this militarized rhetoric seems to be backfiring. Pessimism among doctors about the efficacy of treatment is growing, in spite of the strong advances in chemotherapy and immunotherapy made since 1970. Reporters covering "the war on cancer" frequently caution the public to distinguish between official fictions and harsh facts; a few years ago, one science writer found American Cancer Society proclamations that cancer is curable and progress has been made "reminiscent of Vietnam optimism prior to the deluge." Still, it is one thing to be skeptical about the rhetoric that surrounds cancer, another to give support to many uninformed doctors who insist that no significant progress in treatment has been made, and that cancer is not really curable. The bromides of the American cancer establishment, tirelessly hailing the imminent victory over

---

* Drugs of the nitrogen mustard type (so-called alkylating agents)—like cyclophosphamide (Cytoxan)—were the first generation of cancer drugs. Their use with leukemia (which is characterized by an excessive production of immature white cells), then with other forms of cancer—was suggested by an inadvertent experiment with chemical warfare toward the end of World War II, when an American ship, loaded with nitrogen mustard gas, was blown up in the Naples harbor, and many of the sailors died of their lethally low white-cell and platelet counts (that is, of bone-marrow poisoning) rather than of burns or sea-water inhalation.

Chemotherapy and weaponry seem to go together, if only as a fancy. The first modern chemotherapy success was with syphilis; in 1910, Paul Ehrlich introduced an arsenic derivative, arsphenamine (Salvarsan), which was called "the magic bullet."

cancer; the professional pessimism of a large number of cancer specialists, talking like battle-weary officers mired down in an interminable
colonial war—these are twin distortions in this military rhetoric about
cancer.

Other distortions follow with the extension of cancer images in 11
more grandiose schemes of warfare. As TB was represented as the spir-
itualizing of consciousness, cancer is understood as the overwhelming or
obliterating of consciousness (by a mindless It). In TB, you are eating
yourself up, being refined, getting down to the core, the real you. In
cancer, non-intelligent ("primitive," "embryonic," "atavistic") cells are
multiplying, and you are being replaced by the nonyou. Immunologists
class the body's cancer cells as "nonself."

It is worth noting that Reich, who did more than anyone else to 12
disseminate the psychological theory of cancer, also found something
equivalent to cancer in the biosphere.

> There is a deadly orgone energy. It is in the atmosphere. You
> can demonstrate it on devices such as the Geiger counter. It's a
> swampy quality. . . . Stagnant, deadly water which doesn't flow,
> doesn't metabolize. Cancer, too, is due to the stagnation of the flow
> of the life energy of the organism.

Reich's language has its own inimitable coherence. And more and more—
as its metaphoric uses gain in credibility—cancer is felt to be what he
thought it was, a cosmic disease, the emblem of all the destructive, alien
powers to which the organism is host.

As TB was the disease of the sick self, cancer is the disease of the 13
Other. Cancer proceeds by a science-fiction scenario: an invasion of
"alien" or "mutant" cells, stronger than normal cells (*Invasion of the
Body Snatchers, The Incredible Shrinking Man, The Blob, The Thing*).
One standard science-fiction plot is mutation, either mutants arriving
from outer space or accidental mutations among humans. Cancer could
be described as a triumphant mutation, and mutation is now mainly an
image for cancer. As a theory of the psychological genesis of cancer, the
Reichian imagery of energy checked, not allowed to move outward, then
turned back on itself, driving cells berserk, is already the stuff of science
fiction. And Reich's image of death in the air—of deadly energy that
registers on a Geiger counter—suggests how much the science-fiction
images about cancer (a disease that comes from deadly rays, and is treated
by deadly rays) echo the collective nightmare. The original fear about
exposure to atomic radiation was genetic deformities in the next generation; that was replaced by another fear, as statistics started to show much
higher cancer rates among Hiroshima and Nagasaki survivors and their
descendants.

Cancer is a metaphor for what is most ferociously energetic; and 14
these energies constitute the ultimate insult to natural order. In a science-
fiction tale by Tommaso Landolfi, the spaceship is called "Cancer-
queen." (It is hardly within the range of the tuberculosis metaphor that a
writer could have imagined an intrepid vessel named "Consumption-
queen.") When not being explained away as something psychological,
buried in the recesses of the self, cancer is being magnified and projected
into a metaphor for the biggest enemy, the furthest goal. Thus, Nixon's
bid to match Kennedy's promise to put Americans on the moon was,
appropriately enough, the promise to "conquer" cancer. Both were
science-fiction ventures. The equivalent of the legislation establishing the
space program was the National Cancer Act of 1971, which did not
envisage the near-to-hand decisions that could bring under control the
industrial economy that pollutes—only the great destination: the cure.

TB was a disease in the service of a romantic view of the world. 15
Cancer is now in the service of a simplistic view of the world that can
turn paranoid. The disease is often experienced as a form of demonic
possession—tumors are "malignant" or "benign," like forces—and
many terrified cancer patients are disposed to seek out faith healers, to be
exorcised. The main organized support for dangerous nostrums like
Laetrile comes from far-right groups to whose politics of paranoia the
fantasy of a miracle cure for cancer makes a serviceable addition, along
with a belief in UFOs. (The John Birch Society distributes a forty-five-
minute film called *World Without Cancer*.) For the more sophisticated,
cancer signifies the rebellion of the injured ecosphere: Nature taking
revenge on a wicked technocratic world. False hopes and simplified
terrors are raised by crude statistics brandished for the general public,
such as that 90 percent of all cancers are "environmentally caused," or
that imprudent diet and tobacco smoking alone account for 75 percent of
all cancer deaths. To the accompaniment of this numbers game (it is
difficult to see how any statistics about "all cancers" or "all cancer
deaths" could be defended), cigarettes, hair dyes, bacon, saccharine,
hormone-fed poultry, pesticides, low-sulphur coal—a lengthening roll
call of products we take for granted have been found to cause cancer.
X-rays give cancer (the treatment meant to cure kills); so do emanations
from the television set and the microwave oven and the fluorescent clock
face. As with syphilis, an innocent or trivial act—or exposure—in the
present can have dire consequences far in the future. It is also known that
cancer rates are high for workers in a large number of industrial occupations. Though the exact processes of causation lying behind the statistics
remain unknown, it seems clear that many cancers are preventable. But
cancer is not just a disease ushered in by the Industrial Revolution (there
was cancer in Arcadia) and certainly more than the sin of capitalism
(within their more limited industrial capacities, the Russians pollute

worse than we do). The widespread current view of cancer as a disease of industrial civilization is as unsound scientifically as the right-wing fantasy of a "world without cancer" (like a world without subversives). Both rest on the mistaken feeling that cancer is a distinctively "modern" disease.

The medieval experience of the plague was firmly tied to notions of 16 moral pollution, and people invariably looked for a scapegoat external to the stricken community. (Massacres of Jews in unprecedented numbers took place everywhere in plague-stricken Europe of 1347–48, then stopped as soon as the plague receded.) With the modern diseases, the scapegoat is not so easily separated from the patient. But much as these diseases individualize, they also pick up some of the metaphors of epidemic diseases. (Diseases understood to be simply epidemic have become less useful as metaphors, as evidenced by the near-total historical amnesia about the influenza pandemic of 1918–19, in which more people died than in the four years of World War I.) Presently, it is as much a cliché to say that cancer is "environmentally" caused as it was—and still is—to say that it is caused by mismanaged emotions. TB was associated with pollution (Florence Nightingale thought it was "induced by the foul air of houses"), and now cancer is thought of as a disease of the contamination of the whole world. TB was "the white plague." With awareness of environmental pollution, people have started saying that there is an "epidemic" or "plague" of cancer.

## For Discussion and Writing

1. Summarize in your own words the major point of Sontag's writing.

2. According to Sontag, what are the major metaphors used to speak about disease?

3. As Sontag demonstrates, we not only speak of disease in metaphors drawn from other aspects of life, we also use metaphors drawn *from* disease to speak of other things. Which aspect of her discussion of illness as metaphor do you find most surprising, interesting, or controversial? What connections do you find between her essay and Lakoff and Johnson's view of metaphor?

4. Sontag suggests that as science and medicine gain control over diseases, the diseases lose much of their metaphorical power. TB is no longer active in our imaginations as it was for people in the last century. Cancer, as it is brought under control, will lose its power over our minds as its threat to our bodies diminishes. Will other diseases provide metaphors for moral and political matters? AIDS

has been much in the news recently. Write a short essay in which you extend Sontag's study of illness as metaphor to AIDS or some other newly threatening menace to health. Remember, your concern should not be with the actualities of the disease but with the cultural myths and metaphors that surround it—both the metaphors based on the disease and the metaphors from other contexts that are used to describe and discuss it.

# *Arguing With Metaphor: Analogy and Parable*

As we have seen, metaphor is a crucial element of language and thought. In particular, it functions powerfully in texts designed to argue a position or persuade a reader to adopt a particular attitude. The form of metaphor most common in argument is *analogy*.

Basic strategy in the use of analogy is to claim that situation X, which is under disputation, is like or analogous to situation Y, about which there is no dispute. In extreme forms, such arguments go beyond the assertion of likeness and assert sameness. One says not "Abortion is *like* murder," but "Abortion *is* murder." In arguing for such analogies, the writer tends to suppress what Lakoff and Johnson call the "unused" parts of metaphorical concepts. Therefore, counterargument will often consist of using these unused elements, thus calling into question the whole analogy.

A creative element in argument is the generation of fresh analogies that force a reappraisal of the situation. Such arguments may take the form "X is not much like Y; it is more like Z." Often an argument that has a logical structure will be animated by creatively designed analogies, as in the following text by Judith Jarvis Thomson. In her discussion of ethical questions related to abortion, Thomson uses both *analogy* and *parable* to make abstract issues concrete and to support her own views. A parable is simply an extended analogy in the form of an anecdote: the metaphorical principle developed in narrative form. As you read Thomson, pay particular attention to her use of both analogy and parable.

## Abortion and Ethics

*Judith Jarvis Thomson*

Most opposition to abortion relies on the premise that the fetus is a    1
human being, a person from the moment of conception. The premise is argued for, but, as I think, not well. But I shall not discuss any of this. For it seems to me to be of great interest to ask what happens if, for the sake of argument, we allow the premise. How, precisely, are we supposed to

get from there to the conclusion that abortion is morally impermissible? Opponents of abortion commonly spend most of their time establishing that the fetus is a person, and hardly any time explaining the step from there to the impermissibility of abortion. Perhaps they think the step too simple and obvious to require much comment. Or perhaps instead they are simply being economical in argument. Many of those who defend abortion rely on the premise that the fetus is not a person, but only a bit of tissue that will become a person at birth; and why pay out more arguments than you have to? Whatever the explanation, I suggest that the step they take is neither easy nor obvious, that it calls for closer examination than it is commonly given, and that when we do give it this closer examination we shall feel inclined to reject it.

I propose, then, that we grant that the fetus is a person from the    2
moment of conception. How does the argument go from here? Something like this, I take it. Every person has a right to life. So the fetus has a right to life. No doubt the mother has a right to decide what shall happen in and to her body; everyone would grant that. But surely a person's right to life is stronger and more stringent than the mother's right to decide what happens in and to her body, and so outweighs it. So the fetus may not be killed; an abortion may not be performed.

It sounds plausible. But now let me ask you to imagine this. You    3
wake up in the morning and find yourself back to back in bed with an unconscious violinist. A famous unconscious violinist. He has been found to have a fatal kidney ailment, and the Society of Music Lovers has canvassed all the available medical records and found that you alone have the right blood type to help. They have therefore kidnapped you, and last night the violinist's circulatory system was plugged into yours, so that your kidneys can be used to extract poisons from his blood as well as your own. The director of the hospital now tells you, "Look, we're sorry the Society of Music Lovers did this to you—we would never have permitted it if we had known. But still, they did it, and the violinist now is plugged into you. To unplug you would be to kill him. But never mind, it's only for nine months. By then he will have recovered from his ailment, and can safely be unplugged from you." Is it morally incumbent on you to accede to this situation? No doubt it would be very nice of you if you did, a great kindness. But do you *have* to accede to it? What if it were not nine months, but nine years? Or longer still? What if the director of the hospital says, "Tough luck, I agree, but you've now got to stay in bed, with the violinist plugged into you, for the rest of your life. Because remember this. All persons have a right to life, and violinists are persons. Granted you have a right to decide what happens in and to your body, but a person's right to life outweighs your right to decide what happens in and to your body. So you cannot ever be unplugged from

him.'' I imagine you would regard this as outrageous, which suggests that something really is wrong with that plausible-sounding argument I mentioned a moment ago.

In this case, of course, you were kidnapped; you didn't volunteer for    4
the operation that plugged the violinist into your kidneys. Can those who oppose abortion on the ground I mentioned make an exception for a pregnancy due to rape? Certainly. They can say that persons have a right to life only if they didn't come into existence because of rape; or they can say that all persons have a right to life, but that some have less of a right to life than others, in particular, that those who came into existence because of rape have less. But these statements have a rather unpleasant sound. Surely the question of whether you have a right to life at all, or how much of it you have, shouldn't turn on the question of whether or not you are the product of a rape. And in fact the people who oppose abortion on the ground I mentioned do not make this distinction, and hence do not make an exception in case of rape.

Nor do they make an exception for a case in which the mother has to    5
spend the nine months of her pregnancy in bed. They would agree that would be a great pity, and hard on the mother; but all the same, all persons have a right to life, the fetus is a person, and so on. I suspect, in fact, that they would not make an exception for a case in which, miraculously enough, the pregnancy went on for nine years, or even the rest of the mother's life.

Some won't even make an exception for a case in which continua-    6
tion of the pregnancy is likely to shorten the mother's life; they regard abortion as impermissible even to save the mother's life. Such cases are nowadays very rare, and many opponents of abortion do not accept this extreme view. All the same, it is a good place to begin: a number of points of interest come out in respect to it.

Let us call the view that abortion is impermissible even to save the    7
mother's life ''the extreme view.'' I want to suggest first that it does not issue from the argument I mentioned earlier without the addition of some fairly powerful premises. Suppose a woman has become pregnant, and now learns that she has a cardiac condition such that she will die if she carries the baby to term. What may be done for her? The fetus, being a person, has a right to life, but as the mother is a person too, so has she a right to life. Presumably they have an equal right to life. How is it supposed to come out that an abortion may not be performed? If mother and child have an equal right to life, shouldn't we perhaps flip a coin? Or should we add to the mother's right to life her right to decide what happens in and to her body, which everybody seems to be ready to grant—the sum of her rights now outweighing the fetus' right to life?

The most familiar argument here is the following. We are told that    8 performing the abortion would be directly killing[1] the child, whereas doing nothing would not be killing the mother, but only letting her die. Moreover, in killing the child, one would be killing an innocent person, for the child has committed no crime, and is not aiming at his mother's death. And then there are a variety of ways in which this might be continued: (1) but as directly killing an innocent person is always and absolutely impermissible, an abortion may not be performed. (2) As directly killing an innocent person is murder, and murder is always and absolutely impermissible, an abortion may not be performed.[2] (3) As one's duty to refrain from directly killing an innocent person is more stringent than one's duty to keep a person from dying, an abortion may not be performed. (4) If one's only options are directly killing an innocent person or letting a person die, one must prefer letting the person die, and thus an abortion may not be performed.[3]

Some people seem to have thought that these are not further premises which must be added if the conclusion is to be reached, but that they follow from the very fact that an innocent person has a right to life.[4] But this seems to me to be a mistake, and perhaps the simplest way to show this is to bring out that while we must certainly grant that innocent persons have a right to life, the theses in (1) through (4) are all false. Take

9

---

[1] The term "direct" in the arguments I refer to is a technical one. Roughly, what is meant by "direct killing" is either killing as an end in itself, or killing as a means of some end, for example, the end of saving someone else's life.

[2] Cf. *Encyclical Letter of Pope Pius XI on Christian Marriage*, St. Paul Editions, Boston, p. 32: "However much we may pity the mother whose health and even life is gravely imperiled in the performance of the duty allotted to her by nature, nevertheless what could ever be a sufficient reason for excusing in any way the direct murder of the innocent? This is precisely what we are dealing with here." Noonan, in *The Morality of Abortion*, reads this as follows: "What cause can ever avail to excuse in any way the direct killing of the innocent? For it is a question of that."

[3] The thesis in (4) is in an interesting way weaker than those in (1), (2), and (3): they rule out abortion even in cases in which both mother *and* child will die if the abortion is not performed. By contrast, one who held the view expressed in (4) could consistently say that one needn't prefer letting two persons die to killing one.

[4] Cf. the following passage from Pius XII, *Address to the Italian Catholic Society of Midwives*: "The baby in the maternal breast has the right to life immediately from God. Hence there is no man, no human authority, no science, no medical, eugenic, social, economic or moral 'indication' which can establish or grant a valid juridical ground for a direct deliberate disposition of an innocent human life, that is a disposition which looks to its destruction either as an end or as a means to another end perhaps in itself not illicit. The baby, still not born, is a man in the same degree and for the same reason as the mother" (quoted in Noonan, *The Morality of Abortion*, p. 45).

(2), for example. If directly killing an innocent person is murder, and thus is impermissible, then the mother's directly killing the innocent person inside her is murder, and thus is impermissible. But it cannot seriously be thought to be murder if the mother performs an abortion on herself to save her life. It cannot seriously be said that she *must* refrain, that she *must* sit passively by and wait for her death. Let us look again at the case of you and the violinist. There you are, in bed with the violinist, and the director of the hospital says to you, "It's all most distressing, and I deeply sympathize, but you see this is putting an additional strain on your kidneys, and you'll be dead within the month. But you *have* to stay where you are all the same. Because unplugging you would be directly killing an innocent violinist, and that is murder, and that's impermissible." If anything in the world is true, it is that you do not commit murder, you do not do what is impermissible, if you reach around to your back and unplug yourself from that violinist to save your life.

The main focus of attention in writings on abortion has been on 10 what a third party may or may not do in answer to a request from a woman for an abortion. This is in a way understandable. Things being as they are, there isn't much a woman can safely do to abort herself. So the question asked is what a third party may do, and what the mother may do, if it is mentioned at all, is deduced, almost as an afterthought, from what it is concluded that third parties may do. But it seems to me that to treat the matter in this way is to refuse to grant to the mother that very status of person which is so firmly insisted on for the fetus. For we cannot simply read off what a person may do from what a third party may do. Suppose you find yourself trapped in a tiny house with a growing child. I mean a very tiny house, and a rapidly growing child— you are already up against the wall of the house and in a few minutes you'll be crushed to death. The child on the other hand won't be crushed to death; if nothing is done to stop him from growing he'll be hurt, but in the end he'll simply burst open the house and walk out a free man. Now I could well understand it if a bystander were to say, "There's nothing we can do for you. We cannot choose between your life and his, we cannot be the ones to decide who is to live, we cannot intervene." But it cannot be concluded that you too can do nothing, that you cannot attack it to save your life. However innocent the child may be, you do not have to wait passively while it crushes you to death. Perhaps a pregnant woman is vaguely felt to have the status of house, to which we don't allow the right of self-defense. But if the woman houses the child, it should be remembered that she is a person who houses it.

I should perhaps stop to say explicitly that I am not claiming that 11 people have a right to do anything whatever to save their lives. I think, rather, that there are drastic limits to the right of self-defense. If someone threatens you with death unless you torture someone else to death, I think you have not the right, even to save your life, to do so. But the case under consideration here is very different. In our case there are only two people involved, one whose life is threatened, and one who threatens it. Both are innocent: the one who is threatened is not threatened because of any fault; the one who threatens does not threaten because of any fault. For this reason we may feel that we bystanders cannot intervene. But the person threatened can.

In sum, a woman surely can defend her life against the threat to it 12 posed by the unborn child, even if doing so involves its death. And this shows not merely that the theses in (1) through (4) are false; it shows also that the extreme view of abortion is false, and so we need not canvass any other possible ways of arriving at it from the argument I mentioned at the outset.

The extreme view could of course be weakened to say that while 13 abortion is permissible to save the mother's life, it may not be performed by a third party, but only by the mother herself. But this cannot be right either. For what we have to keep in mind is that mother and the unborn child are not like two tenants in a small house which has, by an unfortu-nate mistake, been rented to both: the mother *owns* the house. The fact that she does adds to the offensiveness of deducing that the mother can do nothing from the supposition that third parties can do nothing. But it does more than this: it casts a bright light on the supposition that third parties can do nothing. Certainly it lets us see that a third party who says "I cannot choose between you" is fooling himself if he thinks this is impartiality. If Jones has found and fastened on a certain coat, which he needs to keep him from freezing, but which Smith also needs to keep him from freezing, then it is not impartiality that says, "I cannot choose between you" when Smith owns the coat. Women have said again and again, "This body is *my* body!" and they have reason to feel angry, reason to feel that it has been like shouting into the wind. Smith, after all, is hardly likely to bless us if we say to him, "Of course it's your coat, anybody would grant that it is. But no one may choose between you and Jones who is to have it."

We should really ask what it is that says "no one may choose" in the 14 face of the fact that the body that houses the child is the mother's body. It may be simply a failure to appreciate this fact. But it may be something more interesting, namely, the sense that one has a right to refuse to lay hands on people, even where it would be just and fair to do so, even where justice seems to require that somebody do so. Thus justice might call for somebody to get Smith's coat back from Jones, and yet you have a right to refuse to be the one to lay hands on Jones, a right to refuse to do physical violence to him. This, I think, must be granted. But then what should be said is not "no one may choose, but only "*I* cannot choose," and indeed not even this, but "*I* will not *act*," leaving it open that somebody else can or should, and in particular that anyone in a position of authority, with the job of securing people's rights, both can and should. So this is no difficulty. I have not been arguing that any given third party must accede to the mother's request that he perform an abortion to save her life, but only that he may.

I suppose that in some views of human life the mother's body is only 15 on loan to her, the loan not being one which gives her any prior claim to it. One who held this view might well think it impartiality to say "I cannot choose." But I shall simply ignore this possibility. My own view is that if a human being has any just, prior claim to anything at all, he has a just, prior claim to his own body. And perhaps this needn't be argued for here anyway, since, as I mentioned, the arguments against abortion we are looking at do grant that the woman has a right to decide what happens in and to her body.

But although they do grant it, I have tried to show that they do not 16 take seriously what is done in granting it. I suggest the same thing will reappear even more clearly when we turn away from cases in which the mother's life is at stake, and attend, as I propose we now do, to the vastly more common cases in which a woman wants an abortion for some less weighty reason than preserving her own life.

Where the mother's life is not at stake, the argument I mentioned at 17 the outset seems to have a much stronger pull. "Everyone has a right to life, so the unborn person has a right to life." And isn't the child's right to life weightier than anything other than the mother's own right to life, which she might put forward as ground for an abortion?

This argument treats the right to life as if it were unproblematic. It is 18 not, and this seems to me to be precisely the source of the mistake.

For we should now, at long last, ask what it comes to, to have a right 19 to life. In some views having a right to life includes having a right to be given at least the bare minimum one needs for continued life. But suppose that what in fact *is* the bare minimum a man needs for continued life is something he has no right at all to be given? If I am sick unto death, and the only thing that will save my life is the touch of Henry Fonda's cool hand on my fevered brow, then all the same, I have no right to be given the touch of Henry Fonda's cool hand on my fevered brow. It would be frightfully nice of him to fly in from the West Coast to provide it. It would be less nice, though no doubt well meant, if my friends flew out to the West Coast and carried Henry Fonda back with them. But I have no right at all against anybody that he should do this for me. Or again, to return to the story I told earlier, the fact that for continued life that violinist needs the continued use of your kidneys does not establish that he has a right to be given the continued use of your kidneys. He certainly has no right against you that you should give him continued use of your kidneys. For nobody has any right to use your kidneys unless you give him such a right; and nobody has the right against you that you shall give him this right—if you do allow him to go on using your kidneys, this is a kindness on your part, and not something he can claim from you as his due. Nor has he any right against anybody else that *they* should give him continued use of your kidneys. Certainly he had no right against the Society of Music Lovers that they should plug him into you in the first place. And if you now start to unplug yourself, having learned that you will otherwise have to spend nine years in bed with him, there is nobody in the world who must try to prevent you, in order to see to it that he is given something he has a right to be given.

Some people are rather stricter about the right to life. In their view, it 20 does not include the right to be given anything, but amounts to, and only to, the right not to be killed by anybody. But here a related difficulty arises. If everybody is to refrain from killing that violinist, then everybody must refrain from doing a great many different sorts of things. Everybody must refrain from slitting his throat, everybody must refrain from shooting him—and everybody must refrain from unplugging you from him. But does he have a right against everybody that they shall refrain from unplugging you from him? To refrain from doing this is to allow him to continue to use your kidneys. It could be argued that he has a right against us that *we* should allow him to continue to use your kidneys. That is, while he had no right against us that we should give him the use of your kidneys, it might be argued that he anyway has a right against us that we shall not now intervene and deprive him of the use of your kidneys. I shall come back to third-party interventions later. But certainly the violinist has no right against you that *you* shall allow him to continue to use your kidneys. As I said, if you do allow him to use them, it is a kindness on your part, and not something you owe him.

The difficulty I point to here is not peculiar to the right to life. It 21 reappears in connection with all the other natural rights; and it is something which an adequate account of rights must deal with. For present purposes it is enough just to draw attention to it. But I would stress that I am not arguing that people do not have a right to life—quite to the contrary, it seems to me that the primary control we must place on the acceptability of an account of rights is that it should turn out in that account to be a truth that all persons have a right to life. I am arguing only that having a right to life does not guarantee having either a right to be given the use of or a right to be allowed continued use of another person's body—even if one needs it for life itself. So the right to life will not serve the opponents of abortion in the very simple and clear way in which they seem to have thought it would.

There is another way to bring out the difficulty. In the most ordinary 22 sort of case, to deprive someone of what he has a right to is to treat him unjustly. Suppose a boy and his small brother are jointly given a box of chocolates for Christmas. If the older boy takes the box and refuses to give his brother any of the chocolates, he is unjust to him, for the brother has been given a right to half of them. But suppose that, having learned that otherwise it means nine years in bed with that violinist, you unplug yourself from him. You surely are not being unjust to him, for you gave him no right to use your kidneys, and no one else can have given him any such right. But we have to notice that in unplugging yourself, you are killing him; and violinists, like everybody else, have a right to life, and thus in the view we were considering just now, the right not to be killed. So here you do what he supposedly has a right you shall not do, but you do not act unjustly to him in doing it.

The emendation which may be made at this point is this: the right to 23 life consists not in the right not to be killed, but rather in the right not to be killed unjustly. This runs a risk of circularity, but never mind: it would enable us to square the fact that the violinist has a right to life with the fact that you do not act unjustly toward him in unplugging yourself, thereby killing him. For if you do not kill him unjustly, you do not violate his right to life, and so it is no wonder you do him no injustice.

But if this emendation is accepted, the gap in the argument against 24 abortion stares us plainly in the face: it is by no means enough to show that the fetus is a person, and to remind us that all persons have a right to life—we need to be shown also that killing the fetus violates its right to life, i.e., that abortion is unjust killing. And is it?

I suppose we may take it as a datum that in a case of pregnancy due 25 to rape the mother has not given the unborn person a right to the use of her body for food and shelter. Indeed, in what pregnancy could it be supposed that the mother has given the unborn person such a right? It is not as if there were unborn persons drifting about the world, to whom a woman who wants a child says "I invite you in."

But it might be argued that there are other ways one can have 26 acquired a right to the use of another person's body than by having been invited to use it by that person. Suppose a woman voluntarily indulges in intercourse, knowing of the chance it will issue in pregnancy, and then she does become pregnant; is she not in part responsible for the presence, in fact, the very existence, of the unborn person inside her? No doubt she did not invite it in. But doesn't her partial responsibility for its being there itself give it a right to the use of her body? If so, then her aborting it would be more like the boy's taking away the chocolates, and less like your unplugging yourself from the violinist—doing so would be depriving it of what it does have a right to, and thus would be doing it an injustice.

And then, too, it might be asked whether or not she can kill it even to 27 save her own life: If she voluntarily called it into existence, how can she now kill it, even in self-defense?

The first thing to be said about this is that it is something new. 28
Opponents of abortion have been so concerned to make out the independence of the fetus, in order to establish that it has a right to life, just as its mother does, that they have tended to overlook the possible support they might gain from making out that the fetus is *dependent* on the mother, in order to establish that she has a special kind of responsibility for it, a responsibility that gives it rights against her which are not possessed by any independent person—such as an ailing violinist who is a stranger to her.

On the other hand, this argument would give the unborn person a 29
right to its mother's body only if her pregnancy resulted from a voluntary act, undertaken in full knowledge of the chance a pregnancy might result from it. It would leave out entirely the unborn person whose existence is due to rape. Pending the availability of some further argument, then, we would be left with the conclusion that unborn persons whose existence is due to rape have no right to the use of their mothers' bodies, and thus that aborting them is not depriving them of anything they have a right to and hence is not unjust killing.

And we should also notice that it is not at all plain that this argument 30
really does go even as far as it purports to. For there are cases and cases, and the details make a difference. If the room is stuffy, and I therefore open a window to air it, and a burglar climbs in, it would be absurd to say, "Ah, now he can stay, she's given him a right to the use of her house—for she is partially responsible for his presence there, having voluntarily done what enabled him to get in, in full knowledge that there are such things as burglars, and that burglars burgle." It would be still more absurd to say this if I had had bars installed outside my windows, precisely to prevent burglars from getting in, and a burglar got in only because of a defect in the bars. It remains equally absurd if we imagine it is not a burglar who climbs in, but an innocent person who blunders or falls in. Again, suppose it were like this: people-seeds drift about in the air like pollen, and if you open your windows, one may drift in and take root in your carpets or upholstery. You don't want children, so you fix up your windows with fine mesh screens, the very best you can buy. As can happen, however, and on very, very rare occasions does happen, one of the screens is defective; and a seed drifts in and takes root. Does the person-plant who now develops have a right to the use of your house? Surely not—despite the fact that you voluntarily opened your windows, you knowingly kept carpets and upholstered furniture, and you knew that screens were sometimes defective. Someone may argue that you are responsible for its rooting, and it does have a right to your house, because after all you *could* have lived out your life with bare floors and furniture, or with sealed windows and doors. But this won't do—for by the same token anyone can avoid a pregnancy due to rape by having a

hysterectomy, or anyway by never leaving home without a (reliable!) army.

It seems to me that the argument we are looking at can establish at 31 most that there are *some* cases in which the unborn person has a right to the use of its mother's body, and therefore *some* cases in which abortion is unjust killing. There is room for much discussion and argument as to precisely which, if any. But I think we should sidestep this issue and leave it open, for at any rate the argument certainly does not establish that all abortion is unjust killing.

There is room for yet another argument here, however. We surely 32 must all grant that there may be cases in which it would be morally indecent to detach a person from your body at the cost of his life. Suppose you learn that what the violinist needs is not nine years of your life, but only one hour: all you need to do to save his life is to spend one hour in bed with him. Suppose also that letting him use your kidneys for that one hour would not affect your health in the slightest. Admittedly you were kidnapped. Admittedly you did not give anyone permission to plug him into you. Nevertheless it seems to me plain you *ought* to allow him to use your kidneys for that hour—it would be indecent to refuse.

Again, suppose pregnancy lasted only an hour, and constituted no 33 threat to life or health. And suppose that a woman becomes pregnant as a result of rape. Admittedly she did not voluntarily do anything to bring about the existence of a child. Admittedly she did nothing at all which would give the unborn person a right to the use of her body. All the same it might well be said, as in the newly emended violinist story, that she *ought* to allow it to remain for that hour—that it would be indecent in her to refuse.

Now some people are inclined to use the term "right" in such a way 34 that it follows from the fact that you ought to allow a person to use your body for the hour he needs, that he has a right to use your body for the hour he needs, even though he has not been given that right by any person or act. They may say that it follows also that if you refuse, you act unjustly toward him. This use of the term is perhaps so common that it cannot be called wrong; nevertheless it seems to me to be an unfortunate loosening of what we would do better to keep a tight rein on. Suppose that box of chocolates I mentioned earlier had not been given to both boys jointly, but was given only to the older boy. There he sits, stolidly eating his way through the box, his small brother watching enviously. Here we are likely to say, "You ought not to be so mean. You ought to give your brother some of those chocolates." My own view is that it just does not follow from the truth of this that the brother has any right to any of the chocolates. If the boy refuses to give his brother any, he is greedy, stingy, callous—but not unjust. I suppose that the people I have in mind will say it does follow that the brother has a right to some of the chocolates, and thus that the boy does act unjustly if he refuses to give his brother any. But the effect of saying this is to obscure what we should keep distinct, namely, the difference between the boy's refusal in this case and the boy's refusal in the earlier case, in which the box was given to both boys jointly, and in which the small brother thus had what was from any point of view clear title to half.

A further objection to so using the term "right" that from the fact 35 that A ought to do a thing for B, it follows that B has a right against A that A do it for him, is that it is going to make the question of whether or not a man has a right to a thing turn on how easy it is to provide him with it; and this seems not merely unfortunate, but morally unacceptable. Take the case of Henry Fonda again. I said earlier that I had no right to the touch of his cool hand on my fevered brow, even though I needed it to save my life. I said it would be frightfully nice of him to fly in from the West Coast to provide me with it, but that I had no right against him that he should do so. But suppose he isn't on the West Coast. Suppose he has only to walk across the room, place a hand briefly on my brow—and lo, my life is saved. Then surely he ought to do it, it would be indecent to refuse. Is it to be said, "Ah, well, it follows that in this case she has a right to the touch of his hand on her brow, and so it would be an injustice in him to refuse"? So that I have a right to it when it is easy for him to provide it, though no right when it's hard? It's rather a shocking idea that anyone's rights should fade away and disappear as it gets harder and harder to accord them to him.

So my own view is that even though you ought to let the violinist use 36 your kidneys for the one hour he needs, we should not conclude that he has a right to do so—we should say that if you refuse, you are, like the boy who owns all the chocolates and will give none away, self-centered and callous, indecent in fact, but not unjust. And similarly, that even supposing a case in which a woman pregnant due to rape ought to allow the unborn person to use her body for the hour he needs, we should not conclude that he has a right to do so; we should conclude that she is self-centered, callous, indecent, but not unjust, if she refuses. The complaints are no less grave; they are just different. However, there is no need to insist on this point. If anyone does not wish to deduce "he has a right" from "you ought," then all the same he must surely grant that there are cases in which it is not morally required of you that you allow that violinist to use your kidneys, and in which he does not have a right to use them, and in which you do not do him an injustice if you refuse. And so also for mother and unborn child. Except in such cases as the unborn person has a right to demand it—and we were leaving open the possibility that there may be such cases—nobody is morally *required* to make large sacrifices, of health, of all other interests and concerns, of all other duties and commitments, for nine years, or even for nine months, in order to keep another person alive.

We have in fact to distinguish between two kinds of Samaritan: the Good Samaritan and what we might call the Minimally Decent Samaritan. The story of the Good Samaritan, you will remember, goes like this:

> A certain man went down from Jerusalem to Jericho, and fell among thieves, which stripped him of his raiment, and wounded him, and departed, leaving him half dead.
>
> And by chance there came down a certain priest that way; and when he saw him, he passed by on the other side.
>
> And likewise a Levite, when he was at the place, came and looked on him, and passed by on the other side.
>
> But a certain Samaritan, as he journeyed, came where he was; and when he saw him he had compassion on him.
>
> And went to him, and bound up his wounds pouring in oil and wine, and set him on his own beast, and brought him to an inn, and took care of him.
>
> And on the morrow, when he departed, he took out two pence, and gave them to the host, and said unto him, "Take care of him; and whatsoever thou spendest more, when I come again, I will repay thee.
>
> (Luke 10:30–35)

The Good Samaritan went out of his way, at some cost to himself, to help one in need of it. We are not told what the options were, that is, whether or not the priest and the Levite could have helped by doing less than the Good Samaritan did, but assuming they could have, then the fact they did nothing at all shows they were not even Minimally Decent Samaritans, not because they were not Samaritans, but because they were not even minimally decent.

These things are a matter of degree, of course, but there is a difference, and it comes out perhaps most clearly in the story of Kitty Genovese, who, as you will remember, was murdered while thirty-eight people watched or listened, and did nothing at all to help her. A Good Samaritan would have rushed out to give direct assistance against the murderer. Or perhaps we had better allow that it would have been a Splendid Samaritan who did this, on the ground that it would have involved a risk of death for himself. But the thirty-eight not only did not do this, they did not even trouble to pick up a phone to call the police. Minimally Decent Samaritanism would call for doing at least that, and their not having done it was monstrous.

After telling the story of the Good Samaritan, Jesus said, "Go, and do 39 thou likewise." Perhaps he meant that we are morally required to act as the Good Samaritan did. Perhaps he was urging people to do more than is morally required of them. At all events it seems plain that it was not morally required of any of the thirty-eight that he rush out to give direct assistance at the risk of his own life, and that it is not morally required of anyone that he give long stretches of his life—nine years or nine months—to sustaining the life of a person who has no special right (we were leaving open the possibility of this) to demand it.

Indeed, with one rather striking class of exceptions, no one in any 40 country in the world *is legally* required to do anywhere near as much as this for anyone else. The class of exceptions is obvious. My main concern here is not the state of the law in respect to abortion, but it is worth drawing attention to the fact that in no state in this country is any man compelled by law to be even a Minimally Decent Samaritan to any person; there is no law under which charges could be brought against the thirty-eight who stood by while Kitty Genovese died. By contrast, in most states in this country women are compelled by law to be not merely Minimally Decent Samaritans, but Good Samaritans to unborn persons inside them. This doesn't by itself settle anything one way or the other, because it may well be argued that there should be laws in this country— as there are in many European countries—compelling at least Minimally Decent Samaritanism.[5] But it does show that there is a gross injustice in the existing state of the law. And it shows also that the groups currently working against liberalization of abortion laws, in fact working toward having it declared unconstitutional for a state to permit abortion, had better start working for the adoption of Good Samaritan laws generally, or earn the charge that they are acting in bad faith.

I should think, myself, that Minimally Decent Samaritan laws would 41 be one thing, Good Samaritan laws quite another, and in fact highly improper. But we are not here concerned with the law. What we should ask is not whether anybody should be compelled by law to be a Good Samaritan, but whether we must accede to a situation in which some- body is being compelled—by nature, perhaps—to be a Good Samaritan. We have, in other words, to look now at third-party interventions. I have been arguing that no person is morally required to make large sacrifices to sustain the life of another who has no right to demand them, and this even where the sacrifices do not include life itself; we are not morally required to be Good Samaritans or anyway Very Good Samaritans to one another. But what if a man cannot extricate himself from such a situation?

[5] For a discussion of the difficulties involved, and a survey of the European experience with such laws, see *The Good Samaritan and the Law*, ed. James M. Ratcliffe, New York, 1966.

What if he appeals to us to extricate him? It seems to me plain that there are cases in which we can, cases in which a Good Samaritan would extricate him. There you are, you were kidnapped, and nine years in bed with that violinist lie ahead of you. You have your own life to lead. You are sorry, but you simply cannot see giving up so much of your life to the sustaining of his. You cannot extricate yourself, and ask us to do so. I should have thought that—in light of his having no right to the use of your body—it was obvious that we do not have to accede to your being forced to give up so much. We can do what you ask. There is no injustice to the violinist in our doing so.

Following the lead of the opponents of abortion, I have throughout 42 been speaking of the fetus merely as a person, and what I have been asking is whether or not the argument we began with, which proceeds only from the fetus's being a person, really does establish its conclusion. I have argued that it does not.

But of course there are arguments and arguments, and it may be said 43 that I have simply fastened on the wrong one. It may be said that what is important is not merely the fact that the fetus is a person, but that it is a person for whom the woman has a special kind of responsibility issuing from the fact that she is its mother. And it might be argued that all my analogies are therefore irrelevant—for you do not have that special kind of responsibility for that violinist, Henry Fonda does not have that special kind of responsibility for me. And our attention might be drawn to the fact that men and women both *are* compelled by law to provide support for their children.

I have in effect dealt (briefly) with this argument above; but a (still 44 briefer) recapitulation now may be in order. Surely we do not have any such "special responsibility" for a person unless we have assumed it, explicitly or implicitly. If a set of parents do not try to prevent pregnancy, do not obtain an abortion, and then at the time of birth of the child do not put it out for adoption, but rather take it home with them, then they have assumed responsibility for it, they have given it rights, and they cannot *now* withdraw support from it at the cost of its life because they now find it difficult to go on providing for it. But if they have taken all reasonable precautions against having a child, they do not simply by virtue of their biological relationship to the child who comes into existence have a special responsibility for it. They may wish to assume responsibility for it, or they may not wish to. And I am suggesting that if assuming responsibility for it would require large sacrifices, then they may refuse. A Good Samaritan would not refuse—or anyway, a Splendid Samaritan, if the sacrifices that had to be made were enormous. But then so would a Good Samaritan assume responsibility for that violinist; so would Henry Fonda, if he is a Good Samaritan, fly in from the West Coast and assume responsibility for me.

My argument will be found unsatisfactory on two counts by many of 45 those who want to regard abortion as morally permissible. First, while I do argue that abortion is not impermissible, I do not argue that it is always permissible. There may well be cases in which carrying the child to term requires only Minimally Decent Samaritanism of the mother, and this is a standard we must not fall below. I am inclined to think it a merit of my account precisely that it does *not* give a general yes or a general no. It allows for and supports our sense that, for example, a sick and desperately frightened fourteen-year-old schoolgirl, pregnant due to rape, may *of course* choose abortion, and that any law which rules this out is an insane law. And it also allows for and supports our sense that in other cases resort to abortion is even positively indecent. It would be indecent in the woman to request an abortion, and indecent in a doctor to perform it, if she is in her seventh month, and wants the abortion just to avoid the nuisance of postponing a trip abroad. The very fact that the arguments I have been drawing attention to treat all cases of abortion, or even all cases of abortion in which the mother's life is not at stake, as morally on a par ought to have made them suspect at the outset.

Second, while I am arguing for the permissibility of abortion in some 46 cases, I am not arguing for the right to secure the death of the unborn child. It is easy to confuse these two things in that up to a certain point in the life of the fetus it is not able to survive outside the mother's body; hence removing it from her body guarantees its death. But they are importantly different. I have argued that you are not morally required to spend nine months in bed, sustaining the life of that violinist; but to say this is by no means to say that if, when you unplug yourself, there is a miracle and he survives, you then have a right to turn round and slit his throat. You may detach yourself even if this costs him his life; you have no right to be guaranteed his death, by some other means, if unplugging yourself does not kill him. There are some people who will be dissatisfied by this feature of my argument. A woman may be utterly devastated by the thought of a child, a bit of herself, put out for adoption and never seen or heard of again. She may therefore want not merely that the child be detached from her, but more, that it die. Some opponents of abortion are inclined to regard this as beneath contempt—thereby showing insensitivity to what is surely a powerful source of despair. All the same, I agree that the desire for the child's death is not one which anybody may gratify, should it turn out to be possible to detach the child alive.

# For Discussion and Writing

1. At a certain point in her argument, Thomson introduces and quotes the Biblical Parable of the Good Samaritan. What is a parable, and

how does it work? Have you any idea why Jesus speaks in parables? What is the relationship between parable, analogy, and metaphor? Is the plugged-in violinist a parable?

2. Discuss Thomson's use of analogies and metaphors. Which of her analogies do you find most effective? Which least effective?

3. There are several ways to counter the use of analogy in argument. One is by offering a better analogy that supports a counterargument. Another is by examining the analogy critically, pointing out the "unused" or suppressed features of the analogy so as to weaken or negate its argumentative thrust. One may also attack the logic of the argument—but we are not really concerned with the logic of argumentation at the present time. We suggest, therefore, that you produce a response to Thomson's views in terms of your own values. You should examine critically the "unused" portions of the analogies she uses, and you should also try to develop an alternative to the analogy of the plugged-in violinist that supports your own position.

4. Consider some controversial subject of the moment—either local or national—and present a position on that subject, basing your presentation on an analogy that you develop for the occasion, such as Thomson's image of being plugged into a violinist. Use your analogy as the basis for explaining your own position on the issue you have chosen to discuss.

# Metaphor and Metonymy: Advertising

Metaphor plays a major role in one kind of text that we encounter every day: advertising. To analyze the role of metaphor in advertising we will need one more technical term: *metonymy*. We have been using the term *metaphor* to cover all the ways of talking about one thing in terms of another, but actually we can make an important distinction between metaphor proper and another metaphoric device. This device is called *metonymy*. Metaphor proper is based upon some resemblance between the two things that are brought together in the metaphor. Robert Francis can speak of poetry and baseball in the same language because a poet and a baseball pitcher share certain attributes (pp. 74–75). There is an analogy between the two elements of the metaphor.

We use metonymy, on the other hand, whenever we speak of one thing in terms of another that is usually associated with it. When we say "The White House says . . ." we don't mean that the building actually spoke but that the person who lives there, the president, has taken the position attributed to the building. Cartoonists use this same metonymy whenever they draw a picture of the White House with words coming out of it. A frequently used type of metonymy called *synecdoche* is the substitution of part of something for the whole of it. If we asked a rancher "How many cattle do you own?" he might reply, "Seven hundred head." Obviously, he owns the rest of the beasts also, not just the heads. You can keep clear the difference between metaphor and metonymy by remembering these examples: (1) *head of beer* is a metaphor, based on resemblance, and (2) *head of cattle* is metonymy, based on association—in this case synecdoche, a part for the whole.

In advertising, metonymy or association is very important. When a celebrity endorses a product, an association is formed between them. When a basketball player endorses a basketball shoe, we have a natural metonymy. Such shoes are already associated with the player. What the advertiser wants, however, and will sometimes make very explicit, is to have this metonymy interpreted as a metaphor. That is, the maker of basketball shoes wants us (subconsciously or consciously) to attribute the quality of the player to the shoe. But it would be a courageous maker of baseball gloves who hired Bob Uecker, who has a well-established image as having been a *not* very good player, to endorse his product. Uecker instead advertises beer. Most beer commercials establish a metonymic connection between good times and beer, hoping that the viewer will accept a further metaphoric connection and finally a cause-and-effect connection: the beer *is* good and a *cause* of good times.

Some ads make a very skillful use of metaphor and metonymy to push their products. You owe it to yourself to understand exactly how they are trying to manipulate you. We provide analyses of three ads here and then invite you to do some analytical work of your own.

# "Light My Lucky"

At this point we would like to describe an advertisement for Lucky Strike cigarettes, because cigarette ads are among the cleverest and most technically perfect that one can find, and because their use raises interesting moral problems about the functioning of advertising in general. We assume that you have seen enough Lucky Strike ads so that you will be able to follow our description without too much trouble. (Originally we intended to reprint the ad, but the company denied us permission to do so.) The ad is very simple. It presents a photo of a young woman (perhaps 23 or 24 years old) in a sweater, in a field or meadow, wearing a scarf, with one hand in her pocket and the other resting lightly on her wind-blown hair, holding an unlighted cigarette. She gazes straight out of the frame. The words "Light My Lucky" appear in quotation marks, very prominently displayed, starting just below her chin and extending across to the right margin of the page. In the lower right corner of the frame, also superimposed over the photographic image of the woman, is a large image of an opened package of Lucky Strike Lights. At the bottom of the frame, on the left, is the well known warning from the Surgeon General, which says: "Smoking By Pregnant Women May Result in Fetal Injury, Premature Birth, and Low Weight." You can visualize the ad, we are sure, or find a comparable ad in a current magazine.

The young woman in the ad is very beautiful. She is outdoors and dressed in outdoorsy clothing, a thick scarf and a heavy sweater. The background is blurred, but it looks like a field or wooded area. What has all this got to do with cigarettes? She is holding an unlighted cigarette in a hand that rests on top of her windblown blonde hair. She looks serious, or perhaps sultry. We read the written phrase in quotation marks as what she says, though she does not appear to be speaking—what she might say, perhaps, but certainly what she wants: "Light My Lucky."

The woman is lightly but carefully made up: an unobtrusive lipstick, delicate but effectively applied eye makeup. The ad makes her the central figure in a cluster of metonymic associations: woman/cigarette/outdoors.

This is a healthy, vigorous woman. The makers of the ad expect some of these positive healthy values to attach themselves (in the reader's subconscious mind) to the cigarette.

The woman is also extremely good-looking. Asking someone for a light is a classic sexual approach, presented in countless films, and turned into a metaphor for sex itself in rock songs like "Light My Fire." The phrase in the ad—"Light My Lucky"—quite deliberately suggests these other texts that are now part of our cultural memory. We call this sort of allusion *intertextuality*. (The concept will be presented more fully in the next chapter, but we should note at this point that intertextuality is, like metaphor and metonymy, a way of presenting two or more things at the same time in the same text.) The ad thus associates the cigarette with beauty, health, and erotic pleasures. These metonymies are deliberate: the cigarette is meant to acquire the associations as permanent attributes.

It is worth noting that the word *light* is used in a punning way in the ad, and that a pun, like metaphor and metonymy, is a way of bringing two meanings together in a single place—in a single word, in fact. *Light* is used as a verb to mean set on fire: light my cigarette, light a fire. By a common metaphorical extension it means "inflame" or "arouse," as in "light my fire." But *light* (as opposed to heavy) is used in our weight-conscious and health-conscious society to mean "free from bad ingredients." Light beer has fewer calories; light cigarettes have less tar and nicotine. These uses are slightly metaphorical in themselves. The "light" in "Light My Lucky" thus refers to both the classic sexual approach and the relative healthiness of the "light" cigarette, just as the image of an attractive woman in outdoor clothing refers to the same two things. Always, in such ads, the hope is held out that the desirable qualities metonymically connected to the product will come to the reader if he or she uses the product. Do you want to be healthy and attractive, and experience erotic pleasure? Smoke Lucky Strike Lights.

The "Surgeon General's Warning" that appears in the corner of the ad refers to pregnant women. But the woman in the ad is anything but pregnant. She is as emphatically unattached as she is positively healthy. The Surgeon General associates smoking, pregnancy, and ill-health. The ad associates smoking, sex, and good health. The idea that smoking is unhealthy is obliterated by these contradictory messages, leaving only pregnancy connected to ill health. This is an extremely clever and well-made ad.

# "Finally, Life Insurance as Individual as You Are"

The Prudential Life Insurance Company logo, visible at the bottom of the ad, is a stylized image of the Rock of Gibraltar. By selecting the physical object as their company symbol, the Prudential Company obviously hoped for a metaphorical transfer of qualities from the Rock to the company in the mind of the consumer. Rocks are an ancient symbol of strength and solidity. In the Gospel of Matthew (16.18) Jesus says to Peter, "Thou art Peter, and upon this rock I will build my church." In saying these words, Jesus is playing upon a pun in the name Peter, which means rock (*pet*rified, for instance, means turned into stone). The qualities of a rock—strength, solidity, firmness—are to be extended metaphorically to the institution of a church by means of a man whose character can be described metaphorically in terms of those rocky qualities.

The Rock of Gibraltar is in fact a rocky mountain that looms over the harbor of Gibraltar, on the southern tip of Spain at the gateway to the Mediterranean Sea. A harbor of enormous strategic importance, it is almost impregnable because the Rock makes attacking it from the land side difficult. It has been a major outpost of the British empire for over a century, and thus can stand metaphorically for power and stability beyond any ordinary rock. The viewer doesn't have to know any of these details, of course. He or she has only to perceive the company in terms of the qualities signified by this enormous rock. So Prudential chose the Rock for its symbol, its logo, and has used it in dozens of ads and TV commercials.

The company, like many other insurance companies, faces another advertising problem. If potential customers feel that it is big, strong, safe, and stable, they may also feel that it is enormous, cold, and indifferent. In making the ad we are examining, Prudential needed to find something that would indicate its concern for the individual. The company might be a rock, but it is a delicate, precise, *caring* sort of rock, who treats everybody as a person rather than a number.

What is unique about each one of us? Physically speaking, the handiest method of establishing each person's uniqueness is through the use of fingerprints. Our fingerprints are in fact indexical signs of each one of us, powerful metonyms that can, for instance, indicate that we were present at the scene of a crime. Because each one of us has his or her own set of prints, the fingerprint can function as a metaphor for uniqueness and individuality. Thus, the Prudential Company can use fingerprints to symbolize individuality. By shaping its rocky symbol *out of* a fingerprint in

# FINALLY, LIFE INSURANCE AS INDIVIDUAL AS YOU ARE.

With Prudential offering more types of life insurance than any other insurance company, we're confident we have a policy that's designed to meet your individual needs.

For instance, we have one policy for people who want high interest on their contract fund while taking life easy with a fixed premium schedule.

There's another policy that earns high interest while giving you high premium flexibility.*

There are also two kinds of policies* that let you invest in one or more of five accounts – stock, bond, money market, an aggressively managed account and a conservatively managed account.** All these products offer you guaranteed lifetime protection.

In addition, Prudential offers competitively priced Term insurance. And a new Permanent Life insurance portfolio with current dividend schedules based on today's higher interest rates.

Of course, whichever life insurance matches your lifestyle, you know it is from The Prudential, one of the world's largest, most trusted financial institutions.

Let a Prudential/Pruco Securities representative review your needs to help you put your finger on the one policy that is unmistakably yours.

* These products are offered through Prudential subsidiaries: Pruco Life Insurance Company and Pruco Life Insurance Company of New Jersey.
** For more complete information, including fees and expenses, send for a prospectus. Read it carefully before you invest or send money. Sold through Pruco Securities Corporation, Newark, New Jersey.
Interest rates may vary from year to year.

The **Prudential**

Life Insurance

this ad, it hopes to add individuality to the other qualities that are metaphorically signified by the rock.

However, metaphors are not mathematical, and it is not easy to add them together and reach a predictable result. At this point we ask you to stop and make your own interpretation of the metaphors in the Prudential ad. What do the images of rock and fingerprint, taken together, mean to you? What associations or connotations do they arouse in your mind? Compare your reactions to those of your classmates in trying to assess the effectiveness of the use of metaphors in this ad. Whatever you decide, these two ads taken together, help to illustrate some of the ways in which advertising and poetry draw upon the same aspects of language for their power. One further example should show how important figurative language can be in advertising.

# VISTA

Though it may not appear so in our black and white reproduction of it, the VISTA ad is visually striking. The tanned diver is dressed in red trunks and teeshirt. The water in the foreground is very shallow and transparent, showing the brown sand under it. The sea is green with bright whitecaps. The upper half of the picture is all bright blue sky, without a cloud. The diver is plunging into no more than two or three inches of water. It is a dramatic, arresting picture, and it arrests the viewer's eye as well. What is going on here, we wonder, and what will come of it? Why would anyone dive into two inches of water, anyway?

For answers, we must go to the small white sentences printed over the blue sky in the upper left of the frame. What they tell us is that we shouldn't read the picture literally. It is not about diving but about things for which such a dive may be a metaphor. The printed text picks up these metaphors from the visual image and interprets them in such a way as to connect them to the product being advertised. It says,

> When you dive into a client
> presentation.
> When you hit the dirt in a
> business skirmish.
> When you make a splash with
> the higher-ups.
> And the higher higher-ups.
> When you finally crest the
> wave.
> Come test our waters.

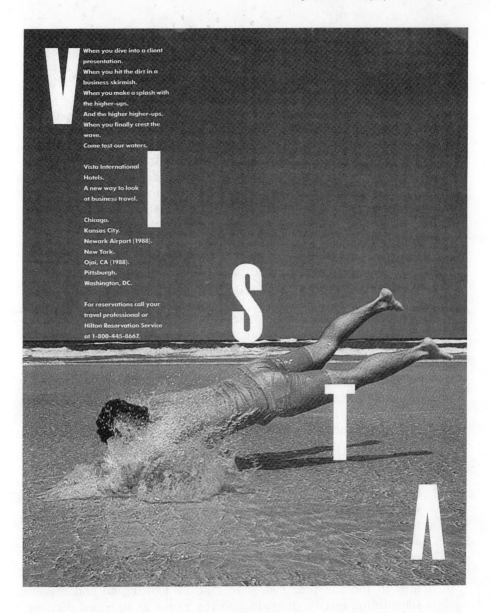

When you dive into a client presentation.
When you hit the dirt in a business skirmish.
When you make a splash with the higher-ups.
And the higher higher-ups.
When you finally crest the wave.
Come test our waters.

Vista International Hotels.
A new way to look at business travel.

Chicago.
Kansas City.
Newark Airport (1988).
New York.
Ojai, CA (1988).
Pittsburgh.
Washington, DC.

For reservations call your travel professional or Hilton Reservation Service at 1-800-445-8667.

After this it introduces the product, a chain of hotels seeking businessmen as customers. The ad takes a collection of dead or inert metaphors that have come to function as clichés about business, and revitalizes them by connecting them to a single, startling visual image. What the image does is take them literally—dive, hit the dirt, make a splash, crest the wave, test our waters. It shows someone doing all these things—or almost doing all these things. After all, it is not easy to hit the dirt and make a splash at the same time. This sounds, in fact, like a clumsily mixed metaphor, but the picture shows how one can indeed hit the dirt and make a splash at the same time. You just dive into two inches of water. This whole process does many of the same things that poems do. It revives inert metaphors that have become clichés; it gives you metaphor where you expect literal meaning and literal meaning where you expect figures of speech. It is also a little bit like a riddle or puzzle on the order of Sylvia Plath's poem "Metaphors." Is it a good ad? Will it sell the product? It is hard to say but it certainly is an attention-getter, and the visual image does indeed lead us to look at the text to find out what is going on here. For our purposes, of course, it also demonstrates once again how poetry and advertising often employ the same dimensions of language for their different purposes.

## For Discussion and Writing

1. Even without the example of these discussions before you, you know a lot about advertising because you see many ads every day. Find two different full-page ads for a particular type of product such as designer perfume, cigarettes, bran cereal, or luxury automobiles. (We suggest a slick magazine designed for a general audience, such as *Sports Illustrated, The New Yorker, Esquire*, or *Vogue* as your best source of skillfully done ads.) Write an essay in which you compare and discuss the metaphoric and metonymic qualities of the two ads. Try to reach some conclusions about how and why certain things work in advertising.

2. Knowing what you know about the workings of advertisements, you should be able to design an ad that works the wrong way. Imagine, for instance, replacing the sultry, outdoorsy blonde in the "Lucky" ad with an obviously pregnant woman. Given the "Surgeon General's Warning" that appears in the ad, this would be a disaster—even if the woman were as lovely and healthy in appearance as the woman now in the ad. Your task is to take an existing ad and make a substitution or two that will ruin the ad for its intended purpose. You should not be too blatant or obvious in your changes nor make too many of them. Just do something that spoils the intended result as you understand it.

# Chapter 3
# Texts and Other Texts

In the previous two chapters we have examined aspects of language and textuality that have been considered important since Aristotle's time. At this point, however, we begin to shift our attention to things that have been the special concerns of modern literature and recent literary theory. As you might expect, from here on, things get more complicated. Our principles, however, remain the same. We will continue to share with you the theory that we have used to shape our presentation of ideas and materials. We will also continue to offer you opportunities to grasp this theory by actual application of it to textual situations.

Our emphasis in this chapter, as you will soon see for yourself, is on the way that texts are always related to and dependent upon other texts. In our culture we have tended to stress "originality" as a supreme value in writing. The pressure to be "original" has often worked to inhibit writers—especially student writers—and thus to prevent them from actually developing their ideas. One of our purposes in this chapter is to reduce the anxiety of originality.

Once you realize that all texts are reworkings of other texts, that writing comes out of reading, that writing is always rewriting, you can see that the desirable quality we call "originality" does not mean creating something out of nothing but simply making an interesting change in what has been done before you. One develops as a writer by playing with material already in existence. The "new" emerges as a function of this play. With this in mind we invite you to enter the world of intertextuality—where you have actually lived all along.

# *Intertextuality*

*One of the surest tests is the way a poet borrows. Immature poets imitate; mature poets steal.*

*—T. S. Eliot*

*In their traffic with art, artists employ preformed images as they employ whatever else feeds into their work. Between their experience of nature and their experience of other art they allow no functional difference.*

*—Leo Steinberg*

Artists and writers do not simply look at nature—or into their own hearts—and transcribe what they find there. This is so because for them the very act of looking is already shaped by the art and writing of the past, as well as by other cultural conventions. The eye of an adult human being is never innocent. The eye of a baby may be "innocent" in some sense, but it is also untrained, and the untrained eye does not see much. As observers of life, we go from ignorance to prejudice without ever passing through the mythical land of objectivity. What a scientist learns is how to see with the prejudices of his or her own science. An artist sees through the prejudices of art.

This is simply the way things are for human beings in this world. Learning to see nature or the human heart is learning how to notice certain things and disregard others. But that is only one side of the problem facing the artist or writer. The writer must not only notice and disregard things. The writer must transcribe the things that he or she notices. That is, the writer must find ways to put experience into verbal form. Experience need not come in the form of an anecdote or a play, but it must be expressed in these or other forms that already exist. A writer, we may say, has one eye on experience and the other on writing that has already been done. No text is produced without awareness of other texts. This is why Labov (see chapter 1) finds a repeated structural pattern in anecdotes told by ordinary speakers. These speakers have already listened to many anecdotes themselves. They know the anecdotal forms.

When a group of people are exchanging anecdotes, stories, or jokes, a further development will be noticed: relationships may be generated between what one person and another person recount. Sometimes the connection is just similarity or association. You will hear a speaker say "That reminds me of . . ." But other times one story will be told in opposition to another, to prove an opposite point or illustrate an alternative view of someone or something. In an extended session, the relationship of one story to another can become very complicated. With written texts—and especially the durable written texts we call literature—such relationships are often of the most elaborate and complex kinds. The technical term for such relationships is *intertextuality*.

Wherever there are texts, there is intertextuality. Even in what we may call minimal texts, like bumper stickers, we can find intertextuality. For instance, in a certain tiny New England state, environmentalists display a red bumper sticker that says SAVE THE BAY. The bay in question suffers from pollution that is a threat to health, to commercial shellfishing, and to the quality of life in general. Many of those concerned with these matters have joined an organization working to preserve or restore the quality of this bay's water. Hence the bumper sticker: SAVE THE BAY.

There are those, however, who do not love environmentalists and do not care about the quality of the bay. They have originated and proudly display a black sticker with their own slogan: PAVE THE BAY. Whatever one's view of the rights and wrongs of the matter, if you are a student of literary language, you have to admit that PAVE THE BAY is the more interesting of the two signs. It is interesting because it is more concrete (so to speak), because it suggests something that is hardly possible (since the bay in question is thirty miles long and five miles wide), and because it is more clearly intertextual.

Paving the bay is sufficiently unlikely to violate our sense of the possible. We readers of this bumper text are forced by this impossibility to find a second way to read the text. If it cannot be meant *literally*, it must, if it means anything, have what we call a *figurative* meaning. That is, it must function like a metaphor. We cannot simply read it; we must interpret it. What does PAVE THE BAY mean? Its meaning depends upon its intertextuality. Without SAVE THE BAY, PAVE THE BAY would be close to nonsense, a mere impossibility. But alongside SAVE THE BAY, from which it is distinguishable by only a single letter, PAVE THE BAY signifies, among other things, the rejection or negation of the environmentalist position that is textualized in SAVE THE BAY. PAVE THE BAY means "Don't let these wimpy environmentalists push you around."

A similar relationship exists between another bumper sticker, WARNING: I BRAKE FOR ANIMALS, and its anti-text, WARNING: I SLOW UP TO HIT LITTLE ANIMALS (both actually exist). Even here the second text signifies mainly a rejection of the first. That is, WARNING: I BRAKE FOR ANIMALS is meant to refer literally to the behavior of the driver; whereas WARNING: I SLOW UP TO HIT LITTLE ANIMALS does not necessarily tell you about the driver's intentions. It does tell you about his attitude toward the sentiment displayed on the first sign. It refers, then, not literally to the world of action but intertextually to the other sign, which it negates.

PAVE THE BAY is a more interesting negation for two reasons. First, it is so economical: a major change in meaning is achieved through the alteration of just one letter. Second, it presents a more startling concept than slowing up to hit animals: It suggests a slightly different world, where strange feats of engineering are possible, whereas going out of one's way to inflict pain on defenseless creatures is distressingly familiar to us. The attitudes motivating the two signs may not be terribly different. They are rooted in dislike of environmentalists who interfere with the rights of others. But one of the two stickers is more interesting than the other—and both are more interesting than their pre-texts, precisely because they are intertextual.

In another case, the "wimps" have the last word. The sticker PRESERVE YOUR RIGHT TO BEAR ARMS has been answered by PRESERVE YOUR RIGHT TO ARM BEARS. Again, the second sign is more interesting because it is both intertextual and figurative. Giving guns to bears is not a possible project in this world. The text that advocates this impossibility thus forces us to look for a nonliteral meaning. To read it we must see it as a transformation of its literal predecessor: ARM BEARS is another minimal change, using exactly the same letters as BEAR ARMS, but inverting the words and relocating the *s* to make ARM a verb and BEARS a noun. Maximum change of meaning with minimal verbal change seems to be a rule of quality here. The second text, which would be nonsense without the first, becomes supersense when connected with its pre-text. For the reader to interpret the second text, he or she must see it as a *transformation* of the first. That is a crucial principle. Intertextuality is active when the reader is aware of the way one text is connected to others.

There are many forms of intertextuality. One text may contain a mention of another, for instance, or a quotation or citation of an earlier text. One text may devote itself extensively to a discussion of another, offering commentary, interpretation, counterstatement, or criticism. One text may be a translation of another, an imitation, an adaptation, a pastiche, or parody. In this chapter, we shall be exploring many—though not all—of these possible relationships. As an introduction to the practice of intertextuality, we ask you to consider and discuss the following three texts. Text (1) is a passage from the biblical Old Testament, in the translation produced in England in the early seventeenth century. Text (2) is a speech delivered by a messenger in a play written in England in the later seventeenth century. Text (3) is an advertisement that appeared in a popular magazine in the later twentieth century.

## Text    (1)

# Judges 16: Samson

21  But the Philistines took him, and put out his eyes, and brought him down to Gaza, and bound him with fetters of brass; and he did grind in the prison house.

22  Howbeit the hair of his head began to grow again after he was shaven.

23  Then the lords of the Philistines gathered them together for to offer a great sacrifice unto Dagon their god, and to rejoice: for they said, Our god hath delivered Samson our enemy into our hand.

24  And when the people saw him, they praised their god: for they said, Our god hath delivered into our hands our enemy, and the destroyer of our country, which slew many of us.

25  And it came to pass, when their hearts were merry, that they said, Call for Samson, that he may make us sport. And they called for Samson out of the prison house; and he made them sport: and they set him between the pillars.

26  And Samson said unto the lad that held him by the hand, Suffer me that I may feel the pillars whereupon the house standeth, that I may lean upon them.

27  Now the house was full of men and women; and all the lords of the Philistines were there; and *there were* upon the roof about three thousand men and women, that beheld while Samson made sport.

28  And Samson called unto the Lord, and said, O Lord God, remember me, I pray thee, and strengthen me, I pray thee, only this once, O God, that I may be at once avenged of the Philistines for my two eyes.

29  And Samson took hold of the two middle pillars upon which the house stood, and on which it was borne up, of the one with his right hand, and of the other with his left.

30  And Samson said, Let me die with the Philistines. And he bowed himself with *all his* might; and the house fell upon the lords, and upon all the people that *were* therein. So the dead which he slew at his death were more than they which he slew in his life.

31  Then his brethren and all the house of his father came down, and took him, and brought *him* up, and buried him between Zorah and Eshtaol in the buryingplace of Manoah his father.

## Text   (2)

# from *Samson Agonistes*

### *John Milton*

*Messenger.* Occasions drew me early to this city,
And as the gates I entered with sun-rise,
The morning trumpets festival proclaimed
Through each high street. Little I had despatched
When all abroad was rumored that this day                          1600
Samson should be brought forth to shew the people
Proof of his mighty strength in feats and games;
I sorrowed at his captive state, but minded
Not to be absent at that spectacle.
The building was a spacious theater                                1605
Half round on two main pillars vaulted high,
With seats where all the lords and each degree
Of sort, might sit in order to behold,
The other side was open, where the throng
On banks and scaffolds under sky might stand;                      1610
I among these aloof obscurely stood.
The feast and noon grew high, and sacrifice
Had filled their hearts with mirth, high cheer, and wine,
When to their sports they turned. Immediately
Was Samson as a public servant brought,                            1615
In their state livery clad; before him pipes
And timbrels, on each side went armed guards,
Both horse and foot before him and behind
Archers, and slingers, cataphracts and spears
At sight of him the people with a shout                            1620
Rifted the air clamoring their god with praise,
Who had made their dreadful enemy their thrall.
He patient but undaunted where they led him,
Came to the place, and what was set before him
Which without help of eye, might be assayed,                       1625
To heave, pull, draw, or break, he still performed
All with incredible, stupendious force,
None daring to appear antagonist.
At length for intermission sake they led him
Between the pillars; he his guide requested                        1630

(For so from such as nearer stood we heard)
As over-tired to let him lean a while
With both his arms on those two massy pillars
That to the arched roof gave main support.
He unsuspicious led him; which when Samson                    1635
Felt in his arms, with head a while inclined,
And eyes fast fixed he stood, as one who prayed,
Or some great matter in his mind revolved.
At last with head erect thus cried aloud,
"Hitherto, Lords, what your commands imposed                  1640
I have performed, as reason was, obeying,
Not without wonder or delight beheld.
Now of my own accord such other trial
I mean to show you of my strength, yet greater;
As with amaze shall strike all who behold."                   1645
This uttered, straining all his nerves he bowed;
As with the force of winds and waters pent
When mountains tremble, those two massy pillars
With horrible convulsion to and fro
He tugged, he shook, till down they came and drew             1650
The whole roof after them, with burst of thunder
Upon the heads of all who sat beneath,
Lords, ladies, captains, counsellors, or priests,
Their choice nobility and flower, not only
Of this but each Philistian city round                        1655
Met from all parts to solemnize this feast.
Samson with these immixed, inevitably
Pulled down the same destruction on himself;
The vulgar only scaped, who stood without.

*Text  (3)*

**FITNESS FOR MEN**

The Rake.
*Ultimate footwear for the club, the court, or the Colosseum.*

## For Discussion and Writing

1. The biblical text is itself, no doubt, a written version of material that was transmitted orally before being set down in the Hebrew Bible.

The English version is a translation made in the early 1600s. It is the immediate pre-text for Milton's verse drama, *Samson Agonistes*, though Milton knew his Bible in Hebrew as well. In the passage we have quoted, a messenger recounts the same crucial events covered by the biblical passage. Discuss the changes Milton has made and the possible reasons for them. How, in other words, has he used his pre-text?

2. Looking at the third text, how can we tell it is part of the same textual network as the others? What specific features indicate this connection? How does this text use the Samson textual network? Try to consider every detail of text (3), such as things like the meaning of "ultimate," for instance.

# *Transforming Texts   (1)*

In this section we will be considering some of the more obvious ways in which new texts are created out of old ones. We can begin with a textual finger exercise devised by the French writer Raymond Queneau. In his book *Transformations*, Queneau presents a very short account of two trivial incidents that do not even make a simple story. He then proceeds to re-present these incidents a hundred times, using a different stylistic principle every time. We have reprinted here, in English translation, Queneau's original "Notation" and six of his revisions. We would like you to examine each of his transformations and discuss exactly what he has done and how he has done it, before proceeding to some transformations of your own.

## Transformations

*Raymond Queneau*

otation

In the S bus, in the rush hour. A chap of about 26, felt hat with a cord instead of a ribbon, neck too long, as if someone's been having a tug-of-war with it. People getting off. The chap in question gets annoyed with one of the men standing next to him. He accuses him of jostling him every time anyone goes past. A snivelling tone which is meant to be aggressive. When he sees a vacant seat he throws himself on to it.

Two hours later, I meet him in the Cour de Rome, in front of the gare Saint-Lazare. He's with a friend who's saying: "You ought to get an extra button put on your overcoat." He shows him where (at the lapels) and why.

 ouble      ntry

Towards the middle of the day and at midday I happened to be on and got on to the platform and the balcony at the back of an S-line and of a Contrescarpe-Champerret bus and passenger transport vehicle which was packed and to all intents and purposes full. I saw and noticed a young man and an old adolescent who was rather ridiculous and pretty grotesque; thin neck and skinny windpipe, string and cord round his hat and tile. After a scrimmage and scuffle he says and states in a lachrymose and snivelling voice and tone that his neighbour and fellow-traveller is deliberately trying and doing his utmost to push him and obtrude himself on him every time anyone gets off and makes an exit. This having been declared and having spoken he rushes headlong and wends his way towards a vacant and a free place and seat.

Two hours after and a-hundred-and-twenty minutes later, I meet him and see him again in the Cour de Rome and in front of the gare Saint-Lazare. He is with and in the company of a friend and pal who is advising and urging him to have a button and vegetable ivory disc added and sewn on to his overcoat and mantle.

 recision

In a bus of the S-line, 10 metres long, 3 wide, 6 high, at 3 km. 600 m. from its starting point, loaded with 48 people, at 12.17 p.m., a person of the masculine sex aged 27 years 3 months and 8 days, 1 m. 72 cm. tall and weighing 65 kg. and wearing a hat 35 cm. in height round the crown of which was a ribbon 60 cm. long, interpollated a man aged 48 years 4 months and 3 days, 1 m. 68 cm. tall and weighing 77 kg., by means of 14 words whose enunciation lasted 5 seconds and which alluded to some involuntary displacements of from 15 to 20 mm. Then he went and sat down about 1 m. 10 cm. away.

57 minutes later he was 10 metres away from the suburban entrance to the gare Saint-Lazare and was walking up and down over a distance of 30 m. with a friend aged 28, 1 m. 70 cm. tall and weighing 71 kg. who advised him in 15 words to move by 5 cm. in the direction of the zenith a button which was 3 cm. in diameter.

# *N arrative*

One day at about midday in the Parc Monceau district, on the back platform of a more or less full S bus (now No. 84), I observed a person with a very long neck who was wearing a felt hat which had a plaited cord round it instead of a ribbon. This individual suddenly addressed the man standing next to him, accusing him of purposely treading on his toes every time any passengers got on or off. However he quickly abandoned the dispute and threw himself on to a seat which had become vacant.

Two hours later I saw him in front of the gare Saint-Lazare engaged in earnest conversation with a friend who was advising him to reduce the space between the lapels of his overcoat by getting a competent tailor to raise the top button.

# *P assive*

It was midday. The bus was being got into by passengers. They were being squashed together. A hat was being worn on the head of a young gentleman, which hat was encircled by a plait and not by a ribbon. A long neck was one of the characteristics of the young gentleman. The man standing next to him was being grumbled at by the latter because of the jostling which was being inflicted on him by him. As soon as a vacant seat was espied by the young gentleman it was made the object of his precipitate movements and it became sat down upon.

The young gentleman was later seen by me in front of the gare Saint-Lazare. He was clothed in an overcoat and was having a remark made to him by a friend who happened to be there to the effect that it was necessary to have an extra button put on it.

 *aiku*[1]

Summer S long neck
plait hat toes abuse retreat
station button friend

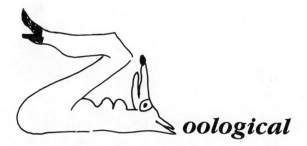 *oological*

In the dog days while I was in a bird cage at feeding time I noticed a young puppy with a neck like a giraffe who, like the toad, ugly and venomous, wore yet a precious beaver upon his head. This queer fish obviously had a bee in his bonnet and was quite bats, he started yak-

---

[1] Haiku: a Japanese poem composed of three lines, of 5, 7, and 5 syllables respectively, and presenting one theme.

king at a wolf in sheep's clothing claiming that he was treading on his dogs with his beetle-crushers. But the sucker got a flea in his ear; that foxed him, and quiet as a mouse he ran like a hare for a perch.

I saw him again later in front of the Zoo with a young buck who was telling him to bear in mind a certain drill about his fevvers.

## For Discussion and Writing

1. Compare "Notation" with each of its transformations. What, specifically, has been done in each adaptation to make it different from the others? How would you describe the "voice" in each one?

2. Using Queneau's six transformations as models, write a set of your own. Use as your "Notation" a short anecdote of your own, or a newspaper report, such as a police report, or the article reprinted here on pp. 138–42.

3. Which transformation was easiest for you to write? Why? Which was most difficult. Why?

4. Try to imagine that "Precision" was written by someone whose composition teacher was always telling him or her to "be more precise" in his writing. What other rules of good writing are being parodied in Queneau's transformations?

# *Transforming Texts*    *(2)*

Writers are always borrowing, or—as T. S. Eliot said in the quotation at the beginning of this chapter—stealing from one another. This is a basic element of textuality. Texts are produced through a combination of the writer's experiences as a human being and the writer's knowledge of earlier texts. Sometimes, however, the intertextual relationship is very much in the foreground: this is true in translation, interpretation, adaptation, and parody. Translation from one language to another is not our concern in this book. Interpretation will be taken up in the next section of this chapter. At the moment, we are concerned with *adaptation* and that special form of adaptation called *parody*.

Adaptation occurs whenever a writer rewrites an earlier work, making significant changes in the original. Raymond Queneau's *Transformations* (pp. 138–42) is one kind of adaptation. The versions of Samson's story produced by John Milton and by the Nike company's copywriters (pp. 134–36) are also adaptations. Milton's adaptation is a reverent development and extension of the biblical original. The Nike ad is more an allusion to the original than a full adaptation of it, but it represents a tendency toward that kind of irreverent adaptation we call *parody*.

A parody is an adaptation that makes fun of its original by exaggerating its most striking and unusual features or by relocating it to a context that renders the original absurd, as in the Nike ad. Exaggeration parodies the form of the original. Relocation parodies its content or meaning. Because it has a critical function, parody points the way to more formal kinds of interpretation and criticism. Parody and other forms of adaptation assume that the original still has some life in it if certain aspects of it are modified, others eliminated, and some new things added. In the following pages, we are going to present for your consideration some adaptations of a well-known text, the fairy tale "Hansel and Gretel," originally published in German by Jacob and Wilhelm Grimm in the year 1812. To begin with, here is a good modern translation of "Hansel and Gretel." We ask you to read it and then move on to the first adaptation.

# Hansel and Gretel

*Jacob and Wilhelm Grimm*

At the edge of a large forest there lived a poor woodcutter with his   1
wife and two children. The little boy's name was Hansel, and the little
girl's was Gretel. There was never much to eat in the house, and once, in
time of famine, there wasn't even enough bread to go around. One night
the woodcutter lay in bed thinking, tossing and turning with worry. All at
once he sighed and said to his wife: "What's to become of us? How can
we feed our poor children when we haven't even got enough for ourselves?" His wife answered: "Husband, listen to me. Tomorrow at
daybreak we'll take the children out to the thickest part of the forest and
make a fire for them and give them each a piece of bread. Then we'll
leave them and go about our work. They'll never find the way home
again and that way we'll be rid of them." "No, Wife," said the man. "I
won't do it. How can I bring myself to leave my children alone in the
woods? The wild beasts will come and tear them to pieces." "You fool!"
she said. "Then all four of us will starve. You may as well start planing the
boards for our coffins." And she gave him no peace until he consented.
"But I still feel badly about the poor children," he said.

The children were too hungry to sleep, and they heard what their   2
stepmother said to their father. Gretel wept bitter tears and said: "Oh,
Hansel, we're lost." "Hush, Gretel," said Hansel. "Don't worry. I'll find a
way." When the old people had fallen asleep, he got up, put on his little
jacket, opened the bottom half of the Dutch door, and crept outside. The
moon was shining bright, and the pebbles around the house glittered like
silver coins. Hansel crouched down and stuffed his pocket full of them.
Then he went back and said to Gretel: "Don't worry, little sister. Just go
to sleep, God won't forsake us," and went back to bed.

At daybreak, before the sun had risen, the woman came and woke   3
the two children. "Get up, you lazybones. We're going to the forest for
wood." Then she gave each a piece of bread and said: "This is for your
noonday meal. Don't eat it too soon, because there won't be any more."
Gretel put the bread under her apron, because Hansel had the pebbles in
his pocket. Then they all started out for the forest together. When they
had gone a little way, Hansel stopped still and looked back in the
direction of their house, and every so often he did it again. His father
said: "Hansel, why do you keep looking back and lagging behind? Wake
up and don't forget what your legs are for." "Oh, father," said Hansel,
"I'm looking at my white kitten; he's sitting on the roof, trying to bid me
good-bye." The woman said: "You fool, that's not your white kitten. It's

the morning sun shining on the chimney." But Hansel hadn't been looking at his kitten. Each time, he had taken a shiny pebble from his pocket and dropped it on the ground.

When they came to the middle of the forest, the father said: "Start 4 gathering wood, children, and I'll make a fire to keep you warm." Hansel and Gretel gathered brushwood till they had a little pile of it. The brushwood was kindled and when the flames were high enough the woman said: "Now, children, lie down by the fire and rest. We're going into the forest to cut wood. When we're done, we'll come back and get you."

Hansel and Gretel sat by the fire, and at midday they both ate their 5 pieces of bread. They heard the strokes of an ax and thought their father was nearby. But it wasn't an ax, it was a branch he had tied to a withered tree, and the wind was shaking it to and fro. After sitting there for some time, they became so tired that their eyes closed and they fell into a deep sleep. When at last they awoke, it was dark night. Gretel began to cry and said: "How will we ever get out of this forest?" But Hansel comforted her: "Just wait a little while. As soon as the moon rises, we'll find the way." And when the full moon had risen, Hansel took his little sister by the hand and followed the pebbles, which glistened like newly minted silver pieces and showed them the way. They walked all night and reached their father's house just as day was breaking. They knocked at the door, and when the woman opened it and saw Hansel and Gretel, she said: "Wicked children! Why did you sleep so long in the forest? We thought you'd never get home." But their father was glad, for he had been very unhappy about deserting them.

A while later the whole country was again stricken with famine, and 6 the children heard their mother talking to their father in bed at night: "Everything has been eaten up. We still have half a loaf of bread, and when that's gone there will be no more. The children must go. We'll take them still deeper into the forest, and this time they won't find their way home; it's our only hope." The husband was heavy-hearted, and he thought: "It would be better if I shared the last bite with my children." But the woman wouldn't listen to anything he said, she only scolded and found fault. Once you've said yes, it's hard to say no, and so it was that the woodcutter gave in again.

But the children were awake; they had heard the conversation. 7 When the old people had fallen asleep, Hansel got up again. He wanted to pick up some more pebbles, but the woman had locked the door and he couldn't get out. But he comforted his little sister and said: "Don't cry, Gretel. Just go to sleep, God will help us."

Early in the morning the woman came and got the children out of 8 bed. She gave them their pieces of bread, but they were smaller than the last time. On the way to the forest, Hansel crumbled his bread in his pocket. From time to time he stopped and dropped a few crumbs on the ground. "Hansel," said his father, "why are you always stopping and looking back? Keep moving." "I'm looking at my little pigeon," said Hansel. "He's sitting on the roof, trying to bid me good-bye." "Fool," said the woman. "That's not your little pigeon, it's the morning sun shining on the chimney." But little by little Hansel strewed all his bread on the ground.

The woman led the children still deeper into the forest, to a place    9 where they had never been in all their lives. Again a big fire was made, and the mother said: "Just sit here, children. If you get tired, you can sleep awhile. We're going into the forest to cut wood, and this evening when we've finished we'll come and get you." At midday Gretel shared her bread with Hansel, who had strewn his on the ground. Then they fell asleep and the afternoon passed, but no one came for the poor children. It was dark night when they woke up, and Hansel comforted his little sister. "Gretel," he said, "just wait till the moon rises; then we'll see the breadcrumbs I strewed and they'll show us the way home." When the moon rose, they started out, but they didn't find any breadcrumbs, because the thousands of birds that fly around in the forests and fields had eaten them all up. Hansel said to Gretel: "Don't worry, we'll find the way," but they didn't find it. They walked all night and then all day from morning to night, but they were still in the forest, and they were very hungry, for they had nothing to eat but the few berries they could pick from the bushes. And when they were so tired their legs could carry them no farther, they lay down under a tree and fell asleep.

It was already the third morning since they had left their father's    10 house. They started out again, but they were getting deeper and deeper into the forest, and unless help came soon, they were sure to die of hunger and weariness. At midday, they saw a lovely snow-white bird sitting on a branch. It sang so beautifully that they stood still and listened. When it had done singing, it flapped its wings and flew on ahead, and they followed until the bird came to a little house and perched on the roof. When they came closer, they saw that the house was made of bread, and the roof was made of cake and the windows of sparkling sugar. "Let's eat," said Hansel, "and the Lord bless our food. I'll take a piece of the roof. You, Gretel, had better take some of the window; it's sweet." Hansel reached up and broke off a bit of the roof to see how it tasted, and Gretel pressed against the windowpanes and nibbled at them. And then a soft voice called from inside:

> "Nibble nibble, little mouse,
> Who's that nibbling at my house?"

The children answered:

>"The wind so wild,
>The heavenly child,"

and went right on eating. Hansel liked the taste of the roof, so he tore off
a big chunk, and Gretel broke out a whole round windowpane and sat
down on the ground to enjoy it. All at once the door opened, and an old,
old woman with a crutch came hobbling out. Hansel and Gretel were so
frightened they dropped what they were eating. But the old woman
wagged her head and said: "Oh, what dear children! However did you get
here? Don't be afraid, come in and stay with me. You will come to no
harm." She took them by the hand and led them into her house. A fine
meal of milk and pancakes, sugar, apples, and nuts was set before them.
And then two little beds were made up clean and white, and Hansel and
Gretel got into them and thought they were in heaven.

But the old woman had only pretended to be so kind. Actually she 11
was a wicked witch, who waylaid children and had built her house out of
bread to entice them. She killed, cooked, and ate any child who fell into
her hands, and that to her was a feast day. Witches have red eyes and
can't see very far, but they have a keen sense of smell like animals, so
they know when humans are coming. As Hansel and Gretel approached,
she laughed her wicked laugh and said with a jeer: "Here come two who
will never get away from me." Early in the morning, when the children
were still asleep, she got up, and when she saw them resting so sweetly
with their plump red cheeks, she muttered to herself: "What tasty morsels they will be!" She grabbed Hansel with her scrawny hand, carried
him to a little shed, and closed the iron-barred door behind him. He
screamed for all he was worth, but much good it did him. Then she went
back to Gretel, shook her awake, and cried: "Get up, lazybones. You
must draw water and cook something nice for your brother. He's out in
the shed and we've got to fatten him up. When he's nice and fat, I'm
going to eat him." Gretel wept bitterly, but in vain; she had to do what
the wicked witch told her.

The best of food was cooked for poor Hansel, but Gretel got nothing 12
but crayfish shells. Every morning the old witch crept to the shed and
said: "Hansel, hold out your finger. I want to see if you're getting fat."
But Hansel held out a bone. The old woman had weak eyes and couldn't
see it; she thought it was Hansel's finger and wondered why he wasn't
getting fat. When four weeks had gone by and Hansel was still as skinny
as ever, her impatience got the better of her and she decided not to wait
any longer. "Ho there, Gretel," she cried out. "Go and draw water and
don't dawdle. Skinny or fat, I'm going to butcher Hansel tomorrow and

cook him." Oh, how the little girl wailed at having to carry the water, and how the tears flowed down her cheeks! "Dear God," she cried, "oh, won't you help us? If only the wild beasts had eaten us in the forest, at least we'd have died together." "Stop that blubbering," said the witch. "It won't do you a bit of good."

Early in the morning Gretel had to fill the kettle with water and light 13 the fire. "First we'll bake," said the old witch. "I've heated the oven and kneaded the dough." And she drove poor Gretel out to the oven, which by now was spitting flames. "Crawl in," said the witch, "and see if it's hot enough for the bread." Once Gretel was inside, she meant to close the door and roast her, so as to eat her too. But Gretel saw what she had in mind and said: "I don't know how. How do I get in?" "Silly goose," said the old woman. "The opening is big enough. Look. Even I can get in." She crept to the opening and stuck her head in, whereupon Gretel gave her a push that sent her sprawling, closed the iron door and fastened the bolt. Eek! How horribly she screeched! But Gretel ran away and the wicked witch burned miserably to death.

Gretel ran straight to Hansel, opened the door of the shed, and cried: 14 "Hansel, we're saved! The old witch is dead." Hansel hopped out like a bird when someone opens the door of its cage. How happy they were! They hugged and kissed each other and danced around. And now that there was nothing to be afraid of, they went into the witch's house and in every corner there were boxes full of pearls and precious stones. Hansel stuffed his pockets full of them and said: "These will be much better than pebbles," and Gretel said: "I'll take some home too," and filled her apron with them. "We'd better leave now," said Hansel, "and get out of this bewitched forest." When they had walked a few hours, they came to a big body of water. "How will we ever get across?" said Hansel. "I don't see any bridge." "And there's no boat, either," said Gretel, "but over there I see a white duck. She'll help us across if I ask her." And she cried out:

> "Duckling, duckling, here is Gretel,
> Duckling, duckling, here is Hansel.
> No bridge or ferry far and wide—
> Duckling, come and give us a ride."

Sure enough, the duck came over to them and Hansel sat down on 15 her back and told his sister to sit beside him. "No," said Gretel, "that would be too much for the poor thing; let her carry us one at a time." And that's just what the good little duck did. And when they were safely across and had walked a little while, the forest began to look more and more familiar, and finally they saw their father's house in the distance. They began to run, and they flew into the house and threw themselves into their father's arms. The poor man hadn't had a happy hour since he had left the children in the forest, and in the meantime his wife had died. Gretel opened out her little apron, the pearls and precious stones went bouncing around the room, and Hansel reached into his pockets and tossed out handful after handful. All their worries were over, and they lived together in pure happiness. My story is done, see the mouse run; if you catch it, you may make yourself a great big fur cap out of it.

## *Transformation (1)*

# The Gingerbread House

## *Robert Coover*

*This is a story called "The Gingerbread House" by the contemporary writer Robert Coover. It consists of forty-two numbered paragraphs that present parts of a story that is clearly an adaptation of "Hansel and Gretel." Read it slowly, pausing after each paragraph to consider its relationship to the Grimm brothers' version of "Hansel and Gretel." Be especially careful to note what Coover has tak n from the original, what he has ignored, what he has added, and what he has taken but changed in some significant way. Then consider the points we have raised for discussion and writing.*

1

A pine forest in the midafternoon. Two children follow an old man, dropping breadcrumbs, singing nursery tunes. Dense earthy greens seep into the darkening distance, flecked and streaked with filtered sunlight. Spots of red, violet, pale blue, gold, burnt orange. The girl carries a basket for gathering flowers. The boy is occupied with the crumbs. Their song tells of God's care for little ones.

2

Poverty and resignation weigh on the old man. His cloth jacket is patched and threadbare, sunbleached white over the shoulders, worn through on the elbows. His feet do not lift, but shuffle through the dust. White hair. Parched skin. Secret forces of despair and guilt seem to pull him earthward.

3

The girl plucks a flower. The boy watches curiously. The old man stares impatiently into the forest's depths, where night seems already to crouch. The girl's apron is a bright orange, the gay color of freshly picked tangerines, and is stitched happily with blues and reds and greens; but her dress is simple and brown, tattered at the hem, and her feet are bare. Birds accompany the children in their singing and butterflies decorate the forest spaces.

### 4

The boy's gesture is furtive. His right hand trails behind him, letting a crumb fall. His face is half-turned toward his hand, but his eyes remain watchfully fixed on the old man's feet ahead. The old man wears heavy mud-spattered shoes, high-topped and leather-thonged. Like the old man's own skin, the shoes are dry and cracked and furrowed with wrinkles. The boy's pants are a bluish-brown, ragged at the cuffs, his jacket a faded red. He, like the girl, is barefoot.

### 5

The children sing nursery songs about May baskets and gingerbread houses and a saint who ate his own fleas. Perhaps they sing to lighten their young hearts, for puce wisps of dusk now coil through the trunks and branches of the thickening forest. Or perhaps they sing to conceal the boy's subterfuge. More likely, they sing for no reason at all, a thoughtless childish habit. To hear themselves. Or to admire their memories. Or to entertain the old man. To fill the silence. Conceal their thoughts. Their expectations.

### 6

The boy's hand and wrist, thrusting from the outgrown jacket (the faded red cuff is not a cuff at all, but the torn limits merely, the ragged edge of the soft worn sleeve), are tanned, a little soiled, childish. The fingers are short and plump, the palm soft, the wrist small. Three fingers curl under, holding back crumbs, kneading them, coaxing them into position, while the index finger and thumb flick them sparingly, one by one, to the ground, playing with them a moment, balling them, pinching them as if for luck or pleasure, before letting them go.

### 7

The old man's pale blue eyes float damply in deep dark pouches, half-shrouded by heavy upper lids and beetled over by shaggy white brows. Deep creases fan out from the moist corners, angle down past the nose, score the tanned cheeks and pinch the mouth. The old man's gaze is straight ahead, but at what? Perhaps at nothing. Some invisible destination. Some irrecoverable point of departure. One thing can be said about the eyes: they are tired. Whether they have seen too much or too little, they betray no will to see yet more.

8

The witch is wrapped in a tortured whirl of black rags. Her long face is drawn and livid, and her eyes glow like burning coals. Her angular body twists this way and that, flapping the black rags—flecks of blue and amethyst wink and flash in the black tangle. Her gnarled blue hands snatch greedily at space, shred her clothes, claw cruelly at her face and throat. She cackles silently, then suddenly screeches madly, seizes a passing dove, and tears its heart out.

9

The girl, younger than the boy, skips blithely down the forest path, her blonde curls flowing freely. Her brown dress is coarse and plain, but her apron is gay and white petticoats wink from beneath the tattered hem. Her skin is fresh and pink and soft, her knees and elbows dimpled, her cheeks rosy. Her young gaze flicks airily from flower to flower, bird to bird, tree to tree, from the boy to the old man, from the green grass to the encroaching darkness, and all of it seems to delight her equally. Her basket is full to overflowing. Does she even know the boy is dropping crumbs? or where the old man is leading them? Of course, but it's nothing! a game!

10

There is, in the forest, even now, a sunny place, with mintdrop trees and cotton candy bushes, an air as fresh and heady as lemonade. Rivulets of honey flow over gumdrop pebbles, and lollypops grow wild as daisies. This is the place of the gingerbread house. Children come here, but, they say, none leave.

11

The dove is a soft lustrous white, head high, breast filled, tip of the tail less than a feather's thickness off the ground. From above, it would be seen against the pale path—a mixture of umbers and grays and the sharp brown strokes of pine needles—but from its own level, in profile, its pure whiteness is set off glowingly against the obscure mallows and distant moss greens of the forest. Only its small beak moves. Around a bread crumb.

12

The song is about a great king who won many battles, but the girl sings alone. The old man has turned back, gazes curiously but dispassionately now at the boy. The boy, too, has turned, no longer furtive, hand poised but no crumb dropping from his fingertips. He stares back down the path by which they three have come, his mouth agape, his eyes startled. His left hand is raised, as if arrested a moment before striking out in protest. Doves are eating his breadcrumbs. His ruse has failed. Perhaps the old man, not so ignorant in such matters after all, has known all along it would. The girl sings of pretty things sold in the market.

### 13

So huddled over her prey is the witch that she seems nothing more than a pile of black rags heaped on a post. Her pale long-nailed hands are curled inward toward her breast, massaging the object, her head lower than her hunched shoulders, wan beaked nose poked in among the restless fingers. She pauses, cackling softly, peers left, then right, then lifts the heart before her eyes. The burnished heart of the dove glitters like a ruby, a polished cherry, a brilliant, heart-shaped bloodstone. It beats still. A soft radiant pulsing. The black bony shoulders of the witch quake with glee, with greed, with lust.

### 14

A wild blur of fluttering white: the dove's wings flapping! Hands clutch its body, its head, its throat, small hands with short plump fingers. Its wings flail against the dusky forest green, but it is forced down against the umber earth. The boy falls upon it, his hands bloodied by beak and claws.

### 15

The gingerbread house is approached by flagstones of variegated wafers, through a garden of candied fruits and all-day suckers in neat little rows.

### 16

No song now from the lips of the girl, but a cry of anguish. The basket of flowers is dropped, the kings and saints forgotten. She struggles with the boy for the bird. She kicks him, falls upon him, pulls his hair, tears at his red jacket. He huddles around the bird, trying to elbow free of the girl. Both children are weeping, the boy of anger and frustration, the girl of pain and pity and a bruised heart. Their legs entangle, their fists beat at each other, feathers fly.

### 17

The pale blue eyes of the old man stare not ahead, but down. The squint, the sorrow, the tedium are vanished; the eyes focus clearly. The deep creases fanning out from the damp corners pinch inward, a brief wince, as though at some inner hurt, some certain anguish, some old wisdom. He sighs.

18

The girl has captured the bird. The boy, small chest heaving, kneels in the path watching her, the anger largely drained out of him. His faded red jacket is torn; his pants are full of dust and pine needles. She has thrust the dove protectively beneath her skirt, and sits, knees apart, leaning over it, weeping softly. The old man stoops down, lifts her bright orange apron, her skirt, her petticoats. The boy turns away. The dove is nested in her small round thighs. It is dead.

19

Shadows have lengthened. Umbers and lavenders and greens have grayed. But the body of the dove glows yet in the gathering dusk. The whiteness of the ruffled breast seems to be fighting back against the threat of night. It is strewn with flowers, now beginning to wilt. The old man, the boy, and the girl have gone.

20

The beams of the gingerbread house are licorice sticks, cemented with taffy, weatherboarded with gingerbread, and coated with caramel. Peppermint-stick chimneys sprout randomly from its chocolate roof and its windows are laced with meringue. Oh, what a house! and the best thing of all is the door.

21

The forest is dense and deep. Branches reach forth like arms. Brown animals scurry. The boy makes no furtive gestures. The girl, carrying her flowerbasket, does not skip or sing. They walk, arms linked, eyes wide open and staring ahead into the forest. The old man plods on, leading the way, his heavy old leather-thonged shoes shuffling in the damp dust and undergrowth.

22

The old man's eyes, pale in the sunlight, now seem to glitter in the late twilight. Perhaps it is their wetness picking up the last flickering light of day. The squint has returned, but it is not the squint of weariness: resistance, rather. His mouth opens as though to speak, to rebuke, but his teeth are clenched. The witch twists and quivers, her black rags whirling, whipping, flapping. From her lean bosom, she withdraws the pulsing red heart of a dove. How it glows, how it rages, how it dances in the dusk! The old man now does not resist. Lust flattens his face and mists his old eyes, where glitter now reflections of the ruby heart. Grimacing, he plummets forward, covering the cackling witch, crashing through brambles that tear at his clothes.

### 23

A wild screech cleaves the silence of the dusky forest. Birds start up from branches and the undergrowth is alive with frightened animals. The old man stops short, one hand raised protectively in front of him, the other, as though part of the same instinct, reaching back to shield his children. Dropping her basket of flowers, the girl cries out in terror and springs forward into the old man's arms. The boy blanches, shivers as though a cold wind might be wetly wrapping his young body, but manfully holds his ground. Shapes seem to twist and coil, and vapors seep up from the forest floor. The girl whimpers and the old man holds her close.

### 24

The beds are simple but solid. The old man himself has made them. The sun is setting, the room is in shadows, the children tucked safely in. The old man tells them a story about a good fairy who granted a poor man three wishes. The wishes, he knows, were wasted, but so then is the story. He lengthens the tale with details about the good fairy, how sweet and kind and pretty she is, then lets the children complete the story with their own wishes, their own dreams. Below, a brutal demand is being forced upon him. Why must the goodness of all wishes come to nothing?

### 25

The flowerbasket lies, overturned, by the forest path, its wilting flowers strewn. Shadows darker than dried blood spread beneath its gaping mouth. The shadows are long, for night is falling.

### 26

The old man has fallen into the brambles. The children, weeping, help pull him free. He sits on the forest path staring at the boy and girl. It is as though he is unable to recognize them. Their weeping dies away. They huddle more closely together, stare back at the old man. His face is scratched, his clothes torn. He is breathing irregularly.

### 27

The sun, the songs, the breadcrumbs, the dove, the overturned basket, the long passage toward night: where, the old man wonders, have all the good fairies gone? He leads the way, pushing back the branches. The children follow, silent and frightened.

### 28

The boy pales and his heart pounds, but manfully he holds his ground. The witch writhes, her black rags fluttering, licking at the twisted branches. With a soft seductive cackle, she holds before him the burnished cherry-red heart of a dove. The boy licks his lips. She steps back. The glowing heart pulses gently, evenly, excitingly.


### 29

The good fairy has sparkling blue eyes and golden hair, a soft sweet mouth and gentle hands that caress and soothe. Gossamer wings sprout from her smooth back; from her flawless chest two firm breasts with tips bright as rubies.


### 30

The witch, holding the flaming pulsing heart out to the boy, steps back into the dark forest. The boy, in hesitation, follows. Back. Back. Swollen eyes aglitter, the witch draws the ruby heart close to her dark lean breast, then past her shoulder and away from the boy. Transfixed, he follows it, brushing by her. The witch's gnarled and bluish fingers claw at his poor garments, his pale red jacket and bluish-brown pants, surprising his soft young flesh.


### 31

The old man's shoulders are bowed earthward, his face is lined with sorrow, his neck bent forward with resignation, but his eyes glow like burning coals. He clutches his shredded shirt to his throat, stares intensely at the boy. The boy stands alone and trembling on the path, staring into the forest's terrible darkness. Shapes whisper and coil. The boy licks his lips, steps forward. A terrible shriek shreds the forest hush. The old man grimaces, pushes the whimpering girl away, strikes the boy.


### 32

No more breadcrumbs, no more pebbles, no more songs or flowers. The slap echoes through the terrible forest, doubles back on its own echoes, folding finally into a sound not unlike a whispering cackle.


### 33

The girl, weeping, kisses the struck boy and presses him close, shielding him from the tormented old man. The old man, taken aback, reaches out uncertainly, gently touches the girl's frail shoulder. She shakes his hand off—nearly a shudder—and shrinks toward the boy. The boy squares his shoulders, color returning to his face. The familiar creases of age and despair crinkle again the old man's face. His pale blue eyes mist over. He looks away. He leaves the children by the last light of day.

### 34

But the door! The door is shaped like a heart and is as red as a cherry, always half-open, whether lit by sun or moon, is sweeter than a sugarplum, more enchanting than a peppermint stick. It is red as a poppy, red as an apple, red as a strawberry, red as a bloodstone, red as a rose. Oh, what a thing is the door of that house!

### 35

The children, alone in the strange black forest, huddle wretchedly under a great gnarled tree. Owls hoot and bats flick menacingly through the twisting branches. Strange shapes writhe and rustle before their weary eyes. They hold each other tight and, trembling, sing lullabyes, but they are not reassured.

### 36

The old man trudges heavily out of the black forest. His way is marked, not by breadcrumbs, but by dead doves, ghostly white in the empty night.

### 37

The girl prepares a mattress of leaves and flowers and pineneedles. The boy gathers branches to cover them, to hide them, to protect them. They make pillows of their poor garments. Bats screech as they work and owls blink down on their bodies, ghostly white, young, trembling. They creep under the branches, disappearing into the darkness.

### 38

Gloomily, the old man sits in the dark room and stares at the empty beds. The good fairy, though a mystery of the night, effuses her surroundings with a lustrous radiance. Is it the natural glow of her small nimble body or perhaps the star at the tip of her wand? Who can tell? Her gossamer wings flutter rapidly, and she floats, ruby-tipped breasts downward, legs dangling and dimpled knees bent slightly, glowing buttocks arched up in defiance of the night. How good she is! In the black empty room, the old man sighs and uses up a wish: he wishes his poor children well.

### 39

The children are nearing the gingerbread house. Passing under mint-drop trees, sticking their fingers in the cotton candy bushes, sampling the air as heady as lemonade, they skip along singing nursery songs. Nonsense songs about dappled horses and the slaying of dragons. Counting songs and idle riddles. They cross over rivulets of honey on gumdrop pebbles, picking the lollypops that grow as wild as daffodils.

40

The witch flicks and flutters through the blackened forest, her livid face twisted with hatred, her inscrutable condition. Her eyes burn like glowing coals and her black rags flap loosely. Her gnarled hands claw greedily at the branches, tangle in the night's webs, dig into tree trunks until the sap flows beneath her nails. Below, the boy and girl sleep an exhausted sleep. One ghostly white leg, with dimpled knee and soft round thigh, thrust out from under the blanket of branches.

41

But wish again! Flowers and butterflies. Dense earthly greens seeping into the distance, flecked and streaked with midafternoon sunlight. Two children following an old man. They drop breadcrumbs, sing nursery songs. The old man walks leadenly. The boy's gesture is furtive. The girl—but it's no use, the doves will come again, there are no reasonable wishes.

42

The children approach the gingerbread house through a garden of candied fruits and all-day suckers, hopping along on flagstones of variegated wafers. They sample the gingerbread weatherboarding with its caramel coating, lick at the meringue on the windowsills, kiss each other's sweetened lips. The boy climbs up on the chocolate roof to break off a peppermint-stick chimney, comes sliding down into a rainbarrel full of vanilla pudding. The girl, reaching out to catch him in his fall, slips on a sugarplum and tumbles into a sticky rock garden of candied chestnuts. Laughing gaily, they lick each other clean. And how grand is the red-and-white striped chimney the boy holds up for her! how bright! how sweet! But the door: here they pause and catch their breath. It is heart-shaped and bloodstone-red, its burnished surface gleaming in the sunlight. Oh, what a thing is that door! Shining like a ruby, like hard cherry candy, and pulsing softly, radiantly. Yes, marvelous! delicious! insuperable! but beyond: what is that sound of black rags flapping?

# For Discussion and Writing

1.  What are the most striking differences between Coover's version and the Grimms'? Discuss the significance of some of these differences.

2.  Select a passage where Coover seems to be following the Grimms' version closely. How does his style of presentation differ from theirs?

3.  Consider the sequence of paragraphs 13–18. A critic has observed that paragraph 15 "presents a Disneyfied version of the scene."

What do you suppose this means? How does paragraph 15 fit into this sequence of four paragraphs? Are the others Disneyfied also?

How do you interpret these paragraphs? What does the behavior of each character mean? What parallels do you find between the behavior of one character and another? What significant contrasts do you find?

4. Consider Coover's story as an interpretation of the Grimms'. What is Coover telling us about the meaning of this story? Examine in particular any images he returns to frequently. Write an essay in which you discuss "The Gingerbread House" as a creative reading or interpretation of "Hansel and Gretel."

*Transformation   (2)*

# Gretel

### *Garrison Keillor*

*Garrison Keillor's "Gretel" is also a contemporary adaptation of "Hansel and Gretel." Keillor, the creator of Lake Woebegon, is a well-known comic writer. This adaptation takes the form of a statement made by Gretel.*

When Hansel and I negotiated the sale of book rights to Grimm  1
Bros., he and I retained the right of final approval of the manuscript and agreed to split the proceeds fifty-fifty. We shook hands on it and I thought the deal was set, but then his lawyers put me under a spell, and when I woke up, they had rewritten the contract and the book too! I couldn't believe it! Not only did the new contract cut me out (under the terms, I was to get ten shiny baubles out of the first fortune the book earned and three trinkets for each additional fortune) but the book was pure fiction.

Suddenly he was portrayed as the strong and resourceful one, a  2
regular little knight, and I came off as a weak sister. Dad was shown as a loving father who was talked into abandoning us in the forest by Gladys, our "wicked" stepmother.

Nothing could be further from the truth.                       3

My brother was a basket case from the moment the birds ate his  4
breadcrumbs. He lay down in a heap and whimpered, and I had to slap him a couple times *hard* to make him walk. Now the little wiener makes

himself out to be the hero who kept telling me, "Don't cry, Gretel." Ha!
The only crying I did was from sheer exhaustion carrying him on my
back.

As for Dad, he was no bleeding heart. He was very much into that 5
whole woodcutter/peasant/yeoman scene—cockfighting, bullbaiting,
going to the village on Saturday to get drunk and watch a garroting or a
boiling—don't kid yourself, Gladys couldn't send us to our *rooms* without his say-so. The truth is that he was in favor of the forest idea from the
word go.

What I can't understand is why they had to lie about it. Many, *many* 6
parents left their children in the forest in those days. It was nothing
unusual.

Nowadays, we tend to forget that famine can be a very difficult 7
experience for a family. For many parents, ditching the kids was not only
a solution, it was an act of faith. They believed that ravens would bring
morsels of food in their beaks, or that wolves would take care of the kids,
or a frog would, or that the fairies would step in. Dwarves, a hermit, a
band of pilgrims, a kindly shepherd, *somebody*. And they were right.

And that is why I was never seriously worried for one single moment 8
while we were there. Deep down, I always knew we would make it.

I don't mean to say that it wasn't a trying experience, an *emotional* 9
experience. It was. And yet there isn't a single documented case of a child
left in the forest who suffered any lasting damage. You look at those
children today and you will find they are better people for having gone
through it. Except for my brother, that is. The little jerk. He and my
father live in luxurious manors with beautiful tapestries and banners and
ballrooms, and I live above an alchemist's shop in a tiny garret they call a
condo. As for Gladys, she was kicked out without so much as a property
settlement. She didn't even get half of the hut. I guess she is the one who
suffered most. Her and the witch.

I often think about the witch—I ask myself, Why did I give her the 10
shove? After all, it wasn't me she was after.

I guess that, back then, I wasn't prepared to understand her type of 11
militance. I couldn't see that she was fattening up Hansel in order to
make a very radical statement. If only I had. Not that I necessarily would
have joined her in making that statement, but I would have seen that from
her point of view it had validity and meaning.

## For Discussion and Writing

1. Keillor's language is different from that of both the original and
   Coover's transformation. How would you describe it? Consider specific expressions.

2. Sum up Gretel's character in your own words. What kind of person is she? What are her values? Consider the last four paragraphs in particular.

3. Consider Keillor's "Gretel" as an interpretation of "Hansel and Gretel" and a criticism of it. What attitude does he seem to adopt toward the original?

4. Write an essay in which you discuss the differences between Coover's and Keillor's transformations of the fairy tale. Consider such matters as style and attitude toward the original. Try to get at the purpose of both transformations.

*Transformation   (3)*

# The Little Brother and the Little Sister
## *Jacob and Wilhelm Grimm*

*We have been speaking of "Hansel and Gretel" as the "original" text, of which Coover and Keillor made transformations. But actually the Grimm brothers were the first transformers. They wrote down stories told to them by various informants. These written manuscripts were then transformed into the first published versions of the tales. As new editions of the book appeared, tales continued to be transformed. For many of them, we have four significantly different versions. The original manuscripts were destroyed, but copies of some of them have survived. What follows here is an English translation of a copy of the Grimms' original manuscript of a story entitled "The Little Brother and the Little Sister."*

There was once a poor woodcutter, who lived in front of a great 1 forest. He fared so miserably, that he could scarcely feed his wife and his two children. Once he had no bread any longer, and suffered great anxiety, then his wife said to him in the evening in bed: take the two children tomorrow morning and take them into the great forest, give them the bread we have left, and make a large fire for them and after that go away and leave them alone. The husband did not want to for a long time, but the wife left him no peace, until he finally agreed.

But the children had heard everything that the mother had said. The 2 little sister began to weep a lot, the little brother said to her she should be quiet and comforted her. Then he quietly got up and went outside in front of the door, the moon shone there and the white pebbles shone in front of the house. The boy picked them up carefully and filled his little coat pocket with them, as many as he could put there. Then he went back to his little sister into bed, and went to sleep.

Early next morning, before the sun had risen, the father and mother   3 came and woke the children up, who were to go with them into the great forest. They gave each a little piece of bread, little sister took it under her little apron, for the little brother had his pocket full of pebbles. Then they set off on their way to the great forest. As they were walking like this, the little brother often stood still, and looked back at their little house. The father said: why are you always standing and looking back; oh, answered the little brother, I am looking at my little white cat, it is sitting on the roof and wants to say goodbye to me but secretly he kept letting one of the little white pebbles drop. The mother spoke: just keep going, it's not your little cat, it is the morning glow which is shining on the chimney. But the boy kept looking back and kept letting another little stone drop.

They walked like this for a long time and at last came to the middle   4 of the great forest. Then the father made a great fire, and the mother says: sleep a while children, we will go into the forest and look for wood, wait until we come back. The children sat down by the fire, and they both ate their little piece of bread. They wait a long time until it was night, but the parents did not come back. Then the little sister began to weep, but the little brother comforted her and took her by the hand. Then the moon shone, and the little white pebbles shone, and showed them the way. And the little brother led the little sister through the whole night. And in the morning they came again in front of the house. The father was glad, for he had not done it willingly; but the mother was angry.

Soon after they had no bread again, and the little brother heard again   5 in the evening in bed, how the mother said to the father, he should take the children out into the great forest again. Then the little sister began again to sob her heart out, and the little brother got up again, and wanted to look for little stones. When he got to the door, however, it was bolted by the mother, then the little brother began to feel sad, and could not comfort the little sister.

They got up again before daybreak, each received a little piece of   6 bread again. When they were on their way, the little brother looks back often. The father said: my child why are you always standing still and looking back towards the little house? Oh! answered the little brother, I am looking at my little dove, it is sitting on the roof, and wants to say goodbye to me, but secretly he crumbled his little piece of bread, and kept letting a crumb fall. The mother spoke: just keep going, it's not your little dove, it's the morning glow shining on the chimney. But the little brother still kept looking back, and kept letting another little crumb drop.

When they had come to the middle of the great forest, the father    7 again made a great fire, the mother again said the same words and both went away. The little sister gave the little brother a half of her little piece of bread, for the little brother had thrown his onto the path. And they waited until evening, then the little brother wanted to lead the little sister back by the moonshine. But the little birds had eaten up the little crumbs of bread and they could not find the way. They walked further and further and got lost in the great forest. On the third day they came to a little house that was made of bread, the roof was covered with cake and the windows of sugar. The children were glad when they saw it and the little brother ate some of the roof and the little sister some of the window. As they stood like this and enjoyed it, a delicate voice cried out:

> nibble, nibble, gnaw!
> who is nibbling at my little house?

The children were badly startled; soon after a small old woman came out, she took the children by the hand in a kindly way, took them into the house, and gave them something good to eat, and put them in a nice bed. But the next morning she put the little brother in a little stable, he was to be a little pig, and the little sister had to bring him water and good food. Every day she went to it then the little brother had to stick out his finger, and she felt if it was already fat. He always stuck out in place of it a little bone, then she thought that he was still not fat, and this went on for a long time. She gave to the little sister nothing to eat but crab-shells, because she was not to be fattened. After four weeks she said in the evening to the little sister, go and fetch water, and heat it tomorrow morning, we will slaughter and boil your little brother, meanwhile I'll make the dough, so that we can also bake as well. The next morning, when the water was hot, she called the little sister to the oven, and said to her: sit on the board, I will push you into the oven, see if the bread is already done; but she wanted to leave the little sister in there and roast her. The little sister notices this and said to her: I don't understand that, sit there first yourself, I will push you in. The old woman sat on it, and the little sister pushed her in, shut the door, and the witch burned to death. Then she went to the little brother and opens his little stable for him. They found the whole little house full of jewels, filled all their pockets with them, and took them to their father, who became a rich man; but the mother was dead.

# For Discussion and Writing

1. We can see now that what we thought was the "original" text was itself a transformation of another "original," a transformation that rewrites significant features of the manuscript version. Please note and discuss the major changes you find, taking "The Little Brother and the Little Sister" as the original and "Hansel and Gretel" as the transformation.

2. Write an essay in which you use the transformation made by the Grimms as your starting point for a discussion of transformation as a form of writing. Consider the possible reasons why the Grimms made the changes they did, moving on to why Coover and Keillor seem to have undertaken their transformations. What is there in the fairy tale that leads people to maintain such a strong interest in it that they wish to rewrite it in a different way? Finally, you might consider how your knowledge of the Grimms' first text changes your view of all the others. Scholars have only recently, and with great reluctance, come to realize how actively the Grimms transformed their source material. To what extent is each of these writers doing something different? To what extent are they all doing the same thing?

3. You, too, can be a transformer. Take some well-known fairy tale and produce your own purposeful transformation of it. This will work best if you look up some familiar story and work with the printed text in front of you. You may follow the leads of Coover and Keillor or find your own principle of transformation, but don't just imitate. Steal! That is, *change* the text you are transforming sufficiently to make it your own.

# Completing Texts: The Reader's Work

*Texts are lazy machineries that ask someone to do part of their job.*
—*Umberto Eco*

What do we do when we read? What does it mean to "complete" a text? Here we shall be considering the act of reading as an act of writing in both a figurative and literal sense. In his book *The Role of the Reader*, Italian semiotician Umberto Eco discusses reading as a collaborative act in which "a well-organized text on the one hand presupposes a model of competence coming, so to speak, from outside the text, but on the other hand works to build up, by merely textual means, such a competence." As readers, we provide "models of competence," bringing to a text our own intellectual equipment to help us understand what we are reading. At the same time, the text directs that reading. When we look at a text that starts out "Once upon a time" or "Once there was" we know we are in the presence of a fairy tale and we therefore accept the conventions of that genre—talking frogs, wicked stepmothers, handsome princes—when we encounter them in the text. In recognizing a text as a particular kind of text, such as fairy tale, mystery, or historical romance, we are drawing on our intertextual knowledge—our reading of other texts like the one in front of us. As Eco reminds us, "no text is read independently of other texts."

When we read the first sentence of William Carlos Williams's story "The Use of Force"—"They were new patients to me, all I had was the name, Olson"—the text assumes that we will know that the speaker is a doctor. When the speaker describes his patient as "One of those picture children often reproduced in advertising leaflets and the photogravure sections of the Sunday papers," the text assumes the reader shares a common cultural frame of reference; specifically, that the reader has seen those American advertisements that feature children, and knows what part the "Sunday papers" play in American culture, and is familiar with the magazine section in them, as well as the type of child (blond and blue-eyed) likely to be featured there as a "beautiful child." These are small examples of the reader's work, and much of this work occurs subconsciously as we read.

The reader's work increases when there is a gap in the narrative and the reader is called upon to infer what took place during that missing time. In Eco's terms, this is called writing (in one's head) a "ghost chapter":

Frequently, given a series of causally and linearly connected events $a \ldots e$, a text tells the reader about the event $a$ and, after a while, about the event $e$, taking for granted that the reader has already anticipated the dependent events $b$, $c$, $d$ (of which $e$ is the consequence, according to many intertextual frames). Thus the text implicitly validates a 'ghost chapter,' tentatively written by the reader.

Writing this ghost chapter in your head can be a very straightforward operation when the information in the gap does not affect the events in the story. If the story tells us, for example, that "John got on the bus in New York," and in the next sentence, "John arrived in Providence," the reader quickly infers that the trip between New York and Providence was both safe and uneventful. The ghost chapter we write between event $a$, "John got on the bus in New York" and event $e$, "John arrived in Providence," might logically contain event $b$, John gave his ticket to the bus driver; event $c$, John found a seat; and event $d$, John watched the scenery go by. We know from our own experience that these are the events most likely to occur on any bus ride between one city and another, and because this is common knowledge, the text does not have to provide this information.

In Kate Chopin's story "The Kiss," there are two gaps in time, the first between the kiss and the reception, and the second between the reception and the wedding. These jumps in time are appropriate to a story with a heroine who acts to get what she wants rather than sitting and brooding about it. Again, the reader may, in writing a ghost chapter, infer that whatever happens in those time periods is not important to the story. Yet Nathalie's final statement before the first gap in time (kiss–reception), "It depends upon—a good deal whether I ever forgive you," leaves the reader as well as Harvy speculating about what the gap in Nathalie's statement signifies: "depends upon—" what? The reader may also be busy speculating as to the nature of the relationship between Nathalie and Harvy. During a second reading of the text, the reader might wonder what plans ran through Nathalie's head; namely, how she plotted the moves that are described to us in the next sequence: the entrapment of Brantain at the reception. (And what information in the text allows us to use the term "entrapment"?) In the second gap, between the reception and the wedding, the reader can logically infer from common knowledge that Brantain and Nathalie become engaged, that she is given an engagement ring, that wedding plans are made. But it is also possible to speculate here about Harvy's reaction to this forthcoming event and to try to forecast what will take place in the final sequence of events.

In other texts, there are gaps that are not so easily filled by the reader because the text wishes to create suspense and so information is deliberately withheld from the reader. At these moments, the reader constructs a *possible world*. Say heroine X enters a room and finds her lover Y in the arms of another woman Z, and the text closes the door in our faces and changes the scene to the battlefield at Waterloo. The thwarted reader, desiring to know what happened in that room, may draw on his or her own frame of reference—"I know what I would do if I were X"—and create a possible world in which the scene is completed, though the imagined completion may be at variance with what actually is to take place in the text. This act is the creation by the reader of a possible world, a new text.

In Eco's terms, possible worlds are "sketches for another story, the story the actual one could have been had things gone differently. . . . They are worlds imagined, believed, wished." A fictional text is itself a possible world because it is composed of a possible set of events chosen by its author. As readers, we most frequently construct possible worlds from texts in which we have become deeply involved, and because we want their stories to continue, we construct our own, adding new endings, proposing new situations. Fans of that problematical heroine Scarlett O'Hara, of *Gone With the Wind*, may construct a possible world in which Scarlett marries Ashley Wilkes, her one true love. But this possible world would have little to do with the possible world that is actualized in Margaret Mitchell's novel, since that world is structured on the proposition that Ashley marries Melanie.

So when we talk about completing a text, we're not being entirely accurate. A text can never be completed. Each reader brings a unique model of competence to a text, and so each reader will fill gaps in the text differently. Because the fictional text is directed at the imagination of the reader, there will always be variables in the interpretation possible in the imaginative spaces of the text. However, a well-organized fictional text will not allow just any interpretation; rather, it directs the reader toward a certain number of possible readings. It is because of the extension of these possible readings by an infinite number of readers, each with a different model of competence, that an infinite number of readings of a text is possible. Which is to say, when John gets on the bus in New York, reader A will put him on a green and white bus; reader B will put him on a blue and white bus; reader C will give him a bumpy ride to Providence; reader D, who has taken that bus ride, will make John bored during the seemingly endless barren stretch from the Connecticut line to East Greenwich, Rhode Island; and so on and on. John's bus ride has endless variations.

In this section, you will be asked to put your work as a reader into the actual writing of ghost chapters and possible worlds. When you compare your reading with those of your classmates, you will have a very clear idea of what we mean by variables in interpretation.


# The Boarding House

*James Joyce*

*This story, which James Joyce termed "a story of adolescence," is one of a group called* Dubliners. *The stories draw on Joyce's experience of growing up in Dublin, Ireland, at the turn of the century.*

Mrs. Mooney was a butcher's daughter. She was a woman who was quite able to keep things to herself: a determined woman. She had married her father's foreman and opened a butcher's shop near Spring Gardens. But as soon as his father-in-law was dead Mr. Mooney began to go to the devil. He drank, plundered the till, ran headlong into debt. It was no use making him take the pledge: he was sure to break out again a few days after. By fighting his wife in the presence of customers and by buying bad meat he ruined his business. One night he went for his wife with the cleaver and she had to sleep in a neighbor's house. 1

After that they lived apart. She went to the priest and got a separation from him with care of the children. She would give him neither money nor food nor house-room; and so he was obliged to enlist himself as a sheriff's man. He was a shabby stooped little drunkard with a white face and a white moustache and white eyebrows, pencilled above his little eyes, which were pink-veined and raw; and all day long he sat in the bailiff's room, waiting to be put on a job. Mrs. Mooney, who had taken what remained of her money out of the butcher business and set up a boarding house in Hardwicke Street, was a big imposing woman. Her house had a floating population made up of tourists from Liverpool and the Isle of Man and, occasionally, *artistes* from the music halls. Its resident population was made up of clerks from the city. She governed her house cunningly and firmly, knew when to give credit, when to be stern and when to let things pass. All the resident young men spoke of her as *The Madam*. 2

Mrs. Mooney's young men paid fifteen shillings a week for board and lodgings (beer or stout at dinner excluded). They shared in common tastes and occupations and for this reason they were very chummy with one another. They discussed with one another the chances of favorites and outsiders. Jack Mooney, the Madam's son, who was clerk to a commission agent in Fleet Street, had the reputation of being a hard case. He 3 was fond of using soldiers' obscenities: usually he came home in the small hours. When he met his friends he had always a good one to tell them and he was always sure to be on to a good thing—that is to say, a likely horse or a likely *artiste*. He was also handy with the mits and sang comic songs. On Sunday nights there would often be a reunion in Mrs. Mooney's front drawing-room. The music-hall *artistes* would oblige; and Sheridan played waltzes and polkas and vamped accompaniments. Polly Mooney, the Madam's daughter, would also sing. She sang:

> I'm a . . . naughty girl.
> You needn't sham:
> You know I am.

Polly was a slim girl of nineteen; she had light soft hair and a small   4
full mouth. Her eyes, which were grey with a shade of green through them, had a habit of glancing upwards when she spoke with anyone, which made her look like a little perverse madonna. Mrs. Mooney had first sent her daughter to be a typist in a corn-factor's office but, as a disreputable sheriff's man used to come every other day to the office, asking to be allowed to say a word to his daughter, she had taken her daughter home again and set her to do housework. As Polly was very lively the intention was to give her the run of the young men. Besides, young men like to feel that there is a young woman not very far away. Polly, of course, flirted with the young men but Mrs. Mooney, who was a shrewd judge, knew that the young men were only passing the time away: none of them meant business. Things went on so for a long time and Mrs. Mooney began to think of sending Polly back to typewriting when she noticed that something was going on between Polly and one of the young men. She watched the pair and kept her own counsel.

Polly knew that she was being watched, but still her mother's per-   5
sistent silence could not be misunderstood. There had been no open complicity between mother and daughter, no open understanding but, though people in the house began to talk of the affair, still Mrs. Mooney did not intervene. Polly began to grow a little strange in her manner and the young man was evidently perturbed. At last, when she judged it to be the right moment, Mrs. Mooney intervened. She dealt with moral problems as a cleaver deals with meat: and in this case she had made up her mind.

It was a bright Sunday morning of early summer, promising heat, but   6
with a fresh breeze blowing. All the windows of the boarding house were open and the lace curtains ballooned gently towards the street beneath the raised sashes. The belfry of George's Church sent out constant peals and worshippers, singly or in groups, traversed the little circus before the church, revealing their purpose by their self-contained demeanor no less

than by the little volumes in their gloved hands. Breakfast was over in the boarding house and the table of the breakfast-room was covered with plates on which lay yellow streaks of eggs with morsels of bacon-fat and bacon-rind. Mrs. Mooney sat in the straw arm-chair and watched the servant Mary remove the breakfast things. She made Mary collect the crusts and pieces of broken bread to help to make Tuesday's bread-pudding. When the table was cleared, the broken bread collected, the sugar and butter safe under lock and key, she began to reconstruct the interview which she had had the night before with Polly. Things were as she had suspected; she had been frank in her questions and Polly had been frank in her answers. Both had been somewhat awkward, of course. She had been made awkward by her not wishing to receive the news in too cavalier a fashion or to seem to have connived and Polly had been made awkward not merely because allusions of that kind always made her awkward but also because she did not wish it to be thought that in her wise innocence she had divined the intention behind her mother's tolerance.

Mrs. Mooney glanced instinctively at the little gilt clock on the man-    7 telpiece as soon as she had become aware through her revery that the bells of George's Church had stopped ringing. It was seventeen minutes past eleven: she would have lots of time to have the matter out with Mr. Doran and then catch short twelve at Marlborough Street. She was sure she would win. To begin with she had all the weight of social opinion on her side: she was an outraged mother. She had allowed him to live beneath her roof, assuming that he was a man of honor, and he had simply abused her hospitality. He was thirty-four or thirty-five years of age, so that youth could not be pleaded as his excuse; nor could ignorance be his excuse since he was a man who had seen something of the world. He had simply taken advantage of Polly's youth and inexperience: that was evident. The question was: What reparation would he make?

There must be reparation made in such cases. It is all very well for    8 the man: he can go his ways as if nothing had happened, having had his moment of pleasure, but the girl has to bear the brunt. Some mothers would be content to patch up such an affair for a sum of money; she had known cases of it. But she would not do so. For her only one reparation could make up for the loss of her daughter's honor: marriage.

She counted all her cards again before sending Mary up to Mr.    9 Doran's room to say that she wished to speak with him. She felt sure she would win. He was a serious young man, not rakish or loud-voiced like the others. If it had been Mr. Sheridan or Mr. Meade or Bantam Lyons her task would have been much harder. She did not think he would face publicity. All the lodgers in the house knew something of the affair; details had been invented by some. Besides, he had been employed for thirteen years in a great Catholic wine-merchant's office and publicity would mean for him, perhaps, the loss of his sit. Whereas if he agreed all might be well. She knew he had a good screw for one thing and she suspected he had a bit of stuff put by.

Nearly the half-hour! She stood up and surveyed herself in the pier- 10 glass. The decisive expression of her great florid face satisfied her and she thought of some mothers she knew who could not get their daughters off their hands.

Mr. Doran was very anxious indeed this Sunday morning. He had 11 made two attempts to shave but his hand had been so unsteady that he had been obliged to desist. Three days' reddish beard fringed his jaws and every two or three minutes a mist gathered on his glasses so that he had to take them off and polish them with his pocket-handkerchief. The recollection of his confession of the night before was a cause of acute pain to him; the priest had drawn out every ridiculous detail of the affair and in the end had so magnified his sin that he was almost thankful at being afforded a loophole of reparation. The harm was done. What could he do now but marry her or run away? He could not brazen it out. The affair would be sure to be talked of and his employer would be certain to hear of it. Dublin is such a small city: everyone knows everyone else's business. He felt his heart leap warmly in his throat as he heard in his excited imagination old Mr. Leonard calling out in his rasping voice: *Send Mr. Doran here, please.*

All his long years of service gone for nothing! All his industry and 12 diligence thrown away! As a young man he had sown his wild oats, of course; he had boasted of his free-thinking and denied the existence of God to his companions in public-houses. But that was all passed and done with . . . nearly. He still bought a copy of *Reynolds's Newspaper* every week but he attended to his religious duties and for nine-tenths of the year lived a regular life. He had money enough to settle down on; it was not that. But the family would look down on her. First of all there was her disreputable father and then her mother's boarding house was beginning to get a certain fame. He had a notion that he was being had. He could imagine his friends talking of the affair and laughing. She *was* a little vulgar; sometimes she said *I seen* and *If I had've known.* But what would grammar matter if he really loved her? He could not make up his mind whether to like her or despise her for what she had done. Of course, he had done it too. His instinct urged him to remain free, not to marry. Once you are married you are done for, it said.

While he was sitting helplessly on the side of the bed in shirt and 13 trousers she tapped lightly at his door and entered. She told him all, that she had made a clean breast of it to her mother and that her mother would speak with him that morning. She cried and threw her arms round his neck, saying:

—O, Bob! Bob! What am I to do? What am I to do at all? 14

She would put an end to herself, she said.                                      15

He comforted her feebly, telling her not to cry, that it would be all 16
right, never fear. He felt against his shirt the agitation of her bosom.

It was not altogether his fault that it had happened. He remembered 17
well, with the curious patient memory of the celibate, the first casual
caresses her dress, her breath, her fingers had given him. Then late one
night as he was undressing for bed she had tapped at his door, timidly.
She wanted to relight her candle at his for hers had been blown out by a
gust. It was her bath night. She wore a loose open combing-jacket of
printed flannel. Her white instep shone in the opening of her furry
slippers and the blood glowed warmly behind her perfumed skin. From
her hands and wrists too as she lit and steadied her candle a faint perfume
arose.

On nights when he came in very late it was she who warmed up his 18
dinner. He scarcely knew what he was eating, feeling her beside him
alone, at night, in the sleeping house. And her thoughtfulness! If the night
was anyway cold or wet or windy there was sure to be a little tumbler of
punch ready for him. Perhaps they could be happy together. . . .

They used to go upstairs together on tiptoe, each with a candle, and 19
on the third landing exchange reluctant good-nights. They used to kiss.
He remembered well her eyes, the touch of her hand and his delirium. . . .

But delirium passes. He echoed her phrase, applying it to himself: 20
*What am I to do?* The instinct of the celibate warned him to hold back.
But the sin was there; even his sense of honor told him that reparation
must be made for such a sin.

While he was sitting with her on the side of the bed Mary came to the 21
door and said that the missus wanted to see him in the parlor. He stood
up to put on his coat and waistcoat, more helpless than ever. When he
was dressed he went over to her to comfort her. It would be all right,
never fear. He left her crying on the bed and moaning softly: *O my God!*

Going down the stairs his glasses became so dimmed with moisture 22
that he had to take them off and polish them. He longed to ascend
through the roof and fly away to another country where he would never
hear again of his trouble, and yet a force pushed him downstairs step by
step. The implacable faces of his employer and of the Madam stared upon
his discomfiture. On the last flight of stairs he passed Jack Mooney who
was coming up from the pantry nursing two bottles of *Bass*. They saluted
coldly; and the lover's eyes rested for a second or two on a thick bulldog
face and a pair of thick short arms. When he reached the foot of the
staircase he glanced up and saw Jack regarding him from the door of the
return-room.

Suddenly he remembered the night when one of the music-hall 23
*artistes*, a little blond Londoner, had made a rather free allusion to Polly.

The reunion had been almost broken up on account of Jack's violence. Everyone tried to quiet him. The music-hall *artiste*, a little paler than usual, kept smiling and saying that there was no harm meant: but Jack kept shouting at him that if any fellow tried that sort of a game on with *his* sister he'd bloody well put his teeth down his throat, so he would.

Polly sat for a little time on the side of the bed, crying. Then she 24 dried her eyes and went over to the looking-glass. She dipped the end of the towel in the water-jug and refreshed her eyes with the cool water. She looked at herself in profile and readjusted a hairpin above her ear. Then she went back to the bed again and sat at the foot. She regarded the pillows for a long time and the sight of them awakened in her mind secret amiable memories. She rested the nape of her neck against the cool iron bed-rail and fell into a revery. There was no longer any perturbation visible on her face.

She waited on patiently, almost cheerfully, without alarm, her memo- 25 ries gradually giving place to hopes and visions of the future. Her hopes and visions were so intricate that she no longer saw the white pillows on which her gaze was fixed or remembered that she was waiting for any-thing.

At last she heard her mother calling. She started to her feet and ran to 26 the banisters.

—Polly! Polly!                                                                                 27
—Yes, mamma?                                                                              28
—Come down, dear. Mr. Doran wants to speak to you.                         29
Then she remembered what she had been waiting for.                          30

## For Discussion and Writing

1. In paragraph 5, the reader must draw on a set of inferences if such phrases as the following are to be interpreted:
   "no open complicity"
   "her mother's persistent silence could not be misunderstood"
   "the affair"
   "a little strange"
   "the young man was evidently perturbed"
   "the right moment"
   "moral problems as a cleaver deals with meat"
   What information in the first four paragraphs can be drawn on by the reader in order to interpret these phrases? How much does the text depend on the reader's model of competence here? What phrases lack interpretive information and act to pique the reader's interest in forthcoming events?

2. Write a ghost chapter of the confrontation of Mr. Doran and Mrs. Mooney. Decide what persuasive strategies Mrs. Mooney will employ to win her case, and how much, if any, resistance Mr. Doran will exhibit. Your chapter may be written as a narrative describing what was said by both parties or as a combination of narrative and dialogue.

# You Were Perfectly Fine

## *Dorothy Parker*

*A New York writer of verse, fiction, plays, and filmscripts, Dorothy Parker was most celebrated for her wit in the 1920s and 1930s. In the story that follows, she presents the aftermath of a fashionable New York dinner party.*

The pale young man eased himself carefully into the low chair, and 1 rolled his head to the side, so that the cool chintz comforted his cheek and temple.

"Oh, dear," he said. "Oh, dear, oh, dear, oh, dear. Oh." 2

The clear-eyed girl, sitting light and erect on the couch, smiled 3 brightly at him.

"Not feeling so well today?" she said. 4

"Oh, I'm great," he said. "Corking, I am. Know what time I got up? 5 Four o'clock this afternoon, sharp. I kept trying to make it, and every time I took my head off the pillow, it would roll under the bed. This isn't my head I've got on now. I think this is something that used to belong to Walt Whitman. Oh, dear, oh, dear, oh, dear."

"Do you think maybe a drink would make you feel better?" she said. 6

"The hair of the mastiff that bit me?" he said. "Oh, no, thank you. 7 Please never speak of anything like that again. I'm through. I'm all, all through. Look at that hand; steady as a humming-bird. Tell me, was I very terrible last night?"

"Oh, goodness," she said, "everybody was feeling pretty high. You 8 were all right."

"Yeah," he said. "I must have been dandy. Is everybody sore at 9 me?"

"Good heavens, no," she said. "Everyone thought you were terribly 10 funny. Of course, Jim Pierson was a little stuffy, there for a minute at dinner. But people sort of held him back in his chair, and got him calmed down. I don't think anybody at the other tables noticed it at all. Hardly anybody."

"He was going to sock me?" he said. "Oh, Lord. What did I do to 11 him?"

"Why, you didn't do a thing," she said. "You were perfectly fine. 12 But you know how silly Jim gets, when he thinks anybody is making too much fuss over Elinor."

"Was I making a pass at Elinor?" he said. "Did I do that?"            13

"Of course you didn't," she said. "You were only fooling, that's all. 14 She thought you were awfully amusing. She was having a marvelous time. She only got a little tiny bit annoyed just once, when you poured the clam-juice down her back."

"My God," he said. "Clam-juice down that back. And every vertebra 15 a little Cabot. Dear God. What'll I ever do?"

"Oh, she'll be all right," she said. "Just send her some flowers, or 16 something. Don't worry about it. It isn't anything."

"No, I won't worry," he said. "I haven't got a care in the world. I'm 17 sitting pretty. Oh, dear, oh, dear. Did I do any other fascinating tricks at dinner?"

"You were fine," she said. "Don't be so foolish about it. Everybody 18 was crazy about you. The maître d'hôtel was a little worried because you wouldn't stop singing, but he really didn't mind. All he said was, he was afraid they'd close the place again, if there was so much noise. But he didn't care a bit, himself. I think he loved seeing you have such a good time. Oh, you were just singing away, there, for about an hour. It wasn't so terribly loud, at all."

"So I sang," he said. "That must have been a treat. I sang."            19

"Don't you remember?" she said. "You just sang one song after 20 another. Everybody in the place was listening. They loved it. Only you kept insisting that you wanted to sing some song about some kind of fusiliers or other, and everybody kept shushing you, and you'd keep trying to start it again. You were wonderful. We were all trying to make you stop singing for a minute, and eat something, but you wouldn't hear of it. My, you were funny."

"Didn't I eat any dinner?" he said.            21

"Oh, not a thing," she said. "Every time the waiter would offer you 22 something, you'd give it right back to him, because you said that he was your long-lost brother, changed in the cradle by a gypsy band, and that anything you had was his. You had him simply roaring at you."

"I bet I did," he said. "I bet I was comical. Society's Pet, I must have 23 been. And what happened then, after my overwhelming success with the waiter?"

"Why, nothing much," she said. "You took a sort of dislike to some 24 old man with white hair, sitting across the room, because you didn't like his necktie and you wanted to tell him about it. But we got you out, before he got really mad.''

"Oh, we got out," he said. "Did I walk?"                                        25

"Walk? Of course you did," she said. "You were absolutely all right. 26 There was that nasty stretch of ice on the sidewalk, and you did sit down awfully hard, you poor dear. But good heavens, that might have happened to anybody.''

"Oh, surely," he said. "Mrs. Hoover or anybody. So I fell down on 27 the sidewalk. That would explain what's the matter with my—Yes. I see. And then what, if you don't mind?''

"Ah, now, Peter!" she said. "You can't sit there and say you don't 28 remember what happened after that! I did think that maybe you were just a little tight at dinner—oh, you were perfectly all right, and all that, but I did know you were feeling pretty gay. But you were so serious, from the time you fell down—I never knew you to be that way. Don't you know, how you told me I had never seen your real self before? Oh, Peter, I just couldn't bear it, if you didn't remember that lovely long ride we took together in the taxi! Please, you do remember that, don't you? I think it would simply kill me, if you didn't.''

"Oh, yes," he said. "Riding in the taxi. Oh, yes, sure. Pretty long 29 ride, hmm?''

"Round and round and round the park," she said. "Oh, and the trees 30 were shining so in the moonlight. And you said you never knew before that you really had a soul.''

"Yes," he said. "I said that. That was me."                                     31

"You said such lovely, lovely things," she said. "And I'd never 32 known, all this time, how you had been feeling about me, and I'd never dared to let you see how I felt about you. And then last night—oh, Peter dear, I think that taxi ride was the most important thing that ever happened to us in our lives.''

"Yes," he said. "I guess it must have been."                                    33

"And we're going to be so happy," she said. "Oh, I just want to tell 34 everybody! But I don't know—I think maybe it would be sweeter to keep it all to ourselves.''

"I think it would be," he said.                                                 35

"Isn't it lovely?" she said.                                                    36

"Yes," he said. "Great."                                                       37

"Lovely!" she said.                                                             38

"Look here," he said, "do you mind if I have a drink? I mean, just 39 medicinally, you know. I'm off the stuff for life, so help me. But I think I feel a collapse coming on.''

"Oh, I think it would do you good," she said. "You poor boy, it's a 40 shame you feel so awful. I'll go make you a highball.''

"Honestly," he said, "I don't see how you could ever want to speak 41

to me again, after I made such a fool of myself, last night. I think I'd
better go join a monastery in Tibet."

"You crazy idiot!" she said. "As if I could ever let you go away now! 42
Stop talking like that. You were perfectly fine."

She jumped up from the couch, kissed him quickly on the forehead, 43
and ran out of the room.

The pale young man looked after her and shook his head long and 44
slowly, then dropped it in his damp and trembling hands.

"Oh, dear," he said. "Oh, dear, oh, dear, oh dear."                          45


# For Discussion and Writing

1. In this story, the reader and the young man learn together the events
   of the previous evening. Both reader and young man must recreate
   out of the girl's report of those events a narrative of the dinner party
   and its aftermath. The young man will write a ghost chapter, because
   the events of the previous evening constitute a gap in his life; the
   reader is asked to construct a possible world of the previous evening,
   to imagine from the information given what may have actually
   occurred. In order to do this, the reader must pay attention to the
   girl's presentation of information and to the young man's interpretation of it. What differences do you find between the two?

2. It is later the same day. The young man's head is beginning to clear
   and he is beginning to remember more details of the night before.
   Write a narrative of the evening's events from the young man's point
   of view. You might want him to answer some questions raised in the
   text, such as why he made a pass at Elinor, why he disliked the old
   man's tie, and how he really feels about the girl he was with.

3. Retell the events of the night before as a series of short narratives
   told by three or more of the following:
   a. Jim Pierson
   b. Elinor
   c. the maître d'hôtel
   d. the waiter
   e. the old man with white hair
   f. the taxi driver

# Interpreting Texts

*Schoolchildren are expected to be able to infer something called the character of Macbeth from indices scattered about Shakespeare's text.*

*—Frank Kermode*

*Directed to art, interpretation means plucking a set of elements (the X, the Y, the Z, and so forth) from the whole work. The task of interpretation is virtually one of translation. The interpreter says, Look, don't you see that X is really—or, really means—A? That Y is really B? That Z is really C?*

*—Susan Sontag*

As the word *interpretation* is normally used in literary study, it means transforming a story, play, or poem into an essay. We have already considered transformation as a form of intertextuality, but the transformations we considered were mainly transformations *within* the same genre: fiction into fiction. We have also considered the way readers must construct ghost chapters and possible worlds in order to complete the texts they read. Both of these activities, transformation and completion, are interpretive. So is the translation of figurative language into literal prose. In short, we have already considered many of the dimensions of interpretation, though not all, but we have not yet faced squarely the problem of writing the interpretive essay.

The purpose of the interpretive essay is not simply to repeat in the form of an essay what has already been said in a story, poem, or play. It *is* that to some extent, but, if that were all, interpretation would be a trivial enterprise. The major function of interpretation is to say what a previous text has left unsaid: to unravel its complications, to make explicit its implications, and to raise its concrete and specific details to a more abstract and general level. That is, as we shall illustrate a few paragraphs later on, the interpreter must find a way of writing about the general principles of human behavior that are embodied in the specific situations and events of any story. The interpreter must say what the story is *about*.

We should also note that interpretation is not something that is entirely avoided in plays, poems, and stories themselves. Authors will often attempt to control the way their texts are read by offering self-interpretations within those texts. Samuel Beckett parodied this desire of the author to control meaning by adding what he called "Addenda" to the end of his novel *Watt*, noting that "The following precious and illuminating material should be carefully studied. Only fatigue and disgust prevented its incorporation.'' The last addendum reads simply, ''no symbols where none intended.''

By forbidding the reader to find symbolic or figurative meanings except where the author intended them to be found, Beckett symbolized the desire of most authors to control the interpretation of their own texts. By saying it so bluntly, he also made this desire faintly ridiculous. But did he *intend* this statement to symbolize what we say it symbolizes? That is a matter of interpretation. We say that when Beckett wrote ''no symbols where none intended'' he was joking, because he knew that no one can control meanings or even realize their intentions perfectly. And we would support our interpretation by pointing to other places where Beckett seems to be saying something similar—an easy task since *Watt* is devoted to the distressing gap between words and things, the constant slippage of meaning. Furthermore, we would add, the expression itself doesn't even specify whose intention is required to make an object into a symbol. If the rule is to be ''no symbols where none intended,'' then perhaps the reader's intention would satisfy the rule in this instance. Then, of course, it would be *our* symbol, and not Beckett's. But doesn't interpretation mean that it must be *his* symbol that we understand? What is the writer's share in meaning and what is the reader's? These are vexed and difficult questions, much debated in literary theory. We cannot and should not try to settle them here. What we hope to accomplish instead is to clarify the possibilities of interpretive writing a bit and to offer a few practical suggestions for entering the world of interpretive discourse.

You may remember the story by William Carlos Williams included in chapter 1 of this book, about a doctor who must struggle physically to diagnose the fever of a lovely and ferocious little girl (pp. 15–18). The story itself is very sparing with interpretive commentary, but it nevertheless makes a strong effort to direct our interpretation of it. The effort is most apparent in the title provided by the author: ''The Use of Force.'' This title takes the concrete events narrated in the text and gathers them under the interpretive umbrella of ''force.'' That is one of the major features of interpretive discourse. Interpretation is constituted by our moving from saying ''The story is about a doctor and a child'' to saying ''The story is about the use of force.'' This move, from the concrete details of doctor and child to the abstraction ''use of force'' is what interpretation is all about. In this case, the author tries hard to guide the interpretive move by providing his own interpretive abstraction in the title of his text.

Kate Chopin, in her story ''The Kiss,'' does not provide us with such guidance. Her title simply names the initial action of the story. To produce an interpretation, we must find our own way of discussing the significance of the events narrated in the text. We might decide the story is about "deception," for instance, and base our interpretation upon this decision. The important point to remember is that interpretation always involves a move from the specific details named in the text to a more general level: from the doctor prying open the child's mouth with a spoon to the abstract concept *force*.

In the epigraph by Frank Kermode at the beginning of this discussion, we can locate one type of interpretation. The reader takes a set of details from a play and constructs from them an abstraction called the "character" of Macbeth. One could do the same for characters in many of the plays and stories we have read. This sort of interpretation appears to be "natural," since we do it all the time, but it is based upon certain assumptions about the psychic unity of human beings and the importance of the individual person that are not, in fact, universal assumptions. Many forms of storytelling exist in which the individuals named in the text are not important in themselves but as representations of something else. This is the case in fables, parables, allegories, and other forms of symbolic fiction. In reading such narratives, the interpreter does what Susan Sontag describes in the epigraph from her essay, "Against Interpretation," quoted at the head of this discussion. That is, the interpreter says, "X is really A, Y is really B."

Being able to say "X is really A" involves knowing the system of values and beliefs that gives the concept "A" its meaning. For instance, Christianity is a system of values and beliefs. The story of Samson, from the Old Testament—a Jewish scripture—is read by Christian interpreters in accordance with their own system of beliefs. Reading and interpreting in this way, they say that Samson is really Christ, or, more technically, that Samson is a "type" of Christ, a symbol of Christ. By his sacrifice of his own life, Samson contributes to the salvation of his people. His death in the temple of the Philistines is equivalent to the death of Jesus at the hands of the Romans; and, just as the Philistines were defeated by Samson's sacrificial death, Rome was Christianized, ultimately conquered, by the One the Romans captured and tortured. This is how interpretation according to a system of values and beliefs works.

Christianity is one of a number of such systems used in literary interpretation. Psychoanalytical systems, such as the Freudian, are also widely used, and so are socioeconomic systems, such as Marxism. It is extremely difficult to generate such interpretations without serious study of the systems involved, which is one of the reasons why we will not ask you to undertake this kind of work. It is possible, however, for someone who is not an expert but is willing to pay close attention to comment on such interpretations, to extend them, and to revise, question, and even reject them. If you have worked on the transformations of "Hansel and Gretel" in the previous section of this book, you are now something of an expert on that story. Therefore, you are in a good position to respond to the following two interpretive essays. The first, from a book by Jack Zipes called *Breaking the Magic Spell*, is a Marxist reading of two tales, including "Hansel and Gretel." The second, from *The Uses of Enchantment* by the noted child psychologist Bruno Bettelheim, is a Freudian interpretation of "Hansel and Gretel."

# The Politics of Fairy Tales

*Jack Zipes*

Perhaps the best-known and most widely circulated collection of   1
folk tales is that of the Brothers Grimm. These *Märchen* were recorded during the first decade of the nineteenth century in the Rhineland. They were told in dialect, largely by servants, housewives, a watchman and inhabitants from towns and small cities and were stylized and transcribed into High German by the Grimms. Consequently, a thorough analysis of the tales must take into account the background of the narrators and their communities, the social upheavals of the times caused by the Napoleonic Wars, the advent of mercantilism and the perspective of the Grimms, including their reasons for choosing certain folk tales for their collection. In dealing with the politics of the tales I want to limit my discussion to an analysis of the socio-historical conditions as reflected in two tales, *How Six Travelled through the World* and *Hansel and Gretel*, to demonstrate how links might be established with the actual struggles of that period. In the first, *How Six Travelled through the World*, the elements of class struggle are most apparent, and the entire feudal system is placed in question. In the second, *Hansel and Gretel*, which is more widely known and has been watered down in modern versions, the social references are at first not as clear. For audiences of the eighteenth and early nineteenth centuries, particularly for the peasantry, the social and political signs were unmistakable.

*How Six Travelled through the World* concerns a man, who "was   2
well-versed in all kinds of skills," served a king valiantly during a war, but was miserably paid and dismissed by the king when the war ended. The soldier swears that he will avenge himself if he can find the right people to help him. Indeed, he encounters five peasants who possess extraordinary powers and agree to assist him. The soldier seeks out the king, who has declared in the meantime that anyone who can defeat his daughter in a foot race can marry her. If she happens to win, death is the reward. With the help of his friends and their supernatural gifts, the soldier wins

the race. However, the king is annoyed, and his daughter even more so, that such a common soldier formerly in his employ should win the wager. The king plots to kill the soldier and his friends, but they outsmart him. The king promises the soldier all the gold he can carry if he renounces his claim to the princess. The soldier agrees and has one of his friends, who has enormous strength, to carry away the entire wealth of the kingdom. The king sends the royal army after the soldier and his friends to retrieve the gold. Of course, they easily defeat the army, divide the gold amongst themselves, and live happily ever after.

It is obvious that this tale treats a social problem of utmost concern  3 to the lower classes. In the eighteenth century it was customary for the state to recruit soldiers for standing armies, treat them shabbily and abandon them when there was no more use for them. Here the perspective of the story is clearly that of the people, and though its origins are pre-capitalist, the narrator and the Grimms were probably attracted to its theme because of its relation to the Napoleonic Wars and perhaps even the Napoleonic Code (instituted in the Rhineland). Common soldiers were indeed treated miserably during these wars; yet, the Code gave rise to hopes for greater democratization. In this tale a common man shows himself to be the equal of a king if not better. The miraculous talents—the magic—are symbolic of the real hidden qualities which he himself possesses, or they might represent the collective energies of small people, the power they actually possess. When these talents are used properly, that is, when they are used to attain due justice and recompense, the people are invincible, a theme common to many other folk tales such as *The Bremen Town Musicians*. Thus, the imaginative elements have a real reference to history and society, for the peasant uprisings and the French Revolution in the eighteenth century were demonstrations of how the oppressed people could achieve limited victories against the nobility. To be sure, these victories were often of short duration, and the peasants and lower estates could be divided or pacified with money as is the case in this tale, where the social relations are not changed. Still, it is important that the tale does *illustrate how common people can work together, assert themselves actively* and achieve clear-cut goals, using their skills and imagination.

The story of "Hansel and Gretel" is also a story of hope and victory.  4 Again the perspective is plebeian. A woodcutter does not have enough food to feed his family. His wife, the stepmother of his children, convinces him that they must abandon *his* children in the woods in order to survive. The children are almost devoured by a witch, but they use their ingenuity to trick and kill her. No fooling around here. Then Hansel and Gretel return home with jewels and embrace their father.

The struggle depicted in this tale is against poverty and against  5 witches who have houses of food and hidden treasures. Here again the imaginative and magic elements of the tale had specific meanings for a peasant and lower-class audience at the end of the eighteenth century. The wars of this period often brought with them widespread famine and poverty which were also leading to the breakdown of the feudal patronage system. Consequently, peasants were often left to shift on their own and forced to go to extremes to survive. These extremes involved banditry, migration or abandonment of children. The witch (as parasite) could be interpreted here to symbolize the entire feudal system or the greed and brutality of the aristocracy, responsible for the difficult conditions. The killing of the witch is symbolically the realization of the hatred which the peasantry felt for the aristocracy as hoarders and oppressors. It is important to note that the children do not turn against their father or stepmother as one might think they would. On the contrary, they reluctantly comprehend the situation which forces their parents to act as they do. That is, they understand the social forces as being responsible for their plight and do not personalize them by viewing their parents as their enemies. The objectification of the tale is significant, for it helps explain the tolerant attitude toward the stepmother (which is not always the case). It must be remembered that women died young due to frequent child-bearing and insanitary conditions. Thus, stepmothers were common in households, and this often led to difficulties with the children by former wives. In this respect, the tale reflects the strained relations but sees them more as a result of social forces. The stepmother is not condemned, either by the narrator or the children. They return home, unaware that she is dead. They return home with hope and jewels to put an end to *all* their problems.

In both these tales class conflict is portrayed in the light of pre-capitalist social conditions which were common in the late eighteenth and early nineteenth centuries in Germany. In neither tale is there a political revolution. What is important is that the contradictions are depicted, whereby the prejudices and injustices of feudal ideology are exposed. The magic and fantastic elements are closely tied to the real possibilities for the peasantry to change conditions, albeit in a limited way. The emphasis is on hope and action. The soldier and his friends *act* and *defeat* the king whenever they are tested. Hansel and Gretel *act* and *kill* the witch. The form of the tale, its closed, compact nature, is shaped by the individual carriers who distribute the stories and allow the common people to learn how they might survive in an unjust society and struggle with hope. Whatever symbols and magic are used can clearly be understood when placed in the historical context of the transition from feudalism to early capitalism. 6

Naturally it could be argued that the folk tale has nothing to do with the socio-political conditions of feudalism. That is, the folk tale originated thousands of years ago, and we cannot be entirely certain about the 7

conditions which gave rise to them. But we do know that it was culti-
vated in an oral tradition by the people and passed on from generation to
generation in essentially 35 different basic patterns which have been
kept intact over thousands of years. As Vladimir Propp has shown, there
have been transformations of elements within the patterns, and these
changes depend on the social realities of the period in which the tales are
told. Linda Dégh clarifies this point in her thorough examination of the
social function of the storyteller in a Hungarian peasant community: "Our
knowledge of European folktale material stems from two sources: literary
works and oral tradition. The most striking characteristic of the traditional tale lies in the fact that the social institutions and concepts which
we discover in it reflect the age of feudalism. Thus the question of the
origin of the folktale coincides with that of the origin of literature in
general." Clearly the folk tales collected in the seventeenth, eighteenth
and nineteenth centuries, though they preserved aesthetic patterns derived from pre-capitalist societies, did so because these patterns plus the
transformed elements and motifs continued to reflect and speak to the
conditions of the people and the dominant ideology of the times to a
great degree. Though primitive in origin, the folk tale in Germany, as told
in the late eighteenth century and collected by the Grimms in the early
nineteenth, related to and was shaped by feudal conditions.

# Hansel and Gretel

## *Bruno Bettelheim*

"Hansel and Gretel" begins realistically. The parents are poor, and 1
they worry about how they will be able to take care of their children.
Together at night they discuss their predicament, and how they can deal
with it. Even taken on this surface level, the folk fairy tale conveys an
important, although unpleasant, truth: poverty and deprivation do not
improve man's character, but rather make him more selfish, less sensitive
to the sufferings of others, and thus prone to embark on evil deeds.

The fairy tale expresses in words and actions the things which go on 2
in children's minds. In terms of the child's dominant anxiety, Hansel and
Gretel believe that their parents are talking about a plot to desert them. A
small child, awakening hungry in the darkness of the night, feels threatened by complete rejection and desertion, which he experiences in the
form of fear of starvation. By projecting their inner anxiety onto those
they fear might cut them off, Hansel and Gretel are convinced that their
parents plan to starve them to death! In line with the child's anxious

fantasies, the story tells that until then the parents had been able to feed their children, but had now fallen upon lean times.

The mother represents the source of all food to the children, so it is 3 she who now is experienced as abandoning them, as if in a wilderness. It is the child's anxiety and deep disappointment when Mother is no longer willing to meet all his oral demands which leads him to believe that suddenly Mother has become unloving, selfish, rejecting. Since the children know they need their parents desperately, they attempt to return home after being deserted. In fact, Hansel succeeds in finding their way back from the forest the first time they are abandoned. Before a child has the courage to embark on the voyage of finding himself, of becoming an independent person through meeting the world, he can develop initiative only in trying to return to passivity, to secure, for himself eternally dependent gratification. "Hansel and Gretel" tells that this will not work in the long run.

The children's successful return home does not solve anything. Their 4 effort to continue life as before, as if nothing had happened, is to no avail. The frustrations continue, and the mother becomes more shrewd in her plans for getting rid of the children.

By implication, the story tells about the debilitating consequences of 5 trying to deal with life's problems by means of regression and denial, which reduce one's ability to solve problems. The first time in the forest Hansel used his intelligence appropriately by putting down white pebbles to mark the path home. The second time he did not use his intelligence as well—he, who lived close to a big forest, should have known that birds would eat the bread crumbs. Hansel might instead have studied landmarks on the way in, to find his way back out. But having engaged in denial and regression—the return home—Hansel has lost much of his initiative and ability to think clearly. Starvation anxiety has driven him back, so now he can think only of food as offering a solution to the problem of finding his way out of a serious predicament. Bread stands here for food in general, man's "life line"—an image which Hansel takes literally, out of his anxiety. This shows the limiting effects of fixations to primitive levels of development, engaged in out of fear.

The story of "Hansel and Gretel" gives body to the anxieties and 6 learning tasks of the young child who must overcome and sublimate his primitive incorporative and hence destructive desires. The child must learn that if he does not free himself of these, his parents or society will force him to do against his will, as earlier his mother had stopped nursing the child when she felt the time had come to do so. This tale gives symbolic expression to these inner experiences directly linked to the mother. Therefore, the father remains a shadowy and ineffectual figure throughout the story, as he appears to the child during his early life when Mother is all-important, in both her benign and her threatening aspects.

Frustrated in their ability to find a solution to their problem in reality   7
because reliance on food for safety (bread crumbs to mark the path) fails
them, Hansel and Gretel now give full rein to their oral regression. The
gingerbread house represents an existence based on the most primitive
satisfactions. Carried away by their uncontrolled craving, the children
think nothing of destroying what should give shelter and safety, even
though the birds' having eaten the crumbs should have warned them
about eating up things.

By devouring the gingerbread house's roof and window, the children   8
show how ready they are to eat somebody out of house and home, a fear
which they had projected onto their parents as the reason for their
desertion. Despite the warning voice which asks, "Who is nibbling at my
little house?" the children lie to themselves and blame it on the wind and
"[go] on eating without disturbing themselves."

The gingerbread house is an image nobody forgets: how incredibly   9
appealing and tempting a picture this is, and how terrible the risk one
runs if one gives in to the temptation. The child recognizes that, like
Hansel and Gretel, he would wish to eat up the gingerbread house, no
matter what the dangers. The house stands for oral greediness and how
attractive it is to give in to it. The fairy tale is the primer from which the
child learns to read his mind in the language of images, the only language
which permits understanding before intellectual maturity has been
achieved. The child needs to be exposed to this language, and must learn
to be responsive to it, if he is to become master of his soul.

The preconscious content of fairy-tale images is much richer than   10
even the following simple illustrations convey. For example, in dreams as
well as in fantasies and the child's imagination, a house, as the place in
which we dwell, can symbolize the body, usually the mother's. A gingerbread house, which one can "eat up," is a symbol of the mother, who
in fact nurses the infant from her body. Thus, the house at which Hansel
and Gretel are eating away blissfully and without a care stands in the
unconscious for the good mother, who offers her body as a source of
nourishment. It is the original all-giving mother, whom every child hopes
to find again later somewhere out in the world, when his own mother
begins to make demands and to impose restrictions. This is why, carried
away by their hopes, Hansel and Gretel do not heed the soft voice that
calls out to them, asking what they are up to—a voice that is their
externalized conscience. Carried away by their greediness, and fooled by
the pleasures of oral satisfaction which seem to deny all previous oral
anxiety, the children "thought they were in heaven."

But, as the story tells, such unrestrained giving in to gluttony   11
threatens destruction. Regression to the earliest "heavenly" state of
being—when on the mother's breast one lived symbiotically off her—
does away with all individuation and independence. It even endangers

one's very existence, as cannibalistic inclinations are given body in the figure of the witch.

The witch, who is a personification of the destructive aspects of 12 orality, is as bent on eating up the children as they are on demolishing her gingerbread house. When the children give in to untamed id impulses, as symbolized by their uncontrolled voraciousness, they risk being destroyed. The children eat only the symbolic representation of the mother, the gingerbread house; the witch wants to eat the children themselves. This teaches the hearer a valuable lesson: dealing in symbols is safe when compared with acting on the real thing. Turning the tables on the witch is justified also on another level: children who have little experience and are still learning self-control are not to be measured by the same yardstick as older people, who are supposed to be able to restrain their instinctual desires better. Thus, the punishment of the witch is as justified as the children's rescue.

The witch's evil designs finally force the children to recognize the 13 dangers of unrestrained oral greed and dependence. To survive, they must develop initiative and realize that their only recourse lies in intelligent planning and acting. They must exchange subservience to the pressures of the id for acting in accordance with the ego. Goal-directed behavior based on intelligent assessment of the situation in which they find themselves must take the place of wish-fulfilling fantasies: the substitution of the bone for the finger, tricking the witch to climb into the oven.

Only when the dangers inherent in remaining fixed to primitive 14 orality with its destructive propensities are recognized does the way to a higher stage of development open up. Then it turns out that the good, giving mother was hidden deep down in the bad, destructive one, because there are treasures to be gained: the children inherit the witch's jewels, which become valuable to them after their return home—that is, after they can again find the good parent. This suggests that as the children transcend their oral anxiety, and free themselves of relying on oral satisfaction for security, they can also free themselves of the image of the threatening mother—the witch—and rediscover the good parents, whose greater wisdom—the shared jewels—then benefit all.

On repeated hearing of "Hansel and Gretel," no child remains un- 15 aware of the fact that birds eat the bread crumbs and thus prevent the children from returning home without first meeting their great adventure. It is also a bird which guides Hansel and Gretel to the gingerbread house, and thanks only to another bird do they manage to get back home. This gives the child—who thinks differently about animals than older persons do—pause to think: these birds must have a purpose, otherwise they would not first prevent Hansel and Gretel from finding their way back, then take them to the witch, and finally provide passage home.

Obviously, since all turns out for the best, the birds must have 16
known that it is preferable for Hansel and Gretel not to find their way
directly back home out of the forest, but rather to risk facing the dangers
of the world. In consequence of their threatening encounter with the
witch, not only the children but also their parents live much more
happily ever afterward. The different birds offer a clue to the path the
children must follow to gain their reward.

After they have become familiar with "Hansel and Gretel," most 17
children comprehend, at least unconsciously, that what happens in the
parental home and at the witch's house are but separate aspects of what
in reality is one total experience. Initially, the witch is a perfectly gratifying mother figure, as we are told how "she took them both by the hand,
and led them into her little house. Then good food was set before them,
milk and pancakes with sugar, apples, and nuts. Afterwards two pretty
little beds were covered with clean white linen, and Hansel and Gretel
lay down in them, and thought they were in heaven." Only on the
following morning comes a rude awakening from such dreams of infan-
tile bliss. "The old woman had only pretended to be so kind; she was in
reality a wicked witch . . ."

This is how the child feels when devastated by the ambivalent 18
feelings, frustrations, and anxieties of the oedipal stage of development,
as well as his previous disappointment and rage at failures on his mother's
part to gratify his needs and desires as fully as he expected. Severely
upset that Mother no longer serves him unquestioningly but makes demands on him and devotes herself ever more to her own interest—
something which the child had not permitted to come to his awareness
before—he imagines that Mother, as she nursed him and created a world
of oral bliss, did so only to fool him—like the witch of the story.

Thus, the parental home "hard by a great forest" and the fateful 19
house in the depths of the same woods are on an unconscious level but
the two aspects of the parental home: the gratifying one and the frustrat-
ing one.

The child who ponders on his own the details of "Hansel and 20
Gretel" finds meaning in how it begins. That the parental home is located
at the very edge of the forest where everything happens suggests that
what is to follow was imminent from the start. This is again the fairy tale's
way to express thoughts through impressive images which lead the child
to use his own imagination to derive deeper understanding.

Mentioned before was how the behavior of the birds symbolizes that 21
the entire adventure was arranged for the children's benefit. Since early
Christian times the white dove has symbolized superior benevolent
powers. Hansel claims to be looking back at a white dove that is sitting on
the roof of the parental home, wanting to say goodbye to him. It is a
snow-white bird, singing delightfully, which leads the children to the

gingerbread house and then settles on its roof, suggesting that this is the right place for them to arrive at. Another white bird is needed to guide the children back to safety: their way home is blocked by a "big water" which they can cross only with the help of a white duck.

The children do not encounter any expanse of water on their way in. 22 Having to cross one on their return symbolizes a transition, and a new beginning on a higher level of existence (as in baptism). Up to the time they have to cross this water, the children have never separated. The school-age child should develop consciousness of his personal unique-ness, of his individuality, which means that he can no longer share everything with others, has to live to some degree by himself and stride out on his own. This is symbolically expressed by the children not being able to remain together in crossing the water. As they arrive there; Hansel sees no way to get across, but Gretel spies a white duck and asks it to help them cross the water. Hansel seats himself on its back and asks his sister to join him. But she knows better: this will not do. They have to cross over separately, and they do.

The children's experience at the witch's house has purged them of 23 their oral fixations; after having crossed the water, they arrive at the other shore as more mature children, ready to rely on their own intelligence and initiative to solve life's problems. As dependent children they had been a burden to their parents; on their return they have become the family's support, as they bring home the treasures they have gained. These treasures are the children's new-won independence in thought and action, a new self-reliance which is the opposite of the passive depen-dence which characterized them when they were deserted in the woods.

It is females—the stepmother and the witch—who are the inimical 24 forces in this story. Gretel's importance in the children's deliverance reassures the child that a female can be a rescuer as well as a destroyer. Probably even more important is the fact that Hansel saves them once and then later Gretel saves them again, which suggests to children that as they grow up they must come to rely more and more on their age mates for mutual help and understanding. This idea reinforces the story's main thrust, which is a warning against regression, and an encouragement of growth toward a higher plane of psychological and intellectual existence.

"Hansel and Gretel" ends with the heroes returning to the home 25 from which they started, and now finding happiness there. This is psy-chologically correct, because a young child, driven into his adventures by oral or oedipal problems, cannot hope to find happiness outside the home. If all is to go well in his development, he must work these problems out while still dependent on his parents. Only through good relations with his parents can a child successfully mature into adoles-cence.

Having overcome his oedipal difficulties, mastered his oral anxieties, 26 sublimated those of his cravings which cannot be satisfied realistically, and learned that wishful thinking has to be replaced by intelligent action, the child is ready to live happily again with his parents. This is symbolized by the treasures Hansel and Gretel bring home to share with their father. Rather than expecting everything good to come from the parents, the older child needs to be able to make some contribution to the emotional well-being of himself and his family.

As "Hansel and Gretel" begins matter-of-factly with the worries of a 27 poor woodcutter's family unable to make ends meet, it ends on an equally down-to-earth level. Although the story tells that the children brought home a pile of pearls and precious stones, nothing further suggests that their economic way of life was changed. This emphasizes the symbolic nature of these jewels. The tale concludes: "Then all worries ended, and they lived together in perfect joy. My tale is ended; there runs a mouse, who catches it may make himself a big fur cap out of it." Nothing has changed by the end of "Hansel and Gretel" but inner attitudes; or, more correctly, all has changed because inner attitudes have changed. No more will the children feel pushed out, deserted, and lost in the darkness of the forest; nor will they seek for the miraculous gingerbread house. But neither will they encounter or fear the witch, since they have proved to themselves that through their combined efforts they can outsmart her and be victorious. Industry, making something good even out of unpromising material (such as by using the fur of a mouse intelligently for making a cap), is the virtue and real achievement of the school-age child who has fought through and mastered the oedipal difficulties.

"Hansel and Gretel" is one of many fairy tales where two siblings 28 cooperate in rescuing each other and succeed because of their combined efforts. These stories direct the child toward transcending his immature dependence on his parents and reaching the next higher stage of development: cherishing also the support of age mates. Cooperating with them in meeting life's tasks will eventually have to replace the child's single-minded reliance on his parents only. The child of school age often cannot yet believe that he ever will be able to meet the world without his parents; that is why he wishes to hold on to them beyond the necessary point. He needs to learn to trust that someday he will master the dangers of the world, even in the exaggerated form in which his fears depict them, and be enriched by it.

The child views existential dangers not objectively but fantastically 29 exaggerated in line with his immature dread—for example, personified as a child-devouring witch. "Hansel and Gretel" encourages the child to explore on his own even the figments of his anxious imagination, because such fairy tales give him confidence that he can master not only the real dangers which his parents told him about, but even those vastly exaggerated ones which he fears exist.

A witch as created by the child's anxious fantasies will haunt him; 30 but a witch he can push into her own oven and burn to death is a witch the child can believe himself rid of. As long as children continue to believe in witches—they always have and always will, up to the age when they no longer are compelled to give their formless apprehensions humanlike appearance—they need to be told stories in which children, by being ingenious, rid themselves of these persecuting figures of their imagination. By succeeding in doing so, they gain immensely from the experience, as did Hansel and Gretel.

## For Discussion and Writing

1. Both Zipes and Bettelheim say things that take the form mentioned by Sontag: "X is really A, Y is really B." Locate some instances of this in each essay. Are you persuaded in all, some, or none of these instances that X really is A, and so on? What are your reasons? What qualities make such assertions acceptable or unacceptable?

2. Because of your previous research, you know some things about "Hansel and Gretel" that Zipes and Bettelheim do not. In particular, you have access to the early version of the tale. Using this knowledge and your own good sense and critical awareness, write a critique of the interpretations of "Hansel and Gretel" by Zipes and Bettelheim. Discuss the strengths and weaknesses of each interpretation as you see them. You may also indicate which interpretation you prefer. Try to be fair, judicious, and critical. Incorporate your own interpretation of the tale in your discussion.

   You are not being asked here to criticize Zipes and Bettelheim from the inside, knowing as much as thcy do about the interpretive methods they use. This is really a chance for you to express your own opinion. What do they say that makes sense to you? What do they say that seems absurd or simply wrong to you? Knowing whatever you know about life and ways of putting life into story form, discuss these two interpretations, considering what they showed you that you hadn't seen before and whether you are persuaded by what they have shown you. Try to make your criticisms as clearly and persuasively as you can, with reasons for every judgment.

3. Looking back at "The Use of Force" or "The Kiss," write an interpretation of one of these stories. Make it as complete and satisfying

as you can. To get started it may help you to reread the introduction to this section on interpretation.

4. Select another tale or children's story (don't rely on your memory; find and reread a version of your choice). Write a script or treatment for a video documentary version of the story. Use Coover's "Gingerbread House" version of "Hansel and Gretel" as a model, since its style is quite similar to that of a script for a filmed translation of the story. But add to the Coover model the part of a narrator or commentator—a Zipes or Bettelheim, or both—who interrupts the action to offer explanations or interpretations of the events.

# Chapter 4

# Experiments with Texts: Fragments and Signatures

## *Textuality*

A major theme of *Text Book* has been the interplay between the use of language in ordinary life and the practices of literacy. In the first chapter, we learned from Pratt and Labov the extent to which literature derives its structure and content from the forms and experiences of everyday life. But literacy can repay in full the debt it owes to ordinary language, as we shall see in this chapter.

The experiments to which you will be introduced in this chapter combine creative and critical writing to investigate your own experience as citizen of a specific culture and language. In some of the earlier chapters, you attempted to capture in literary forms certain life experiences, to express in language something you had already done, thought, felt, or believed. The experimental use of a text in a sense reverses the relationship between writing and knowing, in that you start out with a form and a procedure and use them to invent an idea, to produce or generate a text whose features you may not be able to predict in advance. Instead of trying to make language conform to what you already know, now you may let the form lead you, let the form tell you something or show you something about your cultural existence. In chapter 3 you learned that literary writing can function as a kind of critical or analytical method. The transformations, adaptations, and ghost chapters introduced there took extant works of literature as their raw material. The rewriting of available works, producing new texts from old ones, is already a kind of experimentation with literature, revealing as well as does any analytical procedure how a work produces effects of meaning, emotion, or style.

Our next experiments carry this critical function of literary invention one step farther, and at the same time bring us fully into the practice of textuality in its specialized sense, summarized by the philosopher Martin Heidegger as the feeling that we do not speak language,

language speaks us. This notion of text as *productivity* rather than as representation or communication, giving full play to the generative power of language while reducing its descriptive function, has been developed most extensively in France during the 1960s and 1970s. The strategy of "giving the lead to language" is as old as poetry, of course. The new element in the experiments created by two of the leaders of the French school of textuality—Roland Barthes and Jacques Derrida—is the attempt to apply this technique of creative writing to the ends of critical thinking.

# *The Fragment*

One of Roland Barthes's principal contributions to the practice of textuality was the idea that critical and creative writing are essentially the same—that the old distinction separating fact and fiction, truth and imagination, is less important than the more general condition in which all experience (science as well as art) is equally mediated by language. To explore the consequences of this insight, Barthes developed a hybrid essay combining aspects of critical analysis and artistic expression. One of the texts resulting from this procedure is entitled *A Lover's Discourse: Fragments*.

The poetic or artistic dimension of *Fragments* includes the telling of a love story. The story or anecdote at the heart of this text focuses on the *crisis* or *critical* moment of the love affair. While waiting for the beloved to keep their date at a café (in vain, as it turns out: the beloved stands him up), the lover reads a famous Romantic novel, *The Sorrows of Young Werther*, by Goethe. He begins to compare his own unhappy situation with the story of unrequited love recounted in the novel, which ends with the suicide of the protagonist, Werther. Attempting to free himself from the pain of rejection and jealousy, the lover-reader here decides to end the affair.

This story is never told directly in *A Lover's Discourse*, only in fragments distributed throughout the text, cast in the frame of the lover's meditations. The critical or analytical dimension of *Fragments* thus consists of Barthes casting this highly emotional experience into a collection of stereotypes and clichés that appear in all such love stories. He distances himself from the strong emotions by ordering or classifying the elements of the experience in a scientific manner. Part of his purpose is to identify those aspects of our personal, private attitudes and actions that are in fact directed by public, social, and cultural conventions and beliefs (ideology). He hopes in this way to combine in one text the effects of truth and beauty.

Barthes himself provided a set of instructions at the beginning of *Fragments* itemizing the rhetorical components of his experiment, which could be summarized as follows—as in Pratt's inventory (page 2) of the parts of a natural narrative.

A. Selecting the figures:

   1. Each separate fragment ("Waiting," "The Heart," etc.) is one *figure, pose*, or *topic*. The lover's situation includes a set of poses that anyone who enters into a dating relationship is likely to employ—like the "character contests" described by Goffman (page 27), courting is a "ritual" process. With the term "pose,"

Barthes alludes not only to "role playing" but also to dance figures, a standardized set of movements with which a choreographer might design a ballet.

2. A figure in the lover's discourse is recognizable to the extent that it is something clearly outlined as *memorable*. "You know you have a figure when you can say 'That is so true: I recognize that scene of language.'"

B. Writing the figures:

1. Each figure or topic has a *title* (e.g., "Show me whom to desire," a heading (e.g., "induction"), and an *argument* (e.g., "The loved being is desired because another . . ."). The point of departure for a figure is always something the lover might *say*, even if only to himself or herself, perhaps only unconsciously, in that situation (hence the *discourse*). The argument is a paraphrase *describing* that saying. The figures are arranged in alphabetical order, according to the spelling of the headings (hence the translator had to retain the French—*cacher* comes before *coeur*).

2. Of the body (numbered paragraphs) the following may be observed:

a. Only the topic headings and arguments are general. The meditations or reflections recorded within each topic will be specific to each user of the discourse, who must fill in the figure with his or her own experience (thoughts, feelings, actions) of the pose.

b. The figures do not tell the love story, but instead record the "asides" that might accompany the story, as if one had kept a running commentary on one's experience (not in the manner of a diary, but an analysis, like the color commentary that embellishes the action of a sports broadcast).

c. The content of the commentary in the body is drawn from a combination of three areas of reference, each acknowledged briefly in the margins:

(1) a primary work of art (Goethe's *Sorrows of Young Werther* in this case) relevant to the concerns of the discourse.

(2) the speaker's specialized culture (schooling, training).

(3) the speaker's everyday-life culture—popular arts, mass-media experience, conversations with friends, and the like.

# from *A Lover's Discourse*

## *Roland Barthes*

*Here are five complete "figures" from Barthes's text. As you read them, notice the regular structure (title, heading, argument, and body) and the irregular or flexible size and shape of the body itself. The regular structure directs and stimulates writing; the flexible body allows the writer to stop when he has nothing more to say. As you read, be thinking of how your own meditation on these figures would be different, governed by different cultural and personal experiences.*

**So it is a Lover who Speaks and who Says:**

### *Waiting*

attente / waiting

Tumult of anxiety provoked by waiting for the loved being, subject to trivial delays (rendezvous, letters,
telephone calls, returns).

1.   I am waiting for an arrival, a return, a promised sign. This can be futile, or immensely pathetic: in *Erwartung (Waiting)*, a woman waits for *Schönberg* her lover, at night, in the forest; I am waiting for no more than a telephone call, but the anxiety is the same. Everything is solemn: I have no sense of *proportions*.

2.   There is a scenography of waiting: I organize it, manipulate it, cut out a portion of time in which I shall mime the loss of the loved object and provoke all the effects of a minor mourning. This is then acted out as a play.

The setting represents the interior of a café; we have a rendezvous, I am waiting. In the Prologue, the sole actor of the play (and with reason), I discern and indicate the other's delay; this delay is as yet only a mathe-matical, computable entity (I look at my watch several times); the Pro-logue ends with a brainstorm: I decide to "take it badly," I release the anxiety of waiting. Act I now begins; it is occupied by suppositions: was there a misunderstanding as to the time, the place? I try to recall the moment when the rendezvous was made, the details which were sup-plied. What is to be done (anxiety of behavior)? Try another café? Tele-phone? But if the other comes during these absences? Not seeing me, the other might leave, etc. Act II is the act of anger; I address violent reproaches to the absent one: "All the same, he (she) could have . . ."

"He (she) knows perfectly well . . ." Oh, if she (he) could be here, so that I could reproach her (him) for not being here! In Act III, I attain to (I *Winnicott* obtain?) anxiety in the pure state: the anxiety of abandonment; I have just shifted in a second from absence to death; the other is as if dead: explosion of grief: I am internally *livid*. That is the play; it can be shortened by the other's arrival; if the other arrives in Act I, the greeting is calm; if the other arrives in Act II, there is a "scene"; if in Act II, there is *Pelléas* recognition, the action of grace: I breathe deeply, like Pelléas emerging from the underground chambers and rediscovering life, the odor of roses.

(The anxiety of waiting is not continuously violent; it has its matte moments; I am waiting, and everything around my waiting is stricken with unreality: in this café, I look at the others who come in, chat, joke, read calmly: they are not waiting.)

3.   Waiting is an enchantment: I have received *orders not to move.* Waiting for a telephone call is thereby woven out of tiny unavowable interdictions *to infinity*: I forbid myself to leave the room, to go to the toilet, even to telephone (to keep the line from being busy); I suffer torments if someone else telephones me (for the same reason); I madden myself by the thought that at a certain (imminent) hour I shall have to leave, thereby running the risk of missing the healing call, the return of the Mother. All these diversions which solicit me are so many wasted moments for waiting, so many impurities of anxiety. For the anxiety of waiting, in its pure state, requires that I be sitting in a chair within reach of the telephone, without doing anything.

4.   The being I am waiting for is not real. Like the mother's breast for the *Winnicott* infant, "I create and re-create it over and over, starting from my capacity to love, starting from my need for it": the other comes here where I am waiting, here where I have already created him/her. And if the other does not come, I hallucinate the other: waiting is a delirium.
The telephone again: each time it rings, I snatch up the receiver, I think it will be the loved being who is calling me (since that being should call me); a little more effort and I "recognize" the other's voice, I engage in the dialogue, to the point where I lash out furiously against the importunate outsider who wakens me from my delirium. In the café, anyone who comes in, bearing the faintest resemblance, is thereupon, in a first impulse, *recognized.*

Winnicott:*Playing and Reality.*

And, long after the amorous relation is allayed, I keep the habit of hallucinating the being I have loved: sometimes I am still in anxiety over a telephone call that is late, and no matter who is on the line, I imagine I recognize the voice I once loved: I am an amputee who still feels pain in his missing leg.

5.  "Am I in love?—Yes, since I'm waiting." The other never waits. Sometimes I want to play the part of the one who doesn't wait; I try to busy myself elsewhere, to arrive late; but I always lose at this game: whatever I do, I find myself there, with nothing to do, punctual, even ahead of time. The lover's fatal identity is precisely: *I am the one who waits.*

(In transference, one always waits—at the doctor's, the professor's, the analyst's. Further, if I am waiting at a bank window, an airport ticket counter, I immediately establish an aggressive link with the teller, the stewardess, whose indifference unmasks and irritates my subjection; so that one might say that wherever there is waiting there is transference: I depend on a presence which is shared and requires time to be bestowed—as if it were a question of lowering my desire, lessening my need. *To make someone wait*: the constant prerogative of all power, E.B. "age-old pastime of humanity.")

6.  A mandarin fell in love with a courtesan. "I shall be yours," she told him, "when you have spent a hundred nights waiting for me, sitting on a stool, in my garden, beneath my window." But on the ninety-ninth night, the mandarin stood up, put his stool under his arm, and went away.

### The Heart
*coeur* / heart
This word refers to all kinds of movements and desires, but what is constant is that the heart is constituted into a gift-object—whether ignored or rejected.

1.  The heart is the organ of desire (the heart swells, weakens, etc., like the sexual organs), as it is held, enchanted, within the domain of the Image-repertoire. What will the world, what will the other do with my desire? That is the anxiety in which are gathered all the heart's movements, all the heart's "problems."

E.B.: Letter.

2.    Werther complains of Prince von X: "He esteems my mind and my
*Werther* talents more than this heart of mine, which yet is my one pride . . . Ah,
whatever I know, anyone may know—I alone have my heart."
You wait for me where I do not want to go: you love me where I do not
exist. Or again: the world and I are not interested in the same thing; and
to my misfortune, this divided thing is myself; I am not interested
(Werther says) in my mind; you are not interested in my heart.

3.    The heart is what I imagine I give. Each time this gift is returned to
me, then it is little enough to say, with Werther, that the heart is what
remains of me, once all the wit attributed to me and undesired by me is
taken away: the heart is what remains *to me*, and this heart that lies heavy
on my heart is heavy with the ebb which has filled it with itself (only the
lover and the child have a heavy heart).

(X is about to leave for some weeks, and perhaps longer; at the last
moment, he wants to buy a watch for his trip; the clerk simpers at
him: "Would you like mine? You would have been a little boy when they
cost what this one did," etc.; she doesn't know that *my heart is heavy
within me*.)

### Images
*image* / image
In the amorous realm, the most painful wounds are inflicted more often
by what one sees than by what one
knows.

1.    ("Suddenly, coming back from the coatroom, he sees them in intimate conversation, leaning close to one another.")

The image is presented, pure and distinct as a letter: it is the letter of what
pains me. Precise, complete, definitive, it leaves no room for me, down
to the last finicky detail: I am excluded from it as from the primal scene,
which may exist only insofar as it is framed within the contour of the
keyhole. Here then, at last, is the definition of the image, of any image:
that from which I am excluded. Contrary to those puzzle drawings in
which the hunter is secretly figured in the confusion of the foliage, I am
not in the scene: the image is without a riddle.

2.    The image is peremptory, it always has the last word; no knowledge
can contradict it, "arrange" it, refine it. Werther knows perfectly well
*Werther* that Charlotte is betrothed to Albert, and in fact only suffers vaguely from
the fact; but "his whole body shudders when Albert embraces her

slender waist." *I know perfectly well* that Charlotte does not belong to me, says Werther's reason, *but all the same*, Albert is stealing her from me, says the image which is before his eyes.

3.    The images from which I am excluded are cruel, yet sometimes I am caught up in the image (reversal). Leaving the outdoor café where I must *leave behind* the other with friends, I *see myself* walking away alone, shoulders bowed, down the empty street. I convert my exclusion into an image. This image, in which my absence is reflected as in a mirror, is a *sad* image.

A romantic painting shows a heap of icy debris in a polar light; no man, no object inhabits this desolate space; but for this very reason, provided I am suffering an amorous sadness, this void requires that I fling myself into it; I project myself there as a tiny figure, seated on a block of ice, *Caspar David* abandoned forever. "I'm cold," the lover says, "let's go back"; but there *Friedrich* is no road, no way, the boat is wrecked. There is a *coldness* particular to the lover, the chilliness of the child (or of any young animal) that needs maternal warmth.

4.    What wounds me are the *forms* of the relation, its images; or rather, what others call *form* I experience as force. The image—as the example for the obsessive—is *the thing itself*. The lover is thus an artist; and his world is in fact a world reversed, since in it each image is its own end (nothing beyond the image).

### *"Show me whom to desire"*

*induction* / induction
The loved being is desired because another or others have shown the subject that such a being is desirable:
however particular, amorous desire is
discovered by induction.

1.    Shortly before falling in love, Werther meets a young footman who tells him of his passion for a widow: "The image of that fidelity, that *Werther* tenderness, pursues me everywhere, and as though scorched myself by that fire, I faint, I fail, consuming myself." After which there is nothing left for Werther to do but to fall in love in his turn, with Charlotte. And Charlotte herself will be pointed out to him, before he sees her; in the carriage taking them to the ball, an obliging friend tells him how lovely she is. The body *which will be loved* is in advance selected and manipu-

Friedrich: *The Wreck of the "Hope."*

*Freud*

*La Rochefoucauld*

*Stendhal*

lated by the lens, subjected to a kind of zoom effect which magnifies it, brings it closer, and leads the subject to press his nose to the glass: is it not the *scintillating* object which a skillful hand causes to shimmer before me and which will hypnotize me, capture me? This "affective contagion," this induction, proceeds from others, from the language, from books, from friends: no love is original. (Mass culture is a machine for showing desire: here is what must interest you, it says, as if it guessed that men are incapable of finding what to desire by themselves.)

The difficulty of the amorous project is in this: "Just show me whom to desire, but then get out of the way!": Countless episodes in which I fall in love with someone loved by my best friend: every rival has first been a master, a guide, a barker, a mediator.

*Winnicott*

2.    In order to show you where your desire is, it is enough to forbid it to you *a little* (if it is true that there is no desire without prohibition). X wants me to be there, beside him, while leaving him free *a little*: flexible, going away occasionally, but *not far*: on the one hand, I must be present as a prohibition (without which there would not be the right desire), but also I must go away the moment when, this desire having formed, I might be in its way: I must be the Mother who loves enough (protective and generous), around whom the child plays, while she peacefully knits or sews. This would be the structure of the "successful" couple: a little prohibition, a good deal of play; to designate desire and then to leave it alone, like those obliging natives who show you the path but don't insist on accompanying you on your way.

### *"How blue the sky was"*
*rencontre* / encounter
The figure refers to the happy interval
immediately following the first ravishment, before the difficulties of the amorous relationship begin.

1.    Though the lover's discourse is no more than a dust of figures stirring according to an unpredictable order, like a fly buzzing in a room, I can assign to love, at least retrospectively, according to my Image-repertoire, a settled course: it is by means of this *historical* hallucination that I

La Rochefoucauld: "Some people would never have been in love, had they never heard love talked about."
Stendhal: "Before love is born, beauty is necessary as a sign, it predisposes to this passion by the praises we hear bestowed upon whom we will love" (*On Love*).

sometimes make love into a romance, an adventure. This would appear to assume three stages (or three acts): first comes the instantaneous capture (I am ravished by an image); then a series of encounters (dates, telephone calls, letters, brief trips), during which I ecstatically "explore" the perfection of the loved being, i.e., the unhoped-for correspondence between an object and my desire: this is the sweetness of the beginning, the interval proper to the idyll. This happy period acquires its identity (its *Ronsard* limits) from its opposition (at least in memory) to the "sequel": the "sequel" is the long train of sufferings, wounds, anxieties, distresses, resentments, despairs, embarrassments, and deceptions to which I fall prey, ceaselessly living under the threat of a downfall which would envelop at once the other, myself, and the glamorous encounter that first revealed us to each other.

2.   Some lovers do not commit suicide: it is possible for me to emerge from that "tunnel" which follows the amorous encounter. I see daylight again, either because I manage to grant unhappy love a dialectical outcome (retaining the love but getting rid of the hypnosis) or because I abandon that love altogether and set out again, trying to reiterate, with others, the encounter whose dazzlement remains with me: for it is of the order of the "first pleasure" and I cannot rest until it recurs: I affirm the affirmation, I begin again, without repeating.

(The encounter is radiant; later on, in memory, the subject will telescope into one the three moments of the amorous trajectory; he will speak of "love's dazzling tunnel.")

3.   In the encounter, I marvel that I have found someone who, by successive touches, each one successful, unfailing, completes the painting of my hallucination; I am like a gambler whose luck cannot fail, so that his hand unfailingly lands on the little piece which immediately completes the puzzle of his desire. This is a gradual discovery (and a kind of verification) of affinities, complicities, and intimacies which I shall (I imagine) eternally sustain with the other, who is thereby becoming "my other": I am totally given over to this discovery (I tremble within it), to the point where any intense curiosity for someone encountered is more or less equivalent to love (it is certainly love which the young Moraïte feels for the traveler Chateaubriand, greedily watching his slightest ges- *Chateau-briand*

Ronsard: *"Quand je fus pris au doux commencement
     D'une douceur si doucettement douce . . ."*

   When I was caught up in the sweet beginning
   Of a sweetness so deliciously sweet . . . ("*Doux fut le trait*")
Chateaubriand: *Travels in Egypt, Palestine, Greece and Barbary*.

ture and following him until his departure). At every moment of the
encounter, I discover in the other another myself: *You like this? So do I!*
*Bouvard and* *You don't like that? Neither do I!* When Bouvard and Pécuchet meet for
*Pécuchet* the first time, they marvel over the catalogue of their shared tastes: the
scene, beyond all doubt, is a love scene. The Encounter casts upon the
(already ravished) amorous subject the dazzlement of a supernatural
stroke of luck: love belongs to the (Dionysiac) order of the Cast of the
dice.

(Neither knows the other yet. Hence they must tell each other: "This is
what I am." This is narrative bliss, the kind which both fulfills and delays
*R.H.* knowledge, in a word, *restarts* it. In the amorous encounter, I keep
rebounding—I am *light*.)

## For Discussion and Writing

1. For each of Barthes's five figures, identify the areas of reference
   drawn upon by the writer. Adapting Barthes's system to our own
   purposes, it will be useful to classify these references into three
   broad categories: (1) literature, classical music, fine art; (2) popular
   culture, including music, proverbs or clichés, films, advertising; and
   (3) personal experience, including both things that have happened
   and things that have been said to the lover. When you understand
   Barthes's method you will be in a position to adapt it to your own
   writing. As a first step toward that understanding, select one of
   Barthes's figures and replace its body with your own numbered
   paragraphs. Begin by jotting down notes from your own cultural
   repertory: books, films, TV, things you have heard or said that have
   to do with the figure you have selected. Then, using your notes for
   inspiration, compose your own meditation on your chosen figure.

2. We have reprinted only five figures from the eighty in Barthes's
   book. Assuming that the lover's discourse Barthes describes is shared
   by many people in Western cultures, try to add some of the missing
   pieces of this scenario. Make a list of some of the other objects,
   events, and expressions that constitute the lover's "scenes of language." In class discussion, try to construct the argument that should
   go with each figure. As a group, begin to list some of the cultural
   items that would help you compose the bodies of these figures. You
   can only go so far with this as a group project, because at some point
   the general cultural discourse (all lovers) must be supplemented by

R.H.: Conversation.

your personal repertory of texts (your own experiences as stored in memory).

3.  One way to test the validity and value of an experiment is to see if it is replicable, or if it is applicable to other problems or issues. Write a set of figures, entitled *Fragments of a Student's Discourse*, modeled after Barthes's *Fragments*, applying Barthes's form and procedure to the discourse of the student. You are to write about the conventions and stereotypes of the student experience, identifying the conventions and clichés, figures and poses, myths and expectations of the student life. Do for the student's life*style* what Barthes did for the lover's style of conduct. Use the following questions to guide your extrapolation from the lover's to the student's discourse:

Are any of the figures used in the lover's discourse also relevant to the student's discourse? Of the ones that might be directly translatable across discourses, do they mean the same thing, or function the same way, in both contexts? Some of the figures may not be directly transferable but might have equivalents in the new setting. For example, if the heart is the organ of love sentiment, would the brain be equivalent for the student's situation? What does it mean to *be* "a brain"? Is this the same as *having* one? Can a student be too brainy? What are the sources of a student's anxiety, hope, joy, pain? What are the crucial moments or events in a student's life? Where does this scene of life and language begin? Where does it end? What objects are important to a student? What words, phrases, sayings, clichés preside over our lives as students? To help stimulate your thinking along these lines, we have presented a few cultural references for you to read before composing your fragments. You need neither "cover" them nor be limited by them.

# References for *Fragments of a Student's Discourse*

The three pieces included here may be used in the same way Barthes used Goethe's novel about Werther—as the literary texts to help you identify the conventions of student life as they are represented in writing in our culture. Compare your own experience of the student life with the themes, attitudes, and events of these pieces. Identify any common figures or poses (those items about which you can say, "That's so true!"). Note also those items with which you cannot identify. In writing the *Fragments of a Student's Discourse*, your purpose is to "make a text" for yourself that articulates the central clichés our culture holds regarding "the best years of your life"—college. Part of the interest of Barthes's *Fragments* is the tension that sometimes exists between the general topic and heading and the individual experience of the pose. As you compose your student *Fragments*, you might reflect on the stereotyped notion people tend to have about the student lifestyle. By putting his figures in alphabetical order, Barthes avoids telling the story of love, but he makes this comment about that commonplace anecdote of the unhappy lover:

> every amorous episode can be, of course, endowed with a meaning: it is generated, develops, and dies; it follows a path which it is always possible to interpret according to a causality or a finality— even, if need be, which can be moralized ("I was out of my mind, I'm over it now" "Love is a trap which must be avoided from now on" etc.): this is the *love story*, subjugated to the great narrative Other, to that general opinion which disparages any excessive force and wants the subject himself to reduce the great imaginary current, the orderless, endless stream which is passing through him, to a painful, morbid crisis of which he must be cured, which he must "get over": the love story (the "episode," the "adventure") is the tribute the lover must pay to the world in order to be reconciled with it.

What is the equivalent for the student? What story must the student tell to the great moralizing Other (relatives, friends, parents, employers) in response to the question, "How are things going at school?"

# Graduation

## *Maya Angelou*

*In her four volumes of autobiography, Maya Angelou (b. 1928) has written vividly of her struggles to achieve success as an actress, a dancer, a songwriter, a teacher, and a writer. An active worker in the civil rights movement in the 1960s, Angelou continues to focus much of her writing on racial issues. The following selection is from* I Know Why the Caged Bird Sings *(1969), in which she writes, "I speak to the Black experience, but I am always talking about the human condition."*

The children in Stamps trembled visibly with anticipation.[1] Some    1
adults were excited too, but to be certain the whole young population had come down with graduation epidemic. Large classes were graduating from both the grammar school and the high school. Even those who were years removed from their own day of glorious release were anxious to help with preparations as a kind of dry run. The junior students who were moving into the vacating classes' chairs were tradition-bound to show their talents for leadership and management. They strutted through the school and around the campus exerting pressure on the lower grades. Their authority was so new that occasionally if they pressed a little too hard it had to be overlooked. After all, next term was coming, and it never hurt a sixth grader to have a play sister in the eighth grade, or a tenth-year student to be able to call a twelfth grader Bubba. So all was endured in a spirit of shared understanding. But the graduating classes themselves were the nobility. Like travelers with exotic destinations on their minds, the graduates were remarkably forgetful. They came to school without their books, or tablets or even pencils. Volunteers fell over themselves to secure replacements for the missing equipment. When accepted, the willing workers might or might not be thanked, and it was of no importance to the pregraduation rites. Even teachers were respectful of the now quiet and aging seniors, and tended to speak to them, if not as equals, as beings only slightly lower than themselves. After tests were returned and grades given, the student body, which acted like an extended family, knew who did well, who excelled, and what piteous ones had failed.

Unlike the white high school, Lafayette County Training School    2
distinguished itself by having neither lawn, nor hedges, nor tennis court,

[1] Stamps: a town in Arkansas. [Eds.]

nor climbing ivy. Its two buildings (main classrooms, the grade school and home economics) were set on a dirt hill with no fence to limit either its boundaries or those of bordering farms. There was a large expanse to the left of the school which was used alternately as a baseball diamond or basketball court. Rusty hoops on swaying poles represented the permanent recreational equipment, although bats and balls could be borrowed from the P.E. teacher if the borrower was qualified and if the diamond wasn't occupied.

Over this rocky area relieved by a few shady tall persimmon trees    3
the graduating class walked. The girls often held hands and no longer bothered to speak to the lower students. There was a sadness about them, as if this old world was not their home and they were bound for higher ground. The boys, on the other hand, had become more friendly, more outgoing. A decided change from the closed attitude they projected while studying for finals. Now they seemed not ready to give up the old school, the familiar paths and classrooms. Only a small percentage would be continuing on to college—one of the South's A & M (agricultural and mechanical) schools, which trained Negro youths to be carpenters, farmers, handymen, masons, maids, cooks and baby nurses. Their future rode heavily on their shoulders, and blinded them to the collective joy that had pervaded the lives of the boys and girls in the grammar school graduating class.

Parents who could afford it had ordered new shoes and ready-made    4
clothes for themselves from Sears and Roebuck or Montgomery Ward. They also engaged the best seamstresses to make the floating graduating dresses and to cut down secondhand pants which would be pressed to a military slickness for the important event.

Oh, it was important, all right. Whitefolks would attend the cere-    5
mony, and two or three would speak of God and home, and the Southern way of life, and Mrs. Parsons, the principal's wife, would play the graduation march while the lower-grade graduates paraded down the aisles and took their seats below the platform. The high school seniors would wait in empty classrooms to make their dramatic entrance.

In the Store I was the person of the moment. The birthday girl. The    6
center. Bailey had graduated the year before,[2] although to do so he had had to forfeit all pleasures to make up for his time lost in Baton Rouge.

My class was wearing butter-yellow piqué dresses, and Momma    7
launched out on mine. She smocked the yoke into tiny crisscrossing puckers, then shirred the rest of the bodice. Her dark fingers ducked in and out of the lemony cloth as she embroidered raised daisies around the hem. Before she considered herself finished she had added a crocheted cuff on the puff sleeves, and a pointy crocheted collar.

---

[2] Bailey: the brother of the author. [Eds.]

I was going to be lovely. A walking model of all the various styles of 8
fine hand sewing and it didn't worry me that I was only twelve years old
and merely graduating from the eighth grade. Besides, many teachers in
Arkansas Negro schools had only that diploma and were licensed to
impart wisdom.

The days had become longer and more noticeable. The faded beige 9
of former times had been replaced with strong and sure colors. I began to
see my classmates' clothes, their skin tones, and the dust that waved off
pussy willows. Clouds that lazed across the sky were objects of great
concern to me. Their shiftier shapes might have held a message that in my
new happiness and with a little bit of time I'd soon decipher. During that
period I looked at the arch of heaven so religiously my neck kept a steady
ache. I had taken to smiling more often, and my jaws hurt from the
unaccustomed activity. Between the two physical sore spots, I suppose I
could have been uncomfortable, but that was not the case. As a member
of the winning team (the graduating class of 1940) I had outdistanced
unpleasant sensations by miles. I was headed for the freedom of open
fields.

Youth and social approval allied themselves with me and we tram- 10
meled memories of slights and insults. The wind of our swift passage
remodeled my features. Lost tears were pounded to mud and then to
dust. Years of withdrawal were brushed aside and left behind, as hanging
ropes of parasitic moss.

My work alone had awarded me a top place and I was going to be 11
one of the first called in the graduating ceremonies. On the classroom
blackboard, as well as on the bulletin board in the auditorium, there were
blue stars and white stars and red stars. No absences, no tardinesses, and
my academic work was among the best of the year. I could say the
preamble to the Constitution even faster than Bailey. We timed ourselves
often: "WethepeopleoftheUnitedStatesinordertoformamoreperfectunion
. . ." I had memorized the Presidents of the United States from Washington to Roosevelt in chronological as well as alphabetical order.

My hair pleased me too. Gradually the black mass had lengthened 12
and thickened, so that it kept at last to its braided pattern, and I didn't
have to yank my scalp off when I tried to comb it.

Louise and I had rehearsed the exercises until we tired out ourselves. 13
Henry Reed was class valedictorian. He was a small, very black boy with
hooded eyes, a long, broad nose and an oddly shaped head. I had admired him for years because each term he and I vied for the best grades in
our class. Most often he bested me, but instead of being disappointed I
was pleased that we shared top places between us. Like many Southern
Black children, he lived with his grandmother, who was as strict as
Momma and as kind as she knew how to be. He was courteous, respectful
and soft-spoken to elders, but on the playground he chose to play the

roughest games. I admired him. Anyone, I reckoned, sufficiently afraid or sufficiently dull could be polite. But to be able to operate at a top level with both adults and children was admirable.

His valedictory speech was entitled "To Be or Not to Be." The rigid 14 tenth-grade teacher had helped him write it. He'd been working on the dramatic stresses for months.

The weeks until graduation were filled with heady activities. A group 15 of small children were to be presented in a play about buttercups and daisies and bunny rabbits. They could be heard throughout the building practicing their hops and their little songs that sounded like silver bells. The older girls (nongraduates, of course) were assigned the task of making refreshments for the night's festivities. A tangy scent of ginger, cinnamon, nutmeg and chocolate wafted around the home economics building as the budding cooks made samples for themselves and their teachers.

In every corner of the workshop, axes and saws split fresh timber as 16 the woodshop boys made sets and stage scenery. Only the graduates were left out of the general bustle. We were free to sit in the library at the back of the building or look in quite detachedly, naturally, on the measures being taken for our event.

Even the minister preached on graduation the Sunday before. His 17 subject was, "Let your light so shine that men will see your good works and praise your Father, Who is in Heaven." Although the sermon was purported to be addressed to us, he used the occasion to speak to backsliders, gamblers and general ne'er-do-wells. But since he had called our names at the beginning of the service we were mollified.

Among Negroes the tradition was to give presents to children going 18 only from one grade to another. How much more important this was when the person was graduating at the top of the class. Uncle Willie and Momma had sent away for a Mickey Mouse watch like Bailey's. Louise gave me four embroidered handkerchiefs. (I gave her crocheted doilies.) Mrs. Sneed, the minister's wife, made me an undershirt to wear for graduation, and nearly every customer gave me a nickel or maybe even a dime with the instruction "Keep on moving to higher ground," or some such encouragement.

Amazingly the great day finally dawned and I was out of bed before I 19 knew it. I threw open the back door to see it more clearly, but Momma said, "Sister, come away from that door and put your robe on."

I hoped the memory of that morning would never leave me. Sunlight 20 was itself young, and the day had none of the insistence maturity would bring it in a few hours. In my robe and barefoot in the backyard, under cover of going to see about my new beans, I gave myself up to the gentle warmth and thanked God that no matter what evil I had done in my life He had allowed me to live to see this day. Somewhere in my fatalism I had expected to die, accidentally, and never have the chance to walk up the stairs in the auditorium and gracefully receive my hard-earned diploma. Out of God's merciful bosom I had won reprieve.

Bailey came out in his robe and gave me a box wrapped in Christmas 21 paper. He said he had saved his money for months to pay for it. It felt like a box of chocolates, but I knew Bailey wouldn't save money to buy candy when we had all we could want under our noses.

He was as proud of the gift as I. It was a soft-leather-bound copy of a 22 collection of poems by Edgar Allan Poe, or, as Bailey and I called him, "Eap." I turned to "Annabel Lee" and we walked up and down the garden rows, the cool dirt between our toes, reciting the beautifully sad lines.

Momma made a Sunday breakfast although it was only Friday. After 23 we finished the blessing, I opened my eyes to find the watch on my plate. It was a dream of a day. Everything went smoothly and to my credit. I didn't have to be reminded or scolded for anything. Near evening I was too jittery to attend to chores, so Bailey volunteered to do all before his bath.

Days before, we had made a sign for the Store, and as we turned out 24 the lights Momma hung the cardboard over the doorknob. It read clearly: CLOSED. GRADUATION.

My dress fitted perfectly and everyone said that I looked like a sun- 25 beam in it. On the hill, going toward the school, Bailey walked behind with Uncle Willie, who muttered, "Go on, Ju." He wanted him to walk ahead with us because it embarrassed him to have to walk so slowly. Bailey said he'd let the ladies walk together, and the men would bring up the rear. We all laughed, nicely.

Little children dashed by out of the dark like fireflies. Their crepe- 26 paper dresses and butterfly wings were not made for running and we heard more than one rip, dryly, and the regretful "uh uh" that followed.

The school blazed without gaiety. The windows seemed cold and 27 unfriendly from the lower hill. A sense of ill-fated timing crept over me, and if Momma hadn't reached for my hand I would have drifted back to Bailey and Uncle Willie, and possibly beyond. She made a few slow jokes about my feet getting cold, and tugged me along to the now-strange building.

Around the front steps, assurance came back. There were my fellow 28 "greats," the graduating class. Hair brushed back, legs oiled, new dresses and pressed pleats, fresh pocket handkerchiefs and little handbags, all homesewn. Oh, we were up to snuff, all right. I joined my comrades and didn't even see my family go in to find seats in the crowded auditorium.

The school band struck up a march and all classes filed in as had 29 been rehearsed. We stood in front of our seats, as assigned, and on a signal from the choir director, we sat. No sooner had this been accomplished than the band started to play the national anthem. We rose again and sang the song, after which we recited the pledge of allegiance. We remained standing for a brief minute before the choir director and the principal signaled to us, rather desperately I thought, to take our seats. The command was so unusual that our carefully rehearsed and smooth-running machine was thrown off. For a full minute we fumbled for our chairs and bumped into each other awkwardly. Habits change or solidify under pressure, so in our state of nervous tension we had been ready to follow our usual assembly pattern: the American national anthem, then the pledge of allegiance, then the song every Black person I knew called the Negro National Anthem. All done in the same key, with the same passion and most often standing on the same foot.

Finding my seat at last, I was overcome with a presentiment of worse 30 things to come. Something unrehearsed, unplanned, was going to happen, and we were going to be made to look bad. I distinctly remember being explicit in the choice of pronoun. It was "we," the graduating class, the unit, that concerned me then.

The principal welcomed "parents and friends" and asked the Baptist 31 minister to lead us in prayer. His invocation was brief and punchy, and for a second I thought we were getting on the high road to right action. When the principal came back to the dais, however, his voice had changed. Sounds always affected me profoundly and the principal's voice was one of my favorites. During assembly it melted and lowed weakly into the audience. It had not been in my plan to listen to him, but my curiosity was piqued and I straightened up to give him my attention.

He was talking about Booker T. Washington, our "late great leader," 32 who said we can be as close as the fingers on the hand, etc. . . . Then he said a few vague things about friendship and the friendship of kindly people to those less fortunate than themselves. With that his voice nearly faded, thin, away. Like a river diminishing to a stream and then to a trickle. But he cleared his throat and said, "Our speaker tonight, who is also our friend, came from Texarkana to deliver the commencement address, but due to the irregularity of the train schedule, he's going to, as they say, 'speak and run.'" He said that we understood and wanted the man to know that we were most grateful for the time he was able to give us and then something about how we were willing always to adjust to another's program, and without more ado—"I give you Mr. Edward Donleavy."

Not one but two white men came through the door off-stage. The 33 shorter one walked to the speaker's platform, and the tall one moved to the center seat and sat down. But that was our principal's seat, and already occupied. The dislodged gentleman bounced around for a long breath or two before the Baptist minister gave him his chair, then with more dignity than the situation deserved, the minister walked off the stage.

Donleavy looked at the audience once (on reflection, I'm sure that 34 he wanted only to reassure himself that we were really there), adjusted his glasses and began to read from a sheaf of papers.

He was glad "to be here and to see the work going on just as it was in 35 the other schools."

At the first "Amen" from the audience, I willed the offender to 36 immediate death by choking on the word. But Amens and Yes, sir's began to fall around the room like rain through a ragged umbrella.

He told us of the wonderful changes we children in Stamps had in 37 store. The Central School (naturally, the white school was Central) had already been granted improvements that would be in use in the fall. A well-known artist was coming from Little Rock to teach art to them. They were going to have the newest microscopes and chemistry equipment for their laboratory. Mr. Donleavy didn't leave us long in the dark over who made these improvements available to Central High. Nor were we to be ignored in the general betterment scheme he had in mind.

He said that he had pointed out to people at a very high level that 38 one of the first-line football tacklers at Arkansas Agricultural and Mechanical College had graduated from good old Lafayette County Training School. Here fewer Amens were heard. Those few that did break through lay dully in the air with the heaviness of habit.

He went on to praise us. He went on to say how he had bragged that 39 "one of the best basketball players at Fisk sank his first ball right here at Lafayette County Training School."

The white kids were going to have a chance to become Galileos and 40 Madame Curies and Edisons and Gauguins, and our boys (the girls weren't even in on it) would try to be Jesse Owenses and Joe Louises.

Owens and the Brown Bomber were great heroes in our world, but 41 what school official in the white-goddom of Little Rock had the right to decide that those two men must be our only heroes? Who decided that for Henry Reed to become a scientist he had to work like George Washington Carver, as a boot-black, to buy a lousy microscope? Bailey was obviously always going to be too small to be an athlete, so which concrete angel glued to what country seat had decided that if my brother wanted to become a lawyer he had to first pay penance for his skin by picking cotton and hoeing corn and studying correspondence books at night for twenty years?

The man's dead words fell like bricks around the auditorium and too 42 many settled in my belly. Constrained by hard-learned manners I couldn't look behind me, but to my left and right the proud graduating class of 1940 had dropped their heads. Every girl in my row had found something new to do with her handkerchief. Some folded the tiny squares into love knots, some into triangles, but most were wadding them, then pressing them flat on their yellow laps.

On the dais, the ancient tragedy was being replayed. Professor Parsons sat, a sculptor's reject, rigid. His large, heavy body seemed devoid of will or willingness, and his eyes said he was no longer with us. The other teachers examined the flag (which was draped stage right) or their notes, or the windows which opened on our now-famous playing diamond.

Graduation, the hush-hush magic time of frills and gifts and congratulations and diplomas, was finished for me before my name was called. The accomplishment was nothing. The meticulous maps, drawn in three colors of ink, learning and spelling decasyllabic words, memorizing the whole of *The Rape of Lucrece*[3]—it was for nothing. Donleavy had exposed us.

We were maids and farmers, handymen and washerwomen, and anything higher that we aspired to was farcical and presumptuous.

Then I wished that Gabriel Prosser and Nat Turner had killed all whitefolks in their beds and that Abraham Lincoln had been assassinated before the signing of the Emancipation Proclamation,[4] and that Harriet Tubman had been killed by that blow on her head and Christopher Columbus had drowned in the *Santa Maria*.[5]

It was awful to be a Negro and have no control over my life. It was brutal to be young and already trained to sit quietly and listen to charges brought against my color with no chance of defense. We should all be dead. I thought I should like to see us all dead, one on top of the other. A pyramid of flesh with the whitefolks on the bottom, as the broad base, then the Indians with their silly tomahawks and teepees and wigwams and treaties, the Negroes with their mops and recipes and cotton sacks and spirituals sticking out of their mouths. The Dutch children should all stumble in their wooden shoes and break their necks. The French should choke to death on the Louisiana Purchase (1803) while silkworms ate all the Chinese with their stupid pigtails. As a species, we were an abomination. All of us.

Donleavy was running for election, and assured our parents that if he won we could count on having the only colored paved playing field in that part of Arkansas. Also—he never looked up to acknowledge the

---

[3] *The Rape of Lucrece*: an 1,855-line narrative poem by William Shakespeare. [Eds.]
[4] Gabriel Prosser and Nat Turner: leaders of slave rebellions during the early 1800s in Virginia. [Eds.]
[5] Harriet Tubman: an escaped slave who conducted others to freedom on the Underground Railroad and worked as an abolitionist. [Eds.]

grunts of acceptance—also, we were bound to get some new equipment for the home economics building and the workshop.

He finished, and since there was no need to give any more than the 49 most perfunctory thank-you's, he nodded to the men on the stage, and the tall white man who was never introduced joined him at the door. They left with the attitude that now they were off to something really important. (The graduation ceremonies at Lafayette County Training School had been a mere preliminary.)

The ugliness they left was palpable. An uninvited guest who 50 wouldn't leave. The choir was summoned and sang a modern arrange-ment of "Onward, Christian Soldiers," with new words pertaining to graduates seeking their place in the world. But it didn't work. Elouise, the daughter of the Baptist minister, recited "Invictus,"[6] and I could have cried at the impertinence of "I am the master of my fate, I am the captain of my soul."

My name had lost its ring of familiarity and I had to be nudged to go 51 and receive my diploma. All my preparations had fled. I neither marched up to the stage like a conquering Amazon, nor did I look in the audience for Bailey's nod of approval. Marguerite Johnson, I heard the name again, my honors were read, there were noises in the audience of appreciation, and I took my place on the stage as rehearsed.

I thought about colors I hated: ecru, puce, lavender, beige and black. 52

There was shuffling and rustling around me, then Henry Reed was 53 giving his valedictory address, "To Be or Not to Be." Hadn't he heard the whitefolks? We couldn't *be*, so the question was a waste of time. Henry's voice came out clear and strong. I feared to look at him. Hadn't he got the message? There was no "nobler in the mind" for Negroes because the world didn't think we had minds, and they let us know it. "Outrageous fortune"? Now, that was a joke. When the ceremony was over I had to tell Henry Reed some things. That is, if I still cared. Not "rub," Henry, "erase." "Ah, there's the erase." Us.

Henry had been a good student in elocution. His voice rose on tides 54 of promise and fell on waves of warnings. The English teacher had helped him to create a sermon winging through Hamlet's soliloquy. To be a man, a doer, a builder, a leader, or to be a tool, an unfunny joke, a crusher of funky toadstools. I marveled that Henry could go through with the speech as if we had a choice.

I had been listening and silently rebutting each sentence with my 55 eyes closed; then there was a hush, which in an audience warns that something unplanned is happening. I looked up and saw Henry Reed, the

[6] "Invictus": a poem by the nineteenth-century English poet, William Ernest Hen-ley. Its inspirational conclusion is quoted here. [Eds.]

conservative, the proper, the A student, turn his back to the audience and turn to us (the proud graduating class of 1940) and sing, nearly speaking,

"Lift ev'ry voice and sing
Till earth and heaven ring
Ring with the harmonies of Liberty . . ."

It was the poem written by James Weldon Johnson. It was the music composed by J. Rosamond Johnson. It was the Negro National Anthem. Out of habit we were singing it.

Our mothers and fathers stood in the dark hall and joined the hymn 56 of encouragement. A kindergarten teacher led the small children onto the stage and the buttercups and daisies and bunny rabbits marked time and tried to follow:

"Stony the road we trod
Bitter the chastening rod
Felt in the days when hope, unborn, had died.
Yet with a steady beat
Have not our weary feet
Come to the place for which our fathers sighed?"

Each child I knew had learned that song with his ABC's and along 57 with "Jesus Loves Me This I Know." But I personally had never heard it before. Never heard the words, despite the thousands of times I had sung them. Never thought they had anything to do with me.

On the other hand, the words of Patrick Henry had made such an 58 impression on me that I had been able to stretch myself tall and trembling and say, "I know not what course others may take, but as for me, give me liberty or give me death."

And now I heard, really for the first time:                               59

"We have come over a way that with tears
has been watered,
We have come, treading our path through
the blood of the slaughtered."

While echoes of the song shivered in the air, Henry Reed bowed his 60 head, said "Thank you," and returned to his place in the line. The tears that slipped down many faces were not wiped away in shame.

We were on top again. As always, again. We survived. The depths 61 had been icy and dark, but now a bright sun spoke to our souls. I was no longer simply a member of the proud graduating class of 1940; I was a proud member of the wonderful, beautiful Negro race.

Oh, Black known and unknown poets, how often have your auc- 62
tioned pains sustained us? Who will compute the lonely nights made less
lonely by your songs, or the empty pots made less tragic by your tales?

If we were a people much given to revealing secrets, we might raise 63
monuments and sacrifice to the memories of our poets, but slavery cured
us of that weakness. It may be enough, however, to have it said that we
survive in exact relationship to the dedication of our poets (include
preachers, musicians and blues singers).

# Listen to the White Graduate, You Might Learn Something

## *Roger Rapoport*

*Compare Maya Angelou's piece with this essay from the same
period by Roger Rapoport, a 1968 graduate of the University of Michigan.*

Historians will doubtless rank April 27, 1968, as a landmark in the   1
annals of American education, second only to passage of the Morrill Act.
On that day I completed seventeen years of study, graduated from the
University of Michigan and resigned my commission in the nation's
school system. I knew education would never be the same without me,
nor I the same without it. Still, I would have preferred sleeping through
my own commencement like one more eight-o'clock class. But my
parents were flying in for the occasion. So I woke early and hurried over
to the administration building to get their graduation tickets.

Inside, a secretary explained she didn't have the advertised tickets   2
and directed a long line of seniors to the site of the ceremony, the domed
University Events Building. While janitors obscured the basketball court
with maize and blue bunting, ushers ran us around the perimeter of the
building to the ticket window. A uniformed guard said: "There are no
tickets left and besides you're not supposed to be inside this early."

In frustration I drove directly to the home of University President   3
Robben Fleming. His wife opened the door just as the President descended the staircase with houseguest and commencement speaker
Robert Weaver. After being introduced to the Secretary of Housing, I sat
down on the living-room couch and explained the dilemma. Fleming
made some unsuccessful phone calls and sent me back to the administra-

tion building. There a university administrator directed me to a ticket clerk at the Events Building who was dubious about the authenticity of my yellow plastic I.D. card (362-44-9616-5). I helplessly flipped him my entire wallet—Social Security card, driver's license, draft card and all—in a final effort to get the tickets for my parents, by now stranded at the airport. Tickets in hand, I rushed to pick them up, coming back too late for the pomp and circumstance but soon enough to hear Mr. Weaver talk of promising career opportunities for today's graduates: "So I say to you that the urban frontier, with all of its complexities and problems, is an avenue to exciting and meaningful careers."

Afterward we rushed off to a friend's party and pondered our    4 glorious futures. Here, amidst piles of potato salad, cold cuts, and brownies, was the educational elite of civilization's most advanced state —the breast-fed generation off to conquer the world. In one corner a comely history major was taking her degree to the advertising depart- ment of a Boston false-teeth manufacturer. Another friend, a flaming blonde Marxist, had landed a taskless secretarial post with a New York ad agency. And I was heading for San Francisco and a free-lance writing career. But I wasn't optimistic, for I was following the path of an old friend, a sociology major who had graduated the year before and was now floundering. My new room-mate had been forced to supplement his writing income as a guinea pig for N.A.S.A. in Berkeley. He was paid $25 a day for eating a special diet and depositing the resultant gaseous human waste into a rubber bag stuffed into the back of his pants. The results were used to simulate the effects of astronaut exhaust fumes in the Apollo space capsule. At one point rumor had it that an evaluation of his fumes nearly prompted the scientists to delay the entire Apollo project.

Before embarking upon these remarkable careers, it was natural for    5 our conversation to drift into anecdotes about the good old days. Gradu- ating from college is not just completing a four-year cycle, it's like ending an era. Suddenly you are rid of that inner demon which has been controlling your actions since seventh grade when an adviser waved a manila folder and said in halitosis-filled remarks: "This is C-49—your academic file where we keep records on everything you do in school. To get into college you must build a good one." I studied hard and my teachers wrote soaring evaluations for C-49. Admission to Michigan in my senior year was automatic: B average, student council member, honor society member, editor school paper. So one steamy August afternoon I piled my belongings and a friend in the family Falcon, backed out the driveway and honked good-bye, drove slowly through North Muskegon, Michigan, the town I knew so well, sniffed the sulphurous paper mill, saw the foundry smoke darkening the sky, and said farewell to Muskegon Lake. Soon we were on the superhighway slicing across the Michigan farmland. Three hours later we descended into the Huron River Valley, a forested depression in which nestled Ann Arbor, the technological center of the Midwest and home of the university.

I drove directly to my new residence, South Quadrangle. Built in 6 1951, it was a classic piece of neo-penal architecture—nine stories of cinder block sheathed in red brick. The name South Quad lent proof to Marcuse's theory that words have lost all meaning. It was actually north of East Quadrangle and adjacent to West Quadrangle (the planners gave up and named the northern quadrangle Mary Markley Hall). The quad itself was only a stubby patch of grass virtually consumed by adjacent parking lots reserved for staff. I parked on a side street and lugged my suitcases up to my fourth-floor quarters, which offered a splendid view of the football stadium.

The Quad was drab but never boring. A week after I moved in some- 7 one bombed the cafeteria. Upstairs, wrestlers rattled windows and shook walls during nocturnal practices. When lighted cigarette butts inciner- ated our mailbox, the postmaster put up a warning notice which was promptly burned down. The dim brown corridors were livened by jars of urine splashed under doors, heads jokingly stuffed in flushing toilets, boxes of manure placed on elevators and butyric acid poured into ventilators. Maids opened doors to find naked rear ends mooning them.

Amidst all this horseplay the silver-haired president was kind enough 8 to remind us at our opening convocation that we were "the most talented freshman class in the history of the university." Stressing the quality control which had gone into the selection of our class, he gestured as if he were Moses parting the Red Sea, and summoned wave upon wave of my fellow students to their feet: first the high-school valedictorians, then the salutatorians, finally the student-body presidents.

Orientation week followed. First we learned how to find the health 9 service and get football tickets. Then came a battery of placement tests. I was particularly nervous about the French test (in high school my teacher had passed me on the promise that I would never reveal she was my instructor). I almost flunked the oral part of the placement exam read by a professor from Japan with an unusual French accent. Next came psy- chological testing with true-false questions like: "I prefer eating raw carrots to cooked carrots." (The test presumed a correlation between personal preference and career motivation.) These results were slipped into a folder with my high-school record, which I took to Angell Hall auditorium. My counselor was one of twenty conferring in the au- ditorium. He had the third aisle and I sat down beside him. We turned sideways and shook hands. It took him a mere five minutes to sign me up for history and political science (which I didn't want but needed for a sequence), and French (which I simply didn't want). I tried to protest but he smiled and said: "Don't worry, you've got to take 120 credit hours in four years and that's a lot of hours."

Next was registration, which was like going to camp, a concentra- 10 tion camp. We were herded into the basement of Victorian Waterman gymnasium in small groups. Our pictures were shot in the basement weight room. In the wrestling room student clerks handed out our I.B.M. cards and steered us to the locker room, temporarily fenced into a maze. At a checkpoint, student guards stamped and sorted our papers. The shower room, our next stop, turned out to be a tuition check for in-state students who pay lower fees. Passing under the harmless nozzles we were guided up a stairway to sign up for "psychological experiments." Upstairs, we paid tuition, made last-minute adjustments on courses, and then dribbled off the basketball court with a smudged carbon "class schedule" for the dorm bulletin board.

Although I didn't know who my new teachers were, I figured they 11 would certainly beat my high-school instructors such as the one in world history who ran dry halfway through the period and turned on a radio for the Paul Harvey midday news. But I soon discovered my college professors didn't have much to say either. In Political Science 101, sixteen dull lectures led to a midterm examination asking: "Briefly compare the origins, theory and practice of Communism and Democracy." Small discussion classes weren't better, just harder to sleep in. Under orders from the departmental hierarchy, teaching fellows taught as if we were retarded. In French we got a bowdlerized version of *Candide* and a time card to punch in at the language laboratory three hours a week (where a technician just in from Argentina feebly tried to give aid in Spanish). In English composition we had to write 1500 words on "How to Make a Succulent Hamburger." There was little reassurance when I discovered a copy of the departmental manual which advised the teaching fellows: "Socially, the teacher has to recognize that the students in his section, however inept their prose and surly their manner, are basically reasonable human beings."

In order to fulfill the natural science sequences, I elected astronomy. 12 Class turned out to be a varsity-club meeting. All the athletes sat like the *Playboy* All-America Squad draped across the front row. "The Doc," as we knew her, was a short, elderly woman passionately devoted to the Wolverines. She dressed like a cheerleader in saddle shoes, bobby sox, bulky sweater and pleated skirt. Her grading system was rumored to be "A" for athlete, "B" for boy, and "C" for coed, an exaggeration, of course, but athletes seldom failed.

The Doc's tests were said to be based on old exams. When midterms 13 came along, every Xerox machine in town hummed. The jock fraternity houses kept up their files of old exams as faithfully as they polished their trophies. During my freshman year, Michigan went to the Rose Bowl. The Doc was so excited that she didn't bother to turn in semester grades by the Christmas deadline. The registrar tracked her down in California but she stood her ground: "Fire me if you don't like it," she told them.

Sometime during my first year, I realized the biggest headache was 14 not "depersonalization" but "overpersonalization." If you leave them alone, 30,000 students can probably coexist happily with each other. But like any bureaucracy, a large university has too many of the wrong kind of people in the wrong place. A "resident adviser" with a powerful antenna for marijuana was one example. A dorm "housemother" was another pest. It was rumored she had once dated a young Army officer named Dwight Eisenhower. Now she was a nasty lady muttering like a psychology instructor about "anxiety" and "deviance" and "Spock babies" whenever an ashtray was missing.

Privacy didn't exist. Girls were sequestered on the other side of the 15 dorm and allowed in our rooms for three hours a month during "open-opens" (provided three legs were kept on the floor). The girls often circumvented this nonsense by dating older boys with apartments, since there were no boys around with three legs. (Under dorm rules at the time, a girl coming in five minutes after curfew was penalized; a girl who stayed out all night would not be punished.) We had no place to go. Those freshmen with steady girls resorted to cars, music rooms, church basements or lounges. One couple, a disheveled pair whom we called "Cyclone and Flopsy," used to have a nightly encounter on a high-backed sofa in a main-floor lounge. I'd be reading and suddenly notice a crescent shape rising above the sofa and then disappearing behind the back.

Despite the setbacks in the dorm and the classroom, I never would 16 have comprehended the total frustration of college without the four-story undergraduate library, a sterile, glass-enclosed cage fronted by a gravel-pit lawn. The UGLI, as it was called, was more lonely-hearts club than library. Girls flocked there to distract boys from their studies. The sorority girls who gathered in the art-print gallery were a typical diversion. They were checking out Rubens, Giotto and Brueghel—all I could see was Odalisque lying there waiting for me. Downstairs wasn't much better. My concentration was broken by the creaking chairs and clacking typewriter rooms, the whirring library computer and vulturous cleaning ladies slamming down ashtrays. I usually ended up at a table looking out at the revolving Ann Arbor bank sign down the block. The electric lights enumerated my failure: 7:30 and 20 degrees (page 1), 8:02 and 15 degrees (page 8), 10:35 and 12 degrees (page 22).

Because it was impossible to study efficiently, I would end up in the 17 UGLI seven days a week. By Sunday night, after eight straight hours, the world would be closing in on me. Exhausted and depressed I would try to clear my head by standing out in the chill wind peering through the glass. Amidst the bubbly lights inside I would see thousands of students bent over their books.

One Sunday, something snapped off inside of me. I had been study- 18 ing an astronomy problem. But hung up on a logarithm, I couldn't begin to do the assignment. So finally I just crossed out my name in the front, shut the book, and left it on the table where the cleaning woman would nosily swoop it up.

After freshman year I moved out of the dorm into a series of old, 19 cluttered houses and dilapidated apartments. While the Quad experience gives shape to my memory of freshman year, the remaining three years are a blur. College never led me on to anything. I felt the same as a senior as I did when I was a sophomore. The days were indistinguishable. I spent nights on couches while room-mates and girl friends took the bedroom. In the morning I rose, stretched to the ceiling and a piece of acoustical tile popped out. I ate Life Savers for breakfast, went back to bed for a noonsie at lunchtime, and then feasted on a hamburger for dinner, or I would open a can of lard, flip a glob into the skillet, and then throw in a half pound of frozen ground beef from the freezer. As the hamburger thawed in the bubbling lard, I gradually sliced off melting chunks and formed them into a patty that finally crumbled into a greasy sloppy joe. Afterward I threw the dishes into the three-day-old puddle in the sink and headed for the language lab, which was closed. So I came back, conjugated French, watched Johnny Carson and fell asleep again on the couch.

The days passed emptily and then suddenly slammed smack into the 20 examination period. I can remember the feeling at two a.m. when the snow was falling outside—and only six hours remained before a final exam. I'd put aside lists of key facts, thinking back on those early semester resolutions. Like all courses, it had begun well. The professor had an international reputation and an exciting reading list. But some- where it all fell apart. The books proved to be scholarly treatises only an author's mother could finish. The first-day jokes gave way to disor- ganized soliloquies. I wanted to assimilate material, fitting facts into concepts. The professors wanted overall knowledge accumulation as told to a computer via multiple-choice tests. So at the end of the semester I was not pulling together what I had learned—I was taking it apart. I broke down all the concepts into isolated facts, dates, treaties, and names, the stuff grades are made of. In the morning my class met for the exam. The professor handed out mimeographed questions. When I had filled in all the computer blocks, I turned in the answer sheet (silently, so as not to disturb those still working). Then I went home for vacation to recuperate. Two weeks later a postcard arrived from the professor. No inscription, not even a signature, just a scrawl: "Political Science 110, Grade: C."

As I talked with older, graduating friends it became clear that I had to 21 unpin my hopes from the university classroom. To think of going on to graduate school meant being professionalized into an academic automaton. A friend in dentistry was forced to shave his modest sideburns lest they "pick up infectious bacteria from the spray of the high-speed drill." Unless I was going to become an academic, a lawyer, a C.P.A. or some other carefully defined careerist, school was a liability. So I began to treat it as a part-time job. By no means was I a dropout, I still took my courses and passed. But like my friends I shifted my commitment outside the classroom. There were a variety of alternatives like S.D.S. and student government. As an aspiring writer I chose the student publications building and the campus paper, *The Michigan Daily*.

No prerequisites were required for admission to *The Daily*. There 22 were no examinations or term papers. The hours were ideal—noon to two a.m. A clattering A.P. machine kept *The Daily* contemporary as radical students and staffers engaged in endless discussions where I found both the intimacy and intellectualism lacking in the classroom. Nor was the paper bogged down in the academic seniority system. As a freshman I was sent to Selma to cover the civil-rights demonstrations and wrote numerous signed editorials on how to better mankind.

Outraged administrators accused *Daily* writers and radicals of 23 naïveté. I always felt the *Daily*'s most powerful weapon was its ability to unite the journalist's nose and the child's eye: applied to the stench and confusion of corporate university management, the combination was devastating. My own awakening came in following a tip about one of the most powerful Regents, Eugene Power, who ran a microfilm company with a parasitic relationship to the university's library. Power's firm, University Microfilms Inc., was converting 5000 "borrowed" books a week into salable microfilm copies. In addition, two special microfilm cameras had been installed in the UGLI to copy rare books, some of which would disappear off the shelves for months. When I asked the library director why Power's firm wasn't at least paying a fine for overdue materials, he didn't appreciate it. Regent Power himself stalled on an appointment for three weeks. Finally, flanked by obsequious aides, he sat down with me. He shed little light on his business affairs, ushered me out like a rebellious servant, and admonished, "Behave yourself, son." The story ran (despite a plea by the library director's physician that his coronary patient would suffer a fatal heart attack) and a subsequent attorney general's investigation found Power in conflict of interest. He resigned his post.

The other Regents were no improvement. They were absentee land- 24 lords who visited the plantation two days a month. Their ephemeral presence was the clue that the university was not run by its constituents, but by corporate ambassadors. Chauffeured limousines swept them off campus to deliberations in a baroque mansion blessed by tranquil oaks, rolling lawns, reflecting pools, and a panoramic view of the Huron River Valley. The deliberations normally began on Thursday. All decisions had to be completed by noon Friday in order to give the news service time to prepare releases in advance of the formal two p.m. "public meeting."

The public meetings were required by constitutional statute. The 25 vice-presidents offered faithful little soliloquies while the sleepier Regents dozed behind sunglasses. "A new French house is going into the Oxford Housing Unit," declared the Vice-President for Student Affairs. "Will there be French plumbing," inquired a Regent, convulsing his colleagues.

At first many students thought they could crack this anachronistic 26 structure with liberal administrative allies. It seemed logical that a bright young administrator could work from within to subvert the system to the benefit of the students. Accordingly student radicals worked hard to put a popular liberal psychology professor in office as Vice-President for Student Affairs. On taking office he promised to be a "vice-president presenting the student interest to the Regents and the President." But we soon learned otherwise.

When the House Un-American Activities Committee subpoenaed the 27 names of sixty-five students and faculty members of radical groups he gave in (and withheld announcement of the decision until after *The Daily* had suspended publication for the summer). He refused to honor a campus referendum that had gone two to one against the university's practice of ranking students for the draft. Then he tried to ban sit-ins and finally wound up making secret attempts to discipline S.D.S. leaders for anti-war protests.

Naturally, he was showered with abuse for having "sold out." But 28 rather than try to explain himself to students (he was, after all, still vice-president), he withdrew into his Danish-modern office and brooded. *Daily* reporters were denied interviews. Radicals noticed that he had even drawn the shades and locked his door to thwart imaginary sit-ins. Eventually he became tired of his role and quit, only to be rewarded by an appointment as special adviser on urban problems.

Like adults everywhere he wanted students to reinforce his own 29 expectations, confirm what his generation had done and stabilize his lifetime. At heart the campus administrators were only subtler versions of the forty-two-year-old Ann Arbor police lieutenant who arrested campus cinema leaders for showing a suggestive underground movie. His critical review seemed to be based less on artistic judgment than fear. "The students are going down the same path that caused the Roman Empire to fall," he explained. "When laws break down, that promotes anarchy which leads to dictatorship. Now think what that could do to a man like me. Say I'm in my twenty-fourth year on the police force here and

looking forward to my retirement pension after twenty-five years service. Some dictator could come and cancel that plan and I'd be out of
luck. That's why when you have a good system you have to support it."

But I hadn't signed up for any pension plan yet. Unlike the lieuten- 30
ant I was not committed to perpetuation of the Ann Arbor police. Unlike
the administration I was not committed to perpetuation of the university
in its present form. I saw that obedience to the school system required
people to forget about each other. One had to get out of school to be
human. For taking school seriously meant wrapping oneself up in a
meaningless schedule that did not allow time to know or talk to others. It
meant teachers knew their students better by their handwriting than their
faces. It meant students had to compete with each other needlessly on
the grade-point battlefield. It meant locked offices and silent libraries to
preclude conversation. College cut people instead of bringing them together.

I recall running into a favorite poetry teacher on pulling out of the 31
Thompson Street parking ramp at the end of a hectic day. For the past few
weeks I had unsuccessfully been trying to fit into his tight schedule. But
now we had our chance. We talked hurriedly through my car window
until impatient drivers honked me out of the six-story structure.

Still I tried to reassure myself from time to time—only to have the 32
truth thrown back at me. I remember the night I spent cramming for my
last set of finals with a friend. Lying bewildered on a couch amidst study
guides, Xeroxed notes, and dog-eared old exams I mused: "It's tough
now. But I'll bet twenty-five years from now we'll look back on these as
the best years of our life." My friend, wrestling with incompletes, a late
paper, and the final, could only grimace. "Go ahead and think that if it
makes you feel good. But my memory is better than that."

Disquieting thoughts for a graduation celebration—but they were 33
honest ones. When the party ended I took my parents back to the
airport, and devoted my last evening in Ann Arbor to packing. In the
basement I found forgotten piles of notebooks, paperbacks, love letters
and exams. The ash cans filled quickly, so at midnight I quietly piled the
overflow into a neighbor's backyard. The next morning I called a cab for
the airport. On the way out of town, there was a last sentimental stop.
The driver pulled up in front of UGLI and I raced inside to pay a $3.25
library fine which was blocking my diploma. Now I was free.

# Of This Time, of That Place

*Lionel Trilling*

*The final "primary reference" consists of a series of excerpts from a story published in 1943 by Lionel Trilling, a prominent professor of literature at Columbia University for many years. The excerpts dramatize the figures of the classroom and the office visit.*

. . . He reached the campus as the hour was striking. The students 1 were hurrying to their classes. He himself was in no hurry. He stopped at his dim cubicle of an office and lit a cigarette. The prospect of facing his class had suddenly presented itself to him and his hands were cold, the lawful seizure of power he was about to make seemed momentous. Waiting did not help. He put out his cigarette, picked up a pad of theme paper and went to his classroom.

As he entered, the rattle of voices ceased and the twenty-odd fresh- 2 men settled themselves and looked at him appraisingly. Their faces seemed gross, his heart sank at their massed impassivity, but he spoke briskly.

"My name is Howe," he said and turned and wrote it on the black- 3 board. The carelessness of the scrawl confirmed his authority. He went on, "My office is 412 Slemp Hall and my office hours are Monday, Wednesday, and Friday from eleven-thirty to twelve-thirty."

He wrote, "M., W., F., 11:30–12:30." He said, "I'll be very glad to 4 see any of you at that time. Or if you can't come then, you can arrange with me for some other time."

He turned again to the blackboard and spoke over his shoulder. "The 5 text for the course is Jarman's *Modern Plays*, revised edition. The Co-op has it in stock." He wrote the name, underlined "revised edition" and waited for it to be taken down in the new notebooks.

When the bent heads were raised again he began his speech of 6 prospectus. "It is hard to explain—," he said, and paused as they composed themselves. "It is hard to explain what a course like this is intended to do. We are going to try to learn something about modern literature and something about prose composition."

As he spoke, his hands warmed and he was able to look directly at 7 the class. Last year on the first day the faces had seemed just as cloddish, but as the term wore on they became gradually alive and quite likable. It did not seem possible that the same thing could happen again.

"I shall not lecture in this course," he continued. "Our work will be 8 carried on by discussion and we will try to learn by an exchange of opinion. But you will soon recognize that my opinion is worth more than anyone else's here.''

He remained grave as he said it, but two boys understood and 9 laughed. The rest took permission from them and laughed too. All Howe's private ironies protested the vulgarity of the joke but the laughter made him feel benign and powerful.

When the little speech was finished, Howe picked up the pad of 10 paper he had brought. He announced that they would write an extemporaneous theme. Its subject was traditional, ''Who I am and why I came to Dwight College.'' By now the class was more at ease and it gave a ritualistic groan of protest. Then there was a stir as fountain-pens were brought out and the writing arms of the chairs were cleared and the paper was passed about. At last all the heads bent to work and the room became still.

Howe sat idly at his desk. The sun shone through the tall clumsy 11 windows. The cool of the morning was already passing. There was a scent of autumn and of varnish, and the stillness of the room was deep and oddly touching. Now and then a student's head was raised and scratched in the old elaborate students' pantomime that calls the teacher to witness honest intellectual effort.

Suddenly a tall boy stood within the frame of the open door. ''Is 12 this,'' he said, and thrust a large nose into a college catalogue, ''is this the meeting place of English 1A? The section instructed by Dr. Joseph Howe?''

He stood on the very sill of the door, as if refusing to enter until he 13 was perfectly sure of all his rights. The class looked up from work, found him absurd and gave a low mocking cheer.

The teacher and the new student, with equal pointedness, ignored 14 the disturbance. Howe nodded to the boy, who pushed his head forward and then jerked it back in a wide elaborate arc to clear his brow of a heavy lock of hair. He advanced into the room and halted before Howe, almost at attention. In a loud clear voice he announced, ''I am Tertan, Ferdinand R., reporting at the direction of Head of Department Vincent.''

The heraldic formality of this statement brought forth another cheer. 15 Howe looked at the class with a sternness he could not really feel, for there was indeed something ridiculous about this boy. Under his displeased regard the rows of heads dropped to work again. Then he touched Tertan's elbow, led him up to the desk, and stood so as to shield their conversation from the class.

''We are writing an extemporaneous theme,'' he said. ''The subject 16 is, 'Who I am and why I came to Dwight College.' ''

He stripped a few sheets from the pad and offered them to the boy. 17 Tertan hesitated and then took the paper but he held it only tentatively.

As if with the effort of making something clear, he gulped, and a slow smile fixed itself on his face. It was at once knowing and shy.

"Professor," he said, "to be perfectly fair to my classmates"—he 18 made a large gesture over the room—"and to you"—he inclined his head to Howe—"this would not be for me an extemporaneous subject."

Howe tried to understand. "You mean you've already thought about 19 it—you've heard we always give the same subject? That doesn't matter."

Again the boy ducked his head and gulped. It was the gesture of one 20 who wishes to make a difficult explanation with perfect candor. "Sir," he said, and made the distinction with great care, "the topic I did not expect but I have given much ratiocination to the subject."

Howe smiled and said, "I don't think that's an unfair advantage. Just 21 go ahead and write."

Tertan narrowed his eyes and glanced sidewise at Howe. His strange 22 mouth smiled. Then in quizzical acceptance, he ducked his head, threw back the heavy dank lock, dropped into a seat with a great loose noise and began to write rapidly.

The room fell silent again and Howe resumed his idleness. When the 23 bell rang, the students who had groaned when the task had been set now groaned again because they had not finished. Howe took up the papers and held the class while he made the first assignment. When he dismissed it, Tertan bore down on him, his slack mouth held ready for speech.

"Some professors," he said, "are pedants. They are Dryasdusts. 24 However, some professors are free souls and creative spirits. Kant, Hegel, and Nietzsche were all professors." With this pronouncement he paused. "It is my opinion," he continued, "that you occupy the second category."

Howe looked at the boy in surprise and said with good-natured 25 irony, "With Kant, Hegel, and Nietzsche?"

Not only Tertan's hand and head but his whole awkward body 26 waved away the stupidity. "It is the kind and not the quantity of the kind," he said sternly.

Rebuked, Howe said as simply and seriously as he could, "It would 27 be nice to think so." He added, "Of course I am not a professor."

This was clearly a disappointment but Tertan met it. "In the French 28 sense," he said with composure. "Generically, a teacher."

Suddenly he bowed. It was such a bow, Howe fancied, as a stage- 29 director might teach an actor playing a medieval student who takes leave of Abelard—stiff, solemn, with elbows close to the body and feet together. Then, quite as suddenly, he turned and left.

A queer fish, and as soon as Howe reached his office he sifted 30 through the batch of themes and drew out Tertan's. The boy had filled many sheets with his unformed headlong scrawl. "Who am I?" he had begun. "Here, in a mundane, not to say commercialized academe, is asked the question which from time long immemorably out of mind has accreted doubts and thoughts in the psyche of man to pester him as a nuisance. Whether in St. Augustine (or Austin as sometimes called) or Miss Bashkirtsieff or Frederic Amiel or Empedocles, or in less lights of the intellect than these, this posed question has been ineluctable.''

Howe took out his pencil. He circled "academe" and wrote "vo- 31 cab," in the margin. He underlined "time long immemorably out of mind" and wrote "Diction!" But this seemed inadequate for what was wrong. He put down his pencil and read ahead to discover the principle of error in the theme. "Today as ever, in spite of gloomy prophets of the dismal science (economics) the question is uninvalidated. Out of the starry depths of heaven hurtles this spear of query demanding to be caught on the shield of the mind ere it pierces the skull and the limbs be unstrung.''

Baffled but quite caught, Howe read on. "Materialism, by which is 32 meant the philosophic concept and not the moral idea, provides no aegis against the question which lies beyond the tangible (metaphysics). Existence without alloy is the question presented. Environment and heredity relegated aside, the rags and old clothes of practical life discarded, the name and the instrumentality of livelihood do not, as the prophets of the dismal science insist on in this connection, give solution to the interrogation which not from the professor merely but veritably from the cosmos is given. I think, therefore I am (cogito etc.) but who am I? Tertan I am, but what is Tertan? Of this time, of that place, of some parentage, what does it matter?''

Existence without alloy: the phrase established itself. Howe put aside 33 Tertan's paper and at random picked up another. "I am Arthur J. Casebeer Jr." he read. "My father is Arthur J. Casebeer and my grandfather was Arthur J. Casebeer before him. My mother is Nina Wimble Casebeer. Both of them are college graduates and my father is in insurance. I was born in St. Louis eighteen years ago and we still make our residence there.''

Arthur J. Casebeer, who knew who he was, was less interesting than 34 Tertan, but more coherent. Howe picked up Tertan's paper again. It was clear that none of the routine marginal comments, no "sent. str." or "punct." or "vocab." could cope with this torrential rhetoric. He read ahead, contenting himself with underscoring the errors against the time when he should have the necessary "conference" with Tertan. . . .

II

The question was, At whose door must the tragedy be laid?   35
All night the snow had fallen heavily and only now was abating in 36 sparse little flurries. The windows were valanced high with white. It was very quiet, something of the quiet of the world had reached the class and

Howe found that everyone was glad to talk or listen. In the room there was a comfortable sense of pleasure in being human.

Casebeer believed that the blame for the tragedy rested with hered- 37 ity. Picking up the book he read, "The sins of the fathers are visited on their children." This opinion was received with general favor. Nevertheless Johnson ventured to say that the fault was all Pastor Manders' because the Pastor had made Mrs. Alving go back to her husband and was always hiding the truth. To this Hibbard objected with logic enough, "Well then, it was really all her husband's fault. He *did* all the bad things." De Witt, his face bright with an impatient idea, said that the fault was all society's. "By society I don't mean upper-crust society," he said. He looked around a little defiantly, taking in any members of the class who might be members of upper-crust society. "Not in that sense. I mean the social unit."

Howe nodded and said, "Yes, of course."                                    38

"If the society of the time had progressed far enough in science," De 39 Witt went on, "then there would be no problem for Mr. Ibsen to write about. Captain Alving plays around a little, gives way to perfectly natural biological urges, and he gets a social disease, a venereal disease. If the disease is cured, no problem. Invent salvarsan and the disease is cured. The problem of heredity disappears and li'l Oswald just doesn't get paresis. No paresis, no problem—no problem, no play."

This was carrying the ark into battle and the class looked at De Witt 40 with respectful curiosity. It was his usual way and on the whole they were sympathetic with his struggle to prove to Howe that science was better than literature. Still, there was something in his reckless manner that alienated them a little.

"Or take birth control, for instance," De Witt went on. "If Mrs. 41 Alving had had some knowledge of contraception, she wouldn't have had to have li'l Oswald at all. No li'l Oswald, no play."

The class was suddenly quieter. In the back row Stettenhover swung 42 his great football shoulders in a righteous sulking gesture, first to the right, then to the left. He puckered his mouth ostentatiously. Intellect was always ending up by talking dirty.

Tertan's hand went up and Howe said, "Mr. Tertan." The boy 43 shambled to his feet and began his long characteristic gulp. Howe made a motion with his fingers, as small as possible, and Tertan ducked his head and smiled in apology. He sat down. The class laughed. With more than half the term gone, Tertan had not been able to remember that one did not rise to speak. He seemed unable to carry on the life of the intellect without this mark of respect for it. To Howe the boy's habit of rising seemed to accord with the formal shabbiness of his dress. He never wore the casual sweaters and jackets of his classmates. Into the free and comfortable air of the college classroom he brought the stuffy sordid strictness of some crowded metropolitan high school.

"Speaking from one sense," Tertan began slowly, "there is no blame 44 ascribable. From the sense of determinism, who can say where the blame lies? The preordained is the preordained and it cannot be said without rebellion against the universe, a palpable absurdity."

In the back row Stettenhover slumped suddenly in his seat, his heels 45 held out before him, making a loud dry disgusted sound. His body sank until his neck rested on the back of his chair. He folded his hands across his belly and looked significantly out of the window, exasperated not only with Tertan but with Howe, with the class, with the whole system designed to encourage this kind of thing. There was a certain insolence in the movement and Howe flushed. As Tertan continued to speak, Howe walked casually toward the window and placed himself in the line of Stettenhover's vision. He stared at the great fellow, who pretended not to see him. There was so much power in the big body, so much contempt in the Greek-athlete face under the crisp Greek-athlete curls, that Howe felt almost physical fear. But at last Stettenhover admitted him to focus and under his disapproving gaze sat up with slow indifference. His eyebrows raised high in resignation, he began to examine his hands. Howe relaxed and turned his attention back to Tertan.

"Flux of existence," Tertan was saying, "produces all things, so that 46 judgment wavers. Beyond the phenomena, what? But phenomena are adumbrated and to them we are limited."

Howe saw it for a moment as perhaps it existed in the boy's mind— 47 the world of shadows which are cast by a great light upon a hidden reality as in the old myth of the Cave. But the little brush with Stettenhover had tired him and he said irritably, "But come to the point, Mr. Tertan."

He said it so sharply that some of the class looked at him curiously. 48 For three months he had gently carried Tertan through his verbosities, to the vaguely respectful surprise of the other students, who seemed to conceive that there existed between this strange classmate and their teacher some special understanding from which they were content to be excluded. Tertan looked at him mildly and at once came brilliantly to the point. "This is the summation of the play," he said and took up his book and read, " 'Your poor father never found any outlet for the overmastering joy of life that was in him. And I brought no holiday into his home, either. Everything seemed to turn upon duty and I am afraid I made your poor father's home unbearable to him, Oswald.' Spoken by Mrs. Alving."

Yes, that was surely the "summation" of the play and Tertan had hit 49 it, as he hit, deviously and eventually, the literary point of almost everything. But now, as always, he was wrapping it away from sight. "For most mortals," he said, "there are only joys of biological urgings, gross and crass, such as the sensuous Captain Alving. For certain few there are the transmutations beyond these to a contemplation of the utter whole."

Oh, the boy was mad. And suddenly the word, used in hyperbole, 50 intended almost for the expression of exasperated admiration, became literal. Now that the word was used, it became simply apparent to Howe that Tertan was mad.

It was a monstrous word and stood like a bestial thing in the room. 51 Yet it so completely comprehended everything that had puzzled Howe, it so arranged and explained what for three months had been perplexing him that almost at once its horror became domesticated. With this word Howe was able to understand why he had never been able to communicate to Tertan the value of a single criticism or correction of his wild, verbose themes. Their conferences had been frequent and long but had done nothing to reduce to order the splendid confusion of the boy's ideas. Yet, impossible though its expression was, Tertan's incandescent mind could always strike for a moment into some dark corner of thought.

And now it was suddenly apparent that it was not a faulty rhetoric 52 that Howe had to contend with. With his new knowledge he looked at Tertan's face and wondered how he could have so long deceived himself. Tertan was still talking and the class had lapsed into a kind of patient unconsciousness, a coma of respect for words which, for all that most of them knew, might be profound. Almost with a suffusion of shame, Howe believed that in some dim way the class had long ago had some intimation of Tertan's madness. He reached out as decisively as he could to seize the thread of Tertan's discourse before it should be entangled further.

"Mr. Tertan says that the blame must be put upon whoever kills the 53 joy of living in another. We have been assuming that Captain Alving was a wholly bad man, but what if we assume that he became bad only because Mrs. Alving, when they were first married, acted toward him in the prudish way she says she did?"

It was a ticklish idea to advance to freshmen and perhaps not 54 profitable. Not all of them were following.

"That would put the blame on Mrs. Alving herself, whom most of 55 you admire. And she herself seems to think so." He glanced at his watch. The hour was nearly over. "What do you think, Mr. De Witt?"

De Witt rose to the idea, wanted to know if society couldn't be 56 blamed for educating Mrs. Alving's temperament in the wrong way. Casebeer was puzzled, Stettenhover continued to look at his hands until the bell rang.

Tertan, his brows louring in thought, was making as always for a 57 private word. Howe gathered his books and papers to leave quickly. At this moment of his discovery and with the knowledge still raw, he could not engage himself with Tertan. Tertan sucked in his breath to prepare for speech and Howe made ready for the pain and confusion. But at that moment Casebeer detached himself from the group with which he had been conferring and which he seemed to represent. His constituency remained at a tactful distance. The mission involved the time of an assigned essay. Casebeer's presentation of the plea—it was based on the freshmen's heavy duties at the fraternities during Carnival Week—cut across Tertan's preparations for speech. "And so some of us fellows thought," Casebeer concluded with heavy solemnity, "that we could do a better job, give our minds to it more, if we had more time."

Tertan regarded Casebeer with mingled curiosity and revulsion. 58 Howe not only said that he would postpone the assignment but went on to talk about the Carnival and even drew the waiting constituency into the conversation. He was conscious of Tertan's stern and astonished stare, then of his sudden departure. . . .

Howe, as he lectured on the romantic poets, became conscious of 59 Blackburn emanating wrath. Blackburn did it well, did it with enormous dignity. He did not stir in his seat, he kept his eyes fixed on Howe in perfect attention, but he abstained from using his notebook, there was no mistaking what he proposed to himself as an attitude. His elbow on the writing-wing of the chair, his chin on the curled fingers of his hand, he was the embodiment of intellectual indignation. He was thinking his own thoughts, would give no public offense, yet would claim his due, was not to be intimidated. Howe knew that he would present himself at the end of the hour.

Blackburn entered the office without invitation. He did not smile, 60 there was no cajolery about him. Without invitation he sat down beside Howe's desk. He did not speak until he had taken the blue-book from his pocket. He said, "What does this mean, sir?"

It was a sound and conservative student tactic. Said in the usual way 61 it meant, "How could you have so misunderstood me?" or "What does this mean for my future in the course?" But there were none of the humbler tones in Blackburn's way of saying it.

Howe made the established reply, "I think that's for you to tell me."   62

Blackburn continued icy. "I'm sure I can't, sir."   63

There was a silence between them. Both dropped their eyes to the 64 blue-book on the desk. On its cover Howe had penciled: "F. This is very poor work."

Howe picked up the blue-book. There was always the possibility of 65 injustice. The teacher may be bored by the mass of papers and not wholly attentive. A phrase, even the student's handwriting, may irritate him unreasonably. "Well," said Howe, "let's go through it."

He opened the first page. "Now here: you write, 'In *The Ancient* 66 *Mariner*, Coleridge lives in and transports us to a honey-sweet world where all is rich and strange, a world of charm to which we can escape from the humdrum existence of our daily lives, the world of romance. Here, in this warm and honey-sweet land of charming dreams we can relax and enjoy ourselves.' "

Howe lowered the paper and waited with a neutral look for Black- 67 burn to speak. Blackburn returned the look boldly, did not speak, sat stolid and lofty. At last Howe said, speaking gently, "Did you mean that, or were you just at a loss for something to say?"

"You imply that I was just 'bluffing'?" The quotation marks hung 68 palpable in the air about the word.

"I'd like to know. I'd prefer believing that you were bluffing to 69 believing that you really thought this."

Blackburn's eyebrows went up. From the height of a great and firm- 70 based idea he looked at his teacher. He clasped the crags for a moment and then pounced, craftily, suavely. "Do you mean, Dr. Howe, that there aren't two opinions possible?"

It was superbly done in its air of putting all of Howe's intellectual life 71 into the balance. Howe remained patient and simple. "Yes, many opinions are possible, but not this one. Whatever anyone believes of *The Ancient Mariner*, no one can in reason believe that it represents a—a honey-sweet world in which we can relax."

"But that is what I *feel*, sir." 72

This was well done too. Howe said, "Look, Mr. Blackburn. Do you 73 really relax with hunger and thirst, the heat and the sea-serpents, the dead men with staring eyes, Life in Death and the skeletons? Come now, Mr. Blackburn."

Blackburn made no answer and Howe pressed forward. "Now you 74 say of Wordsworth, 'Of peasant stock himself, he turned from the effete life of the salons and found in the peasant the hope of a flaming revolution which would sweep away all the old ideas. This is the subject of his best poems.' "

Beaming at his teacher with youthful eagerness, Blackburn said, 75 "Yes, sir, a rebel, a bringer of light to suffering mankind. I see him as a kind of Prothemeus."

"A kind of what?" 76

"Prothemeus, sir." 77

"Think, Mr. Blackburn. We were talking about him only today and I 78 mentioned his name a dozen times. You don't mean Prothemeus. You mean—" Howe waited but there was no response.

"You mean Prometheus." 79

Blackburn gave no assent and Howe took the reins. "You've done a 80 bad job here, Mr. Blackburn, about as bad as could be done." He saw Blackburn stiffen and his genial face harden again. "It shows either a lack of preparation or a complete lack of understanding." He saw Blackburn's face begin to go to pieces and he stopped.

"Oh, sir," Blackburn burst out, "I've never had a mark like this 81 before, never anything below a B, never. A thing like this has never happened to me before."

It must be true, it was a statement too easily verified. Could it be that 82 other instructors accepted such flaunting nonsense? Howe wanted to end the interview. "I'll set it down to lack of preparation," he said. "I know you're busy. That's not an excuse but it's an explanation. Now suppose you really prepare and then take another quiz in two weeks. We'll forget this one and count the other."

Blackburn squirmed with pleasure and gratitude. "Thank you, sir. 83 You're really very kind, very kind."

Howe rose to conclude the visit. "All right then—in two weeks."       84

## For Discussion and Writing

1. Compare these pieces with your own experience. Has schooling changed very much in the 1980s from what it was in the 1940s or 1960s? What figures do you recognize? What aspects of the student's discourse do these authors ignore?

    Think about the way stereotypes function in life and the way they are used as organizing devices in literature, film, television. What *image* of teachers and students predominates in the popular media today? Can you think of any examples of times you have been treated as a "typical student" rather than as an individual?

    Has your experience of college lived up to your expectations?

2. As a group project, assemble all the figures identified in the individual papers on *Fragments of a Student's Discourse*. Distribute this composite thesaurus and use it, reversing the direction of Barthes's project, to tell the story of the "typical student." In other words, you should transform the alphabetized figures into a narrative or dramatic representation of the story you might tell in response to the question "How's school going?" or to the observation "College— the best years of your life."

# *The Signature*

Another leader in the development of textualism is the French philosopher Jacques Derrida. Like Roland Barthes, Derrida experiments with a kind of writing that combines creativity and criticism. He no longer wants to write *about* literature but *with* literature. The reason for this approach is the textualist belief that literature cannot be fully understood by the traditional methods of interpretation, description, and analysis. For the textualist, a work of literature becomes intelligible through imitation of the work's own principle of composition—that is, the critic explains the work by using the artist's compositional technique to produce a new text. The textualist no longer tries to tell artists or students what a work of literature means, but seeks to learn from literature how to write criticism. To write as a textualist one must transfer the artist's invention strategy from fiction or poetry to criticism or theory.

To test his theory that literature functions not only as an object of study but as a source of knowledge, Derrida designed an experiment involving one of the oldest and most honored topics in the humanistic tradition—"know thyself." In previous epochs, this project had been understood as an attempt to comprehend one's identity in terms of life experience by means of introspection. In our own time, in which language has become the model for explaining everything else, Derrida proposes to investigate not so much our identity in "life" but our identity in language—the identity not of our person but of our name.

By calling his experiment the "signature," Derrida reminds us of an ancient belief in the similarity or correspondence between the world outside and the interior life of a person, between the macro and micro worlds. The link mediating nature and society, joining one's biological existence to one's cultural experience, is language, with one's proper name bridging these dimensions of reality. The experiment includes the musical sense of "signature"—the set of signs at the beginning of a staff indicating the key (and/or time) of the piece. The letters of the proper name constitute the "key" in which one's life is played out. We shall be returning to Derrida's technique of the "signature" after an excursion through the world of names. We can begin with the question asked by Shakespeare's teenage heroine, Juliet.

# from *Romeo and Juliet* (II.ii.33–61)

## *William Shakespeare*

### *What's in a Name*

*The scene is set in the Italian city of Verona, four centuries ago. In a dark corner of the orchard behind the house of the Capulet family stands Romeo, young son of the Capulets' bitter enemies, the Montagues. He has just met and fallen in love with the Capulet daughter Juliet. At that moment Juliet comes to a window of the house (or out on a balcony, as it is often staged) brooding to herself about this young Montague, who has obviously caught her fancy.*

*This is, of course, one of the most famous love scenes in all of literature—but we ask you to read it in another way, as a scene about language: specifically, as an interrogation of the relationship between words and things. We pick up the action just as Juliet's frustration bursts out in speech. She is not aware, of course, that the person on her mind is actually lurking in her father's orchard, where he will hear every word she says.*

*Juliet*  O Romeo, Romeo! wherefore art thou Romeo?
Deny thy father and refuse thy name;
Or, if thou wilt not, be but sworn my love,
And I'll no longer be a Capulet.
*Romeo [aside]* Shall I hear more, or shall I speak at this?          5
*Juliet* 'Tis but thy name that is my enemy.
Thou art thyself, though not a Montague.
What's Montague? It is nor hand, nor foot,
Nor arm, nor face, nor any other part
Belonging to a man. O, be some other name!          10
What's in a name? That which we call a rose
By any other name would smell as sweet.
So Romeo would, were he not Romeo called,
Retain that dear perfection which he owes
Without that title. Romeo, doff thy name;          15
And for thy name, which is no part of thee,
Take all myself.
*Romeo*        I take thee at thy word.
Call me but love, and I'll be new baptized;
Henceforth I never will be Romeo.          20
*Juliet* What man art thou that, thus bescreened in night,
So stumblest on my counsel?

*Romeo*          By a name
I know not how to tell thee who I am.
My name, dear saint, is hateful to myself,                                25
Because it is an enemy to thee.
Had I it written, I would tear the word.
*Juliet* My ears have yet not drunk a hundred words
Of thy tongue's uttering, yet I know the sound.
Art thou not Romeo, and a Montague?                                30
*Romeo* Neither, fair maid, if either thee dislike.

## For Discussion and Writing

1.  Make a list of all the statements about names in the text. Separate
    them into statements about proper names (Romeo, Montague) and
    statements about common nouns (rose, love). First, try to put each
    statement into your own words. Then discuss the larger implications
    of each statement. What assumptions about the way names work are
    being made by the speaker?

2.  What aspects of names and naming are causing the problems here?
    What can and cannot be changed with respect to names? Could we
    call a rose something else? Try to imagine how you might go about
    changing the common name for something. What about proper
    names? What does it mean to be "Romeo, and a Montague"?

### The History of Names

*The material we have collected here is designed to provide you
with background on the subject of proper names, before you undertake
some research into your own.*

# Names and Magic
# (from *Language and Myth*)

### *Ernst Cassirer*

As the Word is first in origin, it is also supreme in power. Often it is    1
the *name* of the deity, rather than the god himself, that seems to be the
real source of efficacy. Knowledge of the name gives him who knows it
mastery even over the being and will of the god. Thus a familiar Egyptian

legend tells how Isis, the great sorceress, craftily persuaded the sun-god Ra to disclose his name to her, and how through possession of the name she gained power over him and over all the other gods. In many other ways, too, Egyptian religious life in all its phases evinces over and over again this belief in the supremacy of the name and the magic power that dwells in it. The ceremonies attending the anointment of kings are governed by minute prescriptions for the transference of the god's several names to the Pharaoh; each name conveys a special attribute, a new divine power.

Moreover, this motive plays a decisive role in the Egyptian doctrines of the soul and its immortality. The souls of the departed, starting on their journey to the land of the dead, must be given not only their physical possessions, such as food and clothing, but also a certain outfit of a magical nature: this consists chiefly of the names of the gatekeepers in the nether world, for only the knowledge of these names can unlock the doors of Death's kingdom. Even the boat in which the dead man is conveyed, and its several parts, the rudder, the mast, etc., demand that he call them by their right names; only by virtue of this appellation can he render them willing and subservient and cause them to take him to his destination. 2

The essential identity between the word and what it denotes becomes even more patently evident if we look at it not from the objective standpoint, but from a subjective angle. For even a person's ego, his very self and personality, is indissolubly linked, in mythic thinking, with his name. Here the name is never a mere symbol, but is part of the personal property of its bearer; property which must be carefully protected, and the use of which is exclusively and jealously reserved to him. Sometimes it is not only his name, but also some other verbal denotation, that is thus treated as a physical possession, and as such may be acquired and usurped by someone else. Georg von der Gabelentz, in his book on the science of language, mentions the edict of a Chinese emperor of the third century B.C., whereby a pronoun in the first person, that had been legitimately in popular use, was henceforth reserved to him alone. And the name may even acquire a status above the more or less accessory one of a personal possession, when it is taken as a truly substantial Being, an integral *part* of its bearer. As such it is in the same category as his body or his soul. It is said of the Eskimos that for them man consists of three elements—body, soul, and name. And in Egypt, too, we find a similar conception, for there the physical body of man was thought to be accompanied, on the one hand, by his Ka, or double, and, on the other, by his name, as a sort of spiritual double. And of all these three elements it is just the last-mentioned which becomes more and more the expression of a man's "self," of his "personality." Even in far more advanced cultures this connection between name and personality continues to be 3 felt. When, in Roman law, the concept of the "legal person" was formally articulated, and this status was denied to certain physical subjects, those subjects were also denied official possession of a proper name. Under Roman law a slave had no legal name, because he could not function as a legal person.

In other ways, too, the unity and uniqueness of the name is not only    4
a mark of the unity and uniqueness of the person, but actually constitutes it; the name is what first makes man an individual. Where this verbal distinctiveness is not found, there the outlines of his personality tend also to be effaced. Among the Algonquins, a man who bears the same name as some given person is regarded as the latter's other self, his alter ego. If, in accordance with a prevalent custom, a child is given the name of his grandfather, this expresses the belief that the grandfather is resurrected, reincarnated in the boy. As soon as a child is born, the problem arises which one of his departed ancestors is reborn in him; only after this has been determined by the priest can the ceremony be performed whereby the infant receives that progenitor's name.

# Names and Professions
## (from *Destiny in Names*)

### *A. A. Roback*

It is well known that most of our surnames are derived from the    1
occupation of an individual's progenitors. Thus we have Smith and Baker and Taylor and Butcher, Fisher, and Clark and all the rest. Since the decline of the guilds, and the free choice of a person's calling, it would become quite uncommon to find a man actually in the vocation desig-nated by his surname. Occasionally, especially among Jews, we might find a dynasty of cantors, musicians, who preserve the rationale of their surname (Eddie Cantor, Zimbalist, and Fiedler are several illustrations of such namings), and the Cohens, Kahns, Kohns, Kagans, Kaplans, Katzes (abbreviation of *Kohen Tzedek*, "righteous priest"), are still to be re-garded, for religious purposes, priests, descended from Aaron, the first of the caste, but most of them are not aware of their function and keep assimilating their name to something in keeping with the name-patterns of the ruling culture. (Coan, Conway, Cowan, Kuhn, Coburn, Kane, etc.)

If, then, after many removes from the original bearer, we still find, as    2
if through an atavistic throwback, an individual whose name corre-sponds with his profession, we think of it as a curiosity. That General

Marshall should have risen to the first place in the American army, which, in European countries, would earn for him the title of Chief Marshal, is certainly a notable coincidence, if destiny plays no part here. Or let us, for a moment, scan the name of the man who led all the forces against the Nazis and succeeded in squelching their power through the invasion of France. Is it not worth reflecting that this man's surname is "a hewer of iron" (*Eisenhower* is, in the original German, *Eisenhauer*)? If an honorific sobriquet were to be pondered for the purpose, in recognition of his feat, it could not be more appropriate than the name which he actually inherited. Surely it is just as fitting as the nickname Martel, i.e., "the hammer," which was given to Charles, grandfather of Charlemagne, in celebration of his victory over the Saracens. Another of our first-line generals, Van Fleet, does not seem to be quite at home, onomastically, but after all the fleet and the army are only complementary to one another.

This interlinking, or rather cross linking, is not rare with the army, 3 air force, and navy. We can cite, e.g., Bryant L. M. Boatner, commanding general of the air proving grounds, as one illustration, while his brother, H. J. Boatner, who has become a major general, is not out of place as a high land officer. In W. M. Fechteler (in German *fechten* means to fight), commander-in-chief of the Atlantic Fleet, we have another patronymic worthy of its bearer and vice versa.

All these are names with which any newspaper reader must be 4 familiar. A full list of the high ranking officers in the armed forces would, no doubt, disclose many more such coincidences.

In a sphere far removed from warfare and destruction we have a 5 more agreeable circumstance in the name of Pissarev ("writer") the famous Russian critic and that of Sir Russell Brain, probably the most eminent authority on the nervous system, and particularly the brain. Inasmuch as Brain is such an uncommon name, there must be something more than coincidence in this correspondence. In an adjacent sphere, we have the name of Freud, who tells us that because of his sex theories, his name, a contraction of *Freude*, meaning joy, was used as a taunt by his bitter opponents, associating it with the *filles de joie*, in other words implying that his scientific profession coincided with the world's oldest profession.

## For Discussion and Writing

1. Whether or not a name determines one's destiny, there is evidence that people do form an impression of someone based on that person's name. It was recently reported in the newspapers that half the businessmen on Little Tokyo Street in Los Angeles did not want it renamed after *Challenger* astronaut Ellison Onizuka (killed in the

shuttle explosion). One reason for this opposition had to do with Onizuka's name. Although it is a fairly common Japanese surname, the archaic meaning of Onizuka is "place where the devil lives." More troubling are the studies that show a student's name influences the grade a paper receives (papers signed with common, strong names receive higher marks than those signed with odd, unusual names). Anyone who has ever been teased about his or her name (and who has not at some time during childhood?) knows that we are vulnerable through our names, that our name is an important feature of our identity. Write or tell an anecdote about such teasing, either that you experienced yourself or that you witnessed.

2. You know something about names in general. What do you know about your own names—or what can you find out? Using your library's resources (where you should find information on specific proper names and family names) and calling upon older members of your family, find out what you can about the meaning and history of the names you use regularly. If your names mean something in some other language, find out about that, too. (Don't neglect nicknames and pet names.) Assemble your material so that you can present information about your names in the form of an oral or written report. And *save this material.* You will be using it more creatively later on.

### The Power of Names

*Here are two discussions of the power of names. The first is a brief selection from an autobiographical essay by the well-known black writer Ralph Ellison in which he reveals his full name and discusses its significance and its influence on his own life. The second is from a book on women and language by the social critic Dale Spender, who shows how the absence of names affects the place of women in history, and how titles like "Mr." and "Mrs." reveal structures of cultural power.*

# from "Hidden Name and Complex Fate"

## *Ralph Ellison*

Let Tar Baby, that enigmatic figure from Negro folklore, stand for the 1
world. He leans, black and gleaming, against the wall of life utterly
noncommittal under our scrutiny, our questioning, starkly unmoving
before our naïve attempts at intimidation. Then we touch him playfully
and before we can say *Sonny Liston*! we find ourselves stuck. Our playful
investigations become a labor, a fearful struggle, an *agon*. Slowly we
perceive that our task is to learn the proper way of freeing ourselves to
develop, in other words, technique.

Sensing this, we give him our sharpest attention, we question him 2
carefully, we struggle with more subtlety; while he, in his silent way,
holds on, demanding that we perceive the necessity of calling him by his
true name as the price of our freedom. It is unfortunate that he has so
many, many "true names"—all spelling chaos; and in order to discover
even one of these we must first come into the possession of our own
names. For it is through our names that we first place ourselves in the
world. Our names, being the gift of others, must be made our own.

Once while listening to the play of a two-year-old girl who did not 3
know she was under observation, I heard her saying over and over again,
at first with questioning and then with sounds of growing satisfaction, "I
am Mimi Livisay? . . . *I* am Mimi Livisay. I *am* Mimi Livisay . . . I am *Mimi*
Li-vi-say! I am Mimi . . ."

And in deed and in fact she was—or became so soon thereafter, by 4
working playfully to establish the unit between herself and her name.

For many of us this is far from easy. We must learn to wear our names 5
within all the noise and confusion of the environment in which we find
ourselves; make them the center of all of our associations with the world,
with man and with nature. We must charge them with all our emotions,
our hopes, hates, loves, aspirations. They must become our masks and
our shields and the containers of all those values and traditions which we
learn and/or imagine as being the meaning of our familial past.

And when we are reminded so constantly that we bear, as Negroes, 6
names originally possessed by those who owned our enslaved grandparents, we are apt, especially if we are potential writers, to be more than
ordinarily concerned with the veiled and mysterious events, the fusions
of blood, the furtive couplings, the business transactions, the violations
of faith and loyalty, the assaults; yes, and the unrecognized and unrecog-
nizable loves through which our names were handed down unto us.

So charged with emotion does this concern become for some of us, 7 that we have, earlier, the example of the followers of Father Divine and, now, the Black Muslims, discarding their original names in rejection of the bloodstained, the brutal, the sinful images of the past. Thus they would declare new identities, would clarify a new program of intention and destroy the verbal evidence of a willed and ritualized discontinuity of blood and human intercourse.

Not all of us, actually only a few, seek to deal with our names in this 8 manner. We take what we have and make of them what we can. And there are even those who know where the old broken connections lie, who recognize their relatives across the chasm of historical denial and the artificial barriers of society, and who see themselves as bearers of many of the qualities which were admirable in the original sources of their common line (Faulkner has made much of this); and I speak here not of mere forgiveness, nor of obsequious insensitivity to the outrages symbolized by the denial and the division, but of the conscious acceptance of the harsh realities of the human condition, of the ambiguities and hypocrisies of human history as they have played themselves out in the United States.

Perhaps, taken in aggregate, these European names which (some- 9 times with irony, sometimes with pride, but always with personal investment) represent a certain triumph of the spirit, speaking to us of those who rallied, reassembled and transformed themselves and who under dismembering pressures refused to die. "Brothers and sisters," I once heard a Negro preacher exhort, "let us make up our faces before the world, and our names shall sound throughout the land with honor! For we ourselves are our *true* names, not their epithets! So let us, I say, Make Up Our Faces and Our Minds!"

Perhaps my preacher had read T. S. Eliot, although I doubt it. And in 10 actuality, it was unnecessary that he do so, for a concern with names and naming was very much part of that special area of American culture from which I come, and it is precisely for this reason that this example should come to mind in a discussion of my own experience as a writer.

Undoubtedly, writers begin their *conditioning* as manipulators of 11 words long before they become aware of literature—certain Freudians would say at the breast. Perhaps. But if so, that is far too early to be of use at this moment. Of this, though, I am certain: that despite the misconceptions of those educators who trace the reading difficulties experienced by large numbers of Negro children in Northern schools to their Southern background, these children are, in *their* familiar South, facile manipulators of words. I know, too, that the Negro community is deadly in its ability to create nicknames and to spot all that is ludicrous in an unlikely name or that which is incongruous in conduct. Names are not qualities; nor are words, in this particular sense, actions. To assume that they are could cost one his life many times a day. Language skills depend to a large extent upon a knowledge of the details, the manners, the objects, the folkways, the psychological patterns, of a given environment. Humor and wit depend upon much the same awareness, and so does the suggestive power of names.

"A small brown bowlegged Negro with the name 'Franklin D. Roo- 12 sevelt Jones' might sound like a clown to someone who looks at him from the outside," said my friend Albert Murray, "but on the other hand he just might turn out to be a hell of a fireside operator. He might just lie back in all of that comic juxtaposition of names and manipulate you deaf, dumb and blind—and you not even suspecting it, because you're thrown out of stance by his name! There you are, so dazzled by the F.D.R. image—which you *know* you can't see—and so delighted with your own superior position that you don't realize that it's *Jones* who must be confronted."

Well, as you must suspect, all of this speculation on the matter of 13 names has a purpose, and now, because it is tied up so ironically with my own experience as a writer, I must turn to my own name.

For in the dim beginnings, before I ever thought consciously of 14 writing, there was my own name, and there was, doubtless, a certain magic in it. From the start I was uncomfortable with it, and in my earliest years it caused me much puzzlement. Neither could I understand what a poet was, nor why, exactly, my father had chosen to name me after one. Perhaps I could have understood it perfectly well had he named me after his own father, but that name had been given to an older brother who died and thus was out of the question. But why hadn't he named me after a hero, such as Jack Johnson, or a soldier like Colonel Charles Young, or a great seaman like Admiral Dewey, or an educator like Booker T. Washington, or a great orator and abolitionist like Frederick Douglass? Or again, why hadn't he named me (as so many Negro parents had done) after President Teddy Roosevelt?

Instead, he named me after someone called Ralph Waldo Emerson, 15 and then, when I was three, he died. It was too early for me to have understood his choice, although I'm sure he must have explained it many times, and it was also too soon for me to have made the connection between my name and my father's love for reading. Much later, after I began to write and work with words, I came to suspect that he was aware of the suggestive powers of names and of the magic involved in naming.

I recall an odd conversation with my mother during my early teens 16 in which she mentioned their interest in, of all things, prenatal culture! But for a long time I actually knew only that my father read a lot, and that he admired this remote Mr. Emerson, who was something called a "poet and philosopher"—so much so that he named his second son after him.

I knew, also, that whatever his motives, the combination of names 17 he'd given me caused me no end of trouble from the moment when I could talk well enough to respond to the ritualized question which grownups put to very young children. Emerson's name was quite familiar to Negroes in Oklahoma during those days when World War I was brewing, and adults, eager to show off their knowledge of literary figures, and obviously amused by the joke implicit in such a small brown nubbin of a boy carrying around such a heavy moniker, would invariably repeat my first two names and then to my great annoyance, they'd add "Emerson."

And I, in my confusion, would reply, "No, *no, I'm* not Emerson, he's  18 the little boy who lives next door." Which only made them laugh all the louder. "Oh no," they'd say, "*you're* Ralph Waldo Emerson," while I had fantasies of blue murder.

For a while the presence next door of my little friend, Emerson,  19 made it unnecessary for me to puzzle too often over this peculiar adult confusion. And since there were other Negro boys named Ralph in the city, I came to suspect that there was something about the combination of names which produced their laughter. Even today I know of only one other Ralph who had as much comedy made out of his name, a campus politician and deep-voiced orator whom I knew at Tuskegee, who was called in friendly ribbing, *Ralph Waldo Emerson Edgar Allan Poe*, spelled Powe. This must have been quite a trial for him, but I had been initiated much earlier.

During my early school years the name continued to puzzle me, for  20 it constantly evoked in the faces of others some secret. It was as though I possessed some treasure or some defect, which was invisible to my own eyes and ears; something which I had but did not *possess*, like a piece of property in South Carolina, which was mine but which I could not have until some future time. I recall finding, about this time, while seeking adventure in back alleys—which possess for boys a superiority over playgrounds like that which kitchen utensils possess over toys designed for infants—a large photographic lens. I remember nothing of its optical qualities, of its speed or color correction, but it gleamed with crystal mystery and it was beautiful.

Mounted handsomely in a tube of shiny brass, it spoke to me of  21 distant worlds of possibility. I played with it, looking through it with squinted eyes, holding it in shafts of sunlight, and tried to use it for a magic lantern. But most of this was as unrewarding as my attempts to make the music come from a phonograph record by holding the needle in my fingers.

I could burn holes through newspapers with it, or I could pretend  22 that it was a telescope, the barrel of a cannon, or the third eye of a monster—*I* being the monster—but I could do nothing at all about its proper function of making images, nothing to make it yield its secret. But I could not discard it.

Older boys sought to get it away from me by offering knives or tops, 23 agate marbles or whole zoos of grass snakes and horned toads in trade, but I held on to it. No one, not even the white boys I knew, had such a lens, and it was my own good luck to have found it. Thus I would hold on to it until such time as I could acquire the parts needed to make it function. Finally I put it aside and it remained buried in my box of treasures, dusty and dull, to be lost and forgotten as I grew older and became interested in music.

I had reached by now the grades where it was necessary to learn 24 something about Mr. Emerson and what he had written, such as the "Concord Hymn" and the essay "Self-Reliance," and in following his advice, I reduced the "Waldo" to a simple and, I hoped, mysterious "W.," and in my own reading I avoided his works like the plague. I could no more deal with my name—I shall never really master it—than I could find a creative use for my lens. Fortunately there were other problems to occupy my mind. . . .

# The Male Line (from *Man Made Language*)

## *Dale Spender*

Studies of language have revealed that semantics is only one of the 1 forms through which sexism operates. . . . One of the other features of English language practices which is inherently sexist is the use of names. In our society "only men have real names" in that their names are permanent and they have "accepted the permanency of their names as one of the rights of being male." . . . This has both practical and psychological ramifications for the construction—and maintenance—of male supremacy.

Practically it means that women's family names do not count and 2 that there is one more device for making women invisible. Fathers pass their names on to their sons and the existence of daughters can be denied when in the absence of a male heir it is said that a family "dies out." One other direct result of this practice of only taking cognizance of the male name has been to facilitate the development of history as the story of the male line, because it becomes almost impossible to trace the ancestry of

women—particularly if they do not come into the male-defined categories of importance.

Very little is known about women, says Virginia Woolf . . . for "the 3
history of England is the history of the male line" . . . this point was
brought home to Jill Liddington and Jill Norris . . . when they undertook
to document the story of women's suffrage in Lancashire for "this vital
contribution had been largely neglected by historians." . . . They had
difficulty with sources and one difficulty was not one which would be
encountered in tracing men . . . :

> Sometimes we seemed to be forever chasing down blind alleys.
> For instance, one of the most active women, Helen Silcock, a
> weavers' union leader from Wigan, seemed to disappear after 1902.
> We couldn't think why, until we came across a notice of 'congratula-
> tions to Miss Silcock on her marriage to Mr Fairhurst' in a little
> known labour journal, the *Women's Trade Union Review* . . . it was
> an object lesson for us in the difficulties of tracing women activists.

It is also an extremely useful device for eliminating women from
history and for making it exceedingly difficult to perceive a continuum
and develop a tradition.

When females have no right to "surnames," to family names of their 4
own, the concept of women as the property of men is subtly reinforced
(and this is of course assisted by the title *Mrs.*). Currently many women
are changing their names and instead of taking the name of either their
father or their husband they are coining new, autonomous names for
themselves; for example, Cheris Kramer has become Cheris Kramarae,
Julia Stanley has become Julia Penelope—there are almost countless
examples of this change. A common practice has become that of taking
the first name of a close female friend or relative—such as mother—as the
new family name (for example, Janet Robyn, Elizabeth Sarah). When
asked why she had legally dropped her surname and retained her first
two given names, Margaret Sandra stated that a "surname" was intended
as an indication of the "sire" and was so closely linked socially with the
ownership of women that there was no "surname" that she found acceptable.

Although attempts have been made to trivialize these new naming 5
activities among women, such activities are serious and they do undermine patriarchal practices. At the very least they raise consciousness
about the role men's names have played in the subordination of women,
and at best they confound traditional patriarchal classification schemes
which have not operated in women's interest. I have been told that it
makes it very difficult to "pigeon-hole" women, to "place" them, if they
persist with this neurotic practice of giving themselves new names. One

male stated quite sincerely that it was becoming "jolly difficult to work out whether women were married these days because of the ridiculous practice of not taking their husband's names." In order to operate in the world, however, it has *never* been necessary to know from a name whether someone is married or single, as women can testify. Men have not thought that *not* changing their name upon marriage should present difficulties to women and once more the bias of language practices is revealed.

But many males are confused, and not without cause. The language 6 has helped to create the representation of females as sex objects; it has also helped to signal when a sex object is not available and is the property of another male. The patriarchal order has been maintained by such devices and when women consciously and intentionally abolish them men have reason to feel insecure; they do not however have reason to protest.

There are also other "by-products" of this process of permitting the 7 permanency of names only to males. Miller and Swift . . . ask whether it is because of the unenduring nature of female family names that much more emphasis is placed on their first names. Whatever the reason, it is clear that males are more frequently addressed by their family name (and title) and women by their first name. Psychologically this can also work to produce sexual asymmetry.

The use of first names can be evidence of intimacy or friendship but 8 in such circumstances the practice, generally speaking, has to be reciprocal. When one party is referred to by the first name, and the other by the family name and title, it is usually evidence that one has more power than the other. So, for example, the employer may be Mr. Smith and the employees Bill and Mary. The practice of those "in power" referring to those "out of power" by their first names—while still retaining the use of their own title and family name—is widespread and applies to both sexes in a hierarchical society. But there are still instances where both sexes occupy comparable positions but where males are referred to by their family names and women referred to by their first names, indicating the operation of yet another hierarchy.

This is frequently illustrated in the media. Even where there are both 9 male and female contestants on some "quiz" shows, the women are more likely to be addressed by their first names. Interviewers are also more inclined to use women's first names. News items are more likely to make reference to women by their first name (and of course their colouring, for example, blonde or brunette, and their age and marital status) and the usually male presenter of "talk-back" shows indicates a decided disposition to discriminate between the callers in this way.

But it is not confined to the media. I have never heard a male com- 10 plain that a medical practitioner addressed him (perhaps patronizingly) by his first name at the first consultation, yet this protest is often made by women. It would, however, break the social rules which govern subordination if women were to respond by addressing medical practitioners by their first names. This is precisely why I think they should do so.

Regardless of the reason for the development of this practice of 11 calling women by their first names in formal situations, it assists in making "visible" the subordination of the female.

The practice of labeling women as married or single also serves 12 supremely sexist ends. It conveniently signals who is "fair game" from the male point of view. There is tension between the representation of women as sex objects and the male ownership rights over women and this has been resolved by an explicit and most visible device of designating the married status of women. As women do not "own" men, and as men have many dimensions apart from their sexual ones in a patriarchal order, it has not been necessary to make male marital status visible. On the contrary, it could hinder rather than help male operations in the world, so it has never appeared as a "logical" proposition.

Contrary to the belief of many people, the current usage of *Miss* and 13 *Mrs.* is relatively recent, for until the beginning of the nineteenth century the title *Miss* was usually reserved for young females while *Mrs.* designated mature women. Marital status played no role in the use of these terms. How and why this usage changed is a matter of some speculation,[1] but there is nothing speculative about the ends that it serves.

It labels women for the convenience of men. It also labels those 14 whom men do not want. To be over thirty and *Miss* Jones in times but recently passed was an advertisement of failure and an invitation for ridicule.

[1] Miller and Swift (1976) suggest that the use of *Miss* and *Mrs.* to designate marital status was a response to some of the pressures created by the industrial revolution, which disrupted the familiar patterns of small communities in which relationships were readily known. There was no need for this usage prior to the industrial revolution for a woman's marital status was already known in the community in which she lived, but with the migration of population that occurred at the onset of the revolution and with women's entry into the workforce outside the home or local community,

a simple means of distinguishing married from unmarried women was needed [for men] and it served a double purpose: it supplied at least a modicum of information about women's sexual availability, and it applied not so subtle pressure toward marriage by lumping single women with the young and inexperienced. Attached to anyone over the age of eighteen, Miss came in time to suggest the unattractive or socially undesirable qualities associated with such labels as *old maid* and *spinster* or that dreadful word *barren*. So the needs of patriarchy were served when a woman's availability for her primary role as helper and sexual partner was made an integral part of her identity—in effect, a part of her name (p. 99).

The question arises as to why more women have not objected to this 15 offensive labeling in the past. Why was there not greater protest when in the late nineteenth century women were required to surrender even more of themselves and their identity and to become not just Mrs. *Jane* Smith, but Mrs. *John* Smith? (Casey Miller and Kate Swift point out that there would have been bewilderment if a letter had ever arrived addressed to Mrs. *George* Washington.)

It is I think a mark of the identity options open to women in a 16 patriarchal order that so many women voluntarily and even enthusiastically seek to be labeled as the property of a male. The title *Mrs.* and the abandonment of their father's name (a name which required no effort on their part and could not be construed as an achievement) for their husband's name, appears to confirm their identity. In a patriarchal society it is not unrealistic to perceive that security lies in marriage—even if this is eventually revealed as a myth. That so many women continue to choose to be Mrs. Jack Smart and to become "invisible" is an indication of the success of patriarchal ideology.

This is why the refusal of some women to be designated *Mrs.* is 17 significant. To insist on the title *Ms.* (if titles are unavoidable) does undermine some of the patriarchal practices. If the strength of the resistance is proportionate to the danger posed by the strategy then it is clear that some individuals are aware of the subversive influence of the use of *Ms.*

Numerous arguments other than the fundamental one have been 18 advanced to substantiate the undesirability of the term *Ms.* and they share the common features of being inadequate and illogical—and even absurd. For example, one reason that has been given is that the pronunciation of *Ms.* cannot be determined by its spelling. This is a non-starter in English. If we were to find unacceptable all those words which do not reveal their pronunciation from their spelling we would have to dispense with a sizeable number and we could begin with *Mr.* and *Mrs.*

The (unstated) reason for the undesirability of *Ms.* is that it is of no 19 assistance in the maintenance of the patriarchal order and it can even be problematic for males. Again, this is why I think it extremely important that all women should make use of it as a title—if we are to persist with titles.

# For Discussion and Writing

1. Consider any points in these two excerpts that seem to you especially interesting, surprising, or controversial. See if your classmates agree with your judgment. Try to resolve any differences.

2. What can you find out about the female names in your own heritage? How far back can you go beyond your mother, her mother, and so on? Do you have equal information about the male and female parts of your heritage? Note any interesting names from the female side of your family. Compare your findings with those of others.

3. Consider some of the aspects of naming raised by Ellison. Do you know anyone whose last name was acquired at some recent point in history (for example, through Americanization or religious conversion)? Do you know anyone descended from slaves whose name comes from the family that owned the person's ancestors? Do you know of any well-known people who have changed their names? Have you ever heard of a *nom de plume*, or pen name? How many actors and musicians use their "own" names? What is one's "own" name? Have we "problematized" for you the notion of having a name of one's own?

   If you could have any names you wanted, with no fuss, what names would you take? Why? If you decided to change your names in actuality, would there be a fuss? Who would make it? Why?

   Do you know anyone named after a famous person? If so, how has this affected his or her life? Would you like to bear a famous name? Do you believe that names are important? What's in a name?

### Writing from Signatures

Let us begin with a brief discussion of the ancient practice of *blazoning*. In 1484 King Richard III of England chartered the Herald's College, whose purpose was to assign coats of arms and trace lineages. Within a century a set of rules for *blazoning* (giving a concise verbal description of a shield bearing a coat of arms) had been standardized. Aristocratic families all had a coat of arms, and the practice continues today, with coats of arms being displayed by Colleges and Universities, fraternal organizations and business. There are even people who will provide an "authentic" coat of arms for any of us willing to pay for such a thing.

Derrida's signature experiment is in part an adaptation to the generation (note the pun on lineage) of texts out of one's names of the techniques originally developed for representing symbolically on a shield the lineage of a family name. Some of the terms you will encounter when reading Derrida are derived from the art of heraldry. Besides the term "blazon," Derrida also refers to the "abyss," which means in this context the central point or heart of the shield. A coat of arms often contains at the abyss point a miniature shield representing the paternal (most important) coat of arms (or sometimes the arms of a line to which the "armiger" held a claim). The shield within a shield creates an effect of infinite regression, like that of the label on Morton salt, with the girl pictured holding a package of the salt with a label also picturing the girl holding the package, and so on. The implication of this "putting into the abyss" for the experiment is that the microcosm (in this case the name of the author) constitutes a representation of the macrocosm (the work written by the one who signs that name).

The designers of coats of arms used poetic techniques such as the pun and the rebus. The mottoes inscribed on banners draped above or below the shield, for example, frequently were based on a pun on the family name (replacing the war cries of days of old). The Seton family motto is "Set On." The Bernard family, whose shield bore the image of a bear, covered by a crest with a smaller bear, had the motto "Bear and Forbear." The Winlaw's motto is "What I Win I Keep." The best known of such mottoes is that of the Vernons—*Ver non semper viret*—which may be translated either as "The spring is not always green," or, as intended, "Vernon always flourishes."

A member of the Grafton family devised a rebus of the name, composed of a graft issuing from a *tun* (heraldic name for a beer or wine keg). Arms and crests, in other words, frequently deduce their origin from the family name in the same manner as mottoes, in which case they are called *Armes Parlantes* or Canting Heraldry. The families of Salmon, Sturgeon, Lucy, Herring, Shelley, Talbot, Wolf, Rabbitt, Falconer, and the like, bear the image of their name-sake (lucies are pike, shelley is whelk-stalk, talbot is a hound). The Cardingtons bear three wool-cards, and the Harrows three harrows.

As you read the following selections from James Joyce and Jacques Derrida keep in mind that both writers alluded to the herald's system of blazoning a name as one of the models for their use of language.

# "Shem the Penman"
# (from Finnegans Wake)

### *James Joyce*

*Everyone knows that James Joyce is a major modern writer, with a reputation for being difficult. And some people know that* Finnegans Wake *is his last and most complicated text, which he kept revising for years and years, always making it more complicated. Only those who have actually looked at it, however, also know that it is a funny book, chock full of jokes and puns. Among other things, it is also a book about names and naming, and the way we are all full of ready-made language that we apply to things and people left and write (to use a Joycean sort of pun).*

*In the pages that follow we present you with three versions of a tiny excerpt from Joyce's dream-book: some scraps from the first draft, the same section from a later draft, and the same section as it appears in the published book. In this section of the book Joyce is writing about a character named Shem the Penman, who is a writer very much like himself, Shem being a version of his own first name. In short, Joyce is playing with his signature here, and especially with the similarity of Shem and Sham. Read his work for some clues on how you might do this sort of thing yourself. And please don't be too solemn about it. Joyce is just playing with his names, playing with language, playing with himself, following a process that sociolinguists now recognize as the standard operation of nicknaming in our culture.*

### *From the First Draft of* Finnegans Wake

Shem is as short for Shemus as Jim is for Jacob. Originally of respectable connections his back life simply won't stand being written about.

*    *    *    *    *    *

Cain—Ham (Shem)—Esau—Jim the Penman

---

wellknown for violent abuse of self and others.

lives in inkbottlehouse

boycotted, local publican refuse to supply books, papers, ink, foolscap, makes his own from dried dung sweetened with spittle (ink) writes universal history on his own body (parchment)

hospitality, all drunk & rightly indignant

1 eye halfopen, 1 arm, 42 hairs on his head, 17 on upper lip, 5 on chin, 3 teeth, no feet, 10 thumbs, 1/2 a buttock, 1/2 & 1/2 a testicle,—when is a man not a man?

a forger, can imitate all styles, some of his own.

1st copies of most original masterpieces slipped from his pen

### *From a Later Draft of* Finnegans Wake

Shem is as short for Shemus as Jim is joky for Jacob. A few are still found who say that originally he was of respectable connections (—— was among his cousins) but every honest to goodness man in the land knows that his back life will not stand being written about. Putting truth and lies together some shot may be made at how this hybrid actually looked. His bodily makeup, it seems, included 1 halfopen eye, 1 arm, 42 hairs on his crown, 18 on his upper lip, 5 on his chin, all ears, no feet, 5 thumbs, 2 fifths of a buttocks, a testicle & a half,—so that even Shem himself, when playing with words in the nursery asked his brothers & sisters the first riddle of the universe: When is a man not a man?: offering a prize of a crabapple to the winner. One said when the heavens are rocking, another said when other lips, a third said when the fair land of Poland, the next one said when those angel faces smile, still another said when the wine is in, one of the youngest said when father papered the parlour, still one said when you are old & grey & full of tears, and still another when we were boys, & another when you come down the vale, another *et enim imposuit manus episcopas fecit illum altissimis sacerdotum* & one when pigs begin to fly. All were wrong, he said. So Shem took the cake, the correct solution being: when he is a sham.

### *From Section I, Part vii, of* Finnegans Wake

Shem is as short for Shemus as Jem is joky for Jacob. A few tough- 1 necks are still getatable who pretend that aboriginally he was of respectable stemming (he was an outlex between the lines of Ragonar Blaubarb and Horrild Hairwire and an inlaw to Capt. the Hon. and Rev. Mr. Bbyrdwood de Trop Blogg was among his most distant connections) but every honest to goodness man in the land of the space of today knows that his back life will not stand being written about in black and white. Putting truth and untruth together a shot may be made at what this hybrid actually was like to look at.

Shem's bodily getup, it seems, included an adze of a skull, an eight of 2 a larkseye, the whoel of a nose, one numb arm up a sleeve, fortytwo hairs off his uncrown, eighteen to his mock lip, a trio of barbels from his megageg chin (sowman's son), the wrong shoulder higher than the right, all ears, an artificial tongue with a natural curl, not a foot to stand on, a handful of thumbs, a blind stomach, a deaf heart, a loose liver, two fifths of two buttocks, one gleetsteen avoirdupoider for him, a manroot of all evil, a salmonkelt's thinskin, eelsblood in his cold toes, a bladder tri-stended, so much so that young Master Shemmy on his very first de-bouch at the very dawn of protohistory seeing himself such and such, when playing with thistlewords in their garden nursery, Griefotrofio, at Phig Streat III, Shuvlin, Old Hoeland, (would we go back there now for sounds, pillings and sense? would we now for annas and annas? Would we for fullscore eight and a liretta? for twelve blocks one bob? for four testers one groat? not for a dinar! not for jo!) dictited to of all his little brothron and sweestureens the first riddle of the universe: asking, when is a man not a man?: telling them take their time, yungfries, and wait till the tide stops (for from the first his day was a fortnight) and offering the prize of a bittersweet crab, a little present from the past, for their copper age was yet unminted, to the winner. One said when the heavens are quakers, a second said when Bohemeand lips, a third said when he, no, when hold hard a jiffy, when he is a gnawstick and detarmined to, the next one said when the angel of death kicks the bucket of life, still another said when the wine's at witsends, and still another when lovely wooman stoops to conk him, one of the littliest said me, me, Sem, when pappa papared the harbour, one of the wittiest said, when he yeat ye abblokooken and he zmear hezelf zo zhooken, still one said when you are old I'm grey fall full wi sleep, and still another when wee deader walkner, and another when he is just only after having being semisized, another when yea, he hath no mananas, and one when dose pigs they begin now that they will flies up intil the looft. All were wrong, so Shem himself, the doctator, took the cake, the correct solution being—all give it up?—; when he is a—yours till the rending of the rocks,—Sham.

## For Discussion

The oddity of James Joyce's style may be alleviated if we review it in the context of a study on nicknaming. When you come to the assign-ment asking you to generate a text out of your own name, you might find it useful to imitate the way Joyce extended the play of nicknaming to himself, beating society at its own game by providing his own nick-names, as the process is described in the following excerpt *from Jane Morgan, Christopher O'Neill, and Rom Harré*. Compare the observa-tions made in this sociolinguistic analysis with the style of *Finnegans Wake*.

# Nicknames: Their Origins and Social Consequences

## *Jane Morgan, Christopher O'Neill, and Rom Harré*

During adolescence conception both of self and of others undergoes   1
considerable change. This apparently cataclysmic transition is, however,
apparently unreflected by the various personal labels attached. If nicknames are indeed to justify our claims to their being the surface man-
ifestations of deeper psychological processes, then why aren't these
tremendous personality changes of adolescence also reflected? The explanation must, we think, lie in the multiplicity of factors contributing to
any nickname. We have linked it, true, to thought patterns and the
individual's attempts to structure his [or her] world. Goffman's theories
about social stigma also show a similarity to nicknames too strong to be
ignored. They are closely linked, then, to minority and prejudice in a
given society and perhaps even dependent on them. They are subject to
that uncontrollable variable of the individual—his physical, mental, biographical idiosyncrasies, and how adequately he copes with them. All
these—the psychological, the social, the personal—are variables directly
affecting the constant—the nickname. Any change in one of these aspects, thus, for instance the personality changes of adolescence, can
either be accentuated or counteracted by the other two forces exerting
their influences on the situation. Unless these also remain constant, very
little alteration would be apparent.

Another aspect of nicknaming, however, became discernible in the   2
course of research. Again, a definite progression could be traced when
comparing the two lists of nine- and thirteen-year-olds. The change this
time, however, was not in the content of the name itself but in the actual
process of name-giving. We noted previously that the great majority of
nicknames were internal formations—between 55 per cent and 60 per
cent of the entire total. Of this number, in turn, particularly with the
younger age-group, these took the form of very simple, sometimes spontaneous syllabic mutations; "Nicholas-Ridiculous" etc. This variety of
verbal experiment was likened to the "babbling" stage with babies—
both being purely phonic explorations for the sheer joy of articulation,
meaning being largely superfluous. Just as the "babbling" is a transitory
phase in the acquisition of language, so the tendency among children to
respond solely to the aural quality of a name was, in the later survey,
superseded by a reaction to meaning, so that a far more complex thought

pattern was apparent in the actual naming process. Having noticed this phenomenon, the names were analysed again, this time focusing upon the method, rather than the content or origin of the name. Results were as follows:

| Process | 9-yr olds | 13-yr olds |
|---|---|---|
| Simple mutation | 77% | 57% |
| Pun/irony | 8% | 15% |
| Analogy | 15% | 28% |

For these figures to be meaningful obviously an explanation of the categories is essential: Simple mutation entails, as explicated above, merely a slight alteration of the name, usually the addition of a suffix: Bundy-Bundy-o/Bundo; a direct rhyme: Jill-Pill; or simple and often meaningless mutation: Nigel-Niggles, etc. This category, as the table illustrates, is prevalent in the nine-year age-group, but is gradually absorbed into the two others. Pun/irony involves a more complicated and intellectual manipulation of the name, though the response is still predominantly to the phonic rather than the semantic content. Nine-year-olds were capable of the letter play of:

Sarah Tibbets        Stebbit        Tibits

But there is only one notable example of a name undergoing a triple process:

Vincent Parsloe    Lieut. Parslow    Lieut. Pidgeon    Loot

whereas, in the twelve-to-fourteen age-group, this is a far more common occurrence:

| Jackie Amos | Amosquito | Flea |
|---|---|---|
| Steven Hill | Chill | Charlie |
| Joanne R. | Josy | Dozy |
| Richard Cantwell | Tin Cantwell | Tin |
| Tracy F. | Wednesday | "When's dey gonna break" (Thin legs) |

Puns, too, involve a response to meaning rather than the sound of words:

| David Sharp | Acker | Latin equivalent |
|---|---|---|
| Martin Southcott | Eastbed | Antithesis of compounds |
| Andrew Barefield | Barefield Sobers | Pun and allusion |

In the thirteen-year-old selection, too, the nicknames are often ironic:

John O'Derr    Brain of Britain    Cos he's a thick Mick really

This category reveals a far more complicated and sophisticated manipulation of the original name, and a tendency to respond not to the sound of the word but to its meaning. The numbers in the group almost double in the latter survey, suggesting a far more complex thought process emerges proportionately with age.

The third category—that of the allusive names—shows evidence of 3 the children reaching into the realms of their entire experience to supply the name. Again the group demonstrates a remarkable increase at the later stage. The nine-year-olds tended to simply add the "type" names: "Fatty," "Lanky," "Brainbox," "Four Eyes." The thirteen-year-olds, on the other hand, use everyday experience as referents far more frequently. The "Tubby's" of the primary school have become the "Cannon's" and the "Chubby Chequer's" of the high-school comprehensive. The analogy can be triggered off by either appearance or actual name:

| | | |
|---|---|---|
| Debra Brown | Henry | Like that dog on TV |
| Heather Taylor | Tiger | Like that girl on the "Double Deckers" |
| Jane Percy | Percy Thrower | |
| | Percy Parrot | Reasons apparent |
| | Persil Automatic | |
| Sharon Gonsuales | Speedy | Speedy Gonzales |
| Judy Lancaster | Bomber | Lancaster Bomber |

The trend is, we think, worth particular attention because, to a certain extent, it reinforces an aspect of the Peevers and Secord report. The "Tubby's" etc. of the earlier group do seem to imply the process of a type concept being applied, without any significant modification, to individuals. And this validates the American account of the initial method of applying simple "global" referents to personal concepts.

The marked increase in the allusive content of names, too, implies 4 the process of naming by continual reference to personal experience of the environment. The "type" figure is individualised by finding parallel examples in their world—the mass media playing, perhaps, a significant role. This would substantiate tentatively claims about the actual process of differentiation in personal concepts, increasing contact with the environment (directly proportionate to age) shading in the details, helping to discriminate more finely, improving perception and making others, in fact, three-dimensional.

# For Discussion and Writing

1. Does your family have a crest or coat of arms? How much do you know about it? How do these family coats of arms relate to the crests adopted by fraternities and sororities? corporations? Are the logos devised by businesses to represent their companies, or the emblems devised by advertisers to represent products, similar to family crests?

    Imagine that you have been knighted in recognition of your good works, and that you have permission to suggest the design of your own coat of arms. What would it look like?

2. With the three drafts of *Finnegans Wake* before us we can see the progression of the passage both at the level of style and of theme. What is the organizing idea of the piece? What is the stylistic principle? Evaluate the final draft according to the standards of writing normally applied to student essays.

3. Discuss the *Wake* in terms of the theory of nicknames found in Morgan, O'Neill, and Harré. Write a short self-portrait based on your experience with nicknames.

# Signing (The Proper Name)

According to the French philosopher, Jacques Derrida, there are at least three ways in which an author signs a work. The first dimension or register of signing is the signature "proper"—the proper name placed on the title page identifying the source of the writing. The second register refers to what is commonly called "style"—"the inimitable idiom of an artist's work"—such that even without the availability of the proper name an experienced reader might recognize the author of a work. (This second register has been the basis for many an exam question.) There remains, however, one more way in which a piece of writing carries the mark of its owner. This third register of the signature is the most complex, involving the heraldic placement of the name in the depths of the text. At this level the writer's name is seen as the seed out of which the text has grown, by a process of metaphorical and intertextual development. Retracing this process, an interpreter can find the author's name, hidden in the depths—or, to use Derrida's word, the "abyss"—of the text.

As we learned from the reading by Roger Brown in chapter 2, a common noun is the name of a general category—"book" for example. A proper noun, in contrast, is said to have no "meaning" in the ordinary sense of the term. It refers exclusively, picking out in the world not a category of things but a specific individual thing. All the people named "James" or "Robert" do not constitute a set or category in the way that everything named "book" does, because the shared name does not promise any other relationship among the people (other than the fact that people have names), unlike the term "book," which promises that everything by that name will possess certain qualities or attributes.

Or at least such has been the thinking about the operation of proper nouns or names until Derrida came along. Derrida asks us to reconsider the question of how names refer, that is, of the relationship between language and lived reality. We know from some of the readings in this section and from our familiarity with naming practices in non-Western societies, that in some cultures there is a looser, freer passage between common and proper nouns, between a general category and a particular individual who shares some of the qualities of that category; as in nicknames, which continue this tradition of naming a person according to personal attributes, such that the name not only identifies the person, but connotes some aspects of the person's "style."

Derrida's point of departure for reopening the study of reference is the naming process as practiced in literature. Unlike ordinary life in our society in which a person's name is arbitrarily assigned and denotes without connotation the bearer of the name, in literature a name often tells a great deal about a person. One of the first tricks a reader learns about the great symbol hunt for meaning in reading literature is to notice the names of the characters. If a character bears the name "Christian," the reader may expect to find certain religious themes of some use in understanding the work. But what about in life? If you meet people named "Christian" do you expect them to be Christians? And if they are, that is hardly surprising in our culture.

But there is more to it than that, for Derrida finds that not only do authors often give "motivated" names to their characters, but these names also may bear a significant relationship to the author's identity. Jean Genet, the French novelist and dramatist, a reformed criminal, named many of his characters after flowers. His own name, "Genet," means "broomflower" in French, as well as "horse" (among other things). This relationship between the real and fictional proper names is only the beginning of the textual phenomenon identified by Derrida, whose research revealed that the rhetorical figure of antonomasia— taking a common noun for a proper name or a proper name for a common noun—is the key to the process by which the third level of the signature takes place.

At the third level of signing, the relationship between an author's name and his or her literary style becomes the basis for a "poetics"—a theory of the production or making of texts. Derrida calls this process the "double bind" or "double band" of the signature, in which the proper name moves from designating a particular individual to become the key to a general theory of how texts are constructed. Genet provides one model for this process, folding all three levels into one scene in which the botanical properties of the flowers in his books refer both to the proper name "Genet" and to a theory of rhetorical invention. Therefore writing may be produced that follows the linguistic equivalent of the reproductive processes of the specific plants concerned (hence the careful description of "dissemination," or the spreading of seeds as manifested in certain species—cryptogams, angiosperms, and the like).

Derrida's area of application of this idea is unusual, but the metaphor itself is ancient. Fertilization and reproduction in the plant and animal kingdoms have long served as metaphors for creativity in the arts. Indeed, the procedure Derrida uses in the following excerpt— juxtaposing the categories (and vocabulary) of botany and textiles, and these in turn with the terms of literature—is familiar to us from the readings on metaphor in chapter 2. His suggestion that we can find in our own names the conceptual category modeling a personal style of creativity is unusual and provocative, not to mention controversial. Derrida has used the signature theory to read a number of major figures in the fields of literature and philosophy ("Ponge" as "sponge,"

"Blanchot" as "white water," "Kant" as "edge," and so forth), converting their proper names into common nouns using the literal meanings of the name, or puns on the name, to identify the conceptual category which is the clue to that author's principle of invention. In the exercise assigned in this section, you will have an opportunity to extend this experiment to the investigation of your own signature at all three levels, in order to discover, perhaps, your own principle of thinking and writing. Derrida has researched "signing" only with writers, but he intends it to be a theory of language adaptable to thinking in any discipline or field of knowledge. Thus, the style you discover in your experiment based on the readings in this section should be applicable to your work regardless of your intended or eventual major.

In the following excerpt from *Glas* (the book in which he discusses Genet), Derrida offers some elements of his signature theory along with citations from Genet's writings, including statements from autobiographical as well as from fictional works (genres that are not clearly differentiated in Genet's work nor in the signature theory in general) which are meant to support or illustrate the argument.

The blurbs on Genet's books describe him as "the foremost prince in the lineage of French *poètes maudites*—cursed magicians whose lives are as colorful as their work is dangerous, and who distinguish themselves as outlaws as well as masters of language." His peers in American literature would be the likes of Henry Miller and William Burroughs. Genet's masterpiece, *Our Lady of the Flowers*, was written in a prison cell, on brown paper from which the prisoners were supposed to make bags. In 1948 he was condemned to life imprisonment (he was a habitual thief and pervert), but was pardoned by the President of France at the request of France's most eminent writers. Our excerpts from *Glas* do not include the discussions of the more "perverse" themes of Genet's works, but the basic elements of the signature theory come through clearly enough.

# from Glas

## *Jacques Derrida*

Apparently, yielding to the Passion of Writing, Genet has made himself into a flower. . . . What is rhetoric, if the flower (or rhetoric) is the figure of figures and the place of places? Why does the flower dominate all the fields to which it nonetheless belongs? Why does it stop belonging to the series of bodies or objects of which it forms a part? . . .

*Translated by John P. Leavey, Jr., and Richard Rand (Lincoln, U. of Nebraska).

The name of the person who seems to affix, append here his seal (Genet) is the name, as we know, of his mother. . . . *Genêt* names a plant with flowers—yellow flowers (*sarothamnus scoparius, genista*; broom, *genette, genêt-à-balais*, poisonous and medicinal, as distinct from the dyer's broom, dyer's greenweed, woodwaxen, an herb for dying yellow); *genet* a kind of horse. Of Spain, a country of great importance in the text.

If all his literature sings and weaves a funerary hymen to nomination, Genet never sets any value, *noblesse oblige*, on anything but naming himself.

He rides horse(back) on his proper name. He holds it by the bit (*mors*). . . .

Departed are those who thought the flower signified, symbolized, metaphorized, metonymized, that one was devising repertories of signifiers and anthic figures, classifying flowers of rhetoric, combining them, ordering them, binding them up in a sheaf or a bouquet around the phallic arch. . . .

Departed then are, save certain exceptions, duly so considered, the archaeologists, philosophers, hermeneuts, semioticians, semanticians, psychoanalysts, rhetoricians, poeticians, even perhaps all those readers who still believe, in literature or anything else.

Those still in a hurry to recognize are patient for a moment: provided that it be anagrams, anamorphoses, somewhat more complicated, deferred and diverted semantic insinuations capitalized in the depths of a crypt, cleverly dissimulated in the play of letters and forms. Genet would then rejoin this powerful, occulted tradition that was long preparing its coup, its haywire start from sleep, while hiding its work from itself, anagrammatizing proper names, anamorphosing signatures and all that follows. Genet, by one of those movements in (n)*ana*, would have, knowing it or not, silently, laboriously, minutely, obsessionally, compulsively, and with the moves of a thief in the night, set his signatures in (the) place of all the missing objects. In the morning, expecting to recognize familiar things, you find his name all over the place, in big letters, small letters, as a whole or in morsels deformed or recomposed. He is no longer there, but you live in his mausoleum or his latrines. You thought you were deciphering, tracking down, pursuing, you are included. He has affected everything with his signature. He has affected it with everything. . . .

(. . .)

The rhetorical flower organizing this antitrope, this metonymy simulating autonymy, I baptize it anthonymy. One could also say anthonomasia. Antonomasia is a "kind of synecdoche that consists in taking a common noun for a proper name, or a proper name for a common noun" (Littré).

"I was born in Paris on December 19, 1910. As a ward of the *Assistance Publique*, it was impossible for me to know anything but my civil state. When I was twenty-one, I obtained a birth certificate. My mother's name was Gabrielle Genet. My father remains unknown. I came into the world at 22 Rue d'Assas.

" 'I'll find out something about my origin,' I said to myself, and went to the Rue d'Assas. Number 22 was occupied by the Maternity Hospital. They refused to give me any information. I was raised in Le Morvan by peasants. Whenever I come across genêt (broom) flowers on the heaths— especially at twilight on my way back from a visit to the ruins of Tiffauges where Gilles de Rais lived—I feel a deep sense of kinship with them. I regard them solemnly, with tenderness. My emotion seems ordained by all nature. I am alone in the world, and I am not sure that I am not their king—perhaps the fairy of these flowers. They render homage as I pass, bow without bowing, but recognize me. They know that I am their living, moving, agile representative, conqueror of the wind. They are my natural emblem, but through them I have roots in that French soil which is fed by the powdered bones of the children and youths screwed, massacred and burned by Gilles de Rais.''

"Through that spiny plant of the Cevennes [Spain], I take part in the criminal adventures of Vacher. Thus, through her whose name I bear, the vegetable kingdom is my familiar. I can regard all flowers without pity; they are members of my family. If, through them, I rejoin the nether realms—though it is to the bracken and their marshes, to the algae, that I should like to descend—I withdraw further from men.'' . . .

So this flower name would be a cryptogram or a cryptonym. It is not proper because it is common. On the other hand, . . . it is not proper because it also leads back to the nether realms, to the marshes, verily to the depths of the sea. Above the sea, with heavy sides but carried by it, the galley. In the depths of the sea, algae.

Alga is a cryptogam, one of those plants that hide their sexual organs. Like ferns, which in general multiply themselves through the dispersion of spores. Whether one remarks them or not on the surface, the text is full of them. The "ferns" of the "Man Condemned to Death" are "rigid." Certain brackens unfold their fronds several meters below the ground. Cryptogams are evidently not flowers. . . .

The stamin, *l'étamine*, names not only the light material in which nuns are sometimes veiled, or through which precious liquids are filtered. But *étamine*, stamen, is also the male sex organ of plants: according to the *navette* [shuttle, rape]—that's the word—running between the textile code and the botanical code. Situated around the style and its stigma, stamens generally form a thin thread, or filaments (*stamina*). Above the thin thread, a connective with four pollen sacs (microsporangia) that "elaborate and disperse the pollen seeds." . . .

No more than for the flower, is there any univocal semantic or morphological definition of *étamine*. *Etamine* deviates itself from itself, bursts its sheath, at the risk of disseminating the pollen. This always open risk affects not only the androecium, but also the gynoecium. One must argue from the fact that the seed can always burst or remain dormant.

It is concerning the seed, a fertilized ovule, that one thinks one is literally [*proprement*] speaking of dissemination (with angiosperms or gymnosperms). The seeds are sometimes thrown in every direction [*sens*] by the bursting of the fruit. More often, they escape from it through slits or holes open in its wall; wind or animals disperse them. Germination is therefore immediate only if light and moisture permit. . . .

"Botanists know a variety of *genêt which they call winged-genêt*. It describes its flight and theft in the *Journal*:

"As the theft was indestructible, I decided to make it the origin of a state of moral perfection. . . . 'I want to cover the world with its loathsome progeny.' . . . A kind of dissatisfaction inflated each of my acts, including the most simple. I would have liked a visible, dazzling glory to be manifest at my fingertips, would have liked my potency to lift me from the earth, to explode within me and dissolve me, to shower me to the four winds. I would have rained over the world. My powder, my pollen . . . would have touched the stars."

## For Discussion and Writing

1.  Derrida introduces a neologism in his commentary—"anthonomy"—to name the figure of antonomasia specific to Genet's practice. What is the justification for his invention of this hybrid critical term (notice its similarity with "anthology")? What other terms appearing in the selection did you not recognize? In *Glas* Derrida cites many passages from encyclopedic dictionaries, juxtaposing scientific information about botany with Genet's discussion of writing and his descriptions of the sexual life of the characters in his novels. He points out that certain words appear in the vocabularies of both botany and literature. What is the botanical meaning of "style"? Derrida suggests that the punning relationship between the two meanings of "style" justifies a conceptual gathering of the two sets into one category (the signature). Does this possibility make any sense? Look through a glossary of another specialized discipline that interests you, and compare its terminology with a glossary of literary terms.

2.  Select an author whose works are at least somewhat familiar to you and test the signature theory. Write a short account in the manner of Derrida's *Glas* discussing whether or not, or in what way, the author's names are "in the abyss" of the work(s).

3. Drawing on all the readings and exercises provided in this chapter relevant to the proper name, write a text exploring the words and information that may be generated out of your given and surnames. First identify a "key list" of such terms and topics, then construct a composition (organized as much for aesthetic effect as for the exposition of your discoveries) by writing out a variety of presentations expanding your vocabulary into an account of the third level of the signature. To make the original list you should use every available means to find the common nouns or names that translate your proper names into ordinary discourse. Check the dictionary definitions in the original language of your heritage, as well as encyclopedic dictionaries relevant to the names. You may also use poetic techniques to produce words out of your names—puns, anagrams might be especially useful. You might also want to include photocopied images depicting the things you find in your names. Several of the readings suggest analogies which might guide your experiment: think of the project as a written version of your coat of arms (a kind of improvised blazoning); or as a nicknaming process. Comment along the way on any signs of fate or destiny you notice in the results of your research. Are you "well-named"? Remember finally that the goal of the project is to take whatever material your names provide and turn it into a model for a theory (general description) of how to write.

The following text, composed as an experiment in the signature signing by James Michael Jarrett, provides a model for your own composition. Jarrett writes for a jazz magazine and teaches literature for a living, which accounts for at least part of the content of his signature. Your content will be different, but the kind of thing you do with the content produced out of your name should resemble Jarrett's procedure.

# A Jarrett in Your Text

## *James Michael Jarrett*

*For me, Francis Ponge is someone first of all who has known that, in order to know what goes on in the name and the thing, one has to get busy with one's own, let oneself be occupied by it. . . . (Signsponge, 26)*

The text—this text almost mad in its need to obey the law of my (im)possible signature—always begins at a stopping (stoppering or corking) place. It represents the end of false starts for the one who inscribes it. Like the mason jars that lined my Grandmother Jarrett's pantry—full of pole beans, okra, corn, tomatoes, bread 'n' butter pickles, and all kinds of preserves (peach, pear, watermelon rind, blackberry, and muscadine, to name only five)—it silently marks the work (it is the trace) of canning. (In the South, "puttin' up stuff in cans" is to put up stuff in jars.) And like mason jars, signed and dated, covered and sealed with paraffin (like tomes or tombs "sealed unto the day of redemption"), which wait standing with their strong, well-formed legs locked at attention, the text as jar—a cornucopia—exists to become part of a feast.

But you will notice (for you have opened my jar, are feasting now),   2
the text-jar is not used up. It fills itself as fast as it is emptied. To emphasize this point, consider the following biblical passage which describes Elijah the prophet's visit to the drought stricken town of Zarephath and to a widow whom God promised would provide sustenance:

> [Elijah] arose and went to Zarephath. And when he came to the gate of the city, indeed a widow was there gathering sticks. And he called to her and said, "Please bring me a little water in a cup, that I may drink." And as she was going to get it, he called to her and said, "Please bring me a morsel of bread in your hand." Then she said, "As the LORD your God lives, I do not have bread, only a handful of flour in a bin, and a little oil in a jar; and see, I am gathering a couple of sticks that I may go in and prepare it for myself and my son, that we may eat it, and die." And Elijah said to her, "Do not fear; go and do as you have said, but make me a small cake from it first, and bring it to me; and afterward make some for yourself and your son." "For thus says the LORD God of Israel: 'The bin of flour shall not be used up, nor shall the jar of oil run dry, until the day the LORD sends rain on the earth.' " So she went away and did according to the word of Elijah; and she and he and her household ate for many days. The bin of flour was not used up, nor did the jar of oil run dry, according to the word of the LORD which He spoke by Elijah. (I Kings 17:10-16)

Clearly the jar of Zarephath forms this passage's cynosure. It is a hedge against the wasteland. Because of its fecundity (always enjoyed "out of season" and removed from the place of generation), death becomes pregnant. The oil that flows out of its mouth or orifice (associated with the anointing or sanctifying work of God and his prophet) produces new life.

"Can it!"   3

But I am way ahead of myself, so I stop.   4

Jarrett

Jarrette

Jarrete

J'arrete

J'arrête

I stop to start. I "close (a finger hole of a wind instrument) or press   5
down (a violin string, etc.) to produce a desired tone" (*Webster's New
World Dictionary*, "stop"). But my stopping will not be noted, or rather
notated, in this particular manner again. Instead, it is sufficient to see that
every punctuation mark, every white space, the breaking off of every
letter to make another heralds (like a band of angels) a stopping, marks
my signature.

# Michael Jarrett

My model for this experiment in composition is Derrida's *Sign-*   6
*sponge*. Hence, I use my "own signation to investigate [to invaginate] a
field of study," a field of studs. To make my intentions transparent (so
they will be perfectly clear) and straightforward, merely observe that I
ret ("to impute, ascribe, or attribute"—OED) to composition an essentially jar-like function. This essay, therefore, tests sound principles of
canning. It is itself a recipe for making the most heavenly (literally God-
like) jams and jars, and it follows this recipe:

JAMES MICHAEL JARRETT JAM
(straightforward version)

1 signature (James Michael Jarrett)            1  literary object (genre
                                                   of satire or Menippea)

                                                1  pinch of content

Write an introduction using the generative principle of signature and add a pinch of content; cook until moderately thick; write
the recipe. Remark the proper name's generative principle by exposing the grid of common nouns produced by exploring etymo-
logical and associative (homonyms, anagrams, and such) possibilities of the signature. Copiously elaborate the terms of the grid
into a text by straining the Menippea (the literary object) through
the grid. Season and serve as a specific example of an inexhaustible,
general compositional principle.

The above recipe (which both goes before and follows the essay)  7
also follows the following recipe for "Muscadine Jam," which Mrs. S. R.
Dull (who signs her Foreword as Henrietta Stanley Dull) recorded in her
book *Southern Cooking*—a text "gleaned from over forty years of . . .
experience" and written in response to "the need for an authoritative
source of information on the preparation of foodstuffs the 'Southern
Way' ":

Muscadine Jam

5 lbs. fruit                                                        3 lbs. sugar

> Pulp grapes and put pulp to cook in small quantity of water;
> cook until broken. Put through coarse strainer to remove seed. To
> the hulls put sufficient water to boil until tender. Mix the two
> together, add sugar and cook slowly, stirring often to prevent
> scorching. Season with any spices liked. (p. 333)

Inexplicably, Mrs. Dull omits any reference to the jars that traditionally
hold jam. Many reasons could be suggested, but several possibilities seem
especially promising:

> (1)   The jars are present, but because they constitute the re-
> ceived container of jam making, they are invisible.
> (2)   The jars are absent. Dull—"the first lady of cooking in
> Georgia"—can only conceive of jars in Tennessee (or they are ab-
> sent to spite Wallace Stevens).
> (3)   The jars are both absent and present, and the absent/
> present opposition is jammed by the jars (as texts or marks). Mrs.
> Dull's omission typifies logocentrism's habit of establishing dual-
> isms, that is, of privileging content over form, inside over outside,
> and presence over absence.

My signature, though, explicitly demonstrates the interpenetration, or at least the interdependence, of jams and jars.

My papa Jarrett was named James—James Lloyd. But when I think of    8
my first name, the memory usually recalled is not an image of Papa, but
of the hand-tinted photograph that hung over the bed I slept in when
visiting my grandparents. This photograph, which both comforted and
frightened me as a child, portrayed my uncle James—who died of leukemia when he was three years old. My father—Richard Eugene, the only
surviving son and oldest of three children—never saw his brother, so, of
course, neither did I.

## CARROT
## JARRETT

On December 10, 1953, my parents named me James Michael Jarrett.   9
They decided that I would be called Michael (a law broken by telephone
solicitors and teachers on the first day of school). However, when I sign
my signature, I sign it as James M. Jarrett, because my father said that was
best. Thus, in the signing of my name, Michael all but erases itself, and
James—the mark of the ghost-like, absent child—appears. I mark his absence, his never appearing, as his mark in turn marks mine.

James, the Hellenistic version of Jacob (Iakòbõs), means supplanter 10
(supplement) or literally "heel-catcher." A man always in a tight spot,
Jacob usually improvised a way to get out of sticky situations. For
instance, at his birth, foreshadowing the Olympic games (now held in
gyms), Jacob ham-strung his older twin Esau. Nevertheless, God loved
Jacob and hated Esau (Romans 9:13). God thought Jacob had the potential to become a real gem.

When I was in Junior High School, people called me Micajarrett, one 11
word, said real fast. And I loved it, for its rhythm and for its association
with mica.

No mineral matched mica. Its thin, somewhat flexible, crystalline 12
layers (called isinglass), which could be separated into transparent planes
with one's fingernail, fascinated me. I looked at the freckles it made in
granite. I searched for it in the red, Georgia clay. And I marveled at the
tops of electric fuses—little windows of mica resistant to heat and electricity. If Jacob was God's gem, mica was mine.

Mica, actually Michael, asks the question, "Who is like God?" I know 13
the answer well. Its emphatic "nobody"—an answer that certainly demonstrates its asker's unwillingness to elicit the banter of light conversation—booms like Pavarotti singing through an expensive microphone.

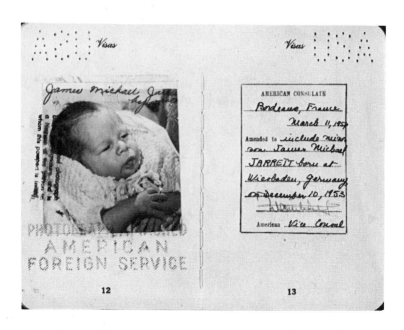

WIESBADEN Hauptbahnhof                                    Aufnahme K. H. Mitschke

But herein lies a problem; who asks the question of Michael, and to whom is the question addressed? What questions are raised in my signature, and what shall I make of this apocalyptic scene?

Gently but firmly tap on Jarrett, and it will easily open up, making its contents available. Cut it in half with a jarrit ("a wooden javelin, about five feet long, used in games by Persian, Turkish, and Arabian horsemen"—OED), and it will reveal two parts as distinct as a *jaret* (a *"variété de prune"*—Littré). It will neatly divide into a common noun—"jar"— and an uncommon verb—"ret." But before I investigate this (reveal its contents to you), notice my Mother's maiden name—"Jordan." Its origin is uncertain, but

> the suggestion has been made that *Jordan* is short for *Jordan-bottle*, and meant originally a bottle of water brought from the Jordan by crusaders or pilgrims; that it was thence transferred to 'a pot or vessel used by physicians and alchemists', and thence to the chamber utensil. But the earlier steps of this conjecture apparently rest upon nothing but the later form of the word (which may actually be a corruption of something else), and the external probabilities of such an origin. (OED)

Thus, "jordan" involves a complex series of displacements, until finally patriarchal law (the law of Dick Jarrett and the OED) puts a lid on the whole subject, screws meaning down, and declares that, henceforth jordan shall be:

(1)  a kind of pot or vessel formerly used by physicians and alchemists,
(2)  a chamber-pot,
(3)  applied derisively to a person (OED),
(4)  or, in a word, a jarrett.

Jarrett supplements jordan. The alchemist's vessel of healing/poison becomes a piss-pot. The little jar relegates the jordan to "The Lady's Dressing Room," declares it unclean—a *pharmakos*— or at very best a "frail *China* Jar [ready to] receive a Flaw" (*Rape of the Lock*, Canto II). But undeniably a trace or whiff of jordan remains, for, after all, a jarrett is a jordan as we have seen, and as I shall point out again.

I married Pamela Gail Dill. She now signs her name Pamela Gail 15 Jarrett. Did I take her name? Was it freely given? Did I erase her name? Does it palimpsestically remain? What is the nature of the idiomatic law by which dill (a plant of the carrot family) disappears into the abyss of a pickle jar only to emblazon itself upon the label or signature of the jar? In what way do the three boys she bore resemble (remark) a pickle jar, which at once carries the signature of both mother and father? These are questions I shall only pose, preserve (for later) by placing them into this text-jar, this *jahr's* text.

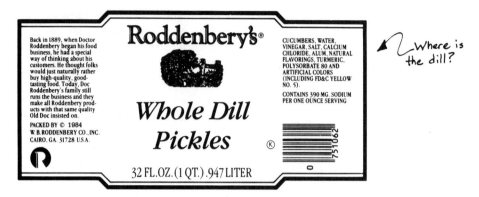

Back in 1889, when Doctor Roddenbery began his food business, he had a special way of thinking about his customers. He thought folks would just naturally rather buy high-quality, good-tasting food. Today, Doc Roddenbery's family still runs the business and they make all Roddenbery products with that same quality Old Doc insisted on.

PACKED BY © 1984
W. B. RODDENBERY CO., INC.
CAIRO, GA. 31728 U.S.A.

Roddenbery's®

*Whole Dill Pickles*

32 FL. OZ. (1 QT.) .947 LITER

CUCUMBERS, WATER, VINEGAR, SALT, CALCIUM CHLORIDE, ALUM, NATURAL FLAVORINGS, TURMERIC, POLYSORBATE 80 AND ARTIFICIAL COLORS (INCLUDING FD&C YELLOW NO. 5).

CONTAINS 390 MG. SODIUM PER ONE OUNCE SERVING

*Where is the dill?*

As I noted earlier, Jarrett—to measure out, sound out, or partly open its principle of generation—yields a "jar" and a "ret." *Jar*, whose noun form rates three separate entries in the OED (a kind of jar in its own rite), suggests: (1) a harsh, inharmonious, grating sound or combination of sounds, which by extension signifies dissension, discord, dispute, and want of harmony, (2) a vessel without spout or handle (or having two handles) usually more or less cylindrical in form, and hence, a measure of volume, and (3) something (like a door) "on the turn, partly open." *Ret*, a verb, signifies the actions of: (1) accusing, charging, reckoning, imputing, and ascribing, (2) soaking (especially flax or hemp) in water and exposing to moisture, in order to soften or season, and (3) rotting (eg., hay spoiled by water). Ret is also an obsolete form ("3 sing. pres. indic.") of "read." Jarrett, I ret, equals (among other things) a rotten, slightly opened jar. A jarrett is a jordan—a truly jarring fact.

In French, the definition of *jarret* is expressed as: (1) "bend of the knee, popliteal space, ham (in man); hough, hock (of horse, etc.)," (2) "knuckle (of veal); shin (of beef)," and (3) "unevenness, bulge, break of outline (in curve of arch, etc.)" or "an elbow, knee-joint (of pipe)" (*Heath's Standard French and English Dictionary*). Phrases employing my signature are as follows:

> *Plier le jarret*, to bend the knee.
> *Avoir du jarret*, to be strong in the leg.
> *Couper les jarrets à quelqu' un*, to take the wind out of someone's sails.
> *S' avancer le jarret tendu*, (i) (of courtier, etc.) to advance making a leg, (ii) (of fencer, etc.) to advance on his toes.
> *Couper les jarrets à un cheval*, to hamstring a horse.

Also, note that *jarrettes* are socks or half-hose. The verb *jarreter* refers to the act of putting on one's garters or stockings or to stripping a tree of its side branches.

Obviously, then, I find myself attracted to Menippean satire because 18 my signature makes the genre possible. I say this, rather write this, because as I study the menippea, it seems purely fanciful (i.e., scientific) to think that my signature—myself as subject—can remain outside the text (establishing an inside and outside of the text). Therefore I insert my signature into the genre (or jar) called menippea, but in so doing, I lose my identity, my title of ownership over the text. I let james michael jarrett—a chain of common nouns—"become a moment or a part of the [menippean] text" (*Signsponge*, 56).

On the simplest level this means that I like satire for its jars. For 19 example, Petronius' character, Seleucus, asked:

> What are men anyway but balloons on legs, a lot of blown-up bladders? Flies, that's what we are. No, not even flies. Flies have something inside. But a man's a bubble, all air, nothing else. (*Satyricon*, trans. Arrowsmith, 50)

People, to Seleucus, were empty jars, and whatever Petronius' position on this issue was, one thing is clear. The *Satyricon* concerned itself with what was later called the Cartesian jar/jelly split. Swift worked the same image when he wrote:

> in most corporeal beings, which have fallen under my cognizance, the outside hath been infinitely preferable to the in; whereof I have been farther convinced from some late experiments. Last week I saw a woman flayed, and you will hardly believe how much it altered her person for the worse.
>
> Yesterday I ordered the carcass of a beau to be stripped in my presence, when we were all amazed to find so many unsuspected faults under one suit of clothes. Then I laid open his brain, his heart, and his spleen; but I plainly perceived at every operation, that the farther we proceeded, we found the defects increase upon us in number and bulk. (*A Tale of a Tub*, Section IX)

This often cited passage presents a jarrish or jordanean episteme. It 20 forcefully argues that people are jelly jars—tubs. It implies that *A Tale of a Tub* should be renamed *A Tale of a Jarrett*.

The menippea features tons of other famous jars. Here are a few 21 examples. Rabelais organized the whole of *Gargantua and Pantagruel* around "the Holy Bottle of Bacbuc." Sir Thomas Browne wrote a piece entitled *Urne Buriall*. Voltaire wrote *CANdide*. Sterne has Mr. Shandy call his servant-girl, Susannah's mind "a leaky vessel" (Vol. IV, ch. 14). And Carlyle, following Swift's lead, wrote *Sartor Resartus* or the *Canner Recanned* or the *Jarrer Rejarred*.

But identifying jars in menippean texts is like making jelly using 22 commercial pectin. It works, but it is nothing to be proud of. Anyone equipped with a box of sure-jel can move into cannery row. James Michael Jarrett, though, offers much more than this. As a sock or half-hose, *jarrettes* resemble the cornucopia, a horn of plenty, whose sheer abundance—*copia*—jars my mind, creating cognitive dissonance, over-loading or jamming all channels.

The menippea too, in its encyclopedic storing up of information, 23 jams signals. It most often features itself as God-like—right—a beautiful, well-heeled angel (messenger) sent to warn mankind of coming apoc-alypse. It hooks into meaty issues, exposes rottenness, calls a jordan a jordan (really puts them in a pickle if done right), and ham-strings (de-limbs) evil doers. Inherently conservative, it keeps the door to a tradi-tional past ajar. In other words, if the menippea had its way everything would be unscrewed: virginity would be endlessly recovered.

Make no mistake, though, the menippea rettes people of villainy, but 24 it soils itself as it cans and contains putrification. At one and the same time it desires to poison and heal by jarring texts (people, language, and reality), by making them bend the knee. Some say it would jam everyone into one mold; others say it has no mold, that it only jars what it does not want or what it fears. Like all jars

it has no spout.
It is without spout.
Its spout is off.
It spouts off.

It has seen the "excremental vision" (Norman O. Brown's term for the jarrettean moment). Again, *it contains rottenness*. It knows its way around jakes (outhouses were supplanted by modern, giant underground jordans called septic tanks). And it prefers "to fall at jar"—that is, to dissent or vary—on and about the outlying districts or margins society and language has inscribed. Aristotle rammed this point home when he wrote in chapter 4 of the *Poetics* that comedy arose in the outlying districts from those who led

*Jazziz:* I read once that you don't like to talk about Carla Bley. Is that still true?

*Bley:* Well, you know, the questions that critics always ask me are not usually the ones I want them to ask. You tell your life story 25,000 times, and pretty soon you begin lying to keep it interesting.

*Jazziz:* So what do you find most interesting at this point in your career?

*Bley:* Oh God. o.k. Let me think for a second. The thing that's most interesting to me right now is my garden. I'm leaving for Europe in three days, and I have to eat all my peas before I go.

*Jazziz:* You're not canning any?

*Bley:* No, I'm not canning any. They're snap peas. They're better if they're eaten fresh. So, I'm really working hard to eat the peas, and I'm trying to figure out—you know—roast peas, pea soup, pea ice cream, pea gravy—anything to get rid of the peas.

*Jazziz:* You ought to check out some recipe books from Latin America that tell how to prepare bananas a million different ways. They might give some possibilities you could improvise upon.

*Bley:* Yeah well, the problem is these snap peas are new. This is a new thing. It's a five year old discovery—a fully edible pea, and it's as big as a real pea. But you eat the pod and everything. It's not like a snow pea.

*Jazziz* What is a typical day like for the world's foremost, pea farming composer, that is, if there is such a thing as a typical day at home?

*Bley:* Yeah, there is. A typical day would be writing music, starting at about 9:00, after having a very quick breakfast—about a five minute breakfast. I get up at a-quarter-to-nine. In fifteen minutes, I manage to get the juice, coffee and toast down, and then I work for about three hours. Then I start taking breaks, going out to the garden or reading the news or something, and I work until about 5:30 or 6:00. Then I cook dinner, and then I work some more.

*Jazziz:* On the road is another schedule.

*Bley:* Aah, on the road is a vacation. When we're not traveling or laying in the sun, we're playing music, but that's just the tip of the iceberg—a month of music, all those months preparing the material. So that's the typical day—writing, pacing up and down.

That special blend of legend and fact, which flavors the lives of many great jazz musicians, has it that Buddy Bolden was "the first to play the hard jazz and blues for dancing," and that on his last and finest gig — a parade down New Orleans' Iberville Street with Henry Allen's Brass Band in 1907 — he went totally insane. "Dementia Praecox, Paranoid Type."

But there's more to Bolden's story than its archetypal tragic ending. For one thing, although he never recorded, Bolden's innovation of mixing secular and sacred music — hymns and blues cooked up together like some beautiful, hellish gumbo — cuts its way into every recording in jazz history. For another thing, his mandate to mix, create farragoes, also suggests a model for jazz journalism, because Bolden was jazz's first publisher.

His newspaper was named *The Cricket*, and Michael Ondaatje, in his novel, *Coming Through Slaughter*, writes that *The Cricket* "respected stray facts, manic theories, and well-told lies," and that "Bolden took all the thick facts and dropped them into his pail of sub-history."

Bolden, it seems, would have dug Carla Bley. For like Bolden, Bley has made musical jambalaya from the materials of her life. She has taken facts, theories, and lies, folded them all together, and cooked up what the Romans called a *satura* — a word originally signifying a *mixture* or *medley*, and interestingly, the word from where we get the English word satire.

So then, fix yourself a cool drink, stretch out in a comfortable chair, and let Bley — as the French say — *faire la cuisine*.

*Jazziz:* I'm especially interested in one thing in your past, because we share this, and that's your background in Fundamentalist, Jerry Falwellean, "Onward Christian Soldiers" type Christianity.

*Bley:* AMEN!

*Jazziz:* How does that influence your music right now? I'm thinking specifically about the gospel—that is, the white, mainstream churchy feel of some of your compositions and the titles like "The Lord Is Listenin' to Ya, Hallelujah!," "A New Hymn" and "Joyful Noise."

*Bley:*   Yeah, well that's a tremendous influence. It would have to be, because that was my only music until I was twelve.

*Jazziz:*   When you wrote "Joyful Noise," were you conscious of that tradition?

*Bley:*   No I wasn't. But I wrote a piece last year called "Healing Power," and that definitely was. I tried to actually heal a person who was dying in a hospital in Germany. I wrote the piece for one week, and I called everyday to find out if the guy was still alive. Finally I finished the piece, and I thought it worked! And then, of course, the punch line is he died the next day.

*Jazziz:*   So what'd you do with that?

*Bley:*   At first I changed the title to "The Healing Impotent," but then I changed it back to the "Healing Power," because it sounded better, and I figured it at least kept him alive for a week. So sometimes, when I announce the piece, I tell the people in the audience: "If you have a headache, if you have a cold, if your feet hurt you, well—listen to this piece. . . ."

*Jazziz:*   When you recorded *Heavy Heart* and *Night-Glo*, did it surprise you that love or sentiment is probably the most scandalous or surprising thing of all? Because I know critics loved it when you were satirical, but when you got romantic it scandalized them more than anything you had done.

*Bley:*   I Know. They hate it. They really hate it.

*Jazziz:*   Did you know it would scandalize them? Did that come as a surprise to you?

*Bley:*   No, I knew.

*Jazziz:*   So you were baiting them?

*Bley:*   No, I wasn't. I'm just not going to do something I don't want to do.

the phallic songs. Comedy (here synonymous with jarrettean literature) is suburban. Like canning and (Wycherley's) country wife, it grew up on the farm; it is a pharmacotic bumpkin, tracing out margins.

Or look at it another way. The menippea is a kind of jazz; (jazz is a 25
kind of menippea, forming a body of work that aurally satirizes mainstream, Caucasian music, art and culture). When it really cooks—lets out
all the stops and hams it up—the result is a high quality jam. This jam,
what Duke Ellington called "such sweet thunder," jars ("cuts") established (generic) ways of playing tunes, because it foregrounds the solo or
group improvisation. Stated succinctly, jazz and the menippea follow the
law of the signature (a hymen making the fold of ensembles and solos);
classical music and literature (e.g., romance and tragedy) follow

*Jazziz*   You've been viewed as something of a musical satirist, something
   along the lines of Brecht and Weill. I've even seen references to Swift
   and Aristophanes. Are you a satirist?
*Bley:*   No, I used to be, and I'm not anymore. I'm terribly serious.
*Jazziz:*   So you're not satirizing anyone?
*Bley:*   No!
*Jazziz:*   No more barbs?
*Bley:*   Well they all think I still am. And that's o.k., if they want to think
   that—if that makes it more acceptable.
*Jazziz:*   What kind of music does your new sextet demonstrate a love
   for?
*Bley.*   It's music that helps you get through the day—or the night. And
   not music that's educational, or interesting, or modern or any of that.
   Deep down it's trying to make people feel better, trying to be music
   that puts people into a very back of the brain mood—like way back
   without your thought processes. I don't know what that's called.

the law of the preestablished score.
   What, then, of this essay? Does it follow the law of the subject (the
idiom) or the law of the object (the recipe)? Hopefully, by miming the
motions of signation, it folds the two laws together. If this is the case,
perhaps a new recipe for essaying is called for, one that can be written
only after all cooking, canning, and jamming is done.

TURN BACK!

1 signature      1 literary object (genre of
satire or menippea)

JAMES MICHAEL JARRETT JAM
(Revised Unstandard Version)

*Jazziz:* If you could wish anything for new music in America, what
would it be?

*Bley:* Well I had an idea a couple of years ago, but I don't think it's coming true. I thought there would be one piece only for everybody, and
that would be the only piece we'd need, but there'd be so many aspects to it that all the people that listened to it would have their own
way of thinking about it. They could hear something with a heavy
backbeat or take the backbeat out. They could make the melody go
up or down so that it was out of sync with anything else or off pitch
with anything else. They could make up their own words, and they
could listen to them scrambled or not scrambled. And everybody
would always be writing on—working on—the same piece. But I
haven't thought about that in a long time. Does that sound reasonable?

*Jazziz:* You may be heading in that direction with your most recent material. I know sometimes when I listen to it my three, young boys are
making noise, stuff is rattling, things are happening. New sounds are
always added to the music. We can always heap it on, personalize it.
So always remember those little kids who add rhythm, melody, and
an occasional harmony to the basic tracks you've laid down.

*Bley:* I like it. It's o.k. with me.

*Jazziz:* Is there anything else interviewers typically fail to ask that you'd
like to say?

*Bley:* One of the great, great quandaries in my life is whether or not it
will ever be possible to make enough money. That sounds like a very
weird thing to talk about. But the older I get the more I find myself
appreciating great restaurants, great cars—just, generally speaking,
the greatest things that the human race has come up with. And I'd
really like to have those things. So I've been thinking, I'd like to
make some money, and I realize that I'm not willing to change the
music in any way, and so I have to think of something else to do. And
maybe that's why I'm starting to do other people's music, hoping that
someone else will, somehow, make the money for me. It'll probably
never happen.

But I certainly wish that . . . well I wish that I had the time to
take two weeks off and go to a warm place in the winter. I wish that I
had a bulldozer. I've always wanted a bulldozer. If I had myself a

bulldozer, I could build myself a pond in my backyard underneath the trees. Little things like that. Every year I think, if I had a bulldozer, if I had two weeks off . . . So that's something I think about almost everyday now. How am I going to pay for these things? and I'm not willing to change *anything*. So I'll just find these young people and try to talk them into doing something crazy with me.

*Jazziz:*  Try to corrupt young minds.

*Bley:*  Yeah, then I'll steal all their royalties. I'll sign them up to my company, then I'll figure out a deal where they benefit me, and they just get the glory. But that's something I *never* talk about.

Cassirer, translated by Susanne K. Langer. Reprinted by permission of Leonard C. R. Langer.

Robert Coover, "The Gingerbread House," from PRICKSONGS AND DESCANTS by Robert Coover. Copyright © 1969 by Robert Coover. Reprinted by permission of the publisher, E. P. Dutton, a division of NAL Penguin, Inc.

Jacques Derrida, reprinted from GLAS by Jacques Derrida, English translation by John P. Leavey, Jr. and Richard Rand, by permission of University of Nebraska Press. Copyright 1986 by the University of Nebraska Press.

Emily Dickinson, reprinted by permission of the publishers and the Trustees of Amherst College from THE POEMS OF EMILY DICKINSON, edited by Thomas H. Johnson, Cambridge, Mass.: The Belknap Press of Harvard University Press, Copyright 1951, © 1955, 1979, 1983 by the President and Fellows of Harvard College.

Ralph Ellison, "Hidden Name and Complex Fate," Copyright © 1964 by Ralph Ellison. Reprinted from SHADOW AND ACT by Ralph Ellison, by permission of Random House, Inc.

Martin Esslin, "Aristotle and the Advertisers," reprinted by permission of Louisiana State University Press from MEDITATIONS: ESSAYS ON BRECHT, BECKETT, AND THE MEDIA by Martin Esslin. Copyright © 1962, 1965, 1966, 1967, 1970, 1971, 1974, 1975, 1976, 1977, 1980 by Martin Esslin.

Robert Francis, "Pitcher." Copyright © 1953 by Robert Francis. Reprinted from THE ORB WEAVER by permission of Wesleyan University Press.

Sigmund Freud, excerpts reprinted from INTRODUCTORY LECTURES ON PSYCHOANALYSIS by Sigmund Freud translated and edited by James Strachey. By permission of Liveright Publishing Corporation. Copyright © 1966 by W. W. Norton & Company, Inc. Copyright © 1965, 1964, 1963 by James Strachey. Copyright 1920, 1934 by Edward L. Bernays. Reprinted by permission of Sigmund Freud Copyrights Ltd., The Institute of Psycho-Analysis, and The Hogarth Press from THE STANDARD EDITION OF THE COMPLETE PSYCHOLOGICAL WORKS OF SIGMUND FREUD translated and edited by James Strachey.

Louise Glück, "Cottonmouth Country," Copyright © 1968 by Louise Glück. From FIRSTBORN by Louise Glück, published by The Ecco Press in 1983. Reprinted by permission.

Erving Goffman, "Character Contests," from INTERACTION RITUAL by Erving Goffman. Reprinted by permission of Gillian Sankoff, Executrix for Erving Goffman, Dechert, Price & Rhods, Philadelphia, PA 19102.

Brothers Grimm, "Hansel and Gretel," from GRIMM'S TALES FOR YOUNG AND OLD by the Brothers Grimm, translated by Ralph Manheim. Translation copyright © 1977 by Ralph Manheim. Reprinted by permission of Doubleday & Company, Inc.

Brothers Grimm, "The Little Brother and the Little Sister," from ONE FAIRY STORY TOO MANY by John Ellis. Reprinted by permission of The University of Chicago Press and John Ellis.

David Hayman, reprinted from A FIRST-DRAFT OF "FINNEGANS WAKE" edited and annotated by David Hayman, Copyright © 1963, by permission of the University of Texas Press.

James Jarrett, "Put a Jarrett in Your Text," reprinted by permission of the author.

James Joyce, "The Boarding House," from DUBLINERS by James Joyce. Copyright 1916 by B. W. Huebsch. Definitive text copyright © 1967 by the Estate of James Joyce. Reprinted by permission of Viking Penguin, Inc.

James Joyce, "Shem the Penman," from FINNEGANS WAKE by James Joyce. Copyright 1939 by James Joyce. Copyright renewed © 1967 by George Joyce and Lucia Joyce. Reprinted by permission of Viking Penguin, Inc.

X. J. Kennedy, "Ars Poetica," from NUDE DESCENDING A STAIRCASE. Reprinted by permission of Curtis Brown Ltd. Copyright © 1961 by X. J. Kennedy.

Robert W. Keidel, "A New Game for Managers to Play," Copyright © 1985 by The New York Times Company. Reprinted by permission.

Ono no Komachi, "Doesn't He Realize," from Kenneth Rexroth, WOMEN POETS OF JAPAN. Copyright © 1977 by Kenneth Rexroth and Ikuko Atsumi. Reprinted by permission of New Directions Publishing Corporation.

Garrison Keillor, "Gretel," excerpted from "My Grandmother, My Self," in HAPPY TO BE HERE. Copyright © 1982 Garrison Keillor. Reprinted with permission of Atheneum Publishers, a division of Macmillan, Inc.

George Lakoff and Mark Johnson, excerpts from METAPHORS WE LIVE BY. Copyright © 1980 by University of Chicago Press. Reprinted by permission.

W. S. Merwin, "Inscription Facing Western Sea," from THE CARRIER OF LADDERS. Copyright © 1970 by W. S. Merwin. Reprinted with the permission of Atheneum Publishers.

W. S. Merwin, "Separation," from THE MOVING TARGET. Copyright © 1963 W. S. Merwin. Reprinted with the permission of Atheneum Publishers.

J. Morgan, C. O'Neill and R. Harré, "Names as Character Sketches," from NICKNAMES: THE ORIGIN AND SOCIAL CONSEQUENCES. Reprinted by permission of Routledge & Kegan Paul.

Dorothy Parker, "You Were Perfectly Fine," from THE PORTABLE DOROTHY PARKER, edited by Brendan Gill. Copyright 1929, renewed 1957 by Dorothy Parker. Originally published in *The New Yorker*. Reprinted by permission of Viking Penguin, Inc.

Ezra Pound, "Agassiz and the Fish" from *ABC of Reading*. Copyright 1934 by Ezra Pound. Reprinted by permission of New Directions Publishing Corporation.

Mary Louise Pratt, "Natural Narratives," From TOWARD A SPEECH ACT THEORY OF LITERARY DISCOURSE. Reprinted by permission of Indiana University Press.

Raymond Queneau, "Transformations," from EXERCISES IN STYLE. Copyright 1947 by Editions Gallimard. Translated by Barbara Wright. Reprinted by permission of New Directions Publishing Corporation.

Roger Rapoport, "Listen to the White Graduate, You Might Learn Something," published in Esquire Magazine, September 1969. Reprinted by permission of The Sterling Lord Agency, Inc. Copyright © 1969 by Roger Rapoport.

Adrienne Rich, "Moving in Winter," from THE FACT OF A DOORFRAME, Poems Selected and New, 1950–1984, by Adrienne Rich, reprinted by permission of W. W. Norton & Company, Inc. Copyright © 1984 by Adrienne Rich.

# Index

Instructor's Manual
to accompany

# TEXT BOOK

### AN INTRODUCTION
### TO LITERARY LANGUAGE

**Robert Scholes, Nancy R. Comley,**
and **Gregory L. Ulmer**

Instructor's Manual

to accompany

**TEXT BOOK**

An Introduction to Literary Language

Robert Scholes
Nancy R. Comley
Gregory L. Ulmer

St. Martin's Press   New York

# Preface

In **Text Book** we have proposed a new method of introducing students to literature at the college level, a method in which literature is seen not as a body of texts to be covered but as a way of thinking to be mastered. Our aim is to help students learn to think in the modes and to recognize the modes that are best exemplified in literary texts. Each of the first three chapters of the book emphasizes a different mode: First, the representative mode of narration and drama, in which human deeds and situations are recounted or enacted; second, the analogical mode of metaphor, in which one thing is presented in terms of another; and third, the mode of intertextuality, in which one text is seen as a development or transformation of earlier texts. In each of these cases our aim is to show how literary texts use processes that are also found in other kinds of speech and writing.

This whole conception of literary study is heavily influenced by recent developments in literary theory—but this is not a course in theory. Our book is <u>not</u> crammed with difficult theoretical readings. Nor do you need to be a theoretician to use it. All you need is a love for literature and an open mind. This is because the theory that informs this book has led us to present literature in a democratic way—not as a set of untouchable great works, each on its pedestal, but as a way of thinking and writing to which we all have access, indeed to which we all need access if we are to realize our full potential as citizens of a democracy. This is why we present literary texts as objects of interaction and emulation rather than worship.

The first two chapters of the book follow a traditional course, treating fiction, drama, and poetry primarily, though not in the traditional way. The third chapter is more unusual, because in it we introduce the concept of "intertextuality" as a key to literary thought and especially to those modes of writing we call interpretation and criticism. In this way, we situate academic ways of writing about literature in relation to literary processes in general, as simply one sort of intertextuality among others. This is a little unusual, but we feel that our gradual approach to this concept makes it possible for all students to comprehend and practice interpretive and critical writing—surely goals of a course like those this book is intended to serve.

The fourth chapter is a more radical departure from the norm. It should be said at once that it has been placed last because it is meant to be an option for the instructor. It may well be that on first using this book, you will not feel ready to tackle Chapter 4. With a class that needs to proceed slowly, you may never feel that the material in Chapter 4 is appropriate. That is fine. There is plenty of material in the first three chapters for a semester's work, and it should be easy to supplement the material in the earlier chapters with additional texts of your own choosing, if you want to spend more time on a particular form of literature, or if you simply have some favorite works that you want to include because you think your students should read them.

On the other hand, if you and your students are ready for a challenge, then you should consider doing one or both of the parts in Chapter 4. Either one can be chosen—the one based on Roland Barthes's notion of the "fragment" as a literary form, or the one based on Jacques Derrida's notion of the "signature"—but whichever you choose will demand some time for preparation and discussion in class of some rather difficult material. The reward will come when your students write on the major assignments provided in these two sections. If they have covered the reading and discussed it thoroughly enough to understand what they are undertaking, their writing

will astonish both you and themselves. We tend, all too often, to underestimate the creative energy of our students. The trick is to find ways of
unleashing the capabilities that are actually there. Accomplishing just
that is a major purpose of **Text Book,** as it should be of all courses that
introduce students to literary ways of thought.

In this manual, we provide some practical advice on how to use the
readings and writing assignments in **Text Book,** we report on our own experiences in field-testing this material, and we include some samples of student writing that demonstrate the kind of creative energy released by these
assignments. We have attempted, in fact, to do everything in our power to
encourage you to give the book a serious try, and to assist you in the
actual use of it, should you decide to put it to the test. We are convinced that the results of such a test will be the strongest argument that
could be made on behalf of this book. A course in literary study must find
its justification in the way students who have taken such a course can then
use language in reading, thinking, and writing. Their own writing will be
the best measure of all this. That is why we have oriented our book to the
production of interesting writing by students.

# CONTENTS

You will of course want to design your own syllabus, but sometimes it is useful to have something to react against. Therefore we are providing two possible versions of a syllabus for a course that uses **Text Book** as the sole text for a semester's work. Obviously, you can follow a plan like either of these and feed into it works from an anthology or materials from any other source. What we are providing here is meant to be a skeleton that can be the basis for your own planning.

## Version 1
Our basic assumption in this version is that you will use all four sections of the book for about equal periods of time. Recognizing that quarters and semesters vary considerably in length from school to school, we have designed this typical syllabus for twelve units, that we call "weeks," which can be adjusted to fit other actual quarters or semesters.

## Week 1
Concentrate on the first part of Chapter 1: Narrative. Assign and discuss Pratt, "Natural Narrative." Students write a personal anecdote. Assign and discuss Pound or Williams. Raise question of relationship between "natural" and "literary" narratives. Assign Chopin. Second writing assignment on Chopin.

## Week 2
Concentrate on the second part of Chapter 1: Drama. Assign either Wedekind or Chopin, followed by a writing assignment on drama. Use some class time for performances.

## Week 3
Conclude Chapter 1. Assign Goffman. Discuss in class. Then move to either the Strindberg for more drama or the Esslin for an approach to television. A writing assignment can come from either the Goffman or the later reading in this section.

## Week 4
Begin Chapter 2 with Roger Brown's material on language. This is crucial for the rest of the chapter; make sure in discussion that everyone understands this. During the rest of the week, work with the three short poems and the related writing and discussion exercises, to make sure all students begin to get a feel for metaphor. Bring in other poems if you like.

## Week 5
Attend to Freud and the surrealists. This is fairly difficult material, so you may wish to go slowly. Students should write on surrealism this week. If you have time, you can begin looking at the poems in the next section.

## Week 6
Writing a paper on metaphor should be the main business of this week, based on the minianthology included in the text. Close with a discussion of Lakoff and Johnson.

## Week 7
We recommend an extra week on metaphor at this point, concentrating on either argument or advertising. Begin with the Keidel and Sontag readings (assuming you have already discussed Lakoff and Johnson, which is crucial)

and then use either the J. J. Thomson piece or the advertising material as the basis for a written paper.

## Week 8
Begin the study of Chapter 3, with the introduction on intertextuality and the three examples provided. Make sure your students understand the concept before moving on to the Queneau writing assignment. By the end of this week, you should be reading Hansel and Gretel in the third section.

## Week 9
Using the Coover, Keillor, and Grimm material in the third section, prepare your students and have them complete a fairy-tale transformation. This should be a substantial piece of writing.

## Week 10
Complete Chapter 3, by using either the "Completing Texts" or "Interpreting Texts" sections, covering both the reading and writing assignments provided.

## Weeks 11 and 12
At this point, you should probably choose which of the two sections in Chapter 4 you are going to use in any given course. Both of them lead to substantial writing assignments, by way of some relatively difficult reading. It will take a bit of time to negotiate the preparation, so make your choice and follow whichever path suits you. If you are teaching two sections, you might choose a different assignment for each. But whichever section you choose, you will need all of the reading in that section to prepare the students for the writing assignment at the end.

## Version 2
Some instructors may feel unready to tackle Chapter 4 in their first use of this book. No problem. If you want to stick to the first three chapters, you need only give each of Chapters 2 and 3 an extra week, by covering both the material on argument and advertising in Chapter 2 and both the literary short stories and the interpretation of fairy tales in Chapter 3. The course can also be extended by simply going a bit slower in Chapter 1 as well as the later chapters, or by introducing more of your favorite poems, plays, stories, or essays into the framework we have provided. In all these cases, the basic syllabus we have just described should be useful as a point of departure.

### A Possible Addendum to the Syllabus

You may wish to give your students a version of the handout we include here, or simply to use it as a guide for a discussion about the course and its purpose. If you wish to duplicate and distribute it, you have our permission.

One of the goals of this course is to teach you to use models. These models include not only various forms of writing, but also certain styles of speaking. Success in school depends not only on the ability to write, but also on the ability to ask questions and to develop strategies for accessing the information stored in whatever materials you are asked to treat. The university requires this class of all students because of the belief that what you learn about reading, writing, speaking, and thinking in this class will be transferable to other parts of the curriculum. If this goal is to be realized, you must become an independent learner, able to use the learning strategies demonstrated in this course without continual prompting by an instructor. Rather, you must learn to prompt yourself, and to interrogate actively the readings and instructors that you encounter. The following list of questions indicates the kinds of things you should know about all the readings in this class. While it is not exhaustive, the list should also be useful in other classes. While some if not all of the questions are quite obvious, it is our experience that many students are content to leave them unformulated, or unanswered.

1. What is the assignment? Exactly what kind of writing am I expected to produce?

2. What is the model I am to follow? What are its specific features? How is it put together? What techniques or devices does the author use?

3. What is the purpose of the supporting readings? How do they contribute to an understanding of the model?

4. Is it possible to reduce the model to a formula? to a precise generalized description of a few steps that must be followed or a few fundamental techniques that must be performed? If so, what are these steps? Can I think of the model as a blueprint or pattern for making more items of its kind?

5. What is the interest of the readings in their own right? What issues do they raise that might be worth discussing, questioning, challenging? Is the form of the model in any way necessary to the topic it talks about? If it were written in some other manner, would that affect my response to the themes?

6. How do earlier sections of the course readings help me understand the present assignment and model?

7. Assuming that the readings supply most if not all of the information needed to define and carry out the project, which selections are the most helpful? which parts are most confusing or difficult?

Story and Storyteller: Narrative

Mary Louise Pratt, "Natural Narrative" (p. 2)

The way this first reading assignment is used will set the tone for much of your course. Because this text develops from assignment to assignment, if your students do not master this one, they will be handicapped in attempting many of the later assignments. It will be important throughout this book not to move on until you are assured that your students comprehend the major features of the material presented. It will never be more important than during the first assignment. Therefore, we begin with two suggestions.

First, we suggest that you really master this material yourself. That is, read it over more than once, trying to anticipate questions that may come from your students. You may also wish to consult the full text in Pratt's book and Chapter 9 in Labov's Language in the Inner City, which has been used in paperback by the University of Pennsylvania Press. In your preparation you should work out your own answers to the questions we have placed at the end of the reading.

Second, we suggest that you begin your discussion by asking your class if there are things in Pratt's discussion that they do not understand clearly. Try to conduct this discussion in such a way as to elicit whatever problems your students are having, however minor or trivial, without implying that they shouldn't have such problems. Your ability to encourage questions without making the questioner seem dumb will be crucial to getting your course off on the right foot. When you have talked over all the difficulties you can elicit, then it is time to go to the specific questions formulated in the book. In the course of your discussion, you should remind students that they are going to be asked to write an anecdote of their own that conforms to the structure discussed by Labov and Pratt—so if they have questions about that six-part structure, now is the time to ask them.

Discussion and Writing
1. In eliciting answers to these questions, it will be important to get more than one, to allow people to express some disagreement over just where the action turns. The resolution of the discussion should not be an exact determination of the moment of climax, for instance, but a clear sense of how an action rises and turns toward resolution. There may well be more than one good answer to these questions. The important thing is to help students understand why any answers that are really far away from the point should be discarded. You want to work for a consensus that locates climax or resolution within a couple of lines. Your students should be able to point to a reasonable place for dénouement and to argue reasonably for their choice.
2. Because it asks for evaluation, this question will obviously tolerate some range of responses. In conducting discussion of it, the key will be to keep discussion focused on particular passages in the two texts, such as the closing lines of Larry's narrative. You might ask what would be lost if they were missing.
3. This can either be a homework assignment, or something done in class. You might break into small groups, for instance, and let each group prepare a narrative; then, compare them in discussion. Or you might have the whole class collaborate, with you leading discussion and a couple of recorders working on a written version. The point of the exercise lies in what we learn about narrative from trying to construct one.

4. The point of this exercise is to help students realize that written narrative must compensate in some way for the absence of the teller of the tale. Without the tones of voice and the gestures of a speaker, written narrative must try harder to convey tone and expressive quality.
5. This is a writing assignment that looks like "creative" writing in a way, but really has another purpose. The purpose is to demonstrate that the writer has indeed learned to use the analytic structure of Labov and can turn that analysis upon his or her own writing to make sure all the elements are there. Your students should have fun writing these anecdotes, but they should also use them to demonstrate mastery of the concepts concerned. In making your own written responses to the assignment you should praise what is interesting, but also check each one to see that all the parts are there. You may even wish to have your students label the parts on their written essays.

Ezra Pound, "Agassiz and the Fish" (p. 14)

This anecdote is here to show how persistent the anecdote form actually is. It is _not_ here to show how superior a literary anecdote is to a natural narrative. It will be perfectly reasonable for you or some of your students to prefer Labov's natural narratives to Pound's literary anecdote. If you are pressed for time you may wish to choose between using this selection and the following one by William Carlos Williams.

Discussion and Writing
1. Some of the six features are less visible in Pound than in the natural narratives. In particular, at the crucial moment of climax, Pound understates where most natural narratives would emphasize or repeat. Pound says, "the student knew something about it." This anecdote deviates from the natural narrative partly in its compression and understatement, but also in the amount of time it covers. Most natural narratives cover a brief experience. Pound uses "three weeks," which is in fact an exaggeration of the actual time span involved in the incident that Pound is probably using as the basis for this incident. (Further discussion of this anecdote may be found in Robert Scholes, Textual Power, Chapter 8.)
2. The point of the question is to show the role of narrative in argument, just as later we shall be concerned with the role of metaphor in various forms of persuasive and argumentative texts. Pound is trying to show that the study of literary texts can be as serious and precise as scientific study only if one is willing to make a serious effort to "see" the texts in question as if they were biological specimens.
3. This question deflects attention from narrative to the related topic of argument, for a moment. Pound is setting up a formula in which science equals what is good by being opposed to what is bad--medieval superstition cut off from close observation of the object under study ("logic in a vacuum").
4. This assignment probably will not support a paper of great length, but it should serve to produce good short papers for those students who will learn from Pound's anecdote and keep studying the specimens until they know something about them. The point is exactly that they should emulate the example Pound provides: comparative study based on close scrutiny. They can only find a paper in this topic by looking for minute differences between the texts provided for their scrutiny. You should not expect any particular "right" answer, but should reward careful attention to detail.
The stumbling block for students doing this assignment may be the word "important" in the first sentence of the assignment. You should reassure them that they are to provide their own criteria for what is important.

2

William Carlos Williams, "The Use of Force" (p. 15)

This is a strong text that should generate plenty of interest in its own right, but you should be aware that it will also figure in later assignments. In short, this is probably not one to skip. You should remind your students to read it with the anecdote structure in mind.

## Discussion and Writing
1. This is meant to be a discussion question, though it could be used for a written assignment. You might begin a class with students writing short answers to this question that can be collected and used as the basis for discussion. The point is to note how little the text evaluates or interprets itself and how much it seems to invite interpretation. Surely, the title itself is mainly an invitation to interpretation. To stimulate discussion, you might ask whether the story should be interpreted as a kind of rape. The analogies are actually very close and sustained. You will want to keep reminding your students to anchor their interpretations in the text. Try to suppress any impulses you have to close down discussion by providing the "right" interpretation, while at the same time guiding the class away from readings that cannot be justified by citation of the text or its appropriate context.
2. There is no right answer to the last question posed here. The major point of this discussion should be to note how Williams's text has the structure of action and resolution of natural narratives but requires the reader to provide more of the interpretation. Williams also provides much more descriptive detail than would appear in a natural narrative, and some of that detail conceals or suggests evaluation. Discussion can be focused on this aspect of the text by asking questions about the function of particular descriptive details, in the form of, "What would be lost if this sentence [or phrase] were missing?"

Kate Chopin, "The Kiss" (p. 19)

This story will be used for later assignments as well. Its function here is to help students retain and refine their concept of the six-part structure of narrative texts. Perhaps we should say here that we do not feel that "six" is a magic number or that some other system with five or seven divisions would not work in the analysis of narrative. The point is that analysis goes better with a system than without, and this is as good as any other. When your students become very sophisticated, they may be ready to discard this, but for now, learning how to use this system will be a stage on their journey toward literary sophistication. You should feel free to admit this. The system is provisional but learning how to use it is important for now.

## Discussion and Writing
1. In this story there is little orientation--or rather, description takes the place of orientation, and of evaluation, too. In particular, the scene before the wedding cries out for evaluation, but none is provided. Chopin wants her readers to perform that act. But the story definitely has a coda. The discussion of this question should take place after the written assignments (Question 1 or 2) have been made. Students who are going to produce their own versions of this text should take a special interest in refining their understanding of its structure.
2. This is an assignment designed to produce a written text. The student who undertakes to produce this anecdote will discover how what is left to subtle innuendo in the literary text needs to be spelled out in a personal

3

anecdote. This exercise will amount to both a reading of the Chopin story and a demonstration of mastery over the Labovian analytic method. It should be both a creative and critical exercise.
3. This written assignment takes the form of an expository or explanatory essay. It can be an extension or development of ideas the student has already considered if the writing assignments for Pound and Williams have been used. We would hope your serious students will be able to make some clear distinctions between the more explicit methods of the natural narrative and the more subtle, implicit methods of literature. This should help them to understand why so much literary criticism takes the form of interpretation: Literary texts demand interpretation; they are structured so as to be incomplete without it. This does not mean, however, that one should like only the literary. There are perfectly valid reasons for admiring the raw vitality and energy of the natural narrative—once one has realized what it is and why it is that way.

## Character and Confrontation: Drama (p. 22)

One of the purposes of this part of Chapter 1 is to enable students to appreciate clearly the difference between narration and dramatization—and to see how both of them connect to ordinary life and ordinary uses of language. Though acting out dramatic scenes takes time and may seem to be too much like play and not enough like learning, our experience is that time spent on helping students get a feel of what stage action is like is seldom wasted. It is a form of reading and not a trivial one.

Frank Wedekind (a scene from the play) Spring Awakening (p. 22)

### Discussion and Writing
1. Do stage the reading. You won't regret it.
2. This is a straightforward question. Obviously, drama puts the emphasis on action and result (with or without a coda). It has no obvious place for orientation (except in stage directions), abstracts, or evaluations. Sometimes, however, dramatists will work in evaluations by putting them in the mouths of characters—but this is a special problem. The form itself is not so adapted to evaluation as is the narrative form. In discussing this question, you may wish to bring out the way that the literary narratives you have been examining move toward the dramatic by suppressing a certain amount of evaluative commentary. The strength of drama lies in its immediacy and in the way that it forces audiences to participate in evaluating the action it presents. It is not surprising that literary narrators should try to capture some dramatic power by imitating drama in this respect. Nor is it surprising that sometimes playwrights work in evaluative commentary. Artists tend to move toward exceeding the limits of their medium. This is an important point.
We assume that you will have some students who prefer the dramatic and some who prefer narration. Obviously there is no right answer, but it is important for the reasons behind the preferences to get as clear an expression as possible. Don't be afraid to state your own preferences and reasons, but don't foreclose their options, either.
3. The point of this assignment is to learn something about dramatic form—its power and limits—but also to think about how certain cultural practices change over time. You should encourage students to deal with contemporary mores as they understand them. We recommend that you also tell them that they must decide whether the presentation should be serious or light. We would not discourage a bit of exaggeration or caricature in an assignment like this. You may well wish to stage or read some of the most successful results.

4

4. The point of this assignment is that the anecdotal form will allow the evaluation and orientation that is not there in the dramatic scene to be made explicit. It is, in a way, a measure of comprehension of Wedekind as well as of the mastery of dramatic idiom. Such assignments call upon both creative and critical skills.

Kate Chopin (dialogue from the story) "The Kiss" (p. 26)

This text has only one question, but, as Kurt Vonnegut might say, it is a doozy. It asks for the transformation of the dialogue from Chopin's story into a playlet that conveys all the action and evaluation conveyed by the original story. This means, just for openers, that your students must understand the story very well. If they want to talk it over again before going to work, that's fine. Give them all the help you can.

You may feel that this kind of writing is beyond the reach of your students. To some extent, it should be, but a perfect response is not the goal here. Whatever they achieve should be of some satisfaction to them. You may well wish to have this assignment begun in class. You might, for instance, begin by working out the scenic structure in a general discussion, and then divide into several small groups, each group working on a different scene. After some input from you, then each individual could take the project home and try to finish it off. Various combinations of group and individual work ought to be possible here. The main thing is that the problems of drama will be brought home to those who struggle with the form. You are also likely to get some results that surprise you.

Things will go best if you talk over at some length the four options mentioned in the question, making sure that everybody knows what a "confidante," for instance, is. We would discourage any use of a commentator who is not also a character, since that solution does not solve the problem but eliminates it by turning the drama into a narrative. All this should be discussed, either before your class starts writing, or after they have begun and before they have finished. The point is to use the creative struggle as a way of bringing out critical questions.

Erving Goffman, Character Contests (p. 27)

This is a serious piece of writing by a major sociologist. Encourage your students to read it carefully and note any questions they have as they read. Begin your discussion by asking them to raise those questions with you. This means that you must have read the selection very carefully yourself.

Discussion and Writing
1. This question is designed mainly to give you a chance to make sure that Goffman's ideas and terminology have been understood. Be patient, and elicit as many incomprehensions or objections as you can. This will pay off later.
2. If your class needs a chance to personalize the Goffman, this question is designed to allow just that. If you think they are ready to move ahead without bringing the matter home to their own experience, you can skip this one. But pausing here may save time in the long run.
3. The scene from Spring Awakening is certainly a character contest of a sort familiar to all of us who have lived in families. It is not easy to say who wins that contest, so perhaps no one does, but you should see what your students think about it—and ultimately you should tell them what you think about it, too. We are divided in our own opinions on this one.

4. Here again, you should let a hundred flowers bloom. We are inclined to consider Harvy the winner of this one. What do you think?

5. You may not feel the need for this return to Williams, but the question, even if considered briefly, should help convince students that the character contest is a very frequent form in fiction--and that the concept of character contest can be a help in evaluating or interpreting the events in a narrative text.

6. Larry's anecdote is the clearest example of run-in we have studied. Another assignment could involve the rewriting of this in dramatic form. If you wish, you might offer that as an alternative to rewriting one of their own anecdotes, but most students are likely to prefer their own. The point of the exercise is for the student to learn how to compensate in dramatic form for the orientation and evaluation that was there in the anecdote.

7. Pretty important--a tiny bandit and a towering barmaid would complicate the flow of simple emotions that the present journalistic account clearly wants to generate. One suspects that myth has already intervened in this "objective" account.

8. This is a more complicated question. You may wish to focus on whether the bloodshed would damage the gamelike quality of the character contest.

9. The best way to approach this question is probably to invent some other forms of words, ranging from simple insults to high-flown speeches. What is so good about the words we have is that they underline the fact that this is indeed a character contest. It is a game and now it's the bandit's move.

10. In making this writing assignment, emphasize the need for the three scenes. The before and after are essential for the orientation and evaluation to emerge. The best solutions will no doubt indicate some change in the relationship between the two bandits after the fiasco. This is a chance for your students with a sense of humor to excel.

August Strindberg, The Stronger (p. 35)

Remind your students that this is a complete play. Everything they need to know to understand this scene is presented here--but they will have to do a lot of orientation and evaluation on their own. They will even have to fill in a lot of past action on their own. Suggest that they read Question 1 before they read the play itself.

Discussion and Writing

1. This is the question. Probably you should work out the plot in class, getting suggestions from all sides. Your students will need to understand the full situation in order to answer the other questions--which means you had better work out your own written list of events in the lives of these characters as you glean them from the text.

2. This is an assignment for a rather sophisticated written essay. If you feel your students are not up to it, you may wish to skip this assignment-- but don't underestimate them. What most belongs to art in this play is the silence of one character and the way the other's remarks reveal the whole romantic entanglement of three characters. The way the wife maneuvers the slippers in such a way as to make the former mistress laugh at a too familiar gesture of rubbing one foot against the other is typical of the artfulness of the play. No ordinary confrontation would manage to get quite so much of the past into the play so quickly.

3. This is a fairly sophisticated assignment, in that it requires the student to take over the story of this triangle as a story but change all the orientation and evaluation that the present version generates. You might

suggest that one way to solve these problems is to take over as much as possible of Strindberg's outline--to discuss the same events and topics in the same order, but to put a different evaluation on all of them. One is at liberty, of course, to imagine a different future than the one implied by the dialogue (or monologue) we have.

4. This might be an alternate assignment to 3 or a companion piece, if both are to be relatively short. The interest of the piece will depend upon the development of the character of the waitress through her speech or writing. Advise your students to give some thought to what kind of person she is going to be before they try to write about her. Is she, for instance, sweet and sensitive, or brutal and stupid? Is she an innocent bystander or is she implicated in these activities? It might be worthwhile to discuss some possibilities in class before anyone undertakes to write this.

Martin Esslin, "Aristotle and the Advertisers: The Television Commercial as Drama" (passages from the essay) (p. 40)

In our introduction we have tried to provide the terminology from Aristotle that the student will need to follow Esslin. It might not hurt to go over it before the students read the passages from Esslin.

Discussion and Writing

1. This question is designed at the occasion for a review of the whole chapter. Kate Chopin's story is an excellent example of Aristotelian principles at work. Your students may have provided some in dramatizing the bakery robbery, too. Try to cover as many things as possible in the discussion, so as to refresh everyone's memory and to establish the Aristotelian critical principles in the minds of your students.

2. If you have access to video equipment yourself, you may wish to select an appropriate commercial and make it available for your students to transcribe. If not, some appointed group of students who do have such access may be able to provide a transcript for the others to work on.

The point of this assignment is to allow for the application of Aristotelian principles and for the development of a parody by means of some distortion of these principles. That is, after transcribing a commercial that works according to the Aristotelian structure, change the structure and destroy the commercial functioning of the commercial. Acting out some of these should be fun. Afterward, you can try in discussion to elicit the common principles to the versions that were acted out. That is, you can ask which alterations in the Aristotelian structure proved most effective in betraying the purpose of the commercial dramatizations.

Chapter 2: TEXTS, THOUGHTS, AND THINGS

The Linguistic Basis of Metaphor

Roger Brown, "What Words Are: Reference and Categories" (p. 48)

This description of Dr. Itard's efforts to teach the "Wild Child" can serve as an extended metaphor or allegory of the composition classroom. We should never underestimate the extent to which our students tend to ignore or forget the material nature of language. The warning in this exemplary tale is that without language we might all be hunting squirrels in the woods. The more explicit lesson of the essay concerns the specific or material way in which language functions. Students rarely think about language as a technology that works in a particular, often quite odd, way. Metaphor is one of the most common, useful, elementary, yet bizarre features of this technology. If you have access to François Truffaut's Film, The Wild Child, we recommend its use as a means of further stimulating discussion.

## Discussion and Writing

1. Before dealing with metaphor, which is a certain kind of relationship between names, we need to understand something about names themselves. In this chapter, we treat the common noun and its metaphorical possibilities. One of the experiments in Chapter 4—the "signature"—explores the metaphorical potential of proper names.

Brown makes good use of Victor's story to illustrate "concept formation," something that many of our students understand no better than Victor, even if they use concepts correctly in everyday speech. The main point to stress in the example is the power of the name as a generalization covering all the individual items of a given sort. Itard is teaching Victor to generalize: In playing "fetch the referent" Itard and Victor demonstrate what is meant by "semantics." Itard's lesson, while appropriate for Victor, is obviously too simple for the class. If you asked your students to fetch a "book" they would be quite scornful. Similarly, if you asked them to write or recite the alphabet, they would balk at the ease of the task. For this very reason, it is sometimes useful to offer such exercises, to raise the students' awareness of how much they take for granted, and how much they already know of the material quality of language.

Brown goes beyond demonstrating the meaning of the word "semantics" by introducing a few complications into the discussion of concepts. It is useful to note the synonymity of the terms "concept," "category," and "class," all used to refer to or name the way multiple entities are unified and sorted into kinds for ease of recognition or identification. Brown now shifts from "vocabulary" to what some students might think of as "jargon"—the specialized vocabulary of a field of knowledge—linguistics. "Identity category" is a special kind or category of "category." The distinction is worth discussing to clarify the fact that we do not have direct, unmediated knowledge of objects such as books, but come into awareness of them by means of our sense perceptions. The physical properties of a particular book combine to identify it as the same one each time we encounter it or think of it; these properties function, that is, as a proper name. We may define a concept as a "set" of properties collected according to a given criterion of selection. The definition of the criterion of selection turns out to be far more flexible than the students expect.

To establish the status of the general and the particular, and the way they relate in language, by means of such a simple example will be useful later on when we start working with relationships between concepts combined in complex arguments.

2. The purpose of these two questions is simply to familiarize the students with some of the most basic terms used to describe the relationship between thinking and language. To define the more precise distinctions between "identity category" and "category of forms" provides some practice in charting the formal limits of a term in a specialized discourse. This process of setting the parameters of a concept in specialized discourses may serve as a model for a similar delimitation of terms also at work in the discourse of everyday life. The term "category of forms" refers to language itself, reflexively, to point out that it is just as important to be able to recognize the shapes of certain letters, or the sound of a given word as the same each time, and thus to identify its status as a meaningful

unit, as it is to recognize that a given book is the same one, or that an item is a "book" (to stay with Itard's example).

The key term in this discussion is "recurrence" or "repetition." People with different accents from different regions of the country can still understand each other in a conversation by ignoring the variables and attending to the significant features that identify a set of sounds as a category of form.  Again, the students find a point such as this one quite obvious, scarcely worth mentioning, even if they haven't thought about it specifically.  Later, in our discussion of poetry, however, they will be pleased to realize that this simple and obvious phenomenon of recurrence of significant features to establish a set of category is the same material aspect of language exploited by poets to build new, unique, but unstable aesthetic categories of signification.  The idea here, as elsewhere in our approach, is to help the students realize how much they already know about language, and that the acquisition of a vocabulary of categories will enable them to extend their cultural skills as native speakers to the understanding and practice of high literacy.

Roger Brown, "What Words Are:  Metaphor" (p. 53)

The logic of our selections from Brown, as we noted, is to establish first the nature of names of categories (concepts), so that we could better appreciate metaphors as relationships between concepts.

## Discussion and Writing

1.  One way to help students notice the material reality of language is to inventory the various practices of assigning names to things, official and unofficial, authorized and unauthorized, in society.  Brown gives a number of examples that illustrate some of the ways in which language actually grows and evolves over time.  Students often find it liberating to learn that language is not permanently set, fixed, defined absolutely once and for all, as it seemed to them to be in their previous schooling.  This realization will be helpful later when they are asked to manipulate a conceptual category, which for some will feel like breaking a law.

One of the principle ways language evolves is by means of metaphor—extending the features of a given category to name something that previously was excluded from the set.  To make the point that language is essentially and fundamentally metaphorical in nature, Brown uses a figure of "catachresis" for his example of a dead metaphor:  "the foot of a mountain."  His point in part is that our very vocabulary itself is metaphorical in a way that we fail to notice.  He also wants to emphasize that this metaphorical quality is irreducible.  Catachresis is the best figure with which to make this point, since it refers to figurative uses that lack any literal substitute.  There is no other literal name for which the "leg" is a metaphor, although we could describe the referent in other terms.

The special attitude mentioned, then, involves paying attention to language itself, listening for so-called dead metaphors; this requires the student to suspend the habits of daily life.  Brown does not encourage us to extend our attention to puns or homophones, but we could while we are at it, to get into the more playful mood or attitude with which the poet approaches language, especially when we remember that homophones have also played a major role in the growth of language (many words, few sounds).  In any case, the "bored of directors" does produce a kind of meaningful joke, in that it is not hard to imagine the accuracy of this descriptive term applied to the serious, responsible directors.  Moreover, by suspending the context temporarily (the context of the statement "of directors" would eliminate the meaning "bored" as the category appropriate for those

sounds), the student is prepared to appreciate the next step in the production of poetry--the assignment of a term to a new context from which it had
been excluded. At the very least the students will be more sensitive to
the problem of mixed metaphors, avoiding going where the hand of man has
never set foot.

Again, the circulation of words manifested in the passage from living
to dead metaphors and back illustrates at a basic level the cycle of
exchange between popular and high culture, everyday speech and literacy.
Part of our goal is to help the students realize the vitality and practi-
cality of this linguistic cycle for their own needs and purposes. The
attitude of suspending one's habits in order to notice figurative usages is
the same sort of openness required for learning anything new.

2. Once the students become aware of metaphorical usage they will notice
that almost every essayist they read uses metaphors, living and dead--an
insight that should improve their ability to read expository and argumentative writing as well as poetry. If they can understand what it means for a
rhetorical figure to be either living or dead, they should also be able to
understand similar uses of figures in poetry. The strategy is to call
their attention to the fact that they already understand and use metaphors
themselves, in order to give them confidence in the value of their native
knowledge of the language.

Brown, in paragraph 7, talks about metaphors blazing, evoking the category of fire and its attributes to communicate the sense of the death of a
metaphor in terms of the dying out of a fire. A comparison with Herrick's
poem reveals first that the fire image is present in both cases, but that
the poem develops the image more intensely, with greater complexity. The
reason students tend to overlook the metaphor in the poem (and hence to
have no idea what the poet is saying) is that the metaphor is introduced
with great economy--in the term "kindles," which simply goes by them too
quickly. They know poems contain metaphors, or the more dreaded "symbols,"
but the concentrated quality such usage gives to the language leaves them
at a loss unless they have already developed the strategies needed to read
such language. They overlook metaphors in essays for similar reasons, not
only because the figures may be dead or commonplace, but because the
reader, not expecting to find a metaphor, fails to exercise the strategy
needed to grasp the meaning of the figure (the comparison of the two sets
or concepts evoked by the metaphor). Language is a material process, we
keep saying, and our students need to be reminded that the usage of language requires effort--reading is as active a process as writing. You
can't hit a tennis ball without swinging at it; you can't read (understand)
a metaphor without "unpacking" it.

3. For this question a little dictionary work will be in order. You might
advise your students to look up these words in a good dictionary, or even
make available some material on these words from the Oxford English
Dictionary, a resource they should be introduced to. The question of difference in our understanding of a word and Herrick's may be discussed with
reference to a word's meaning in the context of a poem versus a dictionary
meaning.

"Wild civility" introduces paradox, a statement that, like metaphor,
depends upon two apparently contradictory terms.

4. We have been insisting on some very basic, obvious points, but our
experience with teaching some of the more difficult texts included in this
book indicates that many writing problems may be reduced to the fact that
the students lack any start-up strategies or problem-solving tactics. Part
of learning to use models involves learning some of the strategies needed
to extract information from written text and from classroom instructors.
They know, for example, that on a multiple-choice exam one of the answers

for a given question is correct. A similar confidence in the prepared setup of a textbook would improve their ability to use the materials provided for their use. Almost everything needed to answer any of the questions posed for discussion or undertake any of the writing assignments is provided in the readings. Hence, a student need not try to guess or remember the definition of a metaphor, only refer to that part of the readings in which the figure is defined. A question such as this one, then, which lends itself as much to class discussion as to writing, simply checks the students' basic reading habits, forcing them to review the selections for the information they will need to manage the next sections illustrating metaphorical practice in various kinds of writing. The best strategy for reading **Text Book,** or any textbook for that matter, turns out to be similar to the strategy needed to read poetry--to look actively for the unifying principle of each section, asking why a given selection has been provided, what function it serves specifically in furthering an understanding of the theme and assignment. Read in this way, even the academic prose of a textbook may blaze with a certain figurative life, as we have already seen in the pedagogical parable of the "Wild Child," and as may be noted again in the theme of "disorder" in Herrick's poem, alluding to the disorder that the poetic attitude of play may introduce into prosaic usage.

Metaphor in Three Poems (p. 60)

Before looking at the poems, you might ask your class how many of them noticed the plant metaphor in the first paragraph of the introduction to this section. This will give you some idea of how well or badly they are doing as students of metaphor. If many of them missed it, you had better stop right there and discuss it.

W. S. Merwin, "Separation" (p. 60)

You can find a discussion of this poem in Chapter 3 of Semiotics and Interpretation by Robert Scholes (New Haven: Yale University Press, 1982). For classroom study of this and all other poems, we recommend that you begin with a couple of readings aloud of the text--by students or yourself.
1. The obvious expectation here is a sharp object, like a knife or needle. What makes Merwin's metaphor poetic is that it uses the blunt end of the needle: unexpected but appropriate.
2. Merwin's metaphor signifies the speaker's inability to escape from awareness of separation. The thread of memory is everywhere for him.

W. H. Auden, "Let us honor..." (p. 61)

This poem and its suggested rewriting should lead to a useful discussion of metaphor and literary interpretation. You can ask students to put some rewritings on the board as a way of starting things. One useful version to discuss looks like this:

> Let us praise if we can
> The living man
> Though we admire none
> But the dead one

All the questions posed in the last paragraph of the text are important. Try to find time for each one to be discussed.

Sylvia Plath, "Metaphors" (p. 62)

1. For those students who have always found poetry to be a complete
enigma, Plath's poem sometimes has the effect of those gestalt-shift per-
ceptual effects--the "rabbit-duck" for example:  When the image is suddenly
perceived as a duck rather than as the rabbit it first appeared to be there
is genuine surprise and pleasure.  Similarly, when the reader realizes that
all the lines of the poem inventory ways of saying "I'm pregnant," thus
supplying the missing meaning, there is a shift in understanding.  The
reader now has at least a rough and ready strategy for discerning the outlines of a referent in poetic language.  The poem shows in addition the way
in which clichés and commonplaces may be revived in a poetic context to
express, through accumulation and its effect of insistence if nothing else,
the feeling of gestation as well as the social attitude toward pregnant
women.
     In class discussion, it will be useful to go through the poem line by
line and metaphor by metaphor, considering how the images are connected to
different aspects of the verbal category or abstraction:   pregnancy.
2.  It will take a little time for students to accomplish this.  You might
start them working on their lists in class and have them complete their
riddle poems at home.  This can also be done as a group effort, with the
poem taking shape on the board.  The purpose of the exercise is to get them
thinking about metaphor from the writer's point of view.

Metaphor and Dream (p. 63)

     This Freudian material will function best if used with the surrealist
poems that follow it in the text.  We have tried to present Freud's concept
of dream-work in the briefest possible span.  If you wish to do more with
it, you can supplement this material with examples from either the relevant
chapters of the Introductory Lectures or from the chapter on the dream-work
in The Interpretation of Dreams.  The major point to be made is that poems
resemble dreams in their use of images and figures of speech both to
express and conceal meaning.  The act of interpretation is the raising of
the latent content of a text to the manifest level.  As a reminder, here
are some capsule definitions:

latent--hidden
manifest--apparent
dream-work--encoding
interpretation--decoding
condensation--part for whole
displacement--one thing for another
imagery--a sensory image for an abstraction

Surrealist Metaphor (p. 66)

     This examination of extreme cases of figuration should help students
understand one limit of metaphor, which is madness or nonsense.  The other
limit is banality or cliché.

Discussion
     You can no doubt find your own illustrations, but here are some chosen
from the material in the text.
1.  apparent contradiction--"sparkling sewer grill"
2.  hidden term--"clown of the eclipse" (moon)
              --"sparkling sewer grill" (stars)

3.  concrete for abstract—any image; Freud's example is a picture of
    someone sitting on an object to indicate possession of it.
4.  abstract for concrete—think of Auden's abstractions, "vertical" and
    "horizontal."

André Breton, "Broken Line" (p. 68)

You may discover that the strangeness of Breton's poetry arouses your
students' interest in the man. If you want to give them more information,
you will find a useful guide in Mary Ann Caws, André Breton (Twayne,
1973). There is also a useful introduction in the Cauvin and Caws edition
of The Poems of André Breton, from which our selection was taken.

Discussion and Writing
1.  What is asked for here, in a somewhat cryptic way, is some consideration of the relationship between poetic charm or pleasure and the fragmented nature of some poetic language. The peculiar charm of certain kinds
of poetry, like the charm of certain dreams, is based on these texts' need
for interpretation. They are charming because they invite us to play a
role in their games of meaning.
2.  This is meant as a writing assignment. If you use it, you may wish to
point out that many of these lines might occur in contemporary popular
music. A whole song might be developed starting with any one of these
lines. Encourage your students to produce such a song.
    In class you might select just one of these lines and have the group
free-associate on it. See what ideas turn up. You might also try to
understand the line by translating it into a prose statement or paraphrase. Then begin to shape the results of these processes into a meditation or a song.
    For the writing assignment, remind your class that they are not inter-
preting; they are not seeking some meaning already in the line; they are
using their own thoughts. It's what it means to them that counts. (You
might remind them also that interpretation is something different.)
3.  This is a fairly sophisticated writing assignment. Even if you choose
not to use it, you may find it worthwhile to go over the four lines that
have been turned into normal prose by changing a single word. Understanding how this was done should enable your students to understand also how
the lines were surrealized in the first place.
4.  Before turning your class loose on this one, you should discuss the
examples in Question 3.
5.  This question is meant to serve as the occasion for a review of the
material on surrealist metaphor. In leading discussion, you should begin
sometimes by directing attention to a specific line and sometimes by asking
about a specific device.

Wallace Stevens, "Domination of Black" (p. 71)

1.  One of the points to stress in the discussion of both Breton and
Stevens concerns the particular way poems are organized. Students are
often more familiar with the other two principal ways to organize a body of
though, narration and exposition. They readily follow a story line or
plot, and an argument (somewhat less readily, not through lack of understanding the process so much as through failure of attention). Many students, however, are not aware that poetry has an ordering principle that in
essence is as straightforward as the other two arrangements. That principle, as we noted earlier, is repetition, the recurrence of items to compose
a pattern. Breton's poem is more chaotic than Stevens's, but the process

of signification is similar--the effect of meaning is produced by means of
a concatenation of items. His poem does not cohere at the level of individual sentences, but only as a whole, as a collection of features into a
set, exactly in the manner of concept formation, except that the resultant
signification in the poem is not a generalization but a particularization
at the opposite end of the scale of meaning from the concept. Or, we could
say that Breton has used the process of concept formation to form a unique
concept (a contradiction in terms, logically). Every poet uses this process of collection of terms into a set by means of repetition and juxtaposition. The set is more apparent in Stevens because the "beat" of repetition is more pronounced and regular. What does the pattern add up to?
What does it mean? Both poems seem to be about the same thing--about a
feeling of depression that we learn about as an inference based on the collection of items in the set. We answer the riddle according to the associations we have with peacocks or spiders. Of course there is a level of
aesthetic power communicated in the poems, but students often find that
dimension to be inaccessible until they have mastered the trick of refer-
ence--what does the poem "name"? One goal of this chapter is to help the
students see that whether or not they are ready to accept the pleasure of
poetic language, they can still learn to use the poetic strategy of
arrangement to build arguments for which they will have plenty of use, even
if they never write a poem.

Poetic Uses of Metaphor (p. 73)

A substantial paper on metaphor should come out of this material.
Your job is to help your students prepare for the paper and even to help
them get started on it. You should be willing to discuss the poems in
class. You might even invite students to submit a draft of a sample paragraph to make sure they are on the right track. One danger of discussing
the poems in class, of course, is that they will get too much repeated on
the papers. You can try to avoid this by concentrating in class on simply
understanding the poems and just pointing out directions for the student to
investigate. It will be useful, though, to identify the major metaphors in
the various poems, and to help students see how every metaphor involves
some kind of comparison, in which both sides must be identified. If X and
Y are being compared, the reader needs a good idea of what X and Y are in
order to follow the metaphoric process. You should avoid following the
process all the way through in too many cases, but help identify the directions in which further study should go.
      In their papers, they will need to identify some interesting meta-
phors, to explain what things are brought together in the metaphor, and to
consider how such features as strangeness and appropriateness function--
sometimes simultaneously--to make certain metaphors especially effective or
interesting. One process they may find useful will be to think of each
poem in terms of Breton's list of poetic strategies. This will help them
begin to talk about metaphoric process. The text makes a start on discussing Francis's poem, "Pitcher." You might continue discussing the images
in that poem, showing how the effect depends upon the metaphor functioning
well in both its contexts: baseball and poetry.
      Here are some thoughts about the poems that may help you generate dis-
cussion while the students are getting familiar enough with the poems to
write their papers.

One no Komachi, "Doesn't he realize..." (p. 74)

Ask the class to rewrite the poem with a new metaphor: Doesn't he
(she) realize/ that I am not/ like...

14

Stephen Spender, "Word" (p. 74)

Note the rhyme scheme. The rhyme for fish is saved until the last line, where it does "rhyme upon a dish." The poem may be said to exist because fish and dish do rhyme. Ask your students what it means for a word to be "free." This is a useful poem to consider early because the metaphor is so obvious. Every student should see that fish and words are being compared here. What they should also see is the way that the comparison (or metaphor) leads to some interesting thoughts about the way words exist and function in poems. What does it mean to "rhyme upon a dish?"

Robert Francis, "Pitcher" (p. 74)

Some students will resist the notion that the poem is about anything but baseball. Our response to this line of resistance would begin by saying, Suppose it is, but what is the metaphor for baseball here? To what is baseball being compared? In terms of what is baseball being discussed? This question must be answered in terms of such expressions as "comprehended," "misunderstood," "communicate," and "understand." If the poem is about baseball (and it is), it discusses baseball through a metaphor of communication, and it emphasizes a type of communication with certain peculiarities that correspond closely, for instance, to what Breton and Stevens identified as the special features of poetry: in particular, the delaying of the process of comprehension. Try suggesting that "The others" are the other fielders on a team--who are not pitchers--or the writers of prose-- who are not poets. And note the second word of the poem.

X. J. Kennedy, "Ars Poetica" (p. 75)

Note the pun on the Latin word for art and British slang for backside. Ask students to interpret the last line of the poem--that is, to extend the meaning beyond golden geese. What, in particular, does the word "lay" signify here?

Louise Glück, "Cottonmouth Country" (p. 75)

This will go best if perceived as based on a single episode: a couple ("us") swimming in North Carolina ("Hatteras"), finding some fish bones floating in the water, seeing a poisonous snake when they come to shore. The last two lines turn the images into metaphor. These lines do not destroy the literal level of what has gone before, but they cannot be read literally themselves. Like a dream, they must be interpreted. Let different interpretations be proposed. In every case, you must ask what is being compared to what.

William Carlos Williams, "A Sort of a Song" (p. 75)

The first metaphor connects snake and words. Don't let your students miss one of Williams's most famous expressions: "No ideas but in things." Ask them what that has to do with metaphor. Look up saxifrage in a dictionary, or ask your students to do it. Is this an idea or a thing? Invent! Compose.

Richard Wilbur, "Praise in Summer" (p. 76)

In the poem the poet offers some metaphors that tend toward the surreal, and then rejects metaphor ("_instead_") as a perversion--but he's at it again (though less obviously) in the last line ("sweep the ceiling"). What does this mean?

Emily Dickinson, "How Soft This Prison Is" (p. 77)

The last line gives us the abstractions behind the metaphors. The poem's power comes from the universality of the feeling and the concreteness of the image—along with the perverse eeriness of the soft prison, the Dungeon of the King of Down.

Adrienne Rich, "Moving in Winter" (p. 77)

Ideas in things, as Williams says. These are not metaphors or similes but associations or metonymies between things and events. The moving of furniture through the snow seems to unleash ideas of the life that has been lived in and around these objects. You might ask how the poet makes the objects convey an attitude toward the marriage: looking at the word "grey" in line 9, for instance.

Mark Strand, "Eating Poetry" (p. 78)

The poem has a surrealist quality. The speaker says "I am a new man," but he snarls and barks. Has eating poetry turned him into something less than a human being? Is eating poetry a metaphor for reading it—or a special way of reading it? These questions should start a good discussion.

W. S. Merwin, "Inscription Facing Western Sea" (p. 78)

This poem simply describes one thing—waves breaking on a shore—in terms of an elaborate metaphor or deep image of another thing—an ancient war. Discussion should focus on the appropriateness of the different parts of the image to the object that it—metaphorically—describes.

Wallace Stevens, "Of Mere Being" (p. 79)

This is another elaborate or deep image, but it doesn't represent anything as concrete as waves breaking on the shore. It is an attempt to represent the essential quality that is common to everything that exists: Being, itself. This is a poet's answer to a philosopher's question: What is Being? In this poem we find metaphor pushed toward surrealism, metaphor at its furthest stretch.

Metaphor as a Basis for Thought (p. 80)

George Lakoff and Mark Johnson, "Concepts We Live By," "Argument Is War," "Some Further Examples," "The Partial Nature of Metaphorical Structuring" (pp. 80-90)

That our "ordinary conceptual system is metaphorical in nature" (paragraph 4), and that metaphors control our thinking and actions, is a revelation to students. In discussing the "argument is war" metaphor, you might point out, in reference to "the culture where arguments are not viewed in terms of war" (paragraph 7), that the Chinese and Japanese are such cultures. A Japanese garden, with its graceful placement of stones and shrubs, invites, indeed requires, the spectator to view it from various perspectives. So it is with a subject or an issue; it is to be contemplated from various points of view. ESL teachers can tell you how difficult it is to teach the American forms of argumentative essays to their Asian composition students.

## Discussion and Writing

1. Practical-minded American students will find in this section the payoff for careful attention to the functioning of metaphor in the previous section. The boundaries separating poetic language from other dimensions of discourse turn out to be much less rigid than they had been led to believe. We learned from Brown that metaphor is a relationship between categories (or concepts) in which the attributes or members of one set are applied to the name of the other set. Lakoff and Johnson understand metaphor in a similar way. Their discussion shows that the term "metaphorical concept" is essentially redundant. Indeed, when they insist that the phrase "argument is war" is to be taken literally--meaning that the concept of argument is structured precisely by means of this metaphor and has no status apart from the metaphor--they indicate the extent to which the opposition between "literal" and "figurative" has lost its meaning. This distinction in a more empirically positivistic attitude toward language was used to suggest that metaphor was at once removed from "truth," serving to help express a signification that could stand on its own, denotatively.

The term "metaphorical concept" is still useful to extend our understanding of concept formation. We noted earlier that metaphor is a relationship between concepts (one way among others of bringing concepts into relationship). Now we learn that concepts themselves are structured internally as metaphors--that the set of attributes constituting a category is itself a certain kind of relationship, and that relationship is metaphorical in nature. The redundancy is necessary also because while the juxtaposition of categories in poems tends to be innovative, producing living metaphors, the metaphors in everyday usage or in expository prose tend to be dead, assimilated into popular usage--hence they pass unnoticed. The most successful metaphors, that is, are those that have become concepts-- those that have passed from the unique status of a surprising juxtaposition to the socially approved and adopted status of a generalization.

A review of the examples is interesting because many students realize for the first time that they have been using figurative terms literally. They had not noticed the continuous circulation between the realms of the concrete and the abstract. You may even want to remind them of the two functions of the verb "to be"--one copulative and the other ontological. When we say that "argument is war," the "is" functions to link the two semantic domains without asserting the actual reality of the connection.

2. Both discussions of "foot of a mountain" stress the conventional nature of the attribution, and both identity it as a "dead" metaphor, but without noting its status as a "catachresis." Brown suggests that the geological "foot" and the anatomical one are homophones, implying that the "foot" of the mountain has a historical derivation unrelated to the human "foot," or at least that in practice a speaker uses the geological foot without ever thinking of anatomy. Lakoff and Johnson make a similar point in a different way, by saying that although the "foot of the mountain" is a metaphor, it is unsystematic, meaning that the transfer of the word from anatomy to geology does not involve a juxtaposition of the two sets, with all their features, but is a singular borrowing without resonance. The mark of a dead metaphor is precisely the transfer of a term without its associated set.

There seems to be some conflict between the two discussions, in that Brown suggests that we will notice metaphor better if we suspend the context of a term, whereas Lakoff and Johnson note that metaphor is living only when we relate two contexts in which the term is used. There is

finally no real disagreement here, since Brown's point in suspending the
habitual context of usage is to take note of all the possible referents of
a term (we haven't taken into account "foot" as a unit of measurement, for
example); that is, the term enters into a living usage when the full
extension of its possible meanings--the sets of attributes it controls as a
name--are brought into play.

The value of sorting out these differing approaches to living and dead
metaphor has to do with the practice it provides in close reading of expository prose and the variations possible in the definition of a concept--the
concept of "metaphor" in this case.

3. This question offers another way to talk about the enlivening of metaphor, or the exchange between ordinary and literary discourses. Students
are often warned to avoid clichés in their writing. The discussions here
indicate that the strategy is not so much to avoid them as to remotivate or
refunction them. Plath's poem shows that the sheer act of collection, of
accumulation, of clichés into a set renews their meaning, enlivens them
through a display of variety. The poem is useful for our purposes because
it calls attention to the existence of metaphor in everyday discourse. Her
demonstration supplements the insight into the inventive, literary nature
of everyday discourse encountered in the section of anecdotes.

One of the most valuable lessons to be learned from Lakoff and Johnson
involves their discussion of "the partial nature of metaphorical structuring." The transfer of attributes across sets tends to be quite selective,
with catachresis representing one end of the scale, exemplifying minimum
transfer, and surrealism representing the other end, maximum transfer.
While it may be reasonable to think of the prop holding up a table as a
"leg," we would not expect this transfer to include a concern for clothing
the leg. The power of metaphor to revive, however, may be seen in the fact
that the prudish Victorians are said to have considered exposure of table
legs to be as indecent as exposure of human legs. But the scientist who
discovered that he could figure the dispersion of gas molecules by treating
them as if they were billiard balls bouncing off one another did not also
imagine that gas molecules are wooden and painted (nor did this lack of
resemblance weaken the power of the comparison).

One of the most fundamental procedures of invention in any field, scientific and literary alike, is the discovery of a new context in which to
consider a term and its referent. That metaphorical juxtaposition bring
together whole sets or semantic fields suggests that the procedure of
invention may be simulated or generated "artificially," by comparing systematically the full range of meanings available in a metaphor. What
begins as a surrealistic exercise may lead to a strategy of thought applicable to other disciplines and practices. It also has considerable value
in making and refuting arguments, as we shall see.

4. Remind students that an editorial that uses metaphor poorly will be as
useful for their essay as one that uses metaphor well.

5. In this exercise the students begin to put into practice the systematic
exploration of the exchanges of meaning that are possible in the juxtaposition of two categories in a metaphorical concept. Several lessons may be
learned here. First there is the strategy of invention available in the
notion of systematic extension of one category to the other. To write a
brief essay on the topic "love is madness" is a matter of setting up the
category "madness" as a model, as a reservoir of information constituting
potential analogies for "love." One of the most basic problems the student
faces when assigned the conventional theme paper--the location of the raw
materials for discussion--is at least partly solved by this approach. Some
research into the various kinds of madness may be necessary in order to
fully explore the concept beyond its partial activation by the culture.

The second lesson has to do with how much one can learn about our cultural attitudes and ideologies by observing what parts of the metaphor are activated and what parts are left out of account. That a murder might be treated more leniently in the court system if it were a "crime of passion," relating love to the "diminished capacity" defense used in "insanity" pleas, tells us something about our common understanding of love. The metaphor legitimated in metaphorical concepts, that is, reflect a general attitude of the culture. What do we mean when we say we are "crazy" about someone? What parts of the cultural attitude toward madness actually carry over to love? The sense of compulsion or obsession is there, but not the stigmas that go with these behaviors—depending, of course, on the context. In general we might observe that reason and rational behavior has a higher status in our culture than does irrationality. At the same time, we expect and approve of certain qualities in given areas of life: someone who approaches love as if it were a science is acting against the grain of our cultural expectation (approved and standardized commonplaces).

The third lesson of this exercise is the introduction to the possibility of going beyond the accepted organization of a concept either to activate some unused portion of the metaphor, or to substitute a new category to replace the conventional one. The point for now, however, is to experience the inventive capacity of metaphor to generate the materials needed for an essay. To say that "ideas are fashions" is more than just the assertion of a link between two terms: every facet of the category of "fashion" becomes available for our understanding of "idea." The next step will be to learn how to extrapolate from this possibility to the construction of arguments.

Metaphorical Concepts (p. 92)

Robert W. Keidel, "A New Game for Managers to Play" (p. 92)

Discussion and Writing
1. Keidel's article provides an illustration of some of the points made in the preceding theoretical explanations of metaphor. His use of "structure" here is the same point made by Lakoff and Johnson regarding the systematic way in which a category is organized by metaphor. The claim in both cases is that the way we talk about something is not merely incidental, but actually directs our thinking about a given activity or situation. Students do not always accept this possibility readily, despite the strong medicine of Lakoff and Johnson's evidence. They are not in the habit of giving that much credit to language. Nor have they always given much thought to the possibility of modeling behavior in one area of life on behavior in another area. They are familiar with the notion of "role model," but they have not thought about the systematic transfer of role behavior from one area to another.
2. We encounter here the figurative-literal distinction. There is often expressed at this point a curiosity about why people talk in this way, by means of metaphors, analogies, and comparisons. This is a question about the material nature of language. Metaphor is one of the properties of discourse. What sort of discussion would be possible that dealt with business only as business, or argument only in terms of argument, and so forth? As we noted earlier, there are other ways to relate concepts besides metaphor, although that still leaves us with the internal metaphorical structuring of categories themselves. The implication of this fact is that concepts themselves—the concept of "business" for example—may be altered.

Lewis Thomas, for example, suggested in Lives of a Cell that we should recognize the socially constructed nature of our concepts, and their metaphorical quality, as the first step toward the invention of a new mythology or ideology more beneficial to our outlook on the world. He points out that the common view of social relationships is Darwinian--a model of competition and struggle the outcome of which must be the survival of the fittest. Thomas suggested that we find some alternative description of nature--one more morally beneficial--to serve as the "vehicle" for the metaphorical concept of society. He suggests, for example, the entities revealed by microbiology, whose symbiotic or cooperative and mutually bene-ficial way of living offers an alternative version of nature to serve as a model for social relationships. Whether or not Thomas's account of nature will be incorporated in our culture's view of society, whether it will become a metaphorical concept, remains to be seen. Indeed, the relation-ship between ideas may itself be figured as a struggle for survival that is either competitive or cooperative.

3. One way to approach this discussion is to think of the way a coach bases a managing strategy on an implied theory of human motivation. This model of human behavior must be inferred by observing the coach's treatment of the players. One proof that the managing style is based on a model is that the coach tends to apply the motivating formula to all players uni-formly, regardless of the individual differences in personality.

4. This essay helps the student get a feel for the systematic exploitation of a category. Most important is the experience of working through what will later prove to be a prewriting stage of preparation--the inventory of the features or attributes of a category to see what it provides to think with, what it makes available informationally as the "vehicle" for the "tenor" or theme of the comparison. The set as a reservoir for invention will generate materials ranging from commonplace expressions to (appar-ently) absurd nonsense. How far can one extend the comparison of marriage to tennis? What is the equivalent in marriage of the double fault in ten-nis? When does the literal quality of metaphorical concepts pass over into reality? If a couple actually hit each other, is this like boxing, or is it boxing itself? The important lesson of this selection, then, is to grasp what is meant by the systematic structuring of metaphorical con-cepts. The writer's strategy is to attempt to identify the equivalent of a given item in the parallel set. This matching (or imposition) may not be readily predicted in advance, intuitively, but requires a kind of calcula-tion, as if filling in the blanks of a formula. Indeed, you will recognize in this strategy Aristotle's proportional formula, in which three of the four terms are known, the fourth term being a product of the logic of the relationship set up by the three familiar terms: A is to B as C is to ---.

Susan Sontag, "Illness as Metaphor" (p. 96)

1., 2. & 3. Part of the purpose of these questions is to be sure the stu-dents have followed closely Sontag's argument. Her essay builds on the earlier definitions of metaphor to show how the way we talk about disease (or anything else) reflects dominant cultural attitudes to the phenomenon. The students have little trouble understanding the general line of thought in the piece and they identify the metaphors Sontag describes. But Sontag makes one turn too many for many of her student readers when she shows that a category can pass from being the tenor of one metaphor (that which is in need of explanation) to being the vehicle of a different metaphor (that which does the explaining). At first the unknown is the concept of "can-cer," for example. It is not unknown scientifically or analytically. We know what it is biologically and medically. But a culture lives not by science or reason alone, but also by mythology or ideology. What is can-cer? To understand the disease culturally includes a review of the terms used to talk about it, as Sontag shows, so that a science fiction scenario comes to mind when we think about cancer—a story of the invasion of the body snatchers.

The twist in Sontag's essay comes when she goes on to explain that diseases in turn are used to talk about other things. "Cancer" itself is one of the metaphors we live by, as Sontag demonstrates in the context of politics. The interesting aspect of this situation is that, as some theorists have noted, people are able to communicate well enough using two categories in relation without understanding either of the two categories in question. A person may know little or nothing in a scientific sense about cancer and politics, yet feel comfortable with a statement using one as a metaphor for the other. The meaning is in the relationship. Sontag's discussion reveals a major resource of most arguments made using metaphor, which is that this switch in the course of an argument of a key term from tenor to vehicle is quite common, even central to the success of the argument. Having established that cancer is like an invasion from outer space, a polemicist could then hope to control the reader's response to a later use of cancer as itself an image in the argument.

4. The shift in position between vehicle and tenor of a given category such as cancer reveals two different levels at which metaphor structures our thinking, as well as two different strategies for generating arguments by means of metaphorical concepts. When "cancer" is the tenor of the metaphor, our focus is on the other semantic domains brought into play to represent the disease. The nature of these vehicles reveals or expresses the fantasies, as Sontag says, that our culture entertains with respect to disease—war, moral violation, science fiction aliens, and so forth. But when "cancer" is the vehicle, its usage requires an inventory of the actual properties of the disease, which will then in turn generate the materials for application to other tenors. The incredibly rapid multiplication of cancer cells, for example, would be a feature of the disease that might lend itself to characterizing some phenomenon in another domain of reference.

To extrapolate from Sontag's essay on cancer a model for an essay on AIDS (for example) it is useful to review exactly Sontag's approach to the topic. The pedagogy depends, in any case, on the students' learning to attend carefully to the strategies of other authors with the idea of borrowing or stealing these strategies for their own writing. We noted that poetry often attempts to produce a certain unified emotion in the reader through the accumulation of concrete details likely to evoke certain associations in our culture. Sontag's procedure in "Illness as Metaphor" reverses the poetic procedure. Her essay, after all, is a piece of criticism. She finds the emotion already in place, and then seeks the details or concrete elements that constitute the feeling. She notes that the very name "cancer" evokes strong feelings—a feeling of terror, perhaps, whose attributes she then identifies. Her approach, in short, is analytical, intended to demythicize "cancer." She is not herself arguing by means of metaphor, but analyzing how metaphorical thinking works. This distinction helps clarify the strategy of the next reading.

## Arguing with Metaphor: Analogy and Parable (p. 104)

### Judith Jarvis Thomson, "Abortion and Ethics" (p. 104)

1. A parable, of course, is an anecdote that presents a plain tale used to signify something else. It is an extended metaphor, a deliberate dream, with a latent and manifest level of content. Jesus speaks in parables as a way of illustrating certain principles of faith—for those who know how to

interpret them. The plugged-in violinist is not quite a parable, since it is presented as a provisional way of thinking about a problem rather than as the illustration of a truth already known. But both analogy and parable are based upon the metaphorical dimension of language.

2. Thomson's essay--a classic frequently assigned in university courses on ethics--is useful for our purposes for several reasons. The controversial topic, for one thing, makes explicit, as did the Sontag piece, the symbolic, metaphorical dimension of cultural issues. Like cancer, abortion has a scientific, biological, medical dimension as well as a moral dimension. The terms needed to account for these two dimensions are quite different and equally real and valid. This existence at two levels of discourse is typical of most cultural phenomena, and is something a citizen must be aware of in order to communicate effectively within society. Indeed, in the issue of abortion the ideologies or mythologies of science and religion come into direct conflict, as they did with the issue of evolution in the previous century (a debate that has been revived in the name of "creationism"). A controversial topic so obviously weighted with a symbolic dimension reveals a lesson relevant to all interpretive disagreements, including those that occur in literary criticism. The resolution of the disagreement can not always be achieved by an appeal to the text or phenomenon itself, because the basis of the disagreement has its origins in the different assumptions--the different conceptual categories--operating for the parties to the debate. A creationist and a humanist, for example, have different concepts of "man" or "human being." Their sets are organized differently, structured by different metaphors, containing different if overlapping attributes. This is why one of the strategies of argument is to get an opponent to accept one's metaphor, and never, if possible, to engage the opponent on his or her own ground.

Thomson's article is also useful because her principal analogy is so obvious, so extreme, so lacking in subtlety that the reader can't miss it. In addition to the violinist analogy, the article blazes with living metaphors. Your students should have little trouble going through the article and identifying the various figures: the expanding child in the tiny house, the house-body comparison, the Henry Fonda hypothesis, the brother's candy, and so forth. They could not be expected to notice the way the essay as a whole relates metaphorically to the theme of the chapter, unless they have begun to read for the unity of **Text Book** as if it were a poem (the strategy we suggested as a learning skill or heuristic device for problem solving)--the metaphorical concept for thinking as conceiving a child, fertility and the gestation of ideas. However low this pun on conception might be, it has been used in discussions of knowing going back to Plato and to the Bible, with the term "abortion" having an active life in other areas of reference in contemporary discourse besides the medical one.

Students may at first find the most exaggerated images to be the least effective in terms of persuasion, but the most effective for understanding how this style of argument works.

3. While it is true that we are not foregrounding argumentative writing in this section, it is also true that we want to note the interpenetration of literary language with other discourses. Our pedagogy involves the close examination of a piece of writing taken as a model in order not only to discern its form but to extrapolate from that form a formula for the generation or invention of our own "original" writing. Therefore it is valuable to discuss with the class not only Thomson's analogies and metaphors, but also the way she combines these figures into arguments.

Argument, as we noted earlier, is one way to bring concepts into relationship. There is more than one way to draw these relationships, of course. The most common form of argument (keeping things at the basic level appropriate for our needs) relates categories by means of cause and effect. The concept of "love," for example, might be used to explain the cause of someone's "crazy" behavior.

Another way to relate categories, a way with which the students are also quite familiar, is comparison and contrast. It is worth discussing the difference between comparison and contrast and metaphor. Metaphor is a figure of comparison, with sets being formed on the basis of resemblance of attributes among the members. To make the distinction we must fall back on the difference between the literal and figurative dimensions of meaning, keeping in mind the unstable character of this opposition. Comparisons are usually expected to be literal—that two terms brought into relation are actually similar at the level of the referents, whereas metaphorical comparisons are figurative, with the vehicle providing an image or representation of the tenor. Comparison and contrast is juxtaposition in the interest of analysis, rather than representation, while argument by metaphor attempts to communicate those aspects of the issue that don't lend themselves to analysis—the experience or feeling of the issue. We might relate the Soviet and American systems, for example, by comparing the two forms of government or the two economic theories; we might also use images to convey what we take to be the freedom of one and the oppression of the other. The metaphor as image would tell what the item in question is _like_.

The representation of the body as a house is a good one with which to explore the unused part of the metaphor. Thomson herself does this when she passes from the initial situation of the expanding baby already inside the house (womb) to the question how an alien might enter the house (a window left open through which a burglar might enter). This analogy makes available the full range of things we can say about houses, including, for example, the contractual and legal status of property rights and ownership. In fact, the recent New Jersey court case of the surrogate mother (Mary Beth Whitehead) was decided against the biological mother and for the biological father (William Stern) on the basis of the contract signed by both parties promising the delivery of a baby for ten thousand dollars. The law, too, works by analogy, transferring the precedents set by one case to the circumstances of another one. In the case of surrogacy the familiar area—property and contracts—was extended to cover an unfamiliar and "unprecedented" situation. To continue Thomson's line of thought, then, we might propose that the baby is a squatter who has occupied premises without making payment and who may hence be evicted. We could then point out the absurdity of this extension as reason to invalidate the metaphor. Or we might argue that the body constitutes an attractive nuisance (like a swimming pool) for which the owner may be held liable. The woman's kidneys attracted the violinist the way a kidney-shaped pool might attract a small child. If the child drowns in the pool the owner may be sued; if the violinist is unplugged the owner of the kidneys may be sued as well.

Our concern is not that arguments constructed in this way be completely convincing, only that the students begin to experience the literary of fictive, poetic play of the production of such analogies. There will be time enough later to make the analogies as convincing or persuasive as possible. For now it will suffice to have the students find images and figures with which to represent the values they find relevant to this topic. They should also discover that the category they choose to work with (property, for example) will actively guide them in deciding what to say about the issue in question.

4. Preparation for this assignment might include an attempt in class to derive from Thomson's essay a formula for the production of analogical argument. To treat a piece of writing as a model is to generalize its features into the steps of a method. The steps manifested here begin with the

selection of the controversial topic. A list of possible topics might be established by means of suggestions from the students. A typical list includes gun control, nuclear disarmament, women's rights, the Palestinian question, terrorism, drunk driving, apartheid, drugs in sports, and so on.

The essay is argumentative, meaning that the writer should take sides and not try to do a report covering all positions fairly. The strategy will be to link the categories of the topic together in a way that supports one's preference, taking advantage of the flexible nature of concepts as sets.

The formula requires next a review of the opponent's point of view. An important part of redrawing the configuration of the concept is an account of the rival position. The terms of the argument are considerably clearer if we know the main features of both sides. To avoid taking anything for granted, you could also review the most basic features of an argument—a premise from which certain consequences logically follow. In this case, the premise of an absolute "right to life" entails moral and legal obligations restricting the rights of women. An argument is always "dialogical," anticipating and manifesting in its arrangement the assumptions of the other position. Thomson's essay makes little sense unless the reader realizes that she is constructing arguments to refute this logic.

The third step in the formula, then, is to break the connections among categories drawn by the opponent and reconnect them in ways more favorable to the writer's position. This can be done either between categories or within the category. At this point, following Thomson's model, our assignment asks the student to argue by means of metaphor, analogy, parable. We can see here also the strategy of demythicizing the opponent's metaphors as a negative step, taken before the positive act of offering one's own metaphors. The technique of arguing from metaphor includes not only the representation of one's position in a scene or image, but also a brief commentary following the figure that explains the consequences, the logic or reasons that follow from the figure. Poets sometimes do this too, explaining the conclusions of their image, as may be seen in X. J. Kennedy's "Ars Poetica" when he adds, after the image of the goose who died trying to look up its sphincter, "Would you lay well? Don't watch." Of course he still leaves the application of the lesson open (we applied it to a theory of writing). In short, reasoning from metaphors, by analogy, is itself a kind of modeling. One lays out the features of a vehicle, and shows how these features guide the understanding of the tenor in question.

In generalizing Thomson's essay into a model, then, the students may look for two kinds of language marking the two discourses cooperating in the essay: the discourse of logic, indicated by talk about premises, stronger and weaker versions of a case, errors and strict interpretations; the discourse of literature, embodied in the examples, hypothetical scenes, analogies, images, and parables. This formula may be generated in class discussion, thus providing the students with the genre they are to practice in this final substantial paper. (Indeed, it would make sense to use the earlier assignments as in-class exercises and topics for group discussion, all undertaken with this final paper in mind.)

The generic formula:

1. Establish a position on a controversial issue.
2. Review the opposing arguments and metaphors.
3. Demythicize opposing metaphors (if any).
4. Offer alternative metaphors.
5. Reason from these metaphors to their consequences, explaining and justifying the initial position.

It would be possible to write a shorter version of the assignment, eliminating the acknowledgment of the opponent and focusing only on the production of one's own metaphor, thus skipping steps 2 and 3 of the formula. Some students find it easier to develop their own position, however, by reasoning negatively from the position of a real or imagined adversary. You can delimit the lessons of Thomson's model in any way that suits your goals for this section. If the students are not to be confused by the model in doing the shorter version, however, they need to work through the two levels of discourse in class, in order to be sure they understand which part of the model they are following.

The final lesson of such a project, unifying the chapter as a whole, is an insight into the unstable, contestable nature of the categories classifying our experience and organizing our thinking. In Thomson's case, the concept at issue is "human rights." The question is not limited to "abortion," but necessarily extends to the concept of a "right," given the position taken by those who oppose abortion on the basis of a right to life. The prochoice and the right-to-life advocates don't agree on this specific concept, nor on any of the concepts that name the question (what is "life"?--the answer depends on the category one chooses as the vehicle of the explanation). As we noted earlier, this insight into the openness of concepts comes to many students as a revelation. To approach argument from the side of literary discourse exposes this fictional or constructed quality of belief systems and formal disciplines alike, and helps the students appreciate the fluid border joining high literacy with everyday life.

## Metaphor and Metonymy: Advertising (p. 121)

"Light My Lucky," "Finally, Life Insurance as Individual as You Are,"
    "VISTA" (pp. 122-128)

We have tried to keep terminology to a minimum here: metaphor, metonymy, and synechdoche (described here as a kind of metonymy). In class, you should probably talk over these figures, coming up with additional examples, until everyone feels comfortable using the terms--which will be important in doing analyses of texts.

Our discussions of the three ads should be assigned and talked over in class. You might ask students to find some version of the "Light My Lucky" ad and bring it to class. We were surprised when Lucky Strike refused us permission to use the ad, because our discussion mainly pointed out how clever the ad was--but cigarette manufacturers seem to be running scared these days.

It is worth pointing out to your students that the advertisers are indeed concerned about critical scrutiny of ads. In order to get permission to use the Prudential ad, we had to revise our discussion to eliminate certain remarks critical of the ad's effectiveness. This puts a greater burden on you and your students to supply the missing critical thought. The VISTA ad is especially useful for demonstrating how advertising texts are often put together using many of the same processes of thought and language that go into the composition of poetry.

## Discussion and Writing
1. Advise your students that for best results they should put some real thought into selecting their ads. To end up with two that work well, they should select several and do preliminary analyses of them. It will be easier to write a good paper if they select ads that use clearly different methods and generate different effects. This may or may not mean that one ad will be successful and one not--they may simply be different--but a clear, discussible difference will make the writing much easier to accomplish.

2. This problem can be solved by merely describing the changes that would be required or by actually remaking the ad, using letters and pictures cut out from somewhere else and pasted into the ad that is the basis of the project. Actually making the changes is probably the best way to go on this, though it involves more work. With something as visual as advertising, you almost have to see it to be certain that the effect you anticipate will actually be generated by the changes you make. The least possible change with the most disastrous effect will be the best response to this assignment.

You may wish to ask your students to submit a few paragraphs along with their redone ad, explaining why they made the changes they did and what they believe to be the effect of those changes. These altered ads should be displayed and discussed in class. This section on advertising closes the chapter on metaphor, but it also anticipates the following chapter on intertextuality.


Chapter 3:   TEXTS AND OTHER TEXTS

Intertextuality (p. 130)

Students should be reminded that they have been working intertextually all along. In this section, the process of intertextuality is highlighted. Discussion of the introductory material might start with the epigraph from T. S. Elliot. In stealing, one makes something one's own, takes it over and transforms it. Imitations, however, are lesser forms of the original. (For a truly awful example of imitation, compare the poetry of Thomas Holly Chivers to that of Edgar Allan Poe. Another would be the comparison of Dürer's praying hands to all those ghastly ones painted on velvet. The discussion of bumper stickers can be used to illustrate the difference between imitating and stealing. Ask students to provide other examples. (At this writing, the yellow caution sign proclaiming "Baby on Board" has spawned many poor imitations, such as Golfer, Dentist, Surfer, etc. on Board. Can we consider "Mother-in-Law in Trunk" an effective transformation?)

For further reading on intertextuality, see the American Journal of Semiotics. Vol. 3, No. 4 (1985), a special issue on intertextuality. The critical introduction by Thaïs Morgan is especially useful and has an extensive bibliography.

Three Texts:   "Samson" Judges 16, "Samson Agonistes," Nike (pp. 133-137)

Discussion and Writing
1.  Judges 16 presents a chronicle of events. Milton has taken these and elaborated on them. He has used a messenger as an eyewitness, one who is "sorrowed at [Samson's] captive state," but who is eager to see the sport Samson is to provide. Milton imparts spectacle to the scene through description of the theatre, the parade escorting Samson, the types of sport Samson provided. Milton only hints at Samson's prayer to the Lord for strength, and his wish to die. Rather, he emphasizes the way Samson tricked the Philistines, and thus Samson's final speech is rich with irony. Certainly one of the messages of the biblical text is that the Lord God of Israel is stronger than the (false) god, Dagon. This message can be read as implicit in Milton's text—if the reader is familiar with the biblical pre-text (and Milton could assume that his readers were).

2. Part of the discussion might concern the different ways words and pictures carry information. The ad assumes our familiarity with the story, counting on instant recognition of the scene. As E. D. Hirsch pointed out in his book on cultural literacy, these inferences work by means of stereotypes and cliches, meaning that only part of the story--its typical features--will be recalled, while much of the detail will not be activated. The process resembles the partial activation of metaphors discussed in the previous chapter. The designers of the ad place considerable stakes on being able to predict the response of the targeted audience. The experts on cultural literacy, that is, are the ad agencies who sponsor research into the "values and life styles" of consumers. The tone of the ad, for example, is witty, humorous, light--obviously not intended for seriously religious people. It is not clear whether or not the "Rake" alludes to the love interest of the story. For many students "Samson" goes with "Delilah" the way "bacon" goes with "eggs," and some discussion could be directed to the sales appeal of this unrepresented part of the inference. Also, the ad seems to joke with the notion of "ultimate," since this is Samson's last event. Do you suppose it also means to suggest that the ultimate Ultimate also wears Nikes?

## Transforming Texts (p. 138)

### Raymond Queneau, Transformations (p. 138)

This exercise provides a pleasurable introduction to the workings of intertextuality: adaptation, to be specific. As we note in the next section, where adaptation is distinguished from parody, adaptation requires that the writer make significant changes in the original text. This is what Queneau does to his original text ("Notation").

1. and 2. Students enjoy doing this exercise and sharing the results in class. They are fascinated with the diversity of responses, and find this a useful introduction to style as well. Queneau's means of transformation are fairly obvious, but be sure to spend some time going over each transformation before students try their own. For example, "Narrative" should be compared with "Notation" for differences and similarities (as in the use of the first person), because the style of "Narrative" is usually the most difficult for students to analyze. From "Passive," the rules for generating the passive voice should be discussed. Though students frequently overuse the passive voice in writing for academic purposes, they find it the most difficult to produce for this assignment, perhaps because they've been trained to haul it out only for serious academic occasions.

3. This discussion will allow students to share (sometimes gleefully) the rules they've absorbed in their academic careers. We have found this to be both enlightening and depressing. Here are some of the rules we learned in the dim past:

"Notation": Be concise.

"Double Entry": Use descriptive language; make your subject clear to your reader.

"Precision": Be precise.

"Narrative": Stories should have a beginning, middle, and end. (Is "Narrative" a story? This might be a good place to remind everyone of Labov's six-part structure of a well-formed anecdote. It could be quite useful to consider how "Narrative" fails to be an anecdote.)

"Passive": Be objective, not subjective; always use the passive voice in formal writing.

"Haiku" doesn't conform to the rules--it doesn't present a single image-- but it does have the feel of a haiku.

"Zoological": Use figurative language to enliven your prose; use a metaphore to organize your thoughts.

Transforming Texts: (p. 143)

Jacob and Wilhelm Grimm, "Hansel and Gretel" (p. 144)

Transformation (1) Coover, "The Gingerbread House" (p. 149)
1. The students' recollection of this story is a good occasion for testing the "decay" of memory, or the selective process by which parts of a unit of signification (which come in all sizes) are retained and other parts suppressed. Many students are surprised by the cruelty perceived in the action of the parents in the Grimms' story. Some students may notice at this point a connection with the story of the "Wild Child," suggesting that he was left in the woods by his evil stepmother. Zipes (see the end of this chapter) makes this possibility explicit in his discussion of the historical context of the Grimms' tales.

As in the relationship between the Bible and Milton's version of "Samson," there is a shift from an emphasis on plot line in the earlier telling to a more psychological emphasis on character and point of view in Coover. We get a different idea of the children in Coover, who reduces the Grimms' emphasis on the trickery, replacing it with a more emotional and sensual representation.

The most striking difference between the two tales is the style in which each is told, taken up in the next question.
2. In looking for comparisons with which to characterize the differences in style, the students might be encouraged to draw on earlier sections of the book to express their observations. The Grimms' version is closer to the arrangement of an anecdote, reflecting its oral origins, while Coover's version is closer to poetry, reflecting the complex temporality of high literacy. In Coover the story line is available but subordinated to the patterns set up by the repetition of images. It is also sometimes deliberately "jammed" or led into self-contradiction.

Precisely because Coover's arrangement is poetic, some students (who, as we have noted in Chapter 2, have much less experience with this ordering principle) will not be able to follow it. They may claim the story makes no sense. Discussion in class, by focusing on the visual nature of Coover's descriptions, and the relationships set up between and among the numbered fragments, helps the students see that the story has an ordering principle. Asked to think of where else this style might be used, or other media in which the style might appear, a few of the students may notice the resemblance of Coover's telling to the style of television drama. As soon as this analogy is offered, whether by a student or the instructor, most of the difficulty of the piece disappears, and the technique begins to seem straightforward. Coover's fragments may then be read as if they constituted a shot list for a video translation of the story (we offer this possibility as an assignment in the last part of this chapter). Most of the students are quite familiar, at least tacitly, with the editing styles of television, and can recognize in Coover's imagery the effects of close-ups and cutting back and forth (parallel editing, montage).

It may also help if they conceive of Coover's fragments as shots that have not yet been assembled into a coherent, chronological narrative. In this and other stories by Coover (like "The Baby-Sitter") the reader is often given several versions of the same episode, some of which contradict each other. Final assemblage, including the discarding of irrelevant material, is left to the reader. This responsibility makes some readers uneasy. This would be a good place to discuss why freedom makes us uneasy,

28

and whether art should allow the reader any freedom or should dominate readers completely.

3. Paragraph 15's description of the gingerbread house could be taken for a cartoon version--an innocuous, sweet picture it is, with those lollipops in "neat little rows." The house contrasts vividly with the witch, its dark occupant, yet her description is that of a typical Disney evil witch. It is the contrast between these Disneyfied elements and the violence of the witch's seizure of the dove, and the boy's, and his struggle with his sister--these actions indicative of intense desires--that pervert the cartoon elements.

Disney classics may be counted on to compose part of the cultural literacy of most of the students. Coover's representation of the witch will remind them of Disney's Snow White. Specialists in children's literature object to the way Disney classics sanitize or censor the negative elements out of the old tales, just as naturalists object to the Disney nature films for their anthropomorphic treatment of the animals, presenting the struggle for survival as a comedy in which the weaker animal escapes from the predator. This section on transformations and intertextuality provides an occasion to discuss the uses our culture makes of such material.

Coover's retelling of the Grimms' tale exemplifies a technique common among proponents of "metafiction"--literature generated self-consciously as a commentary on or interpretation of other literature. A number of authors have retold folktales (Angela Carter and Anne Sexton, for example), tales which, like myths, serve as a reservoir of cultural information. Paragraph 18, with its explicit sexual connotations, is obviously not Disneyfied, and manifests the extent to which this story, like all the transformations in Coover's Pricksongs and Descants, is a work of high literature addressed to adult readers.

Students should not be expected to pin down an interpretation of each event or action in discussing this text, but they should not avoid the sexual implications in the struggles that are narrated. As for the question of desire, we might say that the old man can do nothing more than remember desire; the boy and girl now know desire, and experience the death of innocence. The witch seems to be the seat of desire; her house is the place where the connection between life and death cannot be escaped, where the fruit of the tree of knowledge is eaten and found bitter.

4. One way to approach the metafictional quality of "The Gingerbread House" is to discuss the manner in which Coover's story functions not simply as another piece of fiction, but as a work of literary criticism, in that it offers an interpretation of the Grimms' version. In general, Coover uses the tale to express a view of the role such stories play in our culture. If the students are asked to analyze Coover's story by means of the structure of the anecdote, they may notice that he foregrounds the evaluative aspect, especially in contrast with the Grimms. Folk tales often end with a moral, similar to the coda of the anecdote, to make sure that the audience grasps the point of the story. (The Grimms offer a proverbial riddle--"my tale is done, see the mouse run"--which may be read as an invitation to interpretation: catch the meaning if you can.) Coover offers a significantly greater quantity of interpretive commentary along the way, as in paragraphs 24 and 26, for example. Indeed, the character of the father is expanded, with interpolations of a good fairy from the generic category of options, to act as a center of consciousness reflecting or mediating within the story on the implications of the world presented there.

One approach to this assignment, then, is to open the question of the "moral" of the stories: both what they are and how they are conveyed. Does Coover's moral--the moral of the tale as a whole--agree with the

observations of the father? To the extent that Coover's metafiction is
read by adults, while the Grimms' story is read to children, Coover's moral
may be seen as an adult's more pessimistic or demythicized view of life--a
reading of a children's story from a mature perspective in which one realizes that evil is real and things don't always work out for the best nor
people live happily after. In this context we can see that Coover has
evoked the Disney images precisely to reintroduce into this story the
"teeth" it possessed in its earliest versions. The ordering permitted by
the poetic technique of patterns and repetitions allows Coover to end his
tale with the imagistic lesson of the unity or interdependence of the life
and death principles.

Transformation (2) Garrison Keillor, "Gretel" (p. 158)
1. This piece is a segment of Keillor's essay, "My Stepmother, Myself," a
parody of Nancy Friday's book, My Mother, Myself, which is thus a double
parody. Gretel is meant to sound like a contemporary purveyor of pop femi-
nist psychology, mixing the colloquial (paragraphs 1-5) with the unctuous
(paragraphs 6-8).
2. Gretel is a hardheaded, no-nonsense character. However, her values
show that she believes in fairy tales.
3. Keillor's "Gretel" demonstrates the critical capabilities of parody.
Where Coover's transformation constitutes a reinterpretation of "Hansel and
Gretel," Keillor transforms the fairy tale for critical purposes. Coover's
version has the unity of feeling characteristic of poetic texts and presents a coherent vision that can be summarized as the "moral" of his story,
namely that the gingerbread house of sex is irresistible and is also the
house of death:  the mother and the witch are, after all, the same, and
every boy kills his dove. Coover's transformation of the tale, in short,
is organized poetically and is far from comic. It is a transformation, but
not a parody.
    Keillor uses the story in a different manner, to criticize, by means
of comedy, both a certain kind of feminism and what we might call the
fairy-tale vision of life. Parody, then, is a mode of criticism directed
at specific texts or at aspects of what we might call the cultural text,
formulas of thought and behavior:  metaphors and narratives that we live
by. The problem of cultural literacy is related to the functioning of parody, because the recognition of parody depends upon prior knowledge of the
target text or texts. Students unfamiliar with the Grimms' text will not
comprehend the chief part of Keillor's transformation. Similarly, Keillor
depends upon our having some knowledge of My Mother, Myself or of the femi-
nist attitude found in that text. Keillor's narrative is thus more fragile
than Coover's, which depends more squarely upon our acquaintance with folk
tales alone.
    The method of parody, exemplified in the Keillor narrative, begins
with the selection of some specific feature of a previous text (either a
specific work or a cultural text), usually the most characteristic feature
of its style or content. The parodist then caricatures this feature by
carrying it to absurd lengths or developing implications of it that the
author ignored or repressed. By parodying two texts at once--fairy tales
and a certain kind of thoughtless feminine psychology--Keillor can use each
of them against the other. By updating the fairy tale, he reminds us of
how such tales ignore all kinds of realistic details, including the daily
lives the characters must live after the adventure is over; and, by connecting the fairy tale to pop psychology he questions the fairy-tale element in that cultural text.
    One way to discuss parody as a critical transformation that analyzes
the style of a text by exaggerating features of that style is to ask the

class if they notice other elements of the Grimms' tale that neither
Keillor nor Coover have developed.  One such feature that lends itself to
parody is the trickster theme--the war of trickery that informs the relationship between the children and their elders (including the witch as well
as the parents).  A parody might depict these characters as a family of
practical jokers, or otherwise exaggerate and elaborate this element into a
new version of the story.  That the children keep returning to a home in
which their parents are trying to kill them could also serve as the basis
for a parody, combining ineffectual plots by the mother with a naïveté or
stupidity on the part of the children.  The model here would be something
like Peter Sellers in the Pink Panther series.  At the other end of the
intertextual scale from such a story would be the parable of the prodigal
son.  Indeed, discussion might include an attempt to inventory the range of
texts available to the class as a whole dealing with parent-child relationships.  One thing such a discussion reveals is the considerable difference
among students with respect to the quantity and variety of stories held in
their personal "encyclopedias."

Transformation (3) Jacob and Wilhelm Grimm:  "The Little Brother and the
Little Sister" (p. 160)

Discussion and Writing
1.  In "Hansel and Gretel," dialogue is added, as are details such as the
branch tied to the tree to simulate the sound of an ax; the "mother"
becomes the "stepmother" in "Hansel and Gretel" (presumably this change
would explain her insistence on getting rid of the children--or make it
more palatable to the reader); the snow-white bird that leads the children
to the gingerbread house is added, as is the duck that ferries them across
the river; there is more description of the eating of the house, and of the
meal inside; the "old woman" of the manuscript becomes a "wicked witch,"
with appropriate characteristics (nearsighted red eyes, keen sense of
smell); a bolt is added to the oven door, as are the horrible screeches of
the burning witch; the father is made more repentant, and the children run
to his arms as all is presumably forgiven.  The transformed ending of "pure
happiness" and playfulness contrasts markedly with the manuscript ending:
"but the mother was dead."  In the transformed version, the stepmother's
death is presented almost as an afterthought.  Many of these changes may be
discussed as a softening or Disneyfication of the earlier text--a Disneyfication before Disney, of course.
2.  The manuscript version is a highly condensed narrative that concen-
trates on events and employs little descriptive language.  The transformation makes these events into a story, with its addition of details, dialogue, and attention to motivation and plotting.  Some might say that the
folk material has been gussied up to make a more popular story.
    The lure of the fairy tale lies in what is unexplained:  the witch,
her house, the mother's meanness.  In other words, the symbolic nature of
the fairy-tale images invites interpretation and reinterpretation.  A
return to Freud and the dream image might be useful here.
3.  The following is a student transformation of a fairy tale.

# THE GOOD FAIRY MEETS GODZILLA

The girl laying curled in bed slowly stretches out her arms, flexing the fingers and easing the sleep out of her muscles. As the morning sun warms her cheek, she smiles and thinks about the Saturday (her favorite day) that lays before her. She swings her feet from under the warmth of her quilt ("This was given to me by my mother when I was twelve. Now I give it to you for the day you have children," she remembers her mother saying) and onto the cool wooden floor. Even on this fresh day, the morning routine takes over and she heads for the bathroom.

A fluffy white rabbit hops hurriedly across the path thinking of his boss waiting for him at the club. He stops to check his watch then rushes on.

Somewhere else, a bear roars.

The girl brushes her teeth, humming to a song on the radio. Her new stereo was the envy of all her friends, bested only by the phone she had by her bed. Her wardrobe, too, was nothing modest and she stood before it now, imitating the gestures of her older sister in deciding what to wear. Blue looked good on her, she decided, and picked out her blue dress. Turning up the stereo, she does a strip-tease with her nightgown and then collapses, giggling, onto the floor.

The rabbit looks around and realizes he's lost. Nervously checking his watch, he hurries on.

Somewhere else, a bear roars.

The girl's parents lay awake in bed downstairs. They talk the optimistic talk of a suburban family. Their children are everything they wanted and they playfully remark on their success at child rearing. Upstairs, their youngest stands before her mirror (an antique five foot oval on wooden legs) and brushes her hair, complimenting her image on its choice of clothing. The brush flows smoothly through her hair, never snagging or knotting.

The rabbit sees a section of the forest that looks familiar now. Hopping quickly for the path, he sees a human girl. A pretty girl, too. One he's never seen before but there's no time to stop now. Being the gentleman he is, he doesn't want to rush by without saying anything, so he pauses briefly. Breathless, he explains, "I'm late, I'm late," and hops onto the path, now a familiar road to him.

The girl is standing open-mouthed, staring at the reflection in the mirror, unsure how to explain to herself that a white rabbit just hopped through her mirror. With the trusting innocence and naïveté that only a twelve year old would possess she thrusts her hand at her mirror and shakes it, as if disturbing the reflective surface of a lake. Dropping her brush, Goldilox steps through the looking glass.

The fluffy white rabbit hops quickly down the path, thinking of ways to explain his tardiness to his boss. He twitches his little pink nose and stops suddenly, smelling danger. A wolf steps onto the path and smiles slyly.

"Where are you going?" he asks, coating his voice with sickening false sincerity.

The rabbit swallows audibly, twitches his nose, and replies, "I'm on my way to my grandmother's," hoping desperately that the wolf will see fit to pity him. The wolf smiles, showing all his teeth, and grabs the rabbit, tearing into its neck. Blood spills over the rabbit's white fur, covering it with a red coat. The wolf carries its prey far into the woods to devour it.

Goldilox inspected her new surroundings and giggled nervously. Goosebumps prickled along her arms and she looked first at her hands, then at the forest around her, as if trying to impose one reality onto another. Normally tears would have come by now, but she was determined to find out what was going on behind her mirror. She felt she at least had a right to know; she began walking through the forest.

Papa Bear roared again as he stretched and awoke. Unconsciously rubbing his hand on his chin, feeling his beard, he thought to himself that it would be a good day for a walk through the woods. He swung his big hairy legs from under the quilt onto the cool wooden floor and walked out to the kitchen. Mama Bear and Baby were already up and Mama had jut baked an apple pie to eat for dessert that night. To the disappointment of Baby Bear, she placed the pie on the windowsill to cool. Baby Bear's stomach growled its angry protest.

The forest was a fun adventure for suburban Goldilox and, she reasoned, "Saturday's are made for adventures." She wandered off the path and began picking her way through the brush, stepping on small animals and destroying several budding plants. As she traveled further the forest thickened. Her blue dress caught on twigs, and her hair became tangled and torn. Vainly she kept running her fingers along her scalp trying to straighten her hair. Mosquitoes buzzed around her, biting her arms while gnats flew into her face. She began running, waving her arms frantically around her and kicking at the dense underbrush. By the time she got to the clearing she was tired, scared, and hungry. She also smelled apple pie.

The Bear family finished packing their picnic basket, gathered together fishing poles and a blanket, and set out for a day at their favorite spot by the stream. Baby Bear gave the pie one last longing look and followed his family out.

The apple pie lay cooling on the windowsill. Light breezes whistled down through the nearby pines and drifted across the top of the lightly browned, flaky crust. The smell of cinnamon wafted throughout the house. Apples, flour, and sugar began to meld together into filling as the pie cooled and settled.

Goldilox smelled what seemed to be one of her mother's apple pies as she entered the clearing. She approached a cabin in the middle of the small meadow where the smell was coming from.

All the furniture in the Bear cabin was home-made by Papa Bear himself. Each bed was designed to individual specifications. Mama and Papa Bear's bed was large and very firm to support their weight. Baby's bed was smaller and much softer because of his shorter, more sensitive fur. The dinner table was just big enough for the Bears to eat comfortably. Each chair was for a designated family member. Papa's chair was large and high and had thick arms on the side; Mama's chair was smaller with a very straight back and no arms; Baby's chair was smaller still, and had small arms and a cushioned back. Papa Bear was a simple and loving father and made all these things on the Bear's first Christmas in the cabin.

On finding the door open, Goldilox went inside. She thought nothing of whom the pie came from. Instead, she grabbed it from the windowsill and took it to the table. She sat in Papa's big oak chair and began to eat the pie right from the pan, but the chair was too large. She tried Mama's chair but it was too uncomfortable. She found Baby's small cushioned chair to be just right and sat down and devoured the pie. Apples dripped down her chin as she transferred handfuls of material from pan to mouth.

In a den on the other side of the forest, a wolf was devouring a blood soaked rabbit. It tore at the innards, ripping all the meat off the animal's bones and gorging itself. Blood dripped down the wolf's chin.

Papa was just drifting off to sleep when his line tugged. Grabbing the pole from between his knees, he jerked it, sinking the hook into the mouth of the fish. Baby Bear squealed with delight as his shiny, squirming dinner broke the surface.

As Goldilox was getting up (after finishing the pie) the snap on her dress caught the cushion on the chair, ripping a hole in it. Indifferent to the situation she went to the kitchen to get something to drink. After taking a drink of a soda, she left the can on Papa's chair and went exploring the cabin.

Papa rubbed his stomach contentedly and stood up to signal the rest that it was time to go. Mama obediently folded up the blanket and called for Baby Bear. Together, they started back for the cabin.

Having finished his meal, the wolf crawled further into the den and slept.

Mama and Papa Bear's bed was too hard for Goldilox. She was looking for a place to take a nap before going home. Seeing Baby's bed, she crawled in and found it was just like her bed at home. Her stomach was full with the pie and she was tired from walking, and very soon Goldilox was asleep.

Baby Bear could almost taste the apple pie that was waiting for him just beyond the door. As soon as he got inside and put his fishing pole away, he ran to the kitchen to slice the pie, only to find it missing. Mama Bear was the first to notice the table with the pie tray on it. Papa Bear saw the soda can on his chair and knew someone had been in his house. Outraged at the intrusion he began searching each room, seeing if anything was missing or if the intruder was still there. On entering Baby's room, he saw Goldilox and stopped short. It had been a long time since he'd seen an unarmed human and the novelty of a defenseless human girl excited him in a strange way. He watched the girl's young body as her chest raised and lowered with each breath. As he was approaching the girl, Baby Bear came in the door and, startled, screamed. Goldilox awoke and saw the bears around her. Terrified, she jumped out of the bed and out the bedroom window (it was open). Papa ran to get his shotgun to shoot the varmint but by the time he got back with it, the girl was gone. Baby Bear was promised another pie and chair cushion and, after the sheets were changed, Mama read to him to help him sleep after his harrowing experience.

The wolf was awakened from its sleep by the incessant chattering of squirrels. He crept quietly to the mouth of his den, found the noisemaker, and pounced on it. Being full from the rabbit, he only played with the carcass half-heartedly then went back to sleep.

The branches slapped Goldilox in the face as she ran back to the path home. Thorns tore at her dress and her breath rasped in her throat. She felt as if her knees would collapse when she finally saw the mirror in the middle of the path. She thrust her hand at it to disturb the reflective surface, then stepped through into her bedroom. Her hair was matted and full of brambles, her face was smudged with dirt and tears, and her dress was torn nearly beyond repair. Goldilox collapsed on her bed, thankful her Saturday adventure was over. She was quickly asleep and didn't even notice when an ivory chess queen summoned playing card warriors from behind the mirror. Somewhere a cat was smiling.

Completing Texts:  The Reader's Work (p. 164)

In this section, we place the activity of the reader in the foreground by asking students to actualize that activity by writing.  At this point in **Text Book** we would expect students to know that reading is not a passive act of consumption, and that a text can elicit different readings.  The material here is designed to bring that issue up for discussion.  We reject the aesthetic notion that a reader completes a text by "discovering" a particular meaning intended by the author (See Wolfgang Iser, The Implied Reader, Baltimore:  Johns Hopkins University Press, 1974).  On the other hand, we seriously question the notion of "interpretive community" set forth by Stanley Fish in Is There a Text in This Class? (Cambridge:  Harvard University Press, 1983), which comes very close to allowing readers to make whatever they will of a literary text.  We have cited Umberto Eco because his The Role of the Reader (Bloomington:  Indiana University Press, 1979) strikes the best balance between the activity of the reader in creating a new reading of a text and the text's authority in directing the course of that reading.  Eco's word for this process is "collaboration," a term that should be discussed with your students in relation to the reader's engagement with the text.  You might ask your students if the term can be applied to the activity of class discussion.  Your students may wish to discuss the problems of the reader's work in this section.  They might, for example, want to reflect on the kinds of collaboration called for by a surrealistic or a poetic text.

James Joyce, "The Boarding House" (p. 167)

Discussion and Writing
1.  The student is invited here to examine the narrative machinery of which the opening paragraphs are composed:

"no open complicity":  Paragraph 4 shows us that Mrs. Mooney is in charge of Polly's career as typist and as flirt.  The phrase of course suggests its opposite, the hidden complicity that can be inferred from "her mother's persistent silence could not be misunderstood."

"the affair":  The connotations of the unmodified noun are generally negative, in relation to politics or to sex.  The information we are given concerning Polly's character and actions in paragraphs 3 and 4 would seem to validate the use of the term "affair":  her little song, "I'm a ... naughty girl"; her look:  "a little perverse madonna"; her actions:  she is described as being "very lively" and she flirts with the young men.  And they call her mother "The Madam."

"a little strange":  This description of Polly's state, coupled with that of Mr. Doran's ("the young man was evidently perturbed") calls for inference from the reader, as does "the right moment."  We know there's an affair, and it's taking an odd (or can we can predictable) turn.  And we know we're dealing with a moral problem.  When we read that Mrs. Mooney deals with such problems "as a cleaver deals with meat," we should recall the opening of the story, "Mrs. Mooney was a butcher's daughter," and the fact that her husband, also a butcher, had gone after her with a cleaver.  Here the text guides our interpretation by setting up what might be called a cleaver code.  At the end of paragraph 5, the reader is left to forecast the nature of the moral problem and the nature of Mrs. Mooney's intervention, now that "she has made up her mind."

2. Close attention to details is necessary to construct this scene, which can be written as dialogue, monologue, or narrative. Class discussion of the text should emphasize the sense of entrapment felt by Mr. Doran and the reasons for it. How much information does the story provide to allow the reader to infer the cultural codes of Catholic Dubliners of the middle or lower middle class at the turn of the century? The ghost chapter will address the issue of reparation and why it is an issue. Students should consider the nature of the character contest they are to write.

Dorothy Parker, "You Were Perfectly Fine" (p. 173)

Discussion and Writing
1. The girl presents a somewhat rose-colored version of events. Her understatements come to be seen as such when contrasted with the young man's terse summaries of and questions about his behavior. As a story of entrapment, this text can be compared with Joyce's.
2. Students may want to concentrate on two or three events rather than trying to retell each one.
3. Short narratives by these observers or participants can be written in class and read aloud. Students should have some idea of how difficult it is, if not impossible, to report just the facts of a given event.

Interpreting Texts (p. 177)

Jack Zipes, "The Politics of Fairy Tales" (p. 180)
Bruno Bettelheim, "Hansel and Gretel" (p. 183)

In this section the difference between **Text Book** and conventional approaches to "writing about literature" may be clearly observed. As in traditional approaches, we ask the students to look closely at the formal organization of literary texts, but instead of expecting them to write interpretive essays describing a close reading we treat the original as a model whose effects and strategies the students attempt to imitate or use as the basis for an extrapolation to a related exercise. There is no reason that the technique of modeling could not be used to learn how to write interpretive essays of the kind written by professionals in our field to communicate with other specialists. Indeed, the formula for an interpretive essay closely resembles the structure of metaphorical concepts, juxtaposing two sets of information—the literary text and the explanatory system. Such interpretive essays perform the work of concept formation in the specialized discipline. Once the students understand the process of classification operating in concepts, they have the methodology they need to undertake interpretive writing. All they lack is "all" that information needed to carry out a "living" cross-referencing of the two sets. Hermeneutics, in short, is best reserved for a more advanced course.
It is still quite useful to introduce the students at this introductory level to critical interpretations, which in this context may be understood not as authoritative statements of truth closing down the possibilities of meaning opened by the texts, but as further transformations and translations of extant materials. Since they have less experience with critical writing, the students are unlikely to have the confidence needed to recognize the typicality of these two essays by Zipes and Bettelheim. That is, they are not yet ready, for the most part, to recognize the generic predictability (or to judge the reliability) of the things each critic finds to say about the story.

# Discussion and Writing

1. One way to treat interpretive writing is as a system of invention, providing a reader with something to say in response to art. The process of foregrounding certain elements of a text and suppressing others, with which the students are familiar from earlier sections, may be seen here at the level of critical generalization, for the interpretive system excludes some issues from consideration while guiding the interpreter's perception of possible topics of interest. Zipes's Marxist reading will necessarily look at the social and historical context of the story, ignoring the elements of individual psychology noted in Bettelheim's Freudian reading, or offering collective causes to account for those elements.

Students tend to find the Marxist reading more reasonable or recognizable. They now readily note the parallel between Victor (The Wild Child discussed by Roger Brown--p. 48) and Hansel and Gretel, given the fact that the two "stories" share the same historical period. They follow the extended metaphor that Zipes elaborates between the witch and the aristocrats of the period. From the earlier discussion of concept formation, the students even accept the necessity of the employment of specialized vocabulary, identifying as Marxist, but not always being able to define, such terms as "class conflict" or "capitalism."

The students accept the witch/aristocrat/parasite analogy because it is confirmed by their general opinion about the relationship between aristocrats, who are seen as exploitive, and everyone else. They are not ready to grant that capitalists exploit workers, however, although the possibility that the First World exploits the Third World seems more reasonable to them.

2. The comparison of a Freudian and a Marxist reading of "Hansel and Gretel" in the "casebook" form may produce some valuable discussion and insights into the operations and strategies of critical interpretation. Seeing two readings side by side enables students to see how critics actually work. Some of the students will want to know which of the two critics is right, assuming that one must be correct and the other wrong. You might respond to this by asking them whether Coover or Keillor was "right."

Bettelheim's reading is more controversial than Zipes's, and some of the class will simply not accept the Freudian interpretation as having any validity whatsoever. Our assignments do not require belief in the system. The point is to see how intepretation works, which means that it may even be helpful if the interpretation does not seem "natural." But Bettelheim offers the further difficulty that his writing is more abstruse, depending, as it does, upon a detailed allusion to psychoanalytic theory--specifically to the developmental process of personality formation through the oral, anal, and phallic stages. The move obvious (and caricatured) story of Oedipus is not as directly involved, although it is included in a less familiar form (the good and bad mother). Most of the students possess in their cultural repertoires an awareness of Freud's use of the Oedipus story, however, and are able to identify the basic dynamics of Bettelheim's application of it in this case. Thus, the encounter with the witch may be read as a figurative working through of the emotions raised by the hostility of the mother at the beginning of the story. The students may notice that the house-body analogy also appeared in Thomson's essay on abortion.

It is helpful to spend some time in discussion, not trying to convert anyone to psychoanalysis but creating at least some sympathy for the act of interpretation and the pleasures of explanation. Bettelheim, for example, accounts for the insistence of the rejected children on returning home. By pointing out that psychoanalysis addresses real problems, such as the authentic dilemmas of the maturation process and the difficulties of leaving home to face the world on one's own, you can help students attend more carefully to Bettelheim's argument. His general point is that such stories offer a way of symbolically working through the conditions of life, which the reader must experience. This is, of course, a major reason why stories are important and worthy of the kind of attention we give them in courses like this one.

In any case, the purpose of studying critics like Zipes and Bettelheim is not to attain a competency in Marxist or Freudian criticism but to recognize the strategies of all critical interpretation—to note the various ways that critics translate point A of the story into point X of the interpretive system. This would be a useful place for a brief return to Freud's interpretive terms in Chapter 2. There they were related to Breton and surrealist poetry. Here, they can be reconsidered to compare the way that literature constructs images with the way criticism converts them into exposition.

3. If you did not have time to thoroughly discuss "The Kiss" or "The Use of Force" earlier, here is an opportunity to do so—after students have written their interpretations. The introduction, "Interpreting Texts," gives suggestions to help students move from concrete details to the abstract concepts that are characteristic of interpretation.

4. This assignment is another version of the one included in an earlier section of this chapter. The idea now, however, is to translate a folk or fairy tale into a video script, making explicit the videolike quality of Coover's writing (noted in our earlier discussion of "The Gingerbread House"). The writers should imitate Coover's fragmented paragraph, but having in mind that their text will be used as the basis for a shooting script of a film. What will the camera show? What will people say?

The added interest of this exercise is the interpolation of the critic's voice into the script, as if the paper were a translation of one of Siskel and Ebert's television film review programs. Having noted the kinds of things Zipes and Bettelheim say about "Hansel and Gretel," the students should interrupt their tale periodically to insert the critic's observations whenever a similar sort of thing occurs in their story. This interpolation is possible because of the formulaic character of folk tales, which tend to be organized around a highly consistent, repetitive structure. Thus, the sorts of things the Marxist and/or the Freudian say about food, witches, kings, peasants, and so forth in "Hansel and Gretel" may be said about similar items in other tales. This way of reading the tales offers some basic practice in critical interpretation, along with the experience of the similarity between critical writing and other forms of intertextual transformations of extant writing. In this way the stories may be understood as nonconceptual modes of reference, and criticism may be understood as the supplying of the names or categories of referents addressed by the stories. (This would be one line to take in discussing the relationship of this chapter to earlier topics.) The interpretation, that is, accepts the invitation of the tale to find its moral or lesson and make it explicit.

This exercise also lends itself to parody, although it does not require it. Indeed, consideration of the visualization, montage, close-ups, and other devices of editing involved in video or cinematic translation can lead to some powerful, inventive papers. There is no need to follow a highly technical version of a formal script—we would provide a model if that were the kind of writing we expected. Rather, the idea is to perceive that Coover has imitated the film treatment (or informal script) in the style of "The Gingerbread House." It is easier to notice exactly what Coover is doing if one has in mind this analogy with an audiovisual script.

The following is a student response to question 4.

ZIPES AND BETTELHEIM
" AT THE MOVIES"

Siskel:  Hello, I'm Siskel Zipes.

Ebert:  And I'm Ebert Bettelheim.  We're your weekly movie critics at large.

Siskel:  Today we're watching and reviewing the familiar children's movie "Jack and The Beanstalk."  We will be discussing the Marxist and Freudian views hidden within the context of the movie.

Ebert:  So let's turn on the projector and watch a few scenes.

1

    A large meadow in the spring afternoon.  A small weather-beaten cottage isolated in the meadow.  One cow, slowly grazing on bare patches of grass.  A small child in the distance approaching the house. Skipping. Merrily.  Whistling, to himself perhaps.  The child's hair is blond, disheveled.  His face dirty, but cheeks bright red.  His pants are too short, a dirty brown with patches on top of patches sewn in the knees.  His jerkin a faded yellow with worn out stitching.  He is barefoot.  His whistling tells of the innocence and insignificance of life.

2

    Birds and squirrels scatter out of his way as he approaches the cottage.  He stops by the cow he has named Milky-White.  The thin, bony cow lifts its head for a moment uncaring, then resumes its grazing.  He looks in the well covered with brown moss.  He picks up a pebble and drops it into darkness waiting for a reply.  The one received is not pleasant.  The dull sound of rock hitting rock far below.  The over used door to the cottage is on its last hinges.  Paint peeled off long ago leaving bare, rotting wood.  He skips up the front steps throwing open the old door to the cottage anxiously searching for the familiar face of his dear mother.  The cottage is sparingly furnished.  The wood is rotting and the table bare.  Sunlight enters through small holes in the straw roof.

3

    Poverty weighs on the old lady.  Her dress is simple and almost in rags, its color faded.  Her face is full of grief and wrinkles brought about by resignation rather than age.  Her apron is in tatters and is covered in grease and loose pieces of straw.  Gray hair.  She seems sad and tired.  She greets the boy with a scolding and concerned gestures.  Deep in her sad, blue eyes there is love, but no hope.

4

    Jack walks along the cobblestone path, shuffling his feet.  His head hung low.  He is no longer whistling.  His feet have formed hard calluses and are lined with dry mud.  The cow follows behind on leash.  He holds the halter loosely kicking pebbles in his path.  It is almost dusk.  The sky is grey with sunset.  He is hungry.  His stomach empty.  Nothing he is not used to.  His final destination keeps forcing his shuffle to falter.  He would care not if an eternity passed before his destination was reached.

39

Siskel: The elements of class struggle and the entire feudal system is most apparent in the first few scenes of the movie. The social and political signs are unmistakable. It is obvious at first glance that this tale treats a social problem of utmost concern to the lower classes. It depicts a struggle against poverty and hardships of life that the lower classes are forced to maintain. The boy's clothes as well as his mother's clearly depict the condition of life they are living. The old cottage is their only sanctuary and it is a poor one indeed. The dry well and bare tables show that they are constantly starving. Now the cow, their only source of revenue, is useless. Jack and his mother accept their way of life only because they have lost all hope and they know no other.

Ebert: I disagree Siskel. I believe it is the usual story of poverty, but what is actually being depicted is the boy's deep love for his mother. The boy has an oedipus complex toward his mother. She has raised him from birth and cared for him. It is important to note that no mention of a father is said anywhere in the story. This is because he is being viewed as totally insignificant in the child's eyes. We do not know if the father is dead or alive, nor do we care because the child does not care. The mother is all-important and he wishes only to please her. The house symbolizes the mother's body. He dwells within the house during his childhood as a mother nurses the infant from her body.

5

The short man stands on the side of the path. He too wears rags. His boots are worn, his back arched. The cloak over his shoulders has seen many days and nights, survived the scorching sun and pouring rain. His thick grey beard is tangled in knots. His hands and face are parched. He is a loner. The gnarled oak cane bends under his weight worn smooth through the years. Yet there is wise light in the eyes below the thick, busy eyebrows. He smiles. His teeth are rotten and yellow. He presents a few small beans to the boy next to him. The beans are white and dry. Unedible, yet magical. The man is poor, clever, experienced in the ways of the world. Jack's eyes are bright, there is a total innocence behind the caked mug on his face and a little hope. The man ignores the boy's innocence. The cow now walks behind him on leash, uncaring. Jack's face is full of new hope. There is spring in his step, song in his voice and hunger in his stomach. He juggles the beans in one hand. He skips back toward the cottage he calls home. It is almost dark.

6

The ground shakes. The giant is wrapped in huge pelts of fur. He is hugely muscled. Power surges through his body. His legs are as high and wide as the largest tree trunk. His body as big as a house. His head is covered with thick, red, coarse hair as is his chin. His eyes are deep and burn like cinders. His face fat and livid. His snarl conceals the huge man-eating teeth. The rich furs drag behind him as he reaches into the roasting hearth. The powerful hands crack the bones of a roasting pig like a bed of toothpicks. He laughs to himself silently gloating in his power. He bellows to his wife. The pig's bones crush in his jaws. A golden egg lies alone in a nest of twigs.

7

The old woman's face is full of sorrow and anguish more than anger. Her pale blue eyes float deeply in their sockets shrouded by heavy lids and a few tears. She gazes into space. Her mouth is taut. The damage is irrevocable. All at once she throws the tiny beans in her wrinkled little hands out the window. They are forgotten quickly as is any indication of hope. Jack goes to bed hungry. His heart is bruised. His innocence broken. A moist patch of soil. Deeper. Darkness. There is movement, life struggling upwards to breathe for the first time. Pale morning light.

Siskel: We are shown two things in the previous scenes. The lower class, common people are now forced to turn on one another in order to survive. The man is not evil and is considered to be wise by tricking a young boy because this will enable him to survive a little longer. The wars of this period often brought famine and poverty which led to the breakdown of the feudal system. Consequently, peasants were often likely to shift on their own and forced to go to extremes to survive.

    We are also vividly introduced to the giant. The struggles depicted in the movie are against poverty and against giants who have food and hidden treasures. Here again the imaginative and magic elements of this movie had specific meanings for a peasant and lower-class audience at the end of the eighteenth century. The man-eating giant could be interpreted here to symbolize the entire feudal system or the greed and brutality of the aristocracy, responsible for the difficult conditions faced by Jack and his mother.

Ebert: The giant here does not represent a feudal system, but a threatening father figure. A boy while going through the oedipus complex hates and distrusts his father. He is the only thing intervening between himself and his mother. We are introduced to this giant who the boy sees as a giant father figure and must eventually destroy.

    The beans represent the seeds of life. Jack sees them as magical beans. They are fertile eggs which can bring forth more children. Therefore he brings them to his mother wishing her to implant them within herself. They are his "life-line." But the mother cannot afford to bear more children and she tosses them out.

8

    Jack's heart jumps with a new hope. He must avenge his mother. His fists clench. He starts to climb. The stalk is huge. Dark green. Tangled and gnarled roots branching in all directions, yet ever upward. His body tires, but his mind does not. Jack climbs onwards through the clouds. Far below are cottages. They are small, insignificant. Perhaps this is his destiny. His mother calls for him. He is gone. She sees the beanstalk. Her face twists in agony. Now she has nothing.

9

    The giant is huddled over his food. A mountain of rich furs on muscle. His huge fingers point at a small hen in a little nest. His bellow shakes the castle. A pure golden egg falls into the nest. The huge shoulders of the giant shake with delight, with greed, with lust. He smells gold, he smells power, he smells a boy.

10

    The castle looms overhead on a bed of pillowy clouds. The sun radiates above. Jack is amazed. He feels warm, good inside. He is above the clouds, his small hands raised toward the magnificent structure. Its towers disappearing in the sun. He approaches with hunger and caution in every footstep.

The giant woman takes pity on the poor starving boy. She will feed him now. He will be the food later. Jack nibbles at the immense amount of food. He feels as small as a mouse. Perhaps he is. The walls are covered with tapestries. The floor with thick rugs. The ground shakes. The walls quiver. Jack hides himself in the oven. The giant roars about smelling a boy. The giant woman points. Jack bolts for the door. Bricks start flying. He grabs the hen or all will be in vain. Jack slips through the giant's legs and under the door. The ground shakes beneath him. He dares not look back. He shimmeys down the stalk, panting. The cottage looms closer. He is free.

Siskel: The magic and fantasy elements are closely tied to the real possibilities for the peasantry to change conditions. The emphasis is on hope and action. Jack takes action, he always has hope. Jack climbs to heaven. He feels magnificent, yet he is cautious. The peasantry would view this place as unreal or magical. It exists only in their minds. Jack is prepared to steal from God himself. The giant (God) represents the aristocracy, the extremely powerful and wealthy. The peasantry were forced to risk even death in order to obtain a little wealth. For poverty and famine were waiting below.

Ebert: The giant beanstalk now represents Jack's "life-line" grown toward the sky. A child must face a moment in his life when he says "this is the last day of my childhood." Jack tries to climb this long "life-line" and face the father who stands between him and his mother. The child sees he is not ready to kill the giant father-figure yet and makes the wise decision, bringing some wealth (to please his mother), he barely escapes. Jack is still a child and has escaped the grip of maturity.

## 12

The giant's rage will not cease. His roars crash like thunder. He knows no fear. He swears vengeance. He bellows for his golden harp. The harp of pure gold shines like the sun. Strings of pure silk. It sings. Songs of lullabies and poverty in lands far away. It soothes the giant beast. He sleeps for now. The sun shines brightly over the castle.

For the first time there is a glitter in the old woman's eyes. A glitter not of weariness, but of resistance, perhaps almost hope. Her son has returned. A hen lays a golden egg in a small nest of twigs. The grass has returned. The sun refracts off the water in the well. The boy and his mother live peacefully, almost content. Jack is light-hearted. His innocence returns and his curiosity as well. Early morning. He climbs again.

## 14

The giant sits on his throne. Gold coins piled next to him. Deep in his glowing eyes there is lust, there is greed, there is ignorance. Jack approaches the castle. He will not be fooled twice. He hides in a box of copper. The giant eats. The harp sings. Songs of battles won and lost long ago. His huge head falls, he snores. Jack runs, harp in hand. The golden harp cries to its master. The walls shake, the castle shutters. Smoke billows from the giant's flaring nostrils. His roar echoes through Jack's ears drowning the harp's song. Jack runs through the clouds. He can feel the giant's breath on his back. He shivers, the giant blocks the sun with his body. The beanstalk sways and croaks under the immense weight. Yet it holds both boy and giant. Jack reaches the ground calling for his mother. She runs, axe in hand, quickly and lightly toward her son. Jack swings the axe with new found strength. The sharp metal glints in the sun, its bite is true. The stalk falls and with it the giant. The ground shutters, it splits open, swallows the giant. The clouds disperse overhead. He is gone.

15

The cottage shines in the sunlight. A hen lays a golden egg. A harp sings sweet melodies. A boy and his mother, perhaps for the first time, smile together. One cow grazes on new, green grass. A small cottage isolated in the meadow. A large meadow in the spring afternoon.

Siskel: The peasantry and lower-class could not be content even if there was food and water on the table. Their hatred toward the upper-class drove Jack towards heaven once again. This time more clever. Jack, a common boy, shows himself to be the equal of a giant if not better. His miraculous escape might represent the collective energies of the small people, the power they actually possess. When these powers are used to attain justice and compensation the people are invincible. The killing of the giant is symbolically the realization of the hatred which the peasantry felt for the aristocracy as hoarders and oppressors. It shows the people as fair and just. Once the aristocracy has been destroyed they are wealthy and content with life. Yet their overall lifestyles do not change as Jack and his mother remain in the old cottage.

Ebert: Jacks needs to learn to trust that someday he will master the dangers of the world even in the exaggerated form in which he depicts them. Jack, still a child, realizes this and therefore returns to destroy the giant father-figure. When he finally does he returns home and now finds happiness there. This is psychologically correct, because a young child driven into adventure by oedipal problems cannot find happiness outside the home. Only through good relations with his mother can a boy truly mature into adolescence. Having overcome his oedipal difficulties and learned that wishful thinking has to be replaced by intelligent action, Jack is ready to live happily again with his mother.

Siskel: Thus we conclude our film "Jack and the Beanstalk." I have given it a thumbs up.

Ebert: And I have as well. We highly recommend the whole family to see such an enriching tale that was actually not made by Steven Speilberg.

Siskel: May the good movies be yours and remember to save us the aisle seats.

## Chapter 4: EXPERIMENTS WITH TEXTS

### Introduction (p. 193)

Roland Barthes was born in 1915 and studied French literature and classics at the University of Paris. After teaching French at universities in Romania and Egypt, he joined the Centre national de recherche scientifique, where he devoted himself to research in sociology and lexicology. He was a professor at the College de France until his death in 1980.

Such is the information offered about Barthes on the jackets of his
many books, most of which have been translated into English, including his
first one, Writing Degree Zero, and his last, Camera Lucida. These jackets
include blurbs by the likes of Peter Brooks, who describes Barthes as "the
most characteristic and important French intellectual of the structuralist
generation." Barthes, he adds, "detested all forms of authority, worried
about the power wielded by the teacher, and described his main subject,
literature, as 'a grand imposture which allows us to understand speech outside the bounds of power, in the splendor of a permanent revolution of language.'"

Susan Sontag observed that Barthes "compared teaching to play, reading
to eros, writing to seduction. His voice became more and more personal,
more full of grain, as he called it. All of Barthes's work is an exploration of the histrionic or lucid; in many ingenious modes, a plea for savor,
for a festive (rather than dogmatic or credulous) relation to ideas. For
Barthes, as for Nietzsche, the point is not to teach us something in particular. The point is to make us bold, agile, subtle, intelligent,
detached. And to give pleasure."

We come now to the most challenging chapter of **Text Book**. Indeed,
some of the reviewers of this manuscript wondered if the writing by such
theorists as Barthes and Jacques Derrida (considered in the next section),
however important it might be for understanding the debates animating the
contemporary critical scene, wasn't simply too difficult, too obscure, for
introductory work. It is a good idea to apply the best insights of current
critical theory to the problems of composition, and to design a textbook
with these insights in mind, they said. But was it necessary to take the
pun available in the word "textbook" so seriously as to base a whole pedagogy on the theory of text developed by the French? Or, if it was, did
that imply that one had to include texts by the French theorists themselves?

This concern is well taken, requiring a few words of justification in
response. The first thing to keep in mind in teaching this section is that
it is an experiment. The experiment is to test the claim made by these
theorists that textuality offers the means to break the barrier separating
experts from amateurs in the field of literature. This claim does not deny
the difficulty of theoretical discourse for the uninitiated reader.
Rather, it suggests that the best way to understand the textualist insight
into literature may be not by struggling to master their concepts, but by
practicing oneself the form of writing in which textualists have represented their thinking.

This advice seems to be worth taking for several reasons. First of
all, Barthes, at least, believed that "text" was not definable as a concept
in the conventional sense. He invoked the figure of "catachresis" as the
one needed to name what was meant by "text"--"there is no possibility of
saying the thing in terms other than the metaphor." The common example of
catachresis is "the leg of a table." There is no substitute for the word
"leg" here. Barthes never ceased looking for the catachrestic metaphor
capable of denoting "text"--"it is the field of the haruspex, it is a ban-
quette, a faceted cube, an excipient, a Japanese stew, a din of decors, a
braid, some Valenciennes lace, a Moroccan wadi, a broken television screen,
a layered pastry, an onion, and so on." He once wrote that the best model
(understood as a simplified familiar system that provides a map for a more
complex unknown) for "text" was the Marx Brothers film, A Night at the
Opera. If we try to comprehend what Barthes was naming with these metaphors, we might identify it as "the pleasure" of writing, and we might conclude that, however difficult it is to understand the concept of "text"
theoretically, understanding is not in itself necessary for performing tex-
tually.

The second reason, then, that we think this experiment is worthwhile is that, in our experience, Barthes's various projects—his experiments with genres and styles of writing carried out in his numerous books and articles—translate readily into assignments that are in fact quite pleasurable to perform, and even more pleasurable to read. But that experience too is part of the claim our experiment is designed to test—that the effect of textualist writing is to stimulate in the reader the desire to write in turn. And this test could not be conducted with any writing other than that offered by the theorists themselves.

The essence of the two projects attempted or essayed in this chapter— the fragment and the signature—is in both cases the use of literary devices and strategies (metaphor, characterization, narration, image, and so forth) for the purposes of critical analysis. Textuality is in the vanguard of those movements that claim to have merged the genres of creative and critical writing, producing out of this merger a hybrid discourse that for lack of a better term is called "theory." In this last chapter, then, we explicitly encounter the anomaly that textuality poses to conventional notions of "writing about literature." When working in the mode of the "text," the student is not writing criticism about literature, but is producing a text at once critical and literary, that is as aesthetic as it is intelligent.

Let us turn now to a more specific discussion of some possible ways to approach one of Barthes's projects—the fragment.

The Fragment (p. 195)

Students tend to be more willing to undertake a new kind of writing if they understand the rationale motivating the experiment. Why does Barthes want to work with this particular dimension of discourse; why does he decide to write about love in this particular way? At one level it is easy to respond to this curiosity, given the topic itself. Everyone understands the interest of "love" as a theme. Indeed, students often accept the value of the topic at once and are ready to move on to the formal question. Nonetheless, it is interesting to discuss the value of the topic at another level as well, so that students may enter more fully into the stakes of the experiment.

One way to open this discussion is to note Barthes's motives for writing about love. He explained that in the highly sophisticated world of Parisian intellectuals, sentimental love had become an object of scorn not to be taken seriously. Given Barthes's temperament, which was always to avoid being on the side of the obvious, of "that which goes without saying"—which he identified with ideology—he wanted to scandalize his peers by writing sentimentally.

At the same time, Barthes's scientific interest was piqued by the peculiar linguistic status of the communication between lovers. From a certain point of view what lovers say to one another is so trivial, so full of clichés, as to be linguistically invisible—to be a kind of limit-case marking the outer reaches of language. Yet this trivial discourse, at least as practiced in everyday life, marks the conduct of a profound mode of knowledge. In the history of thought, essentially two kinds of knowledge have developed—calculation (best represented in science), and conjecture (best represented, it is said, in love). By expressing his interest in love as a kind of knowledge, Barthes acknowledged the association between love and knowledge that goes back at least to Plato, whose dialectic began with a lover's desire for a specific beautiful person, and ended with the love of truth or wisdom (philosophy).

What kind of knowledge does the lover have? How does the lover know that the beloved is the right one, the perfect one? Barthes offers two analogies for the truth possessed by a lover. One is from a zen story about the monk who held his pupil's head under water until he nearly drowned, then told him that he should desire truth as much as he wanted air; the other is that of a baby calling for its mother. Love is a model for a kind of knowledge that does not work according to the logic of calculation, but according to the association of intuition. The beloved, the object of love, the other, is the great unknown, intractable, about whom the lover experiences, Barthes says, an exalted feeling of knowing what he or she does not know. Barthes's idea is that "love" is not so much a psychological as a social experience—the amorous situation consists of certain positions and schemes that recur across the divisions separating everyday life from literature and science. Thus it is possible to orient oneself to love by means of a kind of triangulation superimposing these three discourses one upon the other.

The point of the previous discussion is to establish the possibility that love is itself a kind of knowledge, one our culture has not fully defined or understood. Since students may be expected to be naturally curious about love, they may the more willingly agree to undertake an experiment in a new way to write based on a lover's experience. Which brings us to a discussion of the formal properties of the experiment. This subsection of the chapter provides in outline form a summary of Barthes's description in the opening pages of Fragments of "how this book is constructed." He provides, that is, the principle of invention for a genre of the fragment. One purpose of our experiment is to test the extendability of this genre to other discourses—to the student discourse, for example. To this extent, when the students write their fragments they will be conducting a true experiment in the full sense of the term, and not just reproducing a familiar, established form.

A discussion of the selection and writing of the figures is best conducted in relation to the excerpts by Barthes.

So it is a lover who Speaks and who Says: (p. 197)
1. Selecting the figure.
"Dis-cursis," Barthes reminds us, originally meant "the action of running here and there, comings and goings, measures taken." The fragments reproduce at once the outbursts of the distracted lover, and a stop-action or freeze-frame fixing of the typical or stereotyped gestures of the scene of love. He has in mind something like the "gest" featured by Brecht, whose stagecraft included the technique of the "freeze," all the actors holding a pose while one of the characters analyzed the situation in an aside. This aside is the lover's true discourse.

Everyone can recognize the scene of waiting. Even if we have not all been "stood up," we all know the situation and how we would feel if it did happen. The first step in generating this discourse, then, is to identify the conventional, repeated moments or positions of being in love. Among the figures listed in Barthes's table of contents are: to be engulfed, absence, adorable, anxiety, annulment, to hide, fulfillment, connivance, declaration, demons, flayed, to write, exile, mad, jealousy, I-love-you, letter, magic, silence, crying, gossip, ravishment, scene, remembrance, suicide, union, will-to-possess.
2. Writing the Figures.
    a. Title, heading, and argument.
    The title functions in the usual way, to identify the organizing theme of the fragment. The heading may or may not be the same as the title, the difference being that the heading is a subtitle, naming the

argument. The argument does not state directly what lovers say, but refers
to it, as a paraphrase. Each fragment, then, represents the unfolding of a
banal phrase, such as the one the lover utters when the beloved finally
shows up: "Where were you?" The class might want to discuss the phrase
referred to by each of the arguments. Part of the test of the validity of
the figure is the extent to which the class could agree, at least approximately, on the wording of these general phrases. Barthes suggests, incidentally, that these discourses of everyday life, found on the margins of
language, exist at the level of the phrase, and not the word. Their basic
units are these idiomatic phrases. The argument of "the Heart" could refer
to the phrase, "don't break my heart." "Images" could refer to the phrase,
"but I saw you," and so on.

The fragments are presented in alphabetical order, following the order
of the headings. The class may be curious why Barthes wanted to avoid
telling a story. In fact, when one reads A Lover's Discourse in its
entirety, a story of unrequited love does emerge--a story with a definite
unity and coherence of feeling. This story is never directly told, but is
inferred by the reader. Barthes's intention may be appreciated in the context of contemporary discussions critical of narrative, which has become
associated historically with the biases of patriarchal ideology. Barthes
wants to liberate the emotions and gestures of love from the standardiza-
tion positioning imposed on them by narrative form. He offers the reader
instead a thesaurus of possible positions, which the reader is free to
recombine according to the dictates of his or her own story. The unity
will be provided by the reader, not the author--an aesthetic reflecting
Peter Brooks's point about Barthes's dislike for "authority." To
appreciate the peculiar effects thus achieved, the class may compare and
contrast the fragment with other approaches to narrative and story
encountered in earlier chapters.

b. The body (numbered paragraphs).

The titling of the fragments is formulaic enough that students have
little difficulty with it. Still, a few continue to wonder if their headings have to be in French, which they don't, or if they have to be in
alphabetical order, which they do. Sometimes, on their own, students will
translate the headings into whatever language they know (Latin, Hebrew,
Spanish), which works fine if they want to capture some of the same flavor
of "system." But the "body" is a different story.

At this point we begin to see the value of unfamiliar or even of "difficult" texts for learning to use models. When encountering a text by
Barthes or Derrida, the students are unlikely to assume they already know
how it works. Now they must apply the motto of our pedagogy: "When in
doubt, ask the model." This advice is easily followed in simple cases such
as wondering if the figures have to be in alphabetical order. But to learn
how the body works requires careful anatomical study. Since Barthes himself introduced the analogy between the human "body" and the "body" of the
text--comparing the figures to the poses of dancers; writing the figures is
a "choreography"--we may use the analogy to guide discussion. Indeed, the
class will be practicing, in its investigation of these experimental forms,
the strategy learned in the chapter on metaphor.

We may use the anatomical analogy in two senses: the analytical
sense, connoting dissection and classification; and the aesthetic sense,
connoting the athletic prowess of the dancer. The body of the fragment
both classified the discourse in question and performs it. The scientist
tells us about the parts of the body, and the dancer shows us what the body
can do. As Barthes said, this approach to an object of study is not
descriptive but "dramatic," a simulation. We could say the same for the
pedagogy of **Text Book.** Part of the interest of this pedagogy is to explore

the benefits of teaching literature in a literary way--to use in classroom
discussion the methodological powers (long exploited by inventors in all
fields) of figurative thinking and speaking. The textualist does not read
a work primarily at the level of meaning, then, but rather considers the
work as a set of instructions for making another one.

To learn how to get from Barthes's inventio to the actual fragments,
the student will have to look closely at the examples. We will point out
the kinds of things to note in linking the generic principles with the par-
ticulars of the sample.

"Waiting" (p. 197)

1. The lover writes in the first person, although at times he/she may
shift to the third person, referring to oneself as he/she. The relationship of the writer to the speaker is "novelsque," to use Barthes's term.
The phrase that links the generic instructions to the figures--"So it is a
lover who speaks and says:"--distances the writer from the statement. What
the student writes, then, will not be a "confessional" at the level of con-
tent--we learn very little biographically in these passages. We know the
situation--the lover waits for the beloved to telephone, as arranged. What
matters, however, is the feeling, the experience of this waiting.

The category of "experience" is very much in question in the Age of
Science. Feminism has created a renewed interest in the value of experience as knowledge. The cognitive value of experience has been questioned
because it did not seem to permit valid generalizations. The fragments
bring together the general (the category "waiting") with the particular
(the peculiar experience of the writer with that category). This structure
suggests that the specific nature of an individual's specific emotions and
behaviors associated with a given category constitute valid representations
of conceptual categories. How does the writer know what to select for
inclusion? The criterion of selection, Barthes explained, is the "sting"
or punctum. Having identified the general category of the figure as that
which is "so true"--something recognized at once as "the way it is"--the
writer then examines her memory in relation to the category for details--
the traces marking one's encounter with this situation, for something that
affected one sufficiently to have left a mark.

At this point we recognize Barthes's innovation in the dualistic
approach to the relationship between the general and the particular,
between knowledge and experience--he does not distinguish between firsthand
and secondhand knowledge. Rather, he shows that these two ways of gaining
information and insight are interdependent. In the generic instructions
Barthes indicated that the body consisted of three areas of "reference,"
including, besides one's immediate life experience, one's "experience" of
literature (or the arts), of popular culture, and of disciplinary knowledge. He is waiting for a phone call, and this waiting reminds him of a
piece by Schönberg (acknowledged in the margin), Erwartung. The circumstances are not the same (a woman waiting for her lover in a forest), but
the anxiety, the feeling of waiting, is similar. And Barthes comments, "I
have of sense of proportions."

We may recognize that in comparing his experience to events described
in literature (his principal comparison throughout is with Goethe's Sorrows
of Young Werther) Barthes, as he acknowledged, is deliberately practicing
the "lowest" form of reading--projection. He explained that his intent was
to attempt a reading that was at once popular and specialized: to observe
himself in the act of identification. He believed that the genres of high
and popular culture shaped behavior as much as they reflected it. His
approach, in any case, formulates at the level of theory the assumption

that has guided **Text Book**--the inescapable interaction, linguistically and
rhetorically, of daily life and high culture.

Barthes's strategy allows us to discuss not only how people should
read but how they do read. Literature has a cultural function outside the
confines of the school. The choice of Werther as the primary reference,
for example, is not casual. It was a best-seller in its day, and many
young men of the period so identified with it (so projected their own feelings into it, so derived their own feelings from it) that they imitated
Werther's decision to commit suicide. Here lines a dilemma or problem
worth discussing. The men who committed suicide after reading Werther
badly misunderstood the book, according to Goethe. Or perhaps Goethe misunderstood the nature of literary experience. In any case, Goethe
explained that he wrote the book to overcome his own impulse to commit suicide over an unhappy love affair, or that the writing of the book was so
therapeutic he lost the inclination to self-destruction. He published it
thinking that the story would have a similar effect upon its readers. He
ignored, we might say, the difference between writing and reading a work.
If his readers had been textualists, they might have understood that the
one to identify with was not Werther but Goethe.

The point to discuss might be the distinction between reading for
pleasure and reading for school. The first issue to arise is likely to be
the fact that few if any students are familiar with Goethe, let alone
Schönberg. No matter, since they need only understand what Barthes is
doing. When it comes to their own writing, they will imitate not Barthes's
content, but his procedure. In the category of waiting perhaps no work
from high culture comes to mind for them. Barthes's version of the "references" filling the body is just one among a potentially infinite number of
versions, of which our students may produce a few more. The troubling
aspect of the problem of projective reading is that, as Kenneth Burke once
said, the humanities are supposed to provide "equipment for living." The
response to Werther suggests that this equipment, like any other machinery,
can be dangerous if not used properly.

2. The "scenography of waiting" recalls the relationship between life
and theater noted by Goffman in Chapter 1. Rhetorically this segment
expands upon the "anxiety" noted in #1 above. It may correspond to the
saying "Don't make a scene," which the beloved might utter if he/she shows
up. Our emotional experience follows a recognizable pattern, to such an
extent that actors can duplicate it in a theater, which is to say as well
that the signs of feeling may be faked or posed.

Students may wonder how Barthes "invents" or finds these things to
say: "I have just shifted in a second from absence to death; the other is
as if dead." The marginal note refers to "Winnicott," a psychologist. A
reference of this sort comes from Barthes's specialized culture. Students
may similarly draw upon their specialized readings, undertaken in their
present classes or recalled from previous schooling. Someone taking
"Introduction to Psychology" might think of relevant information from the
textbook as a reference. In principle, the content of any disciplinary
subject should provide a collection of potential analogies that the writer
may introduce at an appropriate place.

3. It is worth noting the reality, the accuracy, of the feeling in
question. The obsessive focus, the lover's evasion of all distraction, may
be assessed for its validity. Barthes outlines in detail the specific
quality of the situation.

4. Why is the lover's behavior so peculiar? There is more to it than
meets the eye--it is "overdetermined," as the psychologists say. The
active or constructed quality of experience is evident in love: the
lover's expectation is so high that he momentarily recognizes the voice or

face of the anticipated other in the voices and faces of strangers. The technique includes reference to a psychologist, to personal experience, and the introduction of a metaphor: "I am an amputee who still feels pain in his missing leg."

5. The individual experience is placed explicitly in the context of all manner of waiting--is located in the general. "Transference" is the term used in psychoanalysis to name the neurotic behavior in which, in the therapeutic process, the patient projects onto his relationship with the analyst his childhood relationship with the parents. The source of the anxiety which is the theme of this figure is identified as owing to the powerlessness of the lover's position. The initials in the margin refer to the name of a friend who is the source of the observation about power.

6. A proverbial story, an anecdote conveying the experience of the culture, serves to suggest one possible response to the situation, to the anxiety of waiting for someone who is not going to show up. Barthes's lover is in a specific situation, which happens to be an unhappy one. But even in the middle of a happy relationship the structure of the situtation is present to the imagination of the participant--"things could go wrong." What other proverbs might pertain to this situation?

"The Heart" (p. 199)

All that has been said about the strategy of the figures with respect to "Waiting" applies equally to the other fragments. We will make a few additional comments about the remaining selections.

1. You might not be able to get your students to suspend their natural prejudice, as citizens of American culture, against a rhetorically elaborate style. They may not want to write phrases about a heart "held, enchanted, within the domain of the Image-repertoire." The first step is to recognize that Barthes is saying something comprehensible and useful. The "Image-repertoire" (a term borrowed from the psychoanalyst Jacques Lacan) refers to that set or collection of ready-made icons possessed by every member of a given culture: Each of us has a repertoire we share with the collective, and a more private repertoire, a kind of personal mythology, derived from our specific circumstances. The heart as an image exists for most of us in the shape of a valentine. It might be interesting to inventory this repertoire of images and to identify the stock associations that go with it.

The "anxiety" explored in "Waiting" reappears here, suggesting in this repetition a pattern or unity of feeling linking the fragments.

2. The first reference, in our sample, to Werther: the "primary" reference. It consists of both a direct citation and a paraphrase of Werther's belief that one's emotions, not one's ideas, are unique or individualizing. Barthes, however, is suggesting that emotions are as socialized as concepts. A topic for discussion might be the current received understanding of the "romantic."

3. Why is the heart "heavy"? There is something about the quality of emotion associated with sadness, sorrow, loss, the disappointed lover, unrequited love. Perhaps the story Barthes wishes to avoid is the "good" love story, in that a happy affair in which everything goes smoothly is hardly worth telling about, however desirable it might be to live. Werther, as a representative work of Romanticism, expresses the mood of "world weariness," of Weltschmerz, that Goethe identified as the spirit of his age. Barthes tells an anecdote about a situation in which it would be appropriate to use the phrase "my heart is heavy within me." The guiding principle of invention in this experiment, it is worth reminding ourselves, is the lover's discourse--what is said, the linguistic existence of love.

The writer wants to itemize the specific circumstances in which one has encountered the typical features of the system. This project, incidentally, makes A Lover's Discourse a prototype for the poststructuralist project in general: coming after the structuralists, who described the systems of culture, the poststructuralists asked after the status of the individual subject practicing within these systems.

"Images" (p. 200)

1.  The organization or arrangement of the "body" should be clearer by now. Each one follows a certain development, and is not simply a random collection of paragraphs. This one begins with an example of a "scene" that, for a jealous lover, has the coherence of a message--the beloved engaged in intimate conversation with another, a rival. Barthes typically uses an analogy to convey exactly the nature of the process by which this scene acquires the configuration of an image--the example of the puzzle drawings. Here is one important device of his inventio, of how he unfolds the saying to produce a series of paragraphs out of a brief exclamation. When he says that the image is without riddle, he indicates that, despite the fact that he does not know what the conversation was about, the lover already interprets the scene in a way consistent with the love situation-- as a flirtation with a rival.

2.  The inventio continues to clarify itself through repetition: another reference to Werther. Barthes finds an example of the "scene" as image, an example of the lover's way of seeing and of feeling, in his primary reference. The examples from life and from literature converge to suggest precisely the character of a lover's thoughts, in which reason and emotion fail to coincide: what the lover says is, "I know perfectly, but all the same."

3.  A variation on the theme: the lover may strike a pose, act a scene, as well as see one, as it would be seen by the beloved. Here Barthes shows himself as "sad." In another fragment, "to hide," Barthes provides a good instance of the "image" used as a message in a discourse. "I want you to know that I am hiding something from you, that is the active paradox I must resolve: at one and the same time it must be known and not known: I want you to know that I don't want to show my feelings: that is the message I address to the other." The example he offers of this principle is the wearing of dark glasses to hide the fact that one has been weeping, hoping that the unaccustomed glasses will provoke the question, "But what's the matter?"

The reference to Caspar David Friedrich again signals the quality of an intellectual's participation in high culture. The technique, however, may be adapted to any repertoire--analogies for the figure may be drawn from anywhere, from any dimension of the cultural encyclopedia. Even if we do not know the painting, the allusion to a polar scene offers a powerful sense of the feeling of exclusion being analyzed in this aside. The quotidian phrase operating here might be "the cold shoulder." We are familiar with this coldness; the trick is not to be satisfied with the cliché, but to extend it, to find a way to make that "cold" more specific.

4.  Barthes makes this point several times--that the lover is an artist. What would it be like if life and art were fully merged? The lover, according to Barthes, knows. Sometimes he suggests that the lover inhabits a hermeneutic universe--one in which everything signifies. For the lover, everything the beloved does constitutes a sign, has meaning. Beyond that, a lover not only interprets, but performs life as if it had formal coherence. We like to think that we can tell the difference between the form and the substance of an experience. In education, for example, we

talk about the value of getting an education and not just a degree. But we also know that in fact the pursuit of the form may replace the desire for the substance, for learning. In love, we know that the desire to make an image may direct one's choice of a date, or even of a mate.

"Show Me Whom to Desire" (p. 201)

The preceding discussions perhaps establish the pattern firmly enough for our purposes. The point of these discussions is not to teach Barthes as a "literary figure" about whom we need specialized information, but to identify the strategies of invention and arrangement that guide the genera-tion of these fragments. Students quickly pick up the idea of filling in the category with specific personal incidents that embody their own encoun-ter with the form or the cliché. They have more trouble recognizing the strategy of finding cultural references that similarly embody or give expression to the pose. It is worth repeating that they do not need to use Barthes's references, but that they must use some references--their own encyclopedia or repertoire, whatever it is. They need to be reminded also of Barthes's continual reliance upon metaphors and analogies, as in the use of the camera lense and the zoom effect of "scooping out" the beloved's body in the first paragraph here. They also need to keep clearly in mind the purpose of each fragment, which is to elaborate a specific facet of the experience of being (unhappily?) in love.

One justification for the frequent reference to psychoanalysis is that this discipline is explicitly a "scientific," or at least a disciplinary, version of the lover's discourse. The strategy is to line up and coordi-nate all the levels of language addressed to love--literature (and all the arts of high culture), popular culture, science, and everyday conversa-tion. The generic instructions say that the criterion for selection, the principle of generation, should be that something is memorable. The appli-cation of this advice is easy enough with respect to the production of per-sonal experience. But how does it apply to the level of cultural refer-ences? In one way, the "sting" still functions at this level, in that Barthes, we may suppose, calls to mind in the context of the "image" the Friedrich painting; he does not have to research it. At the same time, when we take over this genre for ourselves, and even apply it to a differ-ent discourse, we can see that a little research might produce interesting results. Are there any Romantic paintings that could serve as an example for the prose in question? Take a look and see. In short, the form obliges the writer to include the three levels of reference, so that the writer may not use as an excuse the claim that "nothing stung me." If nothing comes to mind, one will have to "leaf through the encyclopedia."

"How blue the sky was" (p. 202)

However different the American student's encyclopedia might be from that of a French intellectual, the experiment still stands or falls on the commonality of the poses. We have to be able to say of the pose, "That's so true!" In #3 here, for example, Barthes calls attention to the "narra-tive bliss" experienced at the beginning of an affair, before the couple knows one another, so that each must tell the other all his or her anec-dotes. Part of the bliss is the discovery that the identity ("This is what I am") is shared by the other. What all those stories add up to is con-firmed in this exchange in a way that is fundamentally satisfying. What is the nature of this bliss? The effectiveness of the text rests upon the possibility not that the experience described here will be news to us, but that we will recognize it as our own and call to mind our own participation

in this form.  At the same time, we are meant not only to identify with the
text, but to become aware of this identification in a critical sense, to
understand that all our reading experience relies upon the cultural encyclopedia and our powers of inference in order to produce in us the feeling
of understanding.

Discussion and Writing
1.  The purpose of this question is to initiate a discussion of Barthes's
strategy of invention, to see the sources he drew upon for the composition
of the asides.  Our comments on the figures indicate the direction this
discussion might take.  An inventory of Barthes's cultural repertoire,
including both his high and low dimensions, demonstrates a useful prewriting operation that the students will want to perform for their own repertoires.  The exercise calls for them to begin making explicit at least one
aspect of their cognitive map, tracing the conceptual registers organizing
their thoughts and feelings about love.  Part of the interest of this exercise is that it allows students to examine their own cultural resources.
Barthes's example is there to indicate the sort of thing that is possible,
but the real purpose of the study is to discover the equivalent in one's
own reserve.  In the beginning the search is relatively passive--what comes
to mind while thinking about the given category.  The idea, however, is to
recognize the collective, social, shared basis at least of the materials
that turn up in this search, and then to realize that the process may
become active.  The writer is not limited to what happens to come to mind.
He or she is free to ransack the cultural encyclopedia and take whatever is
needed.
        The written exercise could be done in class, or as a one-page take-
home assignment.  By staying within Barthes's own figure the student may
more easily imitate the peculiarities of the written aside.
2.  This exercise is more ambitious than the previous one.  Its execution
draws on the technique of the "ghost chapter" encountered in Chapter 3.
Class discussion of Barthes's text may be more animated if students are
asked from the outset to find their own equivalents for Barthes's examples,
rather than attempting to understand fully what Barthes is saying.  Indeed,
the parallel between Barthes's case and their own clarifies the reading
better than any explanation of Barthes's background.  It is worth noting
how much of the information about the lover's discourse is secondhand,
available from models distributed through the several levels of the culture.  Even if an individual has not lived through an entire affair, he or
she knows at least the form of the story.  We know that generic expectations guide our response to works of literature.  To what extent is our
response to life experience guided by these same generic expectations?
3.  We come now to the central experiment of this section--an extrapolation
from a lover's discourse to a student's discourse.  It would be possible,
in principle, to take the extrapolation in other directions, to other discourses, or subdiscourses, identifiable in daily life, popular or high culture.  The wording of the assignment implies that the concept of "style"
provides a connection linking the various registers of culture--that the
patterns of a student's life-style may be organized and understood in terms
of the rhetorical features organizing a written composition.  The overlapping of this terminology offers another opportunity to discuss the interdependence of language in life and in literature.
        "Are any of the figures used in the lover's discourse also relevant to
the student's discourse?"  Extrapolation involves primarily reasoning by
analogy from the model to a new area of application.  Discussion of the
parallels between the two situations reveals some significant areas of
overlap.  Foremost among these possibilities is the fact that the love

relationship is a prominent feature of the student's experience. Similarly, one of the lover's fragments, entitled "Inexpressible Love," deals with the lover as a writer. The lover's difficulty with "invention," with finding a way to express amorous feeling, overlaps with the student's or any writer's difficulties in overcoming the anxiety of the blank page. Perhaps writer's block could serve as a metaphor for the anxiety of love. The solution to this boundary question is to orient the figure to the specific peculiarities of the discourse in question. In this case, the whole of the lover's discourse may become one pose within the student's text. What are the attributes or references of love as it is encountered in the student's situation? The special relationship between love and knowledge in our culture manifests itself in the student's tendency to use the library the way Barthes's speaker used the cafe—as the place of encounter.

"If the 'heart' is the organ of love sentiment, would the brain be the equivalent for the student's discourse?" It would, obviously, and so the figure of "The Heart" is a good one to use as the sample for class discussion, for working through together the extrapolation process. This figure reveals the focus of the fragments—the anxiety of the lover's emotions focused on the beloved. A similar unity might be identifiable in the student's experience by asking if there were an emotion associated with learning, or indeed if the "object of study" in school has a status similar to that of the "object of desire" in love. What are the myths and stereotypes associated with the "brain" in our culture? The current series of films dealing with the conflict between Nerds and Frat Boys offers some references for the relevant stereotypes and their transformation. Is it possible to identify a single emotion at the core of one's relationship to learning? Anxiety, clearly, is not necessarily the dominant feeling in love or in learning. At the same time, it is often the case that some one emotion does tend to dominate an individual's position in the discourse.

The assignment should consist of three to five fragments, depending on the number of paragraphs included in the body of each one. Some of the headings we have received are "registration," "greeks," "money," "party," "jocks," "library," "profs," "independence," "sanity," "misfit," "cheat," "first day," "the paper," "sleep," "lost," "question," "scamming." The following excerpt is typical of the sort of thing to expect.

GETTING UP FOR CLASSES

Awakening

Even when prearranged, awakening (the act of waking from sleep) is a disturbance, subject to postponement.

J.C.
1. Awakening is an interruption: The alarm rings. I'm not willing to accept the interruption. Regardless of how much sleep I had during the night, I always need about ten more minutes to recuperate from the shock of interruption. I can't simply "put my feet on the floor."

Horace

Milton
2. Awakening too soon causes anger. "Anger is a short madness." To study for a test I will sleep only from 2 a.m. to 7 a.m. The few tense hours are not at all restful or peaceful. At daybreak I awake—an hour too soon. I'm irritated, annoyed by the chirping of the birds. I cannot appreciate their songs about the "sweet breath of morn."

3. My priorities change during awakening. Last-minute cancellations: in a second I decide to skip breakfast in order to have ten more minutes of sleep. I will take a shower after class; I gain another fifteen minutes. If I wear a sweatshirt instead of the blouse that needs ironing I can sleep another five. With this series of cancellations I acquire a useful thirty minutes.

The following is a student composition utilizing Barthes's strategy.

# In The Beginning

begin

The new student enters a foreign world.
He is at first alien to its operation, to
its customs, and to its inhabitants.


1.        "The known is finite, the unknown infinite;
intellectually, we stand on an islet of an illimitable
ocean of inexplicability."
                        -- T. H. Huxley

        "By space, the universe encompasses and swallows
me up like an atom; by thought I comprehend the world."
                        -- Blaise Pascal


Parents, friends, and all sources of familiar guidance have
been stripped. I've been placed in the middle of a new
world, lost (Left to die? To make or break?). How sterile!
How cold! What once was a guiding hand is now a lifeless map
and a few names with telephone numbers. I am expected to
share my thoughts, needs, and deepest concerns with an image
at the end of a receiver. Perhaps I'll keep to myself.

2.        Freedom is another word for lost. I am now a creature
of choice ("the choice is your own."), the master of my                S.M.F.
destiny, fully responsible for my actions and their
consequences. Responsibility has been dumped onto my lap
like a ton of stone -- alien stone of another world. ("There          Angelou
was a sadness about them, as if this old world was not their
home and they were bound for higher ground.")


## Plume

esteem

Acceptance into an institution of selective
admittance sparks pride. The student is at first
dazzled and seldom sees the ground he treads.


1.        ("The statues of the Parthenon's east pediment from
left to right: ...Persephone, Demeter, Hephaestus,
myself...")

The new student projects himself into all that is acclaimed
wonderful. He sees himself pedastaled, surrounded by a
cheering audience, as though he has accomplished some great
task. ("During that period I looked at the arch of heaven          Angelou
so religiously my neck kept a steady ache.")

2.        I see myself as a creature of consequence, of
importance, of gravity.  The fact that I have been accepted
into an institution of higher learning, I see that as the
world's acknowledgement -- its recognition -- of my abilities,
of my promise.  ("These were the days when my heart was          Poe
volcanic.")  And why should I not strut?  Why not preen a few
feathers?  After all, these are the best years of my life.

3.        With my nose in the air I walk about.  I see a whole
new world.  For a while I forget the dirt that lies on the
streets and see only sky.  Ultimately, I trip and I am
reminded of the ground.


## The Leech


harrow

Experience has taught the student that nothing is
without price.  His money's worth is demanded and he
has learned to bleed his environment of its fruit.
In school, he becomes the farmer, his harvest always
knowledge, and the professor, his soil.


1.        The student feels the pangs of a hunger (the starving
student).  He is a vampire, ready to dry wells of information;
the instructor, his prey.  He is a monster but always
dependent, parasitic.  ("Behave well to the priest.  And take      Homer
the ransom.").

2.        I find myself the pest.  I understand the deception
but depend upon the spoils.  So I play the game.  I listen to
Dickinson ("Tell all the truth but tell it slant -- Success in
circuit lies.") and to Machiavelli ("Occasionally words must
serve to veil the truth."), but Barthes's body speaks ("What I
hide by my language, my body utters.").  The deception
escapes.

3.        "He who will be proved right in the end appears to be      Koestler
wrong and harmful before it."  A comforting idea:  the
professors understand and often encourage the motives:  some
because they understand, others out of pity.  Ultimately, the
leech bleeds and the host receives his check.

            "'Tis so appalling, it exhilarates!"
                          -- Emily Dickinson


57

## Bag-eyed

languish

The student is subject to a bombardment of mental
stimulations that often result in a decreased capacity
to learn; frustration sets in, fatigue breeds, more
frustration; ultimately, an exam is sacrificed for
an hour's sleep.

1.          Fabric is the limitation.  Too often, time and pressure
necessitate an approach towards the asymptotic -- towards
the physical barrier (the proverbial midnight oil must
burn).  Why do I push myself so?  There can be no future in
such an obvious neglect for health.

2.          And there can be no future (rhetoric:  an unsuccessful
future) in neglected studies.  My time here is an investment,
and time is precious; so I join the rat race.  "Their future          Angelou
rode heavily on their shoulders..."  And the world is shadowed
by this compulsion.  I begin to lose all sense of time, of
the world about me, and of needs.  "And so the new term             Trilling
advanced rapidly and one day the fields about the town were
all brown, cleared of even the few thin patches of snow which
had lingered so long."  -- a wild pursuit.

3.          But I could not be so driven by a future, so again the
question:  Why do I push myself?  Only a love or passion
can be responsible.  Plato explains that "Love and the lover
desire what they do not possess."  A passion for wisdom?  As
a student it seems likely.  "Who are those who love wisdom if          Diotina
not the wise or the ignorant?  ...she replied, "that they are
those who are in a state between desire and wisdom.

4.          So I am driven.  But ultimately, the fabric is loosened
and the mind must allow it rest; time to repair.  I find
this, however, rarely to happen before the bags under the eyes
find their mark, rarely before the mind, in its compulsion, has
time to test the body, to tear at it with its constraints.


## A White Flag

Surrender

The student is frequently needled with a desire
for the simple life of ignorance.

1.          With knowledge comes an awareness (more appropriate
term:  complications).  Simplicity is lost to the rational,
creativity becomes the subject of experience, and all that is
grand, falls to the known ("What once was heaven, is zenith          Dickinson
now.").  I often wish for the innocence of youth.  What
is expected of a child?  To be naive can be such a powerful tool
of escape.  "I was grateful to be able to answer promptly,
and I did.  I said I didn't know."                                    Twain

2.　　　　Time is irreversible, but what of exposure?  Suppose I
chose to lock myself inside my head, simply ignore what is
reality (Trilling's "classic case"), allow the demise of my
importance, my value as an individual; then might I be free?
Or suppose I were to simply end it all, wane the tick of the
clock?  As Dr. Howe: "...permit the metamorphosis of Tertan　　　　Trilling
from person to fact."  But something always keeps me going.
I am driven.

> "'Dissolve,' says Death.  The Spirit, 'Sir, I have
> another trust.'"
> 　　　　　-- Emily Dickinson


References for "Fragments of a Student's Discourse" (p. 206)

　　　　The three readings, by Angelou, Rapoport, and Trilling, are provided
as materials for the category of primary reference, to serve for the student's discourse the function of literary example for which Barthes used
Werther in his fragments.  You may wish to assign something else, such as
John Updike's "The Christian Roommates," or any work in the genre of "academic fiction" that you prefer.  The pieces are worth reading and discussing in their own right, but their specific purpose is to help students
identify the poses organizing their situation.
　　　　The questions raised during discussion of the lover's discourse may
recur in this context--the question of the narrative, for example.  Barthes
mentions that society expects a certain story from the rejected lover:  It
expects an account of grievances and lessons learned, mistakes not to be
repeated.  Similarly, the students finds that a certain story is required
by society.  In response to the question "How are things at school?" the
student may feel obliged to produce the conventional answers, depending on
who asks the question.  This story need not be told in the fragments, which
would allow another level of unity to emerge.  There is no need to require
this unity.  On the contrary, the insight gained from the experiment may be
weakened if one attempts to impose a unity of event or affect on the series
of poses.  Nonetheless, such a unity often emerges in the papers, expressing the author's particular style of thought about the student's discourse.  Some of these stories concern the party animal, the druggie or
drunk, the grade-conscious achiever, the hopelessly unmotivated.

Discussion and Writing
1.  Maya Angelou's autobiographical story suggests the relevance of earlier
schooling to the student's discourse.  "Graduation" is a figure still fresh
in the memories of most students in a writing course.  Indeed, one dimension of the asides could be a comparison of the experience of the university or college situation with earlier periods of schooling.  A saying that
often appears in figures dealing with the teacher is something like "You
won't get away with this when you get to college!"
　　　　Angelou's piece calls to mind several important areas of reference for
the student--the family context, for example, including the expectations
and hopes of parents and siblings who constitute part of the audience for
the student's performance.  One of the most useful features of "Graduation"
as a reference is the theme of racism represented in the speech by Mr.
Donleavy.  The story makes explicit the cultural tendency to treat individuals in terms of a stereotype expressing a reductive image authorized by
the dominant ideology.  It is not necessary to turn to something like

Leslie Fiedler's essay, "The Student as Nigger," expressive of the difficulties of the Vietnam era, for the class to identify with Angelou's protagonist. Outside the immediate confines of the campus, someone bearing all the signifiers of the "student" may find herself or himself treated as a type rather than as an individual.

There are a number of typical features of this specific figure--graduation--presented in the story (the speech for example), but in a way that is specific to Angelou's circumstances as a black. Angelou's emotions and responses to the graduation day address are distinctive enough, different enough from the common scene, to offer an example of how a typical form may be filled in an individualized way. The assignment does not call for a complete story, of course--"Graduation" is not a model for the fragments, but a resource as a reference.

At the conclusion of "Graduation" Angelou states part of her motivation for writing: "We [the black people] survive in exact relationship to the dedication of our poets (include preachers, musicians and blues singers)." This statement offers an opportunity to discuss the question in more general terms of why people write. She is saying that the values of her people are embodied and perpetuated in the literature produced by black writers. The same is true obviously of all writing. The "projective" mode of reading used with the references relevant to the fragments of a discourse is the one appropriate to identifying this level of a work.

Roger Rapoport's article similarly reviews an academic career--a college career in this case--from the vantage point of graduation. Written in the era of student unrest, this essay shares some of the same tone expressed in Angelou's story. Students have little trouble recognizing the commonplaces of the scene Rapoport describes, although they may not share his point of view. The article offers an occasion to discuss the disparity between the values and purposes of institutions of higher education and the experience of those who live and perform the practices of the institutions. Secretary of Education William Bennett has criticized universities for failing to make good in practice on the promises expressed in their official documents. This discussion may address the more general problem of the disparity that often separates experience and expectation associated with any aspect of life. Where do these expectations come from? The idea is to get at that strange, symbolic level of human culture, whose images and stereotypes frame our understanding of both lived events and written texts.

Lionel Trilling's story is a bit too long to include in full, for our purposes. You may prefer to assign the complete version (the class may become quite curious about what will happen to Tertan). English classes do not seem to have changed much since the 1940s, in that our students have little trouble identifying the poses contained in this story: "the first day of class," "the office visit," and so forth. This ready recognition permitted by the "student's discourse" facilitates a comparison of the use of types and poses in the narrative ordering of a story with the alphabetical listing of the fragments.

It may or may not be necessary to clarify Trilling's intentions with respect to Blackburn in the latter's visit to Howe's office to complain about his grade on the exam. Many students will not catch the fact that what Blackburn has written about Coleridge's "The Ancient Mariner" applies rather to "Kubla Khan." Hence they fall quickly into agreement with the saying evoked in this pose: "One opinion is as good as another, unless it is the teacher's opinion." Indeed, the reception of the story, especially in this excerpted form, tends to be unsympathetic to Howe. For the purposes of projective reading, this reception is appropriate, although it may also occasion some discussion of the pedagogical exchange, and of the role of power in the learning experience.

2. This final exercise is provided for those who might wish to spend more
time on this section. It also suggests a way to let the students share the
results of their experiment. In this case the pieces provided as references become models for a story to be composed out of the thesaurus of
fragments. Discussions preparing for this narrative ordering would provide
an opportunity for reviewing most of what had been learned during the term
about story telling and comprehension, beginning with the anecdote and carrying through to the inferential ghost walks and intertextual transformations. If this exercise is used only as the basis for discussion, it might
be interesting to see what extent the class could agree on the choices that
would have to be made in establishing the character of the "typical" or
representative student emerging out of the collection of poses.

### The Signature (p. 236)

Textualist practice deemphasizes the interpretive approach to literature, asking what the meaning of a work, in favor of a generative approach,
concerned with the production of meaning effects. Music is a good analogy
for the structuralist assumption underlying this approach--like the signifiers in a system of language (phonemes, for example), musical notes have a
"value," but not a meaning. People listening to a musical composition,
however, understand or are affected by the significance of the piece. Both
Barthes and Derrida allude to this musical metaphor for the production of
effects of understanding: Barthes with the comparison of the fragments to
choreography, and Derrida with the pun on "signature," alluding to the key
or time of a musical composition. The signature experiment takes a musical
approach to the production of meaning in language.

### What's in a Name (p. 237)

#### Discussion and Writing

1. To begin with one of the most familiar scenes in all of literature, and
with one of the most familiar phrases ("a rose by any other name..."),
allows us to ease into a most unfamiliar way of thinking about writing. In
fact, most of the readings in the opening sections are included in part to
establish the legitimacy of the experiment. Again, the principle is our
belief that students are more willing to undertake an experiment if they
understand the motivation that accounts for the project.
    The discussion of common and proper names may be used to remind the
class of their earlier encounter with this topic at the beginning of Chapter 2, in Roger Brown's description of Itard trying to teach the Wild Child
the concept of "concept"--that words are names for categories of things.
The word "book," then, applies to all items of that sort, regardless of
their physical differences. The possibility of a confusion between the
functions of common and proper names is the source of the following scene
in Lewis Carroll's Through the Looking Glass in which the White Knight asks
Alice if she would like to hear a song (a musical context, conveniently for
us):

> "The name of the song is called 'Haddocks' Eyes.'"
> "Oh, that's the name of the song, is it?" Alice said,
> trying to feel interested.
> "No, you don't understand," the Knight said, looking a
> little vexed. "That's what the name is called. The name
> really is 'The Aged Aged Man.'"
> "Then I ought to have said 'That's what the song is
> called'?" Alice corrected herself.

"No, you oughtn't: that's quite another thing! The song is called 'Ways and Means': but that's only what it's called, you know!

"Well, what is the song, then?" said Alice, who was by this time completely bewildered.

"I was coming to that," the Knight said. "The song really is 'A-sitting On A Gate':  and the tune's my own invention."

Like Lewis Carroll, Derrida's experiment investigates the possibility of exchanges between common and proper names. The signature concerns itself with what someone's name "is called."

2.   The two most common theories of how names or words mean were first articulated in Plato's dialogue, Cratylus. One view is that names are purely social conventions, with one community agreeing on "tree," another agreeing on "arbre," and so on. The other view is that there is a "motivation" underlying the name--that there is something "tree-like" in the sounds or letters composing the word.

Languages change over time, through historical evolution. One aspect of this development is the regular exchanges between the categories of common and proper names. Most students are familiar with the fact that proper names in our civilization originated in many cases from common nouns, the names for one's occupation or a description of where one lived. As Charles Berlitz reminds us, the most common family name in the languages of Europe is "Smith," referring to the occupation of blacksmith. He provides this list of the names that mean "Smith":

French:   Le Fèvre, La Farge, La Forge, Fernand.
Italian:  Ferrari, Fabbri, Fabroni, Ferraio.
Spanish:  Herrera, Herrero, Hernández, Fernández.
German:   Schmidt, Schmied.
Swedish:  Smed.
Russian:  Kuznetsov.
Hungarian:  Kovács.
Polish:  Kowak, Kowalski.
Lebanese and Syrian Arabic:  Haddad.
Irish:  Magoon.

At the same time, the proper names of inventors serve as the nouns for objects, ideas, techniques, and the like. Indeed, "Romeo" itself names any man who is courting. Other examples of common nouns derived from proper names, according to Berlitz (in Native Tongues, New York:  Grosset & Dunlap, 1982) are bloomer, bowdlerize, boycott, cardigan, raglan, chauvinist, chesterfield, guillotine, hooligan, lynch, macadam, martinet, sadist, masochism, mesmerize, sandwich, silhouette.

The History of Names (p. 238)

Discussion and Writing

1.  Part of the value of this topic is the access it gives to the peculiar nature of language, to the material reality of language. Our students for the most part are understandably oblivious to the extraordinarily odd quality of this "technology." As was the case with the fragments of a student's discourse, this experiment addresses the linguistic and rhetorical materials in terms of something about which the students have a natural curiosity--their own names. The motivation for doing much of the prewriting work necessary for the final project comes from the fact that the "research" involves an extrapolation from the examples to one's own situation.

The class may be able to think of some examples of "well-named" individuals in the public sphere--White House spokesman "Larry Speakes" is a
recent case in point, as is the quarterback for the Chicago Bears, since
"McMahon" means "son of the bear." Journalists often take note of these
coincidences (one suggested that Robin Leach, host of "Lifestyles of the
Rich and Famous," was appropriately named, thinking no doubt of the pun
with "leech").

This exercise may be done in class, putting the form of the anecdote
to use once again. The purpose of writing rather than telling the anecdote
might be the embarrassment that some students still feel about their
names. The advantage of the topic--that everyone has experienced the cultural materiality of names--is also at times a disadvantage, in that the
topic might become uncomfortably personal. One way around this potential
difficulty is to note that a person will be teased through the name
regardless of what the name is (although some names are more vulnerable
than others). The lesson is worth making, to remove any doubts about the
act of identification with language.
2. The students' information about their family names varies considerably
from one individual to the next. Some have access to a complete family
tree, while others don't know the nationality of their name, and assume
that if their name has no meaning in English, it is meaningless. This
exercise assists with the tasks of prewriting, collecting information for
the main experiment. It may serve also as a library assignment, revealing
the amount of materials available on onomastics and its related histories.
In some cases it also may lead to some work in oral history, with the collection of anecdotes from the memory of family members.

The Power of Names (p. 242)

## Discussion and Writing
1. The selections by Ellison and Spender provide the same sort of perspective on names that Angelou and Rapoport provided on student life. They
call our attention to the political and economic aspects of the history of
names. Their experiences and opinions speak to those students who might be
inclined to resist the importance of the issue "What's in a name?" Both
blacks and women have promoted the practice of changing one's name as a
political gesture, marking their protest against one form or another of
slavery. The Flower Children of the late 1960s communes often invented
names for their offspring not found in the standard dictionary lists of
"common" proper names. Frank Zappa's daughter, Moon Unit, is one example
of that trend. Hollywood entertainers frequently changed their names in
order to make them more interesting and evocative, and to remove the possibility of evoking ethnic biases in the mind of the public. Students sometimes learn that their family name was altered at the time of immigration
in order to make it more pronounceable or less recognizable ethnically.
Such shifts or explicit baptisms signal the existence of a dimension of
coding to which the names appeal as a standard of signification. As with
the figures of the fragments, the signature renders manifest the invisible
powers of the symbolic level of existence.
2. Spender and Ellison both pick up on the theme of slavery and bondage
identifiable in the history of naming, as noted in Cassirer's allusion to
the Roman legal system. To juxtapose the issues of race and sex in naming
opens the way for a better understanding of what is at stake in the debate
surrounding unusual naming practices. The uninformed instinctive response
by outsiders to alterations in the community's dominant conventions of
naming tends to be derision or dismissal. A reminder of what it feels like
to be teased about one's name puts the issue into perspective. And most

students readily acknowledge the slurs communicated in the various epithets applied to "foreign groups" (gringo, honky, polack, wop, etc.). There is less ready agreement, perhaps because the consciousness-raising work done by the women's movement is more recent, about the gender bias of naming practices.

A comparison of information among the class with respect to the relative amounts of information for the family name as opposed to the mother's maiden name is a good way to make explicit the reality of selection that such practices effect in our awareness and memory. The issue also calls attention to gender differences in this awareness, in that the women students are likely to know more about the mother's name than will the men.
3. Ralph Ellison's struggle with the namesake Ralph Waldo Emerson indicates perhaps something about how the quality of "destiny" enters into a name, in that he is first made aware that there is something significant, a meaning or expectation, attached to his name, and then attempts to live up to the name. Jean-Paul Sartre's massive biography of Jean Genet interprets Genet's life as a project to become the thief that he was accused of being in a childhood incident. He worked to turn the common noun into his proper name, in other words. Jacques Derrida responded to Sartre's study with an alternative reading in Glas, showing that it was the common noun available in Genet's proper name (genêt is the word in French for "broomflower") that accounts for his identity in life and in letters.

Ellison also proves the point that a person may be teased even for a name that on the face of it might seem objectionable. He adds that in black culture wordplay in the form of nicknaming is a prominent custom. We shall have more to say about nicknames later. For now it is useful to discuss in this context our general theme concerning the relationship between the life of language in everyday culture and high culture. The signature experiment, like most experiments, consists of a systematic and extended investigation of a material feature of linguistic culture.

Class discussion may turn to childhood games, to recall a time in life when most people experience the power and pleasure of taking on a desirable name. What names were preferred, and what ones avoided? One student mentioned that in playing "cowboys" as a child the boys did not want to be "Jesse James" because they thought "Jesse" was a girl's name. This point raised the gender issue again, leading to the compilation of a list of names used for either sex.

Writing from Signatures (p. 252)

The discussion of heraldry is provided because of its importance for Derrida's formulation of the signature experiment. Given the textualist principle of the merger of critical and creative writing, it is not surprising to find Derrida extrapolating for critical or theoretical writing a device from contemporary literature. The heraldic form of the "abyss" (the center of the shield) has long been the image of the reflexive strategy of modernist authors who include at the "heart" of their texts a representation of the text itself—a version of the "play within the play," except that now the inner play comments not on the themes of the frame story, but on its form. As Peter Hutchinson explains in Games Authors Play (Methuen, 1983), "This concept of the 'interior duplication' derives from André Gide, who himself proved a major exponent of it in his novel The Counterfeiters (where a character is himself writing a novel entitled The Counterfeiters). Gide claimed to see a parallel in heraldry, in which he felt that the 'outer' design was reflected in the 'inner' one of the shield." He offers as another example of this "construction en abyme" the game of ombre in The Rape of the Lock. In extending the abyss construction into criticism,

Derrida applies the representation of the family name in heraldry literally to literature, looking for the way in which the author's names might represent the organizing or generative principle of the work.

Although some of the students might know something about coats of arms from family crests, a more likely source of awareness would be members of Greek organizations or business majors who know something about the logos of certain corporations. In any case, when we come to the passage from Derrida's Glas the students should have in mind this heraldic usage. The way in which the family name determines the decoration of the shield provides a model for the signature experiment, in which the writer's name provides the inventio for the text.

James Joyce, "Shem the Penman" from Finnegans Wake (p. 253)
Morgan, O'Neil, and Harré: "Nicknames: Their Origins and Social Consequences" (p. 257)

## Discussion and Writing

1. This topic opens the minds of the more sceptical students to the relevance of heraldry to the contemporary world. The discussion might be preceded by some outside preparation, with volunteers contributing information about the significance of a given crest or logo. The symbolic organization of such designs could be compared to the uses of figures in other systems of meaning.

2. & 3. Joyce's Wake provides one model to be used as a resource in the signature experiment. Discussion might focus on the way in which Joyce's prose style extends the linguistic processes of nicknaming—modifying the proper name by the means listed in the article (mutation, pun/irony, analogy, allusion, and so forth)—to alter not only his own name (moving from "James" to "Sham" in the same way "Joanne," for example, became "Dozy"), but any and all words in the language. His style, that is, represents another one of Derrida's literary sources for the signature theory of invention (promoting the systematic exchange between proper and common nouns).

Several important elements of the social practices of language treated in the discussion of Barthes's fragments, as well as in the selection from Goffman in Chapter 1, recur here in the linguistic register (the link between nicknaming and various aspects of prejudice and stereotyping). The inclusion of several drafts of the passage allow the students to review the compositional process, to identify exactly what Joyce is doing and the invention technique involved. The passage, that is, is a portrait—a self-portrait of the author—written with a mocking, ironic intent. In it the author (but there is the same distance between the real Joyce and the speaker of the text that Barthes created when he wrote "and so it is a lover who speaks") expresses through the description and the nicknames a feeling about himself—a feeling of being a sham or a fraud. Psychologists report that successful people not uncommonly feel that they are fakes. Their success is not necessarily part of their normal, authentic sense of themselves, established in childhood, and so they never quite feel right in this new social position. Whether or not Joyce actually experienced that condition, the portrait offers an account that may serve the students as a model for nicknaming themselves and for drawing a portrait of themselves through the lens of a particular, predominant feeling they may have about their present situation.

The stylistic pressure Joyce applies to the language may be readily imitated by the students when they understand the motivation and the linguistic principle underlying the text (the nicknaming process, now harnessed as a literary technique). The self-portrait in the nicknaming style makes a good exercise on its own. A one-page composition may be produced as an in-class project, to be revised perhaps and included later in the final essay.

Signing (The Proper Name) (p. 261)
Jacques Derrida, Glas (p. 263)

Derrida exemplifies in this project the textualist approach to criticism, which, rather than imposing on literature a set of concepts derived from the social sciences, reads literature as itself a source of concepts capable not only of producing knowledge of literature (an immanent critique), but knowledge in general. It is not hard to understand why language departments rather than philosophy or social science departments have been the sponsors of Derrida's importation into the American university. Against the dominant tradition in philosophy, which attempted to master the tools of language by reducing its ambiguity to the ideal point of univocality, with symbolic logic being the most recent representative of that tendency, Derrida bases his theory of language on James Joyce—specifically, on Finnegans Wake—and attempts to develop a model of knowledge and representation that exploits the maximum potential of ambiguity. If his experiment is successful—if he can demonstrate the productive benefits of his position—literature as a discipline stands to gain considerably in the hierarchy of knowledge, passing from a "debtor" to a "creditor" discourse.

Derrida's reading of Genet, then, may be appreciated as part of this project to find in literary productions a new science of language. In the case of the signature, the experiment is an investigation of the relationship of words to things, a study of referentiality, in which an alternative to the classic theories of reference (motivation versus convention) is proposed. What Derrida discovers in Genet is the model for a self-conscious exploitation of the aleatory or chance associations joining together the different dimensions of discourse with the real. Barthes explored at the level of rhetoric the overlapping of the discourses of everyday life, popular culture, and high culture (including specialized disciplines). Now Derrida, as we will see, carries the study of such convergences into a new dimension. We get a glimpse here of one of the organizing metaphors of "text" as a concept—the textile. A text is made by weaving together the codes of a culture in an idiomatic way, guided by the peculiarities of style and signature.

Jacques Derrida, to quote another blurb (which we accept as representing the norm of an author's identity), is known for correcting a postulate of linguistics that subordinates all language to its spoken form and ties speech to the person, to the will to possess and the passion to assign a unitary structure, a profound meaning to the contradictory play of human appearances. He is widely studied for his researches into the density and complexity of signifying substance—its irreducibility to simple meaning. Derrida is professeur d'art at the École des hautes études en sciences sociales in Paris, and cofounder of the Collège international de philosophie (an experimental university designed to supplement the established, traditional institutions of higher education in France). His best-known work is Of Grammatology (Baltimore: Johns Hopkins University Press, 1974).

Although Derrida is a philosopher whose European reputation rests on his rereadings of the German tradition of phenomenology and other philosophies of consciousness (Hegel, Husserl, Heidegger), his work has been disseminated in this country principally through language departments, English and Comparative Literature especially. He enjoyed a close working relationship with the Yale School critics (Paul de Man, Geoffrey Hartman, J. Hillis Miller, and Harold Bloom) for a number of years, including a teaching appointment at Yale. This group became associated with the critical position known as "deconstruction" about which there has been so much controversy. Derrida continues to teach and lecture regularly in the United States, having formal association with Cornell and the University of California at Irvine. Recently, some of his writings have appeared in English translation before they were published in France.

The signature experiment included in **Text Book** is not representative of American deconstructive criticism, which so far is based not on Derrida's own methodology for writing or with literature, but on some of his theories of language articulated in commentaries on philosophical works. The signature project, however, reflects Derrida's own practice as a literary critic, as reflected in <u>Glas</u> and as applied in essays on such authors as Ponge, Blanchot, and Sollers.

## Discussion and Writing

1. It is not necessary for the students to follow Derrida's exposition in detail, only that they grasp the essence of his argument—the reading of Genet's corpus as an extrapolation generated by the name "Jean Genet."

Once the common noun available within the proper name is discovered the next step in the generation of a signature text, followed both by Genet and Derrida (the latter repeated the former's strategy, applying the principle of textualist criticism, which is to mime the object of study), is to elaborate a discourse out of the object thus named. The antonomasia or transfer from the proper to the common noun is clear and explicit in Genet, although the drawback of this explicitness (the fact that <u>genêt</u> literally beams "broomflower") is that the signature as "science" can only be developed superficially. Derrida makes it clear that the signature is by no means confined to cases in which the proper name directly translates into a common noun. The "key" of a person's cognitive and compositional style, rather, may operate even more profoundly at the level of "rhythm" (musically). We are not concerned in this experiment with this more complex notion of the signature. It is sufficient for now to initiate the experiment in terms of the more literal registers of signing. The point, in any case, is not to take too seriously any "truth" claims for the procedure, but to stress the experimental value of the name as a guide for invention.

Having found the flowers or the horse in "Genet," or the sponge in "Ponge" (another poet he studies), Derrida describes the nature of these things in detail, constructing his text out of information gleaned from reference books. Indeed, he seems to be using the pun on "reference" to develop an alternative theory of referentiality. Words do not "refer" to the real living things but to other words, whose meanings may be found in dictionaries, glossaries, and encyclopedias. We may recognize the strategy as being similar to the models made from metaphors discussed in Chapter 2, except that here the initial juxtaposition of sets or categories is based on the pun, including the "macaronic" pun across languages (the organizing device of <u>Finnegans Wake</u>). The strategy, in short, is to use as a guide for what to say or write both the linguistic or poetic techniques of pun, rhyme, and the like, and a narrative account of the qualities or attributes of the items or things thus produced. In discussion students may want to find examples of both moves.

Having generated the "thing" as name and as referent or meaning, the next step—the move to the level of the third modality of the signature—is to declare that the "thing" is a model or analogy for all metaphor, that is, for poetic or figurative writing as such. Thus the proper name, the most particular register of language there is, designating one individual in the world, is generalized into a generic formula. The process is similar to the construction of an argument by metaphor, studied in Chapter 2.

It is also a common practice in theoretical speculation, which textuality adopts as a basic strategy of writing about literature (the use of literary devices for the production of a writing to represent knowledge of literature). Textuality, in other words, tests the proposition that literary language is as capable of representing an understanding of literature as is the language of social science.

It is worth noting that Derrida attends to "Jean" as well as to "Genet," although in this selection very little if any of that production appears.

2. This exercise is quite ambitious, and may be more appropriate for an advanced class. It would be most usefully assigned if you decided to spend more time on this section than might normally be possible. To carry it out effectively could require considerable outside reading, in order to have a large enough sample of an author's works available to test adequately whether or in what way a particular signature manifests itself. The other problem is that the signature does not always function at the most obvious level--it may be, Derrida suggests, a movement or rhythm in the temporality of the text, such as the coming and going of the eternal return in Nietzsche (rather than the more obvious "nothingness" of the name in Slavic). Unfortunately, the approach is so recent and so unconventional that few if any essays exist, outside of Derrida's corpus, applying the method. The exercise is here in part to stimulate thinking about the relation of authors to works, or of people to life. Is there anything "hawthorne-like" about the works of Hawthorne? Perhaps this question is as much for the instructors as for the students, appealing to you to test the experiment.

3. Much of the interest of the signature experiment arises because one does not stop the lesson at the point of understanding or appreciating the poem and its genre. Rather, the student is expected to replicate the experiment, extrapolating from the models a formula for discovering the poetics latent in one's own name. Again, it is useful to stress the experimental nature of the project. As in the early stages of any "science," or any project within a field of knowledge, the practical value of a given idea will not always be evident. There is no need to accept as truth the results produced by the aleatory or chance operations of this inventio in order to carry out the investigation into the generalizability of one's proper name. At the very least, students will generate prose that bears many of the features of modernist or poetic literary style--replete with enigmas and obscurities--that have tended to baffle them as readers. In short, the piece will be a text with value for them as a heraldic representation of their identities, and for others as an aesthetic composition. It sometimes happens that someone does not identify with the "fate" or destiny prescribed by the name. Ponge, for example, put no special stock in the "sponge"--did not identify with it, did not see himself as a "sponge" or "parasite," to use one of the meanings of the term available in English (alluding, potentially, to the attitude toward poets as unproductive members of society). As one student wrote:

> My last name has always been a depressing subject. I would give my right eye to have my surname teased the way it was when I was a child rather than the way it is now. All through elementary school my classmates and friends turned "Hicks" into "hick-ups." The jest never bothered me, unless it was said with malice. "Hickey" was the nickname I got as an adolescent, although I didn't get the thing it names until college. My last name, in the singular form, also appears in the

dictionary. "A gullible, provincial person; a yokel."
I will admit only to gullibility (and not much of that)
or to provincial (in the most prestigious sense). As
for yokel, I completely and entirely refuse to see
myself as a "country bumpkin." I do not like country
music, I never wear western clothing, and I refuse to
ride in a pickup truck or associate with anyone who
owns one.

We have here the principal project, the major experiment in its full
form. Jarrett's text is the last, and the most complete, model provided
demonstrating the strategy of writing. The students should be reminded, of
course, that Joyce's Wake and Derrida's Glas offer examples of the kind of
writing and thinking involved.

James (Mike) Jarrett, besides writing for Jazziz, is finishing his
doctorate at the University of Florida. His dissertation topic deals with
jazz as a compositional principle and social point of view in modern literary and theoretical writing. In other words, Jarrett is far enough along
in his career to have committed himself to a theme--jazz in his case--that
shows up in or is imposed on, his proper name. Many of our students, if
not all of them, will not have any such objectification of their style of
thought, although they may have declared a major or they may pursue avoca-
tions whose attributes might show up in the signature. Of course the signature might be used predictively, to suggest areas that the individual
might seek out or avoid. In general, however, Roback's question about the
destiny of the name is only of secondary interest, to add a little spice of
mystery to the experiment. Still, it is not unusual for a student to be
quite surprised by the suitability of the name. One thing that becomes
clear about this "destiny" in Jarrett's example is that it is in part if
not entirely a "construction" of the genre. Since Jarrett happens to be
interested in Menippean satire, which informs one aspect of his dissertation (his "corpus"), he turns to a review of a certain "menippea" to see if
he can find any connections with his poetic formula. His discussion of
these satires sometimes confuses his readers, who need to realize that in
miming this model they need not reproduce the same things Jarrett talks
about, but the same procedure or method. The strategy is the same one used
in filling in the poses of the fragments. There had to be references, but
they did not have to be the ones used by Barthes. The students may substitute for the satires any area of particular interest to them.

The real heart of the experiment is the invention of the third modal-
ity--the transformation of the name into a generic principle for the student's own style of thinking and writing. If Barthes's fragments explored
the style of life of the student, the signature may be said to explore the
style of cognition (in a symbolic way) of the student. The fun of the
experiment is the idea that even if an individual does not recognize the
text generated in this way as "proper," he or she should be encouraged to
save it for future reference, to see if it might not become a self-
fulfilling prophecy (this possibility, of course, is presented in a playful
way). We mentioned earlier the steps of the method, but we will review
them again now as a way to appreciate the value of Jarrett's example.

1. The proper names and nicknames serve as the key for the invention
of the text.
2. These names are elaborated into as extensive a list as possible of
common names (verbs, adjectives, and the like, as well as nouns),
using the devices demonstrated by Genet, Joyce, and Derrida.
3. This key list of common names is elaborated into a narrative, part
of which is devoted to a description or "showing" of the objects,

things, or actions named in the list, and part of which is devoted to a commentary explaining the relevance of these items as metaphors for one's life experience.

4. The commentary mounts an argument by analogy, showing how the named items function as a model for making a text.

Jarrett in fact offers two models for invention--the process of canning jam, and the musical style of jazz. The recipe as a form is a lucky find, derived from the "jar." Notice, too, the introduction of anecdotal material as a means to fill out the term (his grandmother's mason jars). The other model of the third modality, jazz, is introduced through the pun on "cooking." This material is developed more for its biographical interest--the fact that the author really is writing about jazz, and has in his signature terms that refer to musical performance. He does not develop the methods of improvisations as a model for writing as much as he could have, but he alludes to it enough to evoke the idea. This partial development is appropriate for a text attempting to be as aesthetic as it is critical. The point is not to say everything--to generate the descriptions and leave some of the explanations to the inferences of the reader, thus preserving some of the enigmatic strangeness of the models.

It would be useful to do an inventory of all the strategies Jarrett uses to build his discourse; to relate his procedures to the previous readings, to see which devices he privileged, and which ones he ignored. He does very little, for example, with Joyce's style, or with the nicknaming self-portrait. He is also selective within the possible range of materials. He does not activate every term, and the term he chooses to develop as his model is not the only one available. This selectivity indicates the constructed dimension of the experiment. He makes special use of the "macaronic" pun--the pun across languages--moving between English and French. The obvious move is to translate one's name from its original language into its English meaning (from "Kovacs" into "Smith"). Jarrett extends this technique to find a French pun for "Jarrett"--"j'arrête"--although again he only chooses to discuss part of the meaning available for this word. Students need not do all of these things, nor is their text likely to be as long as Jarrett's.

One dimension of this model that deserves special emphasis is its use of visual illustrations. One of the elements that enhances the aesthetic effect of the piece, not to mention its heraldic qualities, is its use of visuals. The pleasure of producing a collage of this sort is considerable, and it further enhances one lesson of the experiment--the link between names and things. Perhaps the appeal of such compositions to our students has something to do with their immersion in a video culture.

Two student papers follow that demonstrate the "signature" assignment. The first paper, by Amy Lynn Greenblatt, was originally accompanied by photographs which highlighted the visual quality of her signature. The second paper, by Brian J. Noe, was originally produced on a MacIntosh with various type faces and line art.

AMY LYNN GREENBLATT

Greenblatt--green leaf
green  1.  the color of most plant leaves and growing grass
       2.  not ripe; immature; inexperienced
leaf   1.  a usually green, flattened plant structure attached
           to a stem & functioning as a principle organ of
           photosynthesis

     So my name is a little redundant.  Composed of so few elements it must repeat itself.  It means forever young, never ripe, always growing.  The color of living things, a living thing. Maybe I can absorb energy to create something like food, like the leaf does.  I may get eaten by insects.  I may turn orange and brown when the winter sets in.  The leaf keeps the tree alive.  It has a large surface area within a small volume so that it gets the most exposure to light.  Perhaps I'll never be ready for anything, if I stay green.  Maybe I'll be naive a lot.  Like my middle name, this one is found in nature.  It could be that I am like the outdoors, or that I like the outdoors.  Maybe I am part of a salad, a very vital ingredient in one. This names goes well with my middle name because leaves and waterfalls often go together.  In fact, near every waterfall there must be leaves. One nourishes the other, then grows abundantly by its banks.

     My interesting initials are ALG, or algae.  This is a perfect complement to the rest of my name.  It is green, it floats on rivers, and it is of the plant kingdom.

## THE WATERFALL

The waterfall, a dynamic liquid flow, is my middle name. The moving water that keeps rivers clean is the meaning of "Lynn." It is like kinetic energy, rushing toward an infinite and unseen goal, always confident that the sea refuses no river. It sweeps the banks, taking dirt along with it. It is beauty, a source of pleasure to those who seek it. But it is not easily accessible. (How many do you find per week?) The paradox is that they are so blatently displayed. The waterfall is sometimes dangerous to boatmen who don't know how to ride it, though they really should stay near the bottom because the drop is designed for a flexible (liquid) medium. The waterfall is a secret place of downfall, seldom seen as such, hidden by nature--yet so loudly announced. Pure splendor--very majestic. Allowing breeze to spray cool droplets from the mainstream, it has infinite subsets, like a beach. I once saw a diminished waterfall in a test tube. I shook it and the little salt particles swirled around frenetically. The large waterfall must be chaotic, although its motion is directed by gravity. I see one every time I pour a drink and take a shower. There is a great one between New York and Canada that I have never seen. It is a link between two heights that never runs dry. It will be in motion forever.

Amy means beloved. I'm sure my parents thought so. Amy can be rearranged to form yam, a sweet potato. Perhaps this fits in with my physique. I am often consumed at Thanksgiving meals because people love my taste. I grow on vines that have leaves, so this fits my last name. I am found outdoors, as most of my name is.

I seem to be Nature's daughter.

A dearly loved sweet potato with green leaves. Perhaps I'll marry a man named Underwood and then I'll be a Dearly Loved Waterfall Underwood. Amy, beloved, be loved.

MY NAME

by

BRIAN J. NOE

sec. #1309

What is in a name? Some say it is a label that we attach to ourselves. Then there are those that believe that the names bears the passage to the soul. Still there persist critics that are not even worth mentioning here so I will not. I feel that the best way to start an examination of names is by reciting this verse that I heard somewhere:

"to know thy name is to know thyself"

which I then revise as;

"to know thy name is to Noe thyself"

It is truly here that we must begin to investigate the true meanings of names. And what better name to start with than my own, **Brian Joseph Richard Noe.** One may think not a totally profound name on the surface, but we must look beyond that into its meanings. From the first time a person asked, "Tell me your name," and I replied with some harsh rebuttal, "N0e," I realized that this was a name that I could have fun with.

My next experience in life that led me to believe that my name contained some hint of my destiny was when I saw my first James Bond movie. From that point on in my life I came to the rationalization that I had to get my doctorate. Here my name gave me the clue to what I was to become, a great scientist.

It is now time to see what my name holds and the best place to begin is with the beginning and that is Brian. Brian from the celtic word briar—a craftsman who carves wooden pipes, and with the suffix a meaning an occupation of and after combination and deletion we come up with Brian—a craftsman who carves pipes.

I find it not a coincidence that I have in fact carved quite a few wooden pipes. Could this be sublimital destiny, let us preceed further.

**Joseph** is my baptismal name. It is derived from Joseph, Jacob's son who was given a coat of many colors. And it is from this Joseph that the English word joseph, a multi-colored coat worn in the eighteenth century while horseback riding, came from. But do not forget that colors can stand for many things; such as dimensions.

**Richard** is my confirmation name. Derived from rich and meaning, one who is rich. But there are many things that one can be rich in, there is material wealth, richness in intelligence and intellect, and richness in health to name just a few. And it is from **Richard the Lion-Hearted,** King of England, a brave and fierce warrior.

And there there is **Noe.** Not just no, but _____?
The unmost opposite to positive. Noe is not a very common name but indeed one which holds deep and hidden meanings. If traced back in time Noe can be derived from deleting the l in noel. Noel is the French word for the birth of Christ. From its earlier Latin meanings natalis - relating to one's birth, and nasci- to be born.

It is the practice of many languages to put the last name first, and I feel here it is a good idea to do so. So now shall I say that I was born a great and crafty warrior with many dimensions. Here is a prophecy that is very likely to show up in Antiquity or in the Middle Ages about the birth of a son.

We can now come up with some variations upon the name. Let's start by taking Brian and rearrange the i and the a, and get brain. The brain is the core of all thought, and so being it is there that all intellect is perceived and generated. Then it was not just calling me brain in jest that my childhood companions called me, but a prophecy to the future and a homaging praise they employed to me one of proven superior intellect.

Let's be creative and see what else can be generated.  From my brain will be born great and rich ideas about the theory of dimensional travel. Will I indeed find a way to time travel?  I certainly hope so, that has been my greatest dream since childhood.  But that's enough of that shit. My great grandmother on my father's side was a Cherokee Indian and from my childhood I have been a master at the bow and arrow along with swordsmanship and other warrior attributes, I have progressed along the line to being a great warrior.

How interesting this has become.  Where else can we go now?  Let's say that we taken the b off brain then we get rain.  Here this may lead to an understanding of my personal being dark and gloomy which many have called me.  Or if we may wish to reduce it to in.  This could lead to the meaning of absorption.  Here again we find a comparison with my photographic memory.

Let's now try rewriting my name Bria[neon].  Here we have generated a new word neon.  Neon as in neon lights, being bright and luminous.  Once again we have struck upon another dimension of my personality, bright and shining.

**Noe** one is here.
**Noe** is not a word with
which you can die!!

Predetermination of your nature via your name.  This seems an absurd idea but there may be something in it.

No(e)t signed:

**BRIAN J. NOE**